*Guido Buzzi-Ferraris and
Flavio Manenti*

**Interpolation and
Regression Models for
the Chemical Engineer**

Related Titles

Velten, K.

Mathematical Modeling and Simulation
Introduction for Scientists and Engineers

2009

ISBN: 978-3-527-40758-3

Flaig, R.-M.

Bioinformatics Programming in Python

2008

ISBN: 978-3-527-32094-3

Epperson, J. F.

An Introduction to Numerical Methods and Analysis
Revised Edition

2007

ISBN: 978-0-470-04963-1

Buzzi-Ferraris, G. and Manenti, F.

Fundamentals and Linear Algebra for the Chemical Engineer
Solving Numerical Problems

2010

ISBN: 978-3-527-32552-8

Guido Buzzi-Ferraris and Flavio Manenti

Interpolation and Regression Models for the Chemical Engineer

Solving Numerical Problems

WILEY-VCH Verlag GmbH & Co. KGaA

The Authors

Prof. Guido Buzzi-Ferraris
Politecnico di Milano
CMIC Department
Piazza Leonardo da Vinci 32
20133 Milano
Italia

Dr. Flavio Manenti
Politecnico di Milano
CMIC Department
Piazza Leonardo da Vinci 32
20133 Milano
Italia

All books published by Wiley-VCH are carefully produced. Nevertheless, authors, editors, and publisher do not warrant the information contained in these books, including this book, to be free of errors. Readers are advised to keep in mind that statements, data, illustrations, procedural details or other items may inadvertently be inaccurate.

Library of Congress Card No.: applied for

British Library Cataloguing-in-Publication Data
A catalogue record for this book is available from the British Library.

Bibliographic information published by the Deutsche Nationalbibliothek
The Deutsche Nationalbibliothek lists this publication in the Deutsche Nationalbibliografie; detailed bibliographic data are available on the Internet at http://dnb.d-nb.de.

© 2010 WILEY-VCH Verlag GmbH & Co. KGaA, Weinheim

All rights reserved (including those of translation into other languages). No part of this book may be reproduced in any form – by photoprinting, microfilm, or any other means – nor transmitted or translated into a machine language without written permission from the publishers. Registered names, trademarks, etc. used in this book, even when not specifically marked as such, are not to be considered unprotected by law.

Typesetting   Thomson Digital, Noida, India
Printing and Binding   betz-druck GmbH, Darmstadt
Cover Design   Grafik-Design Schulz, Fußgönheim

Printed in the Federal Republic of Germany
Printed on acid-free paper

ISBN: 978-3-527-32652-5

Contents

Preface *IX*

1   **Interpolation** *1*
1.1   Introduction *1*
1.1.1   Which Model to be Adopted? *2*
1.1.2   Which Points? *2*
1.2   Classes for Function Interpolation *3*
1.3   Polynomial Interpolation *4*
1.3.1   Error in Polynomial Interpolation *6*
1.4   Roots-Product Form *8*
1.5   Standard Form *9*
1.6   Lagrange Method *12*
1.7   Newton Method *17*
1.7.1   Coefficients' Evaluation *17*
1.7.2   Previsions *22*
1.7.3   Additional Data Point *23*
1.7.4   Derivatives Evaluation *24*
1.8   Neville Algorithm *26*
1.9   Hermite Polynomial Interpolation *29*
1.9.1   Lagrange-Type Method *30*
1.9.2   Newton-Type Method *31*
1.10   Interpolation with Rational Functions *33*
1.10.1   Thiele's Continuous Fractions *35*
1.10.2   Bulirsch–Stoer Method *39*
1.11   Inverse Interpolation *42*
1.12   Successive Polynomial Interpolation *44*
1.12.1   Hermite Cubic Polynomials *45*
1.12.2   Cubic Spline *49*
1.13   Two-Dimensional Curves *54*
1.14   Orthogonal Polynomials *54*
1.14.1   Chebyshev Polynomials *56*

2	**Fundamentals of Statistics** 61	
2.1	Introduction 61	
2.2	Fundamentals 62	
2.3	Estimation of Expected Value 65	
2.3.1	Random Selection 66	
2.3.2	Arithmetic Mean 66	
2.3.3	Median 66	
2.3.4	Remedian 67	
2.3.5	Trimmed Mean 68	
2.3.6	Clever Mean 69	
2.3.7	Mode 69	
2.3.8	Symmetric and Nonsymmetric Distributions 69	
2.4	Estimation of Variance 70	
2.4.1	Use of Arithmetic Mean 70	
2.4.2	Using the Median 71	
2.4.3	Clever Variance 72	
2.5	Estimation of Standard Deviation 74	
2.5.1	Square Root of Variance 74	
2.5.2	Unbiased Standard Deviation 74	
2.5.3	Using the Median 74	
2.5.4	Using the Sum of Absolute Errors 75	
2.5.5	Minimum and Maximum Values 75	
2.6	Outlier Detection 76	
2.7	Relevant Probability Distributions 79	
2.7.1	Binomial Distribution 79	
2.7.2	Poisson Distribution 82	
2.7.3	Normal (Gaussian) Distribution 83	
2.7.4	t-Student Distribution 84	
2.7.5	χ^2 Distribution 87	
2.7.6	F (Fisher) Distribution 89	
2.8	Correct Meaning of Statistical Tests and Confidence Regions 91	
2.9	Nonparametric Statistics 98	
2.10	Conditional Probability 99	
3	**Linear Regressions** 101	
3.1	Introduction 101	
3.2	Least Sum of Squares Method 103	
3.3	Some Caveat 111	
3.4	Class for Linear Regressions 114	
3.5	Generalized Toolkit for Linear Problems 124	
3.5.1	Data File Structure 126	
3.5.2	Building a Data File 126	
3.5.3	Data Visualization 128	
3.6	Data Modification 128	
3.7	Data Deletion 129	

3.8	Preliminary Analysis 130
3.9	Multicollinearity 136
3.9.1	When Does the Multicollinearity Occur? 137
3.9.2	How Can Multicollinearity be Detected? 137
3.10	Best Model Selection 140
3.11	Principal Components 145

4	**Robust Linear Regressions** 151
4.1	Introduction 151
4.2	Some Caveat 151
4.3	Outliers and Gross Errors 152
4.3.1	When is an Outlier Generated? 154
4.3.2	How Can We Detect Outliers? 156
4.3.3	What Should be Done When Outliers are Detected? 168
4.4	Studentized Residuals 179
4.5	M-Estimators 181
4.6	Influential Observations 182
4.7	y-Outliers, X-Outliers, and F-Outliers 186
4.8	Secluded Observations 187
4.9	Robust Indices 189
4.10	Normality Condition 189
4.11	Heteroscedasticity Condition 190

5	**Linear Regression Case Studies** 193
5.1	Introduction 193
5.2	Ferrari F1's Test 193
5.3	Best Model Formulation 196
5.4	Outliers 200
5.4.1	Outliers Generated by Poor Quality Data 201
5.4.2	Outliers Originated by Inadequate Models 216
5.4.3	Outliers Generated by Inadequate Design of Experiments 224
5.4.4	Outliers Generated by Heteroscedasticity Condition 226
5.5	Best Model Selection 227
5.6	Principal Components 241

6.	**Nonlinear Regressions** 245
6.1	Nonlinear Regression Problems 245
6.2	Some Caveat 248
6.3	Parameter Evaluation 250
6.3.1	Test to Check the Robustness of a Minimization Program 252
6.4	BzzNonLinearRegression Class 253
6.5	Nonalgebraic Constraints 259
6.6	Algorithms for Outlier Detection 261
6.7	Correlations Among Model Parameters 263
6.8	Preventative Model Analysis 264

6.9	Model Discrimination	267
6.10	Model Collection and Model Selection	272

7 Nonlinear Regression Case Studies 275

7.1	Introduction 275	
7.2	One Dependent Variable with Constant Variance	278
7.3	Multicubic Piecewise Models 322	
7.4	One Dependent Variable and Nonconstant Variance	331
7.5	More Dependent Variables and Constant Variance	337
7.6	More Dependent Variables and Nonconstant Variance	341
7.7	Model Consisting of Ordinary Differential Equations	343
7.8	Model Consisting of Differential Algebraic Equations	352
7.9	Analysis of Alternative Models 356	
7.10	Independent Variables Subject to Experimental Error	362
7.11	Variables with Missing Experiments 369	
7.12	Outliers 370	
7.13	Independent Variables Subject to Experimental Error and Model with Outliers 374	

8 Reasonable Design of Experiments 377

8.1	Introduction 377
8.2	Preliminary Experiments 378
8.3	Using Models to Suggest New Experiments 380
8.4	New Experiments to Improve the Parameter Estimation 381
8.5	Model Selection: The Bayesian Approach 387
8.6	New Experiments for Model Discrimination 389
8.7	Criterion Used in BzzNonLinearRegression Class to Generate New Experiments 389

References 405

Appendix A: Mixed-Language: Fortran and C++ 409

Appendix B: Basic Requirements for Using the BzzMath Library 417

Appendix C: Copyrights 421

Index 423

Preface

This book is addressed to students and professionals that have to numerically solve scientific problems dealing with data analysis, such as interpolations, linear and nonlinear regressions, model discrimination, experimental design...

The reader is assumed to be basically familiar on numerical methods and statistics topics that each undergraduate student in scientific or engineering disciplines should have. Moreover, we kindly recommend at least a basic knowledge of C++ programming language.

Readers that have no these basic requirements may firstly be interested in the companion book:

> Guido Buzzi-Ferraris (1994), Scientific C++ - Building Numerical Libraries, the Object-Oriented Way, 2nd Ed., 479pp, Addison-Wesley, Cambridge University Press, ISBN 0-201-63192-X.

Such a book provides and applies fundamentals of numerical methods in C++.

Whereas many books on statistics and regressions look after these topics from a theoretical point of view only, we wanted to explain theoretical aspects in an informal way, by offering an *applied* point of view of this scientific discipline. Actually, this work is strongly addressed to the solution of concrete problems and it includes several examples, applications, code samples, programming, and overall programs so to give the reader not only the methodology to tackle his specific problem, but even the structure to implement an appropriate program and *ad hoc* algorithms to solve it.

The book describes numerical methods, performing algorithms, specific devices, innovative techniques and strategies that are all implemented in a freeware and well-established numerical library (as testified by the scientific literature): the **BzzMath** library, developed by Prof. Guido Buzzi-Ferraris at Politecnico di Milano and included in the enclosed CD-rom or freely downloadable at the website: www.chem.polimi.it/homes/gbuzzi (Buzzi-Ferraris, 2009).

This gives the reader the great opportunity to use and implement in his code a numerical library that involves some of the most performing algorithms in the solution of differential equations, algebraic systems, optimal problems, data regressions for linear and nonlinear cases...

Unfortunately, contrarily to many other books proposing theoretical aspects only, all these numerical contents cannot be explained in a single book by asking for their application to concrete problems and for specific code examples; thus, we decided to split numerical analysis topics in four distinct areas, each one covered by an *ad hoc* book by the same authors and adopting the same philosophy:

- *Buzzi-Ferraris and Manenti*, **Fundamentals and Linear Algebra for the Chemical Engineer**. Solving Numerical Problems, *WILEY-VCH, Weinheim, Germany*, 2010;
- *Buzzi-Ferraris and Manenti*, **Interpolation and Regression Models for the Chemical Engineer**. Solving Numerical Problems, *WILEY-VCH, Weinheim, Germany*, 2010;
- *Buzzi-Ferraris and Manenti*, **Nonlinear Systems and Optimization for the Chemical Engineer**. Solving Numerical Problems (in progress);
- *Buzzi-Ferraris and Manenti*, **Differential and Differential-Algebraic Systems for the Chemical Engineer**. Solving Numerical Problems (in progress).

This book proposes algorithms and methods for data analysis, whereas all the other companion books concern: linear algebra and linear systems, nonlinear systems and optimization issues, and differential and differential-algebraic systems, respectively. After having introduced theoretical contents, all of them deeply explain their application and provide optimized C++ code samples to solve general problems. By doing so, the reader can use the proposed programs for an easier approach to tackle his specific numerical issues using the *BzzMath* library.

The *BzzMath* library may be adopted in every scientific field where there is the need of solving numerical problems, *in primis* in engineering, but also in statistics, medicine, economics, physics, management and environmental sciences, biosciences...

The *BzzMath* library is well-described in the scientific literature and it is also field-proven by industrial applications and R&D projects.

Outline of this book

This book deals with data analysis, specifically involving interpolation, regression, and model discrimination problems. Analogously to the aforementioned companion books, even this one proposes a series of robust and performing algorithms implemented in the *BzzMath* library to tackle such a multifaceted and well-known hard issues.

It discusses the function interpolation problem (Chapter 1), by explaining their forms, introducing interpolation methods, and providing *ad hoc* algorithms and code samples to validate them.

An introduction of fundamentals of statistics, the description of new robust estimators, and a detailed discussion on the real meaning of statistical tests and confidence limits is given in Chapter 2.

Data regression problems are faced in the central part of this book. Theory and concrete applications were intentionally separated in distinct chapters to give an appropriate, even though informal, overview of the theoretical aspects as well as to propose an exhaustive set of applications so to cover at the best the regression field. Chapter 3 deals with theoretical aspects of linear regressions.

Robust methods for detecting outliers and identifying correlations among parameters are then proposed and compared to traditional methods and the concept of outlier has been defined (Chapter 4). Moreover, a novel approach called *clever least sum of squares* is introduced, discussed, and compared to the existing methods, such as the least sum of squares, the least median of squares, and least trimmed sum of squares. The main benefit coming from this method is given by the feature of automatically set its robustness according to the data set to be analyzed and the model adopted, allowing to overcome some shortcomings arising in using too much robust methods. Examples and case studies for linear regressions is the provided in Chapter 5.

Theoretical contents for nonlinear regressions are deepened in Chapter 6 and a series of selected examples are proposed in Chapter 7 in order to cover a wide range of cases such as with one or more dependent variables, one or more independent variables, constant and non-constant variance, piecewise models. Also, models consisting of ordinary differential equation and differential-algebraic systems are considered as case studies.

At last, the optimal design of experiments and the selection of appropriate additional experimental points to discriminate among an arena of rival models are both discussed in Chapter 8.

Notation

These books contain icons to highlight some important features and concepts, but also to underline the possibility to make some serious mistake either in programming or in selecting the appropriate numerical methods.

New concepts or new ideas. As they may be difficult to understand, it is necessary to change the point of view.

Description and remark of important concepts and interesting ideas.

Positive aspects, benefits, and advantages of algorithms, methods, and techniques in solving a specific problem.

Negative aspects and disadvantages of algorithms, methods, and techniques in solving a specific problem.

Some aspects are intentionally neglected.

Caveat, risk to make sneaky mistakes, and spread errors.

`Class` name or information about the *BzzMath* library style.

 Definitions and properties.

 Conditioning status of the mathematical formulation.

 Algorithm stability.

 Information about computational time.

 The problem, method, ... is obsolete.

 Example folders and paths on the attached CD-rom

BzzMath Library Style

In order to make both implementation and program reading easier, it was necessary to diversify the style of identifiers.

C++ is *case sensitive*, therefore it distinguishes capital letters from the small ones. Moreover, C++ identifiers are not limited in the number of chars of their name, contrarily to identifiers of FORTRAN77. It is then possible, we think indispensable, to use these prerogatives by giving every variable, object, constant, function, *etc.*, an identifier that allows immediately recognizing what we are looking at.

Programmers typically use two different styles to characterize an identifier that consists of two words. One possibility is separating the word by means of an underscore, *i.e.* `dynamic_viscosity`. The other possibility is to use a first capital letter for the second word, *i.e.* `dynamicViscosity`.

The style adopted in the *BzzMath* library is described hereinafter:

- **Constants**: the identifier should have more than two capital letters. If more words have to be used, they must be separated by an underscore.
  Some good examples are: `MACH_EPS`, `PI`, `BZZ_BIG_FLOAT`, and `TOLERANCE`.
  Bad examples are: `A`, `Tolerance`, `tolerance`, `tol`, and `MachEps`.
- **Variables** (standard type, derived type, class object): when the identifier consists of a single word, it may consists either of different chars starting with a small letter or of a single char either capital or small. On the other hand, when the identifier consists of more than a single word, each word should start with capital letter except for the first one, whereas all the remaining letters have to be small.
  Some good examples are: `machEpsylon`, `tol`, `x`, `A`, `G`, `dynamicViscosity`, and `yDoubleValue`.
  Bad examples are: `Aa`, `AA`, `A_A`, `Tolerance`, `tOLerance`, `MachEps`, and `mach_epsilon`.
- **Functions**: the identifier should have at least two chars: the first is capital, whereas the others are not. When the identifier consists of more words, each of them has to start with capital letter.

Some good examples are: `MachEpsilon`, `Tolerance`, `Aa`, `Abcde`, `DynamicViscosity`, and `MyBestFunction`.
Bad examples are: `A`, `F`, `AA`, `A_A`, `tolerance`, `TOL`, and `machEps`.
- **New types of object**: this is similar to the function identifier, but, in order to distinguish it from functions, it is useful to add a prefix. All the classes belonging to the ***BzzMath*** library are characterized by the prefix `Bzz`.
Some good examples are: `BzzMatrix`, `BzzVector`, `BzzMinimum`, and `BzzOdeStiff`.
Bad examples are: `A`, `matrix`, and `Matrix`.

Another decision concerning the style was to standardize the bracket positions at the beginning and at the end of a *block*, to make C++ programs easier to read.

Even in this case, programmers adopt two alternatives: some of them put the first bracket on the same row where the block starts, some others put it on the following line with the same indenting of the bracket that closes the block.

The former case takes to the following style:
```
for(i=1;i<=n;i++){
    ...
}
if(x>1.){
    ...
}
```
whereas the latter case to:
```
for(i=1;i<=n;i++)
    {
    ...
    }
if(x>1.)
    {
    ...
    }
```
This latter alternative is adopted in the ***BzzMath*** library.

A third important decision about style concerned the criterion to pass variables of a function either by value or by reference. In the ***BzzMath*** library, the following criterion is adopted:

- If the variable is standard and the function keeps it unchanged, it is passed by value.
- If the variable is an object and the function keeps it unchanged, it is passed by reference and, if possible, as *const* type.
- If the variable (either standard or object) is to be modified by the function, its pointer must be provided.

The object `C` only is modified in the following statements:
```
Product(3.,A,&C);
Product(A,B,&C);
```

1
Interpolation

Examples of this chapter can be found in the directory `Vol2_Chapter1` within the enclosed CD-ROM.

1.1
Introduction

This chapter deals with the problems of estimating the N parameters a of a model $f(\mathbf{x}, \mathbf{a})$ that exactly satisfy N conditions assigned a priori. A second topic concerns the use of such a model to make previsions.

A common choice of the N conditions is to assign N values $\mathbf{x}_i$, y_i and ask the model to exactly interpolate them, by requiring the solution of the system:

$$y_i = f(\mathbf{x}_i, \mathbf{a}) \qquad (i = 1, \ldots, N) \tag{1.1}$$

The method of *exact interpolation* is based on the solution either of the system (1.1) or of the other systems deriving from the N conditions that have to be satisfied by the N model parameters.

The *exact interpolation* presents two obvious but fundamental limitations.

1) The method can be applied only if $\mathbf{x}$ and y are *unbiased* (not affected by experimental errors); otherwise, the interpolating function would assume the trend of the random error.
2) The points $\mathbf{x}_i$ and the selected interpolating function must allow to univocally evaluate parameters $\mathbf{a}$.

A typical application of the exact interpolation is in the simulation of hard time-computing functions.

Only the case with a single independent variable x is considered.

Support points are the pairs of values (x_i, y_i); specifically, values x_i shall be called *abscissas*, whereas values y_i *ordinate*.

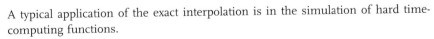
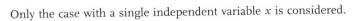

Interpolation and Regression Models for the Chemical Engineer: Solving Numerical Problems
Guido Buzzi-Ferraris and Flavio Manenti
Copyright © 2010 WILEY-VCH Verlag GmbH & Co. KGaA, Weinheim
ISBN: 978-3-527-32652-5

1.1.1
Which Model to be Adopted?

The model adopted for interpolation should have the following features.

1) It should represent the function at the best.
2) It should be easy to use.
3) It should not be time consuming in providing a prevision.
4) Adaptive parameters should be easily and univocally evaluable.

Polynomial functions are one of the most important classes:

$$P_n(x) = a_0 + a_1 x + \cdots + a_n x^n \tag{1.2}$$

When there are numerous points to be interpolated, the use of a single interpolating polynomial function is generally avoided and a series of low-order polynomials are surely preferred. Alternative strategies exist, such as Hermite polynomials, *spline*, and Bézier curves.

Rational functions represent another important class. They are denoted by the ratio between two polynomial functions:

$$Q_{n,m}(x) = \frac{P_n(x)}{P_m(x)} \tag{1.3}$$

Even though it is nonlinear in parameters, this function can be easily linearized to simplify the evaluation of parameters.

It is more difficult to operate with rational functions rather than polynomials (i.e., consider derivative and integral calculations), but rational functions have the advantage to better interpolate many functions.

Other interesting classes of functions are trigonometric functions, which are useful for periodic phenomena, and exponential functions.

1.1.2
Which Points?

Sometimes, values of x required in the exact interpolation cannot be selected, for example, when the experimental data have been already acquired by the field or when the data set is provided by tables and no other experiments can be carried out.

Conversely, it is possible to appropriately select the x_i values in interpolating an evaluable function.

Especially with polynomial interpolations, a bad choice of the experimental points may lead to erroneous results.

Some authors discriminate between two cases: they call *interpolation* the problem with the data stored in a table and *function approximation* the problem where the points can be accurately selected.

1.2 Classes for Function Interpolation

Polynomial and rational interpolations are particularly important and they were both implemented in an appropriate class.

In the ***BzzMath*** library, the class is called `BzzInterpolation`.

The `BzzInterpolation` class has two constructors: the default constructor and a constructor that requires the vectors **x** of abscissas and the corresponding values of ordinates **y** as argument.

Example 1.1

Let $\mathbf{x} = \{1., 2., 3.\}$ be the abscissas. In correspondence with these points, the ordinates $\mathbf{y} = \{1., 2., 4.\}$ are obtained.
The program to initialize `BzzInterpolation` objects is

```
#include "BzzMath.hpp"
void main(void)
  {
  BzzVector x(3,1.,2.,3.);
  BzzVector y(3,1.,2.,4.);
  BzzInterpolation a; // default constructor
  a(x,y);
  a.BzzPrint("BzzInterpolation a");
  BzzPrint("\n\nConstructor");
  BzzInterpolation b(x,y);
  b.BzzPrint("BzzInterpolation b");
  BzzPause();
  }
```

Support points can be changed during the program execution through the operator (,). For example,

```
BzzInterpolation p;
BzzVector x(......),y(......);
p(x,y);
```

Additional examples of the use of `BzzInterpolation` class can be found in

```
BzzMath/Examples/BzzMathBasic/
Interpolation
```

either on the enclosed CD-ROM or at the web site:

```
www.chem.polimi.it/homes/gbuzzi.
```

1.3
Polynomial Interpolation

When the polynomial has a single variable x, it can assume the form

$$P_n(x) = a_0 f_0(x) + a_1 f_1(x) + a_2 f_2(x) + \cdots + a_n f_n(x) \tag{1.4}$$

where $f_0(x), f_1(x), \ldots, f_n(x)$ are polynomial expressions with an order smaller than or equal to n and known coefficients.

For example,

$$P_4(x) = a_0 + a_1 x + a_2 x^2 + a_3 x^3 + a_4 x^4$$
$$P_4(x) = a_0(x+3) + a_1(1-x^2) + a_2(x^2+x)^2 + a_3(x^3-2x^2+4x) + a_4 x^4$$
$$P_4(x) = a_0 + a_1 x + a_2(2x^2-1) + a_3(4x^3-3x) + a_4(8x^4-8x^2+1)$$

are valid formulations of a 4-degree polynomial.

Since a n-degree polynomial has $(n+1)$ coefficients, $(n+1)$ distinct conditions are necessary to evaluate them univocally.

Given $(n+1)$ support points (x_i, y_i) and $(n+1)$ distinct abscissas x, coefficients $a_i (i = 0, \ldots, n)$ can be obtained by solving the linear system with $(n+1)$ equations:

$$\mathbf{F}\mathbf{a} = \mathbf{y} \tag{1.5}$$

A polynomial is in its *standard form* when

$$P_n(x) = a_0 + a_1 x + \cdots + a_n x^n \tag{1.6}$$

If the polynomial is written in the standard form, the linear system (1.5) becomes

$$\mathbf{X}\mathbf{a} = \mathbf{y} \tag{1.7}$$

where the matrix

$$\mathbf{X} = \begin{vmatrix} 1 & x_0 & (x_0)^2 & \ldots & (x_0)^n \\ 1 & x_1 & (x_1)^2 & \ldots & (x_1)^n \\ \ldots & \ldots & \ldots & \ldots & \ldots \\ 1 & x_{n-1} & (x_{n-1})^2 & \ldots & (x_{n-1})^n \\ 1 & x_n & (x_n)^2 & \ldots & (x_n)^n \end{vmatrix} \tag{1.8}$$

is known as Vandermonde matrix.

If the abscissas x_i are different from each other, the following features are valid.

1) The determinant of Vandermonde matrix $\mathbf{X}$ is always nonzero.
2) The system (1.7) has a single solution.
3) An interpolating polynomial passes through support points.

The interpolating polynomial can be obtained with different techniques and it can apparently assume different forms.

Given $n+1$ support points (x_i, y_i), there is a unique n-degree polynomial passing through them.

1.3 Polynomial Interpolation

As a result, even though the polynomial apparently assumes different forms, it is ever the *same polynomial* with *the same maxima, minima, and zeros*.

Polynomials are largely employed in each field of numerical analysis: they are adopted in calculating integrals, in solving differential equations, in function approximation, and so on.

They are used especially for their following properties.

1) They are *easy to manage and use*: polynomial integration and derivatives do not present any problematic issues.
2) Parameter evaluation is quite easy.
3) It is easy to carry out a prevision in a point different from the assigned abscissa.
4) *Some properties that make them unique*: the sum, the subtraction, the product between two polynomials are still polynomial functions; if the scale of the variable x is changed, by adding or multiplying abscissas by any value, a polynomial is again obtained.

Moreover, polynomials were studied for several years and, as a result, the theory of polynomial approximation is well known and well established.

Finally, the analysis of the exact interpolation is *educationally* very important since it allows to analyze some numerical problems.

In spite of these favorable properties, a negative feature is to be underlined: *polynomials obtained through the exact interpolation often do not approximate some classes of function in an accurate manner*. Specifically, the inaccuracy arises when the polynomial interpolation is carried out without an appropriate care and when the polynomial degree is considerably high.

It is incorrect to think a function approximation is better for higher degrees of the polynomial obtained by the exact interpolation.

This thinking originates for three reasons.

1) There are theoretical motivations to think that the polynomial approximation accuracy improves by increasing the polynomial degree.

Weierstrass theorem. If $f(x)$ is a continuous function with continuous derivatives in an interval $[a, b]$, by assigning any positive value δ, there is a polynomial $P_n(x)$ with a degree equal to n that allows the following inequality for any value of x in the interval $[a, b]$:

$$|f(x) - P_n(x)| < \delta \tag{1.9}$$

In this case, the ambiguity is dictated by the fact that the interpolating polynomial in Weierstrass theorem is *not* the function that exactly interpolates some assigned points.

2) There is another theoretical reason that seems to motivate the use of larger polynomial degrees to achieve better approximations.

Taylor polynomials. It is possible to approximate a derivable function $f(x)$ around the point x_0 through a Taylor expansion:

$$P_n(x) = f(x_0) + f'(x_0)(x-x_0) + \cdots + R_{n+1}(x) \quad (1.10)$$

where

$$R_{n+1}(x) = \frac{1}{n!}\int_{x_0}^{x}(x-t)^n f^{(n+1)}(t)\,dt = \frac{(x-x_0)^{n+1}}{(n+1)!}f^{n+1}(\xi) \quad (1.11)$$

for ξ in the range $[x_0, x]$.

The Taylor polynomial is *not* obtained by using the exact interpolation for $n+1$ points; moreover, its validity cannot be extended to the range $[x_0, x_n]$, but it is limited to the neighborhood of x_0.

3) Finally, many examples of polynomial interpolations obtained through the exact interpolation where the error decreases by increasing the polynomial degree are reported in many books on numerical analysis. These examples are generally referred to special functions, such as $\sin(x)$ and $\cos(x)$.

Contrary to the appearance, it is very rare for higher interpolating polynomial degrees to continuously improve the function approximation; usually, the opposite is true.

When the function to be approximate presents asymptotic behaviors and/or discontinuities in the derivatives, the approximation through the method of exact polynomial interpolation must be avoided.

The polynomial coefficients can be evaluated by imposing conditions different from the ones already discussed (that is passing through $n+1$ data points). For example, the first or higher order derivatives may be assigned in some specific support points.

Specifically, if both the ordinate y_i and the first derivative y_i' are assigned for each support point, a Hermite polynomial is obtained.

It is always suitable to exploit the value of first or higher derivatives of the function to be interpolated to improve the accuracy.

The following assumption is made in the first part of this chapter.

The $n+1$ conditions needed for evaluating model parameters require to pass through the $n+1$ support points (x_i, y_i) with $i = 0, \ldots, n$, $x_i \neq x_j$, and $i \neq j$.

1.3.1
Error in Polynomial Interpolation

Suppose to approximate the function $f(x)$ through a polynomial $P_n(x)$ obtained by an exact interpolation with $n+1$ support points. As a certain function is approximated by a simplified model, one should also ask what is the difference between the complete model (the function) and the simplified model (the interpolating polynomial).

1.3 Polynomial Interpolation

Obviously, the gap between the function and the polynomial is negligible in correspondence with the support points. For all the remaining points, the following property is valid.

Error in a polynomial approximation. If the polynomial $P_n(x)$ is adopted to make a prevision of the value that the function $f(x)$ would have in correspondence with a specific point $x = z$, which is not a support point, the error estimation is given by the relation

$$f(z) - P_n(z) = (z-x_0)(z-x_1)\cdots(z-x_n)\frac{f^{n+1}(\xi)}{(n+1)!} \qquad (1.12)$$

where $x_0 < x_1 < \cdots < x_n$ and $x_0 \leq \xi \leq x_n$. The point ξ, where the $(n+1)$th derivative is evaluated, is unknown and varies according to z.

Relation (1.12) is valid for functions $f(x)$ that can be differentiated $n+1$ times. The formula to evaluate the error has some practical limitations.

1) The $(n+1)$th derivative is rarely known.
2) Usually, the error evaluated by the formula is not very useful, as its estimate is inaccurate.

For example, consider the function

$$y(x) = \frac{1}{x}$$

Given the abscissas 1., 2., 3., 4., 5. and using a 4-degree polynomial, the prevision $P_4(4.5) = .216146$ is obtained in correspondence with $z = 4.5$, with an absolute error equal to 0.006076.

The error can be estimated by using formula (1.12).

$$(4.5-1.)(4.5-2.)(4.5-3.)(4.5-4.)(4.5-5.)\frac{5!}{\xi^6 5!}$$

where $1. \leq \xi \leq 5$. As a consequence, the error estimation is in the range of $0.000021 \div 3.28125$ and it is too inaccurate to be useful.

However, this formula allows to make some important considerations.

1) About polynomial degree or the amount of support points.
2) On the prevision point z.
3) On the interval size.
4) About the disposition of abscissas $x_0, x_1, \ldots, x_n$.

1) From the formula, it seems that the error proportionally decreases to $(n+1)!$ by increasing the polynomial degree. It is true only for functions, with derivatives increasing slower than $n!$, that is, $\sin(x)$ and $\cos(x)$, whereas derivatives usually grow faster. For this reason, the ratio between the $(n+1)$th derivative and the term $(n+1)!$ initially decreases and then increases with the polynomial degree. As a consequence, the error of the polynomial interpolation can increase with the polynomial degree beyond a certain value.

2) The function

$$\Phi_{n+1}(z, x_0, x_1, \ldots, x_n) = (z-x_0)(z-x_1) \cdots (z-x_n) \quad (1.13)$$

is a $(n+1)$-degree polynomial with zeros in correspondence with the abscissas; as a result, it should alternate maxima and minima while their value exclusively depends on the location of abscissas.

If the abscissas $x_0, x_1, \ldots, x_n$ are evenly spaced, maxima and minima of the function $\Phi_{n+1}(z)$ are small in the center of the interval $[x_0, x_n]$ and large toward the borders. The higher the polynomial degree, the larger the absolute value of maxima and minima of the function $\Phi_{n+1}(z)$.

3) If the dimensions of the interval $[x_0, x_n]$ increase, the error in polynomial interpolation increases, too, especially when n is large, as the function $\Phi_{n+1}(z, x_0, x_1, \ldots x_n)$ increases. On the other hand, the error generally approaches zero when the interval tends to be zero.
4) Values of both $\Phi_{n+1}(z)$ and error strongly depend on the selection of the abscissas. Therefore, it is possible to select the abscissas for *minimizing the maximum* value of $\Phi_{n+1}(z)$ in the interval $[x_0, x_n]$. We will discuss this problem later.

The following general rules have to be taken into consideration to carry out an exact interpolation.

1) Do not use polynomials with a degree higher than 3–5.
2) The interpolation may become less accurate toward the borders of the interval.
3) If possible, abscissas must be appropriately selected.
4) The error may be very large outside the interval: avoid any extrapolation.

1.4
Roots-Product Form

A n-degree polynomial is equal to zero for n values of x: $w_1, w_2, \ldots w_n$. They are called *polynomial roots* and they can assume either real or complex values.

For example, the polynomial

$$\begin{aligned} P_3(x) &= x^3 - 2x^2 + 4x - 8 \\ &= (x-2)(x^2+4) = (x-2)(x-i2)(x+i2) \end{aligned}$$

has one real root and two complex roots.

A n-degree polynomial may always be written in the following form, called *roots-product form*:

$$P_n(x) = a_n(x-w_1)(x-w_2) \cdots (x-w_n) \quad (1.14)$$

The roots-product form is always well conditioned.

1.5 Standard Form

Knowing the n real roots $w_1, w_2, \ldots, w_n$ of the polynomial function and the value of the coefficient a_n, the *unique* n-degree polynomial can be immediately obtained.

If a polynomial is given in the roots-product form and the roots are all real numbers and the coefficient a_n is known, the prevision p in correspondence with $x = z$ can be evaluated with the following algorithm.

Algorithm 1.1 Roots-product form prevision

Input: the polynomial degree n, the roots $w_1, w_2, \ldots, w_n$, and the abscissa z.
Output: the prevision p in $x = z$.

```
p = aₙ
for i = 1(step 1), n
    p = p*(z−wᵢ)
```

Algorithm 1.1 requires n flops.

Algorithm 1.1 is always stable.

1.5
Standard Form

The most common form to describe an n-degree polynomial is the standard form

$$P_n(x) = a_0 + a_1 x + \cdots + a_n x^n \tag{1.15}$$

This form clearly highlights the fact that $P_n(x)$ is a polynomial with a degree equal to n.

The standard form (1.15) could be ill conditioned.

This means that a small perturbation on coefficients can completely modify the polynomial features, for example, roots can strongly change their values.

For example, if the polynomial (Wilkinson, 1963)

$$P_{20}(x) = (x-1)(x-2)(x-3) \cdots (x-19)(x-20)$$

is written in the standard form, it becomes

$$P_{20}(x) = x^{20} - 210 x^{19} + \cdots + 20!$$

If the coefficient 210 multiplying x^{19} is modified by a factor 10^{-7}, some roots of the new polynomial become complex numbers, even though they are evaluated without any numerical error.

The standard form is important to describe the polynomial and it should be used with care. It is worth noting the following points.

1) One is not obliged to write a polynomial in this form to represent the same polynomial.

2) It is unsuitable to perform operations with this form for evaluating a prevision in an assigned abscissa $x = z$.
3) More performing methods exist to calculate polynomial coefficients.

Point No. 1

If the polynomial is obtained in a different form, it is improper to transform it into the standard form; as already seen in the previous example, some ill-conditioned problems can arise.

For the same reason, it is also unseemly to explicitly get the polynomial in the standard form: since this form is ill conditioned, some problems can arise in evaluating a prevision. In addition, in a specific abscissa, the prevision can differ from the value of the data point adopted to evaluate the coefficients.

The 1-degree polynomial passing through the support points

$$x_0 = 100000., \quad y_0 = 1./3. \quad \text{and} \quad x_1 = 100001., \quad y_1 = -2./3.$$

with a precision of seven significant digits is

$$y = 100000.3 - x$$

Again, using seven significant digits, the value .3 rather than .3333333 in correspondence with $x = 100000.$ is obtained.

A polynomial can be written in its *centered standard form*:

$$P_n(x) = a_0 + a_1(x-c) + \cdots + a_n(x-c)^n \tag{1.16}$$

where the center c is an assigned constant.

Whether a polynomial is obtained through an exact interpolation and if the abscissa $x = 0$ is not a support point, it is inappropriate to use the *standard form*. A partial remedy against round-off errors is to adopt the *centered standard form* by choosing an internal abscissa c of the polynomial interval.

For example, selecting $c = 100000.$ as center, the previous polynomial becomes

$$y = .3333333 - (x - 100000.)$$

Then, $y = .3333333$ is obtained in correspondence with $x = 100000.$

Point No. 2

Suppose to know the parameters a_i of the polynomial in the standard form. These parameters may be obtained by techniques that differ from the exact interpolation, that is, by a Taylor expansion. To calculate the prevision in a specific point $x = z$, it is suitable to adopt the so-called *Horner method*.

Horner procedure:

$$P_n(z) = a_0 + z(a_1 + z(a_2 + z(\ldots z(a_{n-1} + a_n z)))) \tag{1.17}$$

Algorithm 1.2 Standard form prevision

Input: the polynomial degree n, coefficients of the polynomial in the standard form $a_0, a_1, \ldots, a_n$, and the abscissa z.

Output: the prevision p.

```
p = aₙ
for i = n−1(step−1), 0
    p = p*z + aᵢ
```

Algorithm 1.2 requires n flops.

Horner algorithm allows improving performances in computational time while preserving the standard form.
For example, the 4-degree polynomial

$$P_4(z) = a_0 + a_1 z + a_2 z^2 + a_3 z^3 + a_4 z^4$$

requires 10 multiplications and 4 additions; Horner algorithm needs only 4 multiplications and 4 additions.

Sometimes, it can be useful to also evaluate the first derivative in correspondence with z. It can be implemented by slightly modifying the previous algorithm.

Algorithm 1.3 Horner procedure with first derivative

Input: the polynomial degree n, coefficients of the polynomial in the standard form $a_0, a_1, \ldots, a_n$, and the abscissa z.
Output: the prevision p and the first derivative dy.

```
dy = 0
p = aₙ
for i = n−1(step−1), 0
    dy = dy*z + p
    p  = p*z + aᵢ
```

Algorithm 1.3 requires $2n$ flops.

Point No. 3

Usually, it is unsuitable to get parameters a_i by solving system (1.7) for the following reasons.

1) Vandermonde matrix is ill conditioned for high polynomial degrees and for abscissas not cleverly selected.
2) The standard form is ill conditioned when $x = 0$ is not a support point.
3) The solution of system (1.7) requires a number of calculations that are proportional to the cube of the polynomial degree. It will be shown how it is possible to obtain an interpolating polynomial with a computational effort equal to the square of the polynomial degree.

It is for the aforementioned reasons numerous books on numerical analysis consider it unwise the use of the standard form for polynomials.

On the other hand, this form has been revalued and largely used to solve differential equation problems with boundary conditions (see Buzzi-Ferraris and Manenti, 2011b), especially because of the following problem features:

- Polynomials have a relatively small degree (3–5).
- Data points can be accurately selected.
- The zero is one of the data points.
- Many polynomials of the same order and with the same support abscissas are used.
- The first and the second derivatives must be evaluated in some predetermined points within the polynomial validity interval.

It shall be shown how the standard form is significantly advantageous for such polynomials (Buzzi-Ferraris and Manenti, 2011b).

1.6
Lagrange Method

With the Lagrange method, one need not solve the square system (1.5) in $n+1$ equations (Ralston and Rabinowitz, 1988).

The n-degree polynomial is written as the linear combination of $n+1$ polynomials, each one with degree n:

$$P_n(x) = a_0 L_0(x) + a_1 L_1(x) + \cdots + a_n L_n(x) \tag{1.18}$$

In Lagrange method, the polynomials $L_0(x), L_1(x), \ldots, L_n(x)$ are selected in order to make unitary the diagonal of the matrix $\mathbf{F}$ of the system (1.5).

The polynomial

$$L_i(x) = \frac{(x-x_0)(x-x_1) \cdots (x-x_{i-1})(x-x_{i+1}) \cdots (x-x_n)}{(x_i-x_0)(x_i-x_1) \cdots (x_i-x_{i-1})(x_i-x_{i+1}) \cdots (x_i-x_n)} \tag{1.19}$$

is called Lagrange polynomial.

The polynomial $L_i(x)$ is an n-degree polynomial that is null in correspondence with the abscissa $x_j (j = 0, \ldots, n; j \neq i)$ and it is equal to 1 in correspondence with the abscissa x_i.

The system (1.5) becomes

$$\mathbf{Ia} = \mathbf{y} \tag{1.20}$$

and the polynomial $P_n(x)$ passing through the $n+1$ support points is immediately written

$$P_n(x) = \sum_{i=0}^{n} y_i L_i(x) \tag{1.21}$$

For example, given the support points $(1, 1)$, $(2, 2)$, and $(3, 4)$, the 2-degree polynomial in the Lagrange form is

$$P_2(x) = \frac{(x-2)(x-3)}{(1-2)(1-3)} + 2\frac{(x-1)(x-3)}{(2-1)(2-3)} + 4\frac{(x-1)(x-2)}{(3-1)(3-2)}$$

1.6 Lagrange Method

Coefficients a_i of the Lagrange form correspond to the values y_i of the support points.

This version of Lagrange method is useful in manual evaluations or simple programs, but it does not perform so well when it is implemented within a general program.

Therefore, the Lagrange method should be improved to overcome the following weaknesses.

1) The number of calculations required for a prevision in an abscissa $x = z$ is large by adopting equation (1.21).
2) When several previsions are performed in correspondence with different abscissas, shared evaluations are not exploited.
3) The method does not allow to exploit the calculations already performed when a new support point is to be introduced (by increasing the polynomial degree).

It is useful to adopt a rearranged Lagrange form (Hamming, 1962).

A Lagrange polynomial can be written in the *barycentric form*:

$$c_i = \frac{1}{(x_i-x_0)(x_i-x_1) \cdots (x_i-x_{i-1})(x_i-x_{i+1}) \cdots (x_i-x_n)} \quad (1.22)$$

with $(i = 0, \ldots, n)$;

$$v_i = \frac{c_i}{z-x_i} \quad (i = 0, \ldots, n) \quad (1.23)$$

$$w_i = \frac{v_i}{\sum_{k=0}^{n} v_k} \quad (i = 0, \ldots, n) \quad (1.24)$$

$$P_n(z) = \sum_{i=0}^{n} w_i y_i \quad (1.25)$$

Coefficients c_i are called *coefficients of the Lagrange form*.

Coefficients c_i can be iteratively obtained by introducing a support point at a time. In doing so, a limitation of the Lagrange method is overcome: new points can be introduced (so to increase the polynomial degree) without restarting from the beginning.

In fact,

$$c_0 = 1 \quad (1.26)$$

$$c_0 = \frac{1}{(x_0-x_1)}, \quad c_1 = \frac{1}{(x_1-x_0)} = -c_0 \quad (1.27)$$

$$c_0 = \frac{1}{(x_0-x_1)(x_0-x_2)}, \quad c_1 = \frac{1}{(x_1-x_0)(x_1-x_2)}, \quad c_2 = -c_0-c_1 \quad (1.28)$$

and so on.

Algorithm 1.4 Coefficients for Lagrange form

Input: the polynomial degree n, abscissas $x_0, x_1, \ldots, x_n$.
Output: coefficients for Lagrange $c_0, c_1, \ldots, c_n$.

$$
\begin{aligned}
&c_0 = 1 \\
&\text{for } k = 1(\text{step } 1), n \\
&\quad \text{for } i = 0(\text{step } 1), k-1 \\
&\quad\quad c_i = c_i/(x_i - x_k) \\
&\quad c_k = -\sum_{i=0}^{k-1} c_i
\end{aligned}
$$

Algorithm 1.4 requires $n(n+1)/2$ flops.

Once the coefficients are evaluated, it is possible to make a prevision in correspondence with a point $x = z$ using the barycentric formula.

For the reasons that will be explained later, it is suitable to separately evaluate the weight w_i of the barycentric formula and the prevision p.

Algorithm 1.5 Coefficients w_i for Lagrange form

Input: the polynomial degree n, abscissas $x_0, x_1, \ldots, x_n$, coefficients $c_0, c_1, \ldots, c_n$, and abscissa $x = z$.
Output: weights of the barycentric formula $w_0, w_1, \ldots, w_n$.

$$
\begin{aligned}
&\text{for } i = 0(\text{step } 1), n \\
&\quad w_i = \frac{c_i}{z - x_i} \\
&\text{den} = \sum_{i=0}^{n} w_i \\
&\text{for } i = 0(\text{step } 1), n \\
&\quad w_i = \frac{w_i}{\text{den}}
\end{aligned}
$$

Algorithm 1.5 requires $n+1$ flops, $n+1$ divisions, and n addictions.

Once the coefficients w_i are known, the prevision in $x = z$ can be evaluated using the barycentric formula.

Algorithm 1.6 Prevision with the barycentric Lagrange formula

Input: the polynomial degree n, weights $w_0, w_1, \ldots, w_n$, and ordinates of the support points $y_0, y_1, \ldots, y_n$.
Output: prevision p.

$$
\begin{aligned}
&p = 0 \\
&\text{for } i = 0(\text{step } 1), n \\
&\quad p = p + w_i y_i
\end{aligned}
$$

Algorithm 1.6 requires $n+1$ flops. As a result, to make an estimate, the Lagrange method requires $n(n+1)/2$ flops to evaluate c_i, $n+1$ flops, $n+1$ divisions and additions to evaluate w_i, and other $n+1$ flops to get $P_n(z)$.

The Lagrange function in the BzzInterpolation class evaluates polynomial previsions through the Lagrange method.

Example 1.2

Let $\mathbf{x} = \{1., 1.3, 1.6, 1.9, 2.2\}$ be the abscissas for the function $y_i = e^{-x_i^2}$. Evaluate Lagrange previsions for $\mathbf{z} = \{1.8, 1.65, 1.35\}$.
The program is

```
#include "BzzMath.hpp"
void main(void)
   {
   BzzPrint("\n\nLagrange");
   BzzVector x(5,1.,1.3,1.6,1.9,2.2);
   BzzVector y(5);
   for(int i = 1;i <= 5;i++)
       y[i] = exp(-x[i]*x[i]);
   BzzInterpolation p(x,y);
   double prev = p.Lagrange(1.8);
   BzzPrint("\nPrevision %e",prev);
   prev = p.Lagrange(1.65);
   BzzPrint("\nPrevision %e",prev);
   prev = p.Lagrange(1.35);
   BzzPrint("\nPrevision %e",prev);
   BzzPause();
   }
```

The polynomial interpolation using the Lagrange method presents the following shortcomings.

1) The polynomial form is more difficult to use, for example, when the polynomial is adopted to estimate the derivatives of the interpolated function.
2) The error is harder to estimate.
3) Theoretically, it requires a number of calculations slightly larger than the Newton method (explained in the next paragraph). In practice, differences in the computational time are negligible.

The Lagrange method is important from a theoretical point of view, as it allows to simply demonstrate the existence and the uniqueness of an interpolating polynomial. It is even practically important for three features.

1) The value of parameters corresponds to the ordinate of support points.
2) It allows better performances in CPU times when the interpolation is performed for the same points but with different functions.
3) The Lagrange form is always well-conditioned.

Therefore:

1) As the matrix **F** of the system is converted into the identity matrix **I**, model parameters are the values of y in correspondence with the abscissas. Therefore, they have a mathematical (and sometimes physical) meaning, contrary to all other forms. This feature is fundamental for the finite elements method. In fact, in this important method for integrating differential equations with boundary conditions, it is possible to make two polynomials continuous in two adjacent elements by simply imposing the equivalence of their parameters in the shared point.
2) The value of the ordinates y_i are not involved in the evaluation of the coefficients w_i. Hence, if the same procedure is applied to different functions with the same points x_i, the same coefficients w_i are obtained. For this reason, it is suitable to separately evaluate coefficients w_i and the prevision P.

For example, suppose to evaluate a prevision by a parabolic interpolation in an interval L in correspondence with the point $0.75L$ for different functions, once the function values are assigned in correspondence with three points: $0, 0.5L, L$. The 2-degree interpolating polynomial is

$$P_2(x) = y_0 \frac{(x-0.5L)(x-L)}{(-0.5L)(-L)} + y_1 \frac{x(x-L)}{(0.5L)(-0.5L)} + y_2 \frac{x(x-0.5L)}{L(0.5L)}$$

The prevision in $0.75L$ is

$$P_2(0.75L) = y_0 \frac{0.25(-0.25)}{0.5} + y_1 \frac{0.75(-0.25)}{(0.5)(0.5)} + y_2 \frac{0.75(0.25)}{0.5}$$

and by simplifying it

$$P_2(0.75L) = -0.125 y_0 + 0.75 y_1 + 0.375 y_2$$

This feature is fundamental whenever a linear operator is involved, for example, to get formulae for the numerical integration (see Buzzi-Ferraris and Manenti, 2011b). Another advantage of the Lagrange method is the easiness of writing a program based on this algorithm to obtain a polynomial prevision (given $n+1$ support points).

Algorithm 1.7 Prevision with Lagrange

Input: the polynomial degree n, points $x_0, x_1, \ldots, x_n$, ordinates of the support points $y_0, y_1, \ldots, y_n$, and the prevision point $x = z$.
Output: prevision p.

```
p = 0
for i = 0(step 1), n
    r = y_i
    for k = 0(step 1), n
        if (i ≠ k) r = r(z−x_k)/(x_i−x_k)
    p = p+r
```

1.7
Newton Method

This method presents some interesting features to get an n-degree polynomial passing through $n+1$ points (Kincaid and Cheney, 1990).

1) The k-degree polynomial is built by starting from the $(k-1)$-degree polynomial.
2) To build the polynomial and to evaluate the prevision, the required number of flops is small.
3) Round-off errors are small, too, throughout the calculations.
4) It is possible to estimate the error by using the polynomial rather than the function.

An n-degree polynomial in the *Newton form* is

$$P_n(x) = a_0 + a_1(x-x_0) + a_2(x-x_0)(x-x_1) + \cdots \\ + a_n(x-x_0) \cdots (x-x_{n-1}) \tag{1.29}$$

For example, given the support points $(1,1)$, $(2,2)$, and $(3,4)$, the 2-degree polynomial in the Newton form is

$$P_2(x) = 1 + (x-1) + 0.5(x-1)(x-2)$$

1.7.1
Coefficients' Evaluation

If the polynomial is written in the Newton form, system (1.5) becomes

$$\begin{aligned} a_0 &= y_0 \\ a_0 + a_1(x_1-x_0) &= y_1 \\ &\cdots \\ a_0 + a_1(x_n-x_0) + \cdots + a_n(x_n-x_0) \cdots (x_n-x_{n-1}) &= y_n \end{aligned} \tag{1.30}$$

The system solution is immediate as the coefficient matrix is triangular.
For example, given the support points $(1,1)$, $(2,2)$, and $(3,4)$, the system (1.30) is

$$\begin{aligned} a_0 &= 1 \\ a_0 + a_1(2-1) &= 2 & (a_1 = 1) \\ a_0 + a_1(3-1) + a_2(3-1)(3-2) &= 4 & (a_2 = .5) \end{aligned}$$

The solution of system (1.30) requires n^2 flops.

It is useful to change the point of view.

Newton method was considered as a way to get a *linear system with an easier solution*. It can also be considered as a criterion to build polynomials with increasing degree.

The kth coefficient a_k of the polynomial in the Newton form is denoted by expression $f[x_0, x_1, \ldots, x_k]$, where x_i denotes the points adopted to get coefficients $a_0, a_1, \ldots, a_k$.

Using this kind of representation, one can rewrite the polynomial as follows:

$$P_n(x) = f[x_0] + f[x_0, x_1](x-x_0) + f[x_0, x_1, x_2](x-x_0)(x-x_1) + \cdots \\ + f[x_0, x_1, \ldots, x_n](x-x_0)(x-x_1) \cdots (x-x_{n-1}) \qquad (1.31)$$

The k-degree polynomial passing through the support points (x_0, y_0), (x_1, y_1), ..., (x_k, y_k) is denoted by $P_k(x, x_0, x_1, \ldots, x_k)$. The points $x_0, x_1, \ldots, x_k$ are arbitrarily selected from among the possible points.

The polynomial $P_k(x, x_0, x_1, \ldots, x_k)$ does *not* change even when the *sequence* of the support points is changed. However, only the aspect of the polynomial is different.

For example,

$$P_2(x) = f[x_0] + f[x_0, x_1](x-x_0) + f[x_0, x_1, x_2](x-x_0)(x-x_1) \\ = f[x_1] + f[x_1, x_2](x-x_1) + f[x_1, x_2, x_0](x-x_1)(x-x_2)$$

Therefore, by assigning the support points

$$x_0 = 1, y_0 = 1;\ x_1 = 2, y_1 = 2;\ x_3 = 3, y_3 = 4$$

it takes place

$$P_2(x) = 1 + (x-1) + 0.5(x-1)(x-2) \\ = 2 + 2(x-2) + 0.5(x-2)(x-3)$$

By knowing the $(k-1)$-degree polynomial $P_{k-1}(x, x_0, x_1, \ldots, x_{k-1})$, it is possible to evaluate the polynomial $P_k(x, x_0, x_1, \ldots, x_k)$ as follows.

Denoting by $\Phi_k(x, x_0, x_1, \ldots, x_{k-1})$ the k-degree polynomial:

$$\Phi_k(x, x_0, x_1, \ldots, x_{k-1}) = (x-x_0)(x-x_1) \cdots (x-x_{k-1}) \qquad (1.32)$$

This polynomial is equal to zero in correspondence with the points $x_0, x_1, \ldots, x_{k-1}$ and it has also the coefficient $a_k = 1$.

The k-degree polynomial

$$S_k(x) = P_{k-1}(x, x_0, x_1, \ldots, x_{k-1}) + \lambda_k \Phi_k(x, x_0, x_1, \ldots, x_{k-1}) \qquad (1.33)$$

is a linear combination of the two polynomials $P_{k-1}(x, x_0, x_1, \ldots, x_{k-1})$ and $\Phi_k(x, x_0, x_1, \ldots, x_{k-1})$. Therefore, it passes through the support points (x_0, y_0), (x_1, y_1), ..., (x_{k-1}, y_{k-1}). Varying the parameter λ_k, a family of k-degree polynomials all passing through the support points is generated. By imposing a new support point (x_k, y_k) selected from among the data points not yet used, λ_k can be determined and, therefore, the polynomial P_k passing through the support points $(x_0, y_0), \ldots,$ (x_{k-1}, y_{k-1}), (x_k, y_k).

Since

$$\lambda_k = \frac{y_k - P_{k-1}(x_k)}{(x_k-x_0)(x_k-x_1) \cdots (x_k-x_{k-1})} \qquad (1.34)$$

it results

$$P_k(x) = P_{k-1}(x) + (y_k - P_{k-1}(x_k))\frac{(x-x_0)(x-x_1)\cdots(x-x_{k-1})}{(x_k-x_0)(x_k-x_1)\cdots(x_k-x_{k-1})} \quad (1.35)$$

For example, suppose to find out the 2-degree polynomial passing through the support points $(1,1)$, $(2,2)$, and $(3,4)$.

The zero-degree polynomial passing through the first point is

$$P_0(x) = 1$$

The 1-degree polynomial passing through first two points is

$$P_1(x) = P_0(x) + \frac{(y_1 - P_0(x_1))(x-x_0)}{(x_1-x_0)} = 1 + (x-1) = x$$

Finally, the 2-degree polynomial is

$$P_2(x) = P_1(x) + \frac{(y_2 - P_1(x_2))(x-x_0)(x-x_1)}{(x_2-x_0)(x_2-x_1)}$$
$$= x + 0.5(x-1)(x-2)$$

The number of operations required to determine the polynomial parameters is equal to the number of operations required to solve the system (1.30), even though their interpretation is changed. Hence, n^2 flops are required.

The idea to sequentially get the polynomials starting from other polynomial with a small degree can be further improved by developing a more performing algorithm.

Rather than carrying out the linear combination between the $(k-1)$-degree polynomial and the k-degree polynomial, it is worth considering the following linear combination between two $(k-1)$-degree polynomials:

$$S_k(x) = \frac{(x-x_0)P_{k-1}(x,x_1,\ldots,x_k) - (x-x_k)P_{k-1}(x,x_0,\ldots,x_{k-1})}{\lambda_k} \quad (1.36)$$

By varying λ_k, one still obtains a family of k-degree polynomials. Assigning the value $x_k - x_0$ to λ_k, the k-degree polynomial is obtained:

$$P_k(x,x_0,x_1,\ldots,x_k) = \frac{(x-x_0)P_{k-1}(x,x_1,\ldots,x_k) - (x-x_k)P_{k-1}(x,x_0,\ldots,x_{k-1})}{(x_k-x_0)}$$
$$(1.37)$$

passing through the support points $(x_0,y_0),\ldots,(x_{k-1},y_{k-1}),(x_k,y_k)$.

It is worth noting that expression $f[x_0,x_1,\ldots,x_k]$ is coefficient a_k of $P_k(x,x_0,x_1,\ldots,x_k)$.

Coefficient a_{k-1} of $P_{k-1}(x,x_1,x_2,\ldots,x_k)$ can be rewritten with expression $f[x_1,\ldots x_k]$, whereas coefficient a_{k-1} of $P_{k-1}(x,x_0,\ldots,x_{k-1})$ is $f[x_0,\ldots x_{k-1}]$. From relation (1.37), it can be deduced that coefficient a_k of the polynomial P_k should be

$$f[x_0,x_1,\ldots,x_k] = \frac{(f[x_1,\ldots,x_k] - f[x_0,\ldots,x_{k-1}])}{x_k - x_0} \quad (1.38)$$

Coefficient $f[x_0, x_1, \ldots, x_k]$ is called kth *rational difference* for relation (1.38).

For example, to find out the 2-degree polynomial passing through the points $(1,1)$, $(2,2)$, and $(3,4)$, it is possible to set up the following scheme:

$$\begin{array}{lll} x_0 = 1 & y_0 = f[x_0] = 1 & \\ & & f[x_0, x_1] = 1 \\ x_1 = 2 & y_1 = f[x_1] = 2 & \qquad\qquad f[x_0, x_1, x_2] = 0.5 \\ & & f[x_1, x_2] = 2 \\ x_2 = 3 & y_2 = f[x_2] = 4 & \end{array}$$

Relation (1.38) can be adopted to suitably evaluate the coefficients of the polynomial in the Newton form (1.31).

Algorithm 1.8 Coefficients in the Newton form

Input: the polynomial degree n, abscissas $x_0, x_1, \ldots, x_n$, and ordinates $y_0, y_1, \ldots, y_n$.
Output: coefficient of Newton form $a_0, a_1, \ldots, a_n$.

$$\begin{aligned} &\text{for } i = 0(\text{step } 1), n \\ &\quad d_i = y_i \\ &a_0 = d_0 \\ &\text{for } k = 1(\text{step } 1), n \\ &\quad \text{for } i = 0(\text{step } 1), n-k \\ &\qquad d_i = (d_{i+1} - d_i)/(x_{i+k} - x_i) \\ &\quad a_k = d_0 \end{aligned}$$

Algorithm 1.8 requires $n(n+1)/2$ flops.

It is not necessary to store all the scheme of the rational differences: an auxiliary vector **d** is sufficient.

The rational differences can also be written in the following form:

$$\begin{aligned} f[x_0, x_1, x_2, \ldots, x_k] &= \frac{f[x_0]}{(x_0 - x_1)(x_0 - x_2) \cdots (x_0 - x_k)} \\ &\quad + \frac{f[x_1]}{(x_1 - x_0)(x_1 - x_2) \cdots (x_1 - x_k)} + \cdots \\ &\quad + \frac{f[x_k]}{(x_k - x_0)(x_k - x_1) \cdots (x_k - x_{k-1})} \end{aligned} \qquad (1.39)$$

From relation (1.39), it can be deduced that $f[x_{i_0}, x_{i_1}, \ldots, x_{i_k}]$ is constant against index permutations $i_0, i_1, \ldots, i_k$ in *classical analysis*.

For example,

$$f[x_0, x_1, x_2] = f[x_2, x_0, x_1] = f[x_1, x_2, x_0] = f[x_0, x_2, x_1]$$

From a theoretical point of view, the order of support points is not relevant. In fact,

$$P_2(x) = f[x_0] + f[x_0, x_1](x-x_0) + f[x_0, x_1, x_2](x-x_0)(x-x_1)$$
$$= f[x_1] + f[x_1, x_2](x-x_1) + f[x_1, x_2, x_0](x-x_1)(x-x_2)$$

In *numerical analysis*, permutations are not equivalent.

If the polynomial is used for a prevision in a point $x = z$, which is known before evaluating the polynomial coefficients, it is suitable to sort the points against their distance from z. The prevision is more accurate as the operations are better focused on the final objective and the maximum accuracy is obtained by adjusting the prevision with terms that are gradually less relevant.

As an example, given the support points $(1,1)$, $(2,2)$, and $(3,4)$, it is suitable to introduce the points sorted as $(2,2)$, $(3,4)$, and $(1,1)$ in evaluating a prevision in correspondence with $z = 2.1$.

The fact that the rational differences do not depend on the index permutations leads to another consequence.

There are different ways (equivalent for the classical analysis) to write the rational differences.

For example,

$$f[x_0, x_1, x_2] = \frac{(f[x_0, x_1] - f[x_0, x_2])}{x_1 - x_2} = \frac{(f[x_0, x_1] - f[x_1, x_2])}{x_0 - x_2}$$

Among the possible choices to evaluate the rational differences, the best sequence *in terms of numerical accuracy* is generally the following one, called *Neville sequence*:

$$\begin{array}{llllll}
x_0 & y_0 = f[x_0] & & & & \\
 & & f[x_0, x_1] & & & \\
x_1 & y_1 = f[x_1] & & f[x_0, x_1, x_2] & & \\
 & & f[x_1, x_2] & & f[x_0, x_1, x_2, x_3] & \\
x_2 & y_2 = f[x_2] & & f[x_1, x_2, x_3] & & f[x_0, x_1, x_2, x_3, x_4] \\
 & & f[x_2, x_3] & & f[x_1, x_2, x_3, x_4] & \\
x_3 & y_3 = f[x_3] & & f[x_2, x_3, x_4] & & \\
 & & f[x_3, x_4] & & & \\
x_4 & y_4 = f[x_4] & & & & \\
\end{array}$$

Aitken sequence is a possible alternative, even though it is usually less accurate:

$$\begin{array}{llllll}
x_0 & y_0 = f[x_0] & & & & \\
 & & f[x_0, x_1] & & & \\
x_1 & y_1 = f[x_1] & & f[x_0, x_1, x_2] & & \\
 & & f[x_0, x_2] & & f[x_0, x_1, x_2, x_3] & \\
x_2 & y_2 = f[x_2] & & f[x_0, x_2, x_3] & & f[x_0, x_1, x_2, x_3, x_4] \\
 & & f[x_0, x_3] & & f[x_0, x_2, x_3, x_4] & \\
x_3 & y_3 = f[x_3] & & f[x_0, x_3, x_4] & & \\
 & & f[x_0, x_4] & & & \\
x_4 & y_4 = f[x_4] & & & & \\
\end{array}$$

For example, to find out the 2-degree polynomial passing through the support points $(1,1)$, $(2,2)$, and $(3,4)$ ordered by growing abscissas, the Neville scheme is

$$\begin{array}{lll}
x_0 = 1 & y_0 = f[x_0] = 1 & f[x_0, x_1] = \dfrac{2-1}{2-1} = 1 \\
x_1 = 2 & y_1 = f[x_1] = 2 & \qquad\qquad\qquad\qquad f[x_0, x_1, x_2] = \dfrac{2-1}{3-1} = \dfrac{1}{2} \\
x_2 = 3 & y_2 = f[x_2] = 4 & f[x_1, x_2] = \dfrac{4-2}{3-2} = 2 \\
\end{array}$$

and the Aitken scheme is

$$\begin{array}{llll}
x_0 = 1 & y_0 = f[x_0] = 1 & f[x_0, x_1] = \dfrac{2-1}{2-1} = 1 & \\
x_1 = 2 & y_1 = f[x_1] = 2 & & f[x_0, x_1, x_2] = \dfrac{1.5-1}{3-2} = \dfrac{1}{2} \\
x_2 = 3 & y_2 = f[x_2] = 4 & f[x_0, x_2] = \dfrac{4-1}{3-1} = \dfrac{3}{2} &
\end{array}$$

Many forms of Newton method can be obtained from these two schemes to represent the same polynomial. For example, from the Neville scheme

$$\begin{aligned}
P_2(x) &= f[x_0] + f[x_0, x_1](x-x_0) + f[x_0, x_1, x_2](x-x_0)(x-x_1) \\
&= 1 + (x-1) + 0.5(x-1)(x-2) \\
P_2(x) &= f[x_1] + f[x_1, x_2](x-x_1) + f[x_0, x_1, x_2](x-x_1)(x-x_2) \\
&= 2 + 2(x-2) + 0.5(x-2)(x-3) \\
P_2(x) &= f[x_2] + f[x_1, x_2](x-x_2) + f[x_0, x_1, x_2](x-x_2)(x-x_1) \\
&= 4 + 2(x-3) + 0.5(x-3)(x-2)
\end{aligned}$$

1.7.2
Previsions

Once the coefficients a_k are calculated, the estimate in $x = z$ is obtained by applying the Horner scheme:

$$P_n(z) = a_0 + (z-x_0)(a_1 + (z-x_1)(\cdots)) \tag{1.40}$$

Algorithm 1.9 Prevision with the Newton form

Input: the polynomial degree n, points $x_0, x_1, \ldots, x_n$, coefficients of Newton form $a_0, a_1, \ldots, a_n$, and the point z.
Output: prevision p.

$$\begin{aligned}
&p = a_n \\
&\text{for } i = n-1(\text{step}-1), 0 \\
&\quad p = a_i + p(z-x_i)
\end{aligned}$$

Algorithm 1.9 requires n multiplications and $2n$ additions.

For example, given the polynomial

$$P_2(x) = 1 + (x-1) + 0.5(x-1)(x-2)$$

the prevision in $z = 1.5$ is

$$p = 0.5; \quad p = 1 + 0.5(1.5-2) = 0.75; \quad p = 1 + 0.75(1.5-1) = 1.375$$

The function `Newton` in the `BzzInterpolation` class evaluates polynomial previsions with the Newton method.

Example 1.3

Let $\mathbf{x} = \{1., 1.3, 1.6, 1.9, 2.2\}$ be the abscissas for the function $y_i = e^{-x_i^2}$. Evaluate Newton previsions in correspondence with $\mathbf{z} = \{1.8, 1.65, 1.35\}$.
The program is

```
#include "BzzMath.hpp"
void main(void)
    {
    BzzPrint("\n\nNewton");
    BzzVector x(5,1.,1.3,1.6,1.9,2.2);
    BzzVector y(5);
    for(int i = 1;i <= 5;i++)
        y[i] = exp(-x[i]*x[i]);
    BzzInterpolation p(x,y);
    double prev = p.Newton(1.8);
    BzzPrint("\nPrevision %e",prev);
    prev = p.Newton(1.65);
    BzzPrint("\nPrevision %e",prev);
    prev = p.Newton(1.35);
    BzzPrint("\nPrevision %e",prev);
    BzzPause();
    }
```

1.7.3 Additional Data Point

When a new point is introduced in a polynomial approximation, it is necessary to decide whether the point is to be added to the existing ones (and the interpolating polynomial degree is to be increased) or the point must replace an old point (by maintaining the current polynomial degree).

The former problem is solved by adopting either the Newton method or the barycentric Lagrange method. Evidently, the latter problem can be solved by considering the previous n support points that are still active together with the new point, as if $n+1$ support points were simultaneously assigned.

If the parameters of the previous polynomial were evaluated by using the Newton method, it is possible to exploit the calculations already executed.

In fact, let us consider four support points (x_1, y_1), (x_2, y_2), (x_3, y_3), and (x_4, y_4) adopted to define the polynomial $P_3(x)$. To replace the point $x_4, f[x_4]$ with the new point $x_0 = v, f[x_0] = f(v)$, the rational differences necessary to build the new polynomial are

$$P_3(x) = f[x_0] + f[x_0, x_1](x-x_0) + f[x_0, x_1, x_2](x-x_0)(x-x_1) \\ + f[x_0, x_1, x_2, x_3](x-x_0)(x-x_1)(x-x_2) \quad (1.41)$$

which uses the support points (x_0, y_0), (x_1, y_1), (x_2, y_2), (x_3, y_3) and even the rational differences to build the previous polynomial:

$$P_3(x) = f[x_1] + f[x_1, x_2](x-x_1) + f[x_1, x_2, x_3](x-x_1)(x-x_2) \\ + f[x_1, x_2, x_3, x_4](x-x_1)(x-x_2)(x-x_3) \tag{1.42}$$

$$\begin{array}{llll}
x_0 = v & f[x_0] = f(v) & & \\
& & f[x_0, x_1] & \\
x_1 & f[x_1] & & f[x_0, x_1, x_2] \\
& & f[x_1, x_2] & & f[x_0, x_1, x_2, x_3] \\
x_2 & f[x_2] & & f[x_1, x_2, x_3] & \\
& & f[x_2, x_3] & & f[x_1, x_2, x_3, x_4] \\
x_3 & f[x_3] & & f[x_2, x_3, x_4] & \\
& & f[x_3, x_4] & & \\
x_4 & f[x_4] & & &
\end{array}$$

New terms $f[x_0], f[x_0, x_1], f[x_0, x_1, x_2]$, and $f[x_0, x_1, x_2, x_3]$ of the scheme are the coefficients of the new polynomial. They can be evaluated from coefficients of the previous polynomial, without necessarily re-evaluating the overall scheme.

For example, consider the following support points: $(1, 1), (2, 2)$, and $(3, 4)$. In this case, the polynomial in the Newton form is

$$P_2(x) = 1 + (x-1) + 0.5(x-1)(x-2)$$

Now, by introducing the new support point $(0, 3)$ and, at the same time, removing the existing point $(3, 4)$, the scheme of rational differences becomes

$$\begin{array}{llll}
x_0 = 0 & y_0 = f[x_0] = 3 & & \\
& & f[x_0, x_1] = -2 & \\
x_1 = 1 & y_1 = f[x_1] = 1 & & f[x_0, x_1, x_2] = 1.5 \\
& & f[x_1, x_2] = 1 & \\
x_2 = 2 & y_2 = f[x_2] = 2 & & f[x_1, x_2, x_3] = 0.5 \\
& & f[x_2, x_3] = 2 & \\
x_3 = 3 & y_3 = f[x_3] = 4 & &
\end{array}$$

and the polynomial passing through the support points $(0, 3), (1, 1), (2, 2)$ becomes

$$P_2(x) = 3 - 2x + 1.5x(x-1)$$

1.7.4
Derivatives Evaluation

Let us consider Algorithm 1.9 to evaluate a polynomial prevision with the Newton form.

The same algorithm can be seen from a different point of view: it allows to modify the polynomial parameters a_i in order to replace the last support point through the polynomial prevision in z.

Algorithm 1.10

Input: the polynomial degree n, points $x_0, x_1, \ldots, x_n$, coefficients of Newton form $a_0, a_1, \ldots, a_n$, and the new point z for replacing x_n.

Output: the new $n+1$ coefficients $a_0, a_1, \ldots, a_n$ of the Newton form.

$$\text{for } i = n-1(\text{step}-1), 0$$
$$a_i = a_i + a_{i+1}(z-x_i)$$

As the algorithm is substantially the same as Algorithm 1.9, it results

$$P_n(z) = a_0 \tag{1.43}$$

As a result, the *same* polynomial (apart from round-off errors) is now expressed as if the support points were $(z, P_n(z)), (x_0, y_0), \ldots, (x_{n-1}, y_{n-1})$:

$$P_n(x) = f[z] + f[z, x_0](x-z) + f[z, x_0, x_1](x-z)(x-x_0) + \cdots$$
$$+ f[z, x_0, x_1, \ldots, x_{n-1}](x-z)(x-x_0)(x-x_1) \cdots (x-x_{n-2}) \tag{1.44}$$

It is important to realize the difference between the following problems.

1) An *authentic new support point* is introduced and one of the existing points is deleted: a *new* polynomial is obtained and it is far from the original one.
2) As a new support point, the polynomial prevision is adopted in a specific point and one of the existing support points is deleted: the polynomial is the same as the original one, but it is presented in a Newton form as though support points were changed.

For example, by considering the following support points $(1, 1), (2, 2)$, and $(3, 4)$, the polynomial in the Newton form is

$$P_2(x) = 1 + (x-1) + 0.5(x-1)(x-2)$$

In $x = z = 1.5$, the polynomial prevision is $P_2(x) = 1.375$. The polynomial coefficients can be modified in order to write it into the Newton form with the following points: the polynomial prevision $z = (1.5, 1.375)$ and the two previous points $(1, 1)$ and $(2, 2)$.

The new polynomial form is

$$a_2 = 0.5$$
$$a_1 = 1. + 0.5(1.5-2) = 0.75$$
$$a_0 = 1. + 0.75(1.5-1) = 1.375$$

The same previous polynomial can be rewritten as follows

$$P_2(x) = 1.375 + 0.75(x-1.5) + 0.5(x-1.5)(x-1)$$

If Algorithm 1.10 is repeated n times with ever the same point z, the polynomial in the special Newton form, where all the support points have the same abscissa z, is obtained.

$$P_n(x) = f[z] + f[z, z](x-z) + f[z, z, z](x-z)^2 + \cdots$$
$$+ f[z, z, \ldots, z](x-z)^n \tag{1.45}$$

This special form corresponds to the *standard centered form* with z as the center.

For example, applying the previous algorithm just once results in

$$a_2 = 0.5, \quad a_1 = 0.75 + 0.5(1.5 - 1.) = 1., \quad a_0 = 1.375 + 1(0) = 1.375$$
$$P_2(x) = 1.375 + (x - 1.5) + 0.5(x - 1.5)^2$$

This polynomial form is useful to easily evaluate the derivatives in $x = z$.

In fact, the ith derivative evaluated in $x = z$ is

$$P^{(i)}(z) = i! a_i \tag{1.46}$$

For example, writing the polynomial in the form

$$P_2(x) = 1.375 + (x - 1.5) + 0.5(x - 1.5)^2$$

results in

$$P_2(1.5) = 1.3755, \quad P'_2(1.5) = 1., \quad P''_2(1.5) = 2(0.5) = 1.$$

Once again, it is important to underline that a polynomial can assume different forms: in particular, it can be written in the Newton form, where the support points are highlighted, and in the standard centered form, where the derivatives of the point adopted as center are highlighted.

For example,

$$P_2(x) = 1. + (x - 1) + 0.5(x - 1)(x - 2)$$
$$P_2(x) = 1.375 + (x - 1.5) + 0.5(x - 1.5)^2$$

are two different forms of the same polynomial.

The Newton form that employs a *single* support point shall be very useful in the integration of differential systems through the *multivalue methods* (see Buzzi-Ferraris and Manenti, 2011b), as it allows to vary the integration step without any trouble.

Actually, although in a generic Newton form the abscissa of all the support points is explicit, the form (1.45) refers to a single-point z; hence, all the required information to describe the polynomial is collected on it.

1.8
Neville Algorithm

The development of the aforementioned algorithms consists of two phases: first, the coefficients of the interpolating polynomial are evaluated, and second, a prevision in the assigned z is carried out.

To get only a prevision in correspondence with an assigned abscissa z, one does not require to evaluate the polynomial coefficients by simply adopting one of the techniques described above.

Let us denote by $P_k(z, x_0, x_1, \ldots, x_k)$ the prevision achieved with the k-degree polynomial $P_k(x, x_0, x_1, \ldots, x_k)$ passing through $(x_0, y_0), (x_1, y_1), \ldots, (x_k, y_k)$.

Relation (1.37), which allows to build a new k-degree polynomial starting from two $(k-1)$-degree polynomials, can be used not only to get a new polynomial but also to

1.8 Neville Algorithm

get the prevision in $x = z$ for a k-degree polynomial, starting from the previsions obtained by two $(k-1)$-degree polynomials.

In fact, it is sufficient to write relation (1.37) by using z rather than x to get

$$P_k(z, x_0, x_1, \ldots, x_k) = \frac{(z-x_0)P_{k-1}(z, x_1, \ldots, x_k) - (z-x_k)P_{k-1}(z, x_0, \ldots, x_{k-1})}{x_k - x_0} \quad (1.47)$$

The same rules described for $f[x_0, x_1, \ldots, x_k]$ are valid for $P_k(z, x_0, x_1, \ldots, x_k)$ too, and it is useful, in particular, to adopt the scheme proposed by Neville against the other alternatives (i.e., Aitken method).

The following sequence, exemplified for $n = 3$, allows to evaluate $P_k(z, x_0, x_1, \ldots, x_k)$ by using the Neville method.

$$\begin{array}{llll}
x_0 & y_0 = P_0(z, x_0) & & \\
 & & P_1(z, x_0, x_1) & \\
x_1 & y_1 = P_0(z, x_1) & & P_2(z, x_0, x_1, x_2) \\
 & & P_1(z, x_1, x_2) & & P_3(z, x_0, x_1, x_2, x_3) \\
x_2 & y_2 = P_0(z, x_2) & & P_2(z, x_1, x_2, x_3) \\
 & & P_1(z, x_2, x_3) & \\
x_3 & y_3 = P_0(z, x_3) & &
\end{array}$$

For example, the scheme to evaluate the prevision in $z = 1.5$ obtained by a polynomial interpolation passing through $(1, 1)$, $(2, 2)$, and $(3, 4)$ is

$$\begin{array}{lll}
x_0 = 1 & P_0 = 1 & \\
 & & P_1 = .5(2) + .5(1) = 1.5 \\
x_1 = 2 & P_0 = 2 & \\
 & & P_1 = -.5(4) + 1.5(2) = 1. \\
x_2 = 3 & P_0 = 4 &
\end{array} \quad P_2 = \frac{(.5(1) + 1.5(1.5))}{2} = 1.375$$

Algorithm 1.11 Prevision with the Neville method

Input: the polynomial degree n, abscissas $x_0, x_1, \ldots, x_n$, ordinates $y_0, y_1, \ldots, y_n$, and the new point z where the prevision is to be evaluated.
Output: previsions $p_0, p_1, \ldots, p_n$ obtained with polynomials from 0 to n.

$$\begin{aligned}
&\text{for } i = 0 (\text{step } 1), n \\
&\quad p_i = y_i \\
&\text{for } k = 1 (\text{step } 1), n \\
&\quad \text{for } i = n (\text{step}-1), k \\
&\quad\quad p_i = p_i + (z - x_i)(p_i - p_{i-1})/(x_i - x_{i-k})
\end{aligned}$$

Algorithm 1.11 requires $n(n+1)$ flops.

The algorithm provides the previsions obtainable with growing-order polynomials and, therefore, it is possible to calculate the error generated by excluding a polynomial term. In the `BzzInterpolation` class, the function `Neville` evaluates polynomial previsions through the Neville method. This function returns the previsions obtainable with growing-order polynomials.

Example 1.4

Let $\mathbf{x} = \{1., 1.3, 1.6, 1.9, 2.2\}$ be the abscissas for the function $y_i = e^{-x_i^2}$. Evaluate the Neville previsions in $\mathbf{z} = \{1.8, 1.65, 1.35\}$.
The program is

```
#include "BzzMath.hpp"
void main(void)
    {
    BzzPrint("\n\nNeville");
    BzzVector x(5,1.,1.3,1.6,1.9,2.2);
    BzzVector y(5);
    for(int i = 1;i <= 5;i++)
        y[i] = exp(-x[i]*x[i]);
    BzzInterpolation p(x,y);
    BzzVector prev;
    prev = p.Neville(1.8);
    prev.BzzPrint("Neville Previsions");
    BzzPause();
    prev = p.Neville(1.65);
    prev.BzzPrint("Neville Previsions");
    BzzPause();
    prev = p.Neville(1.35);
    prev.BzzPrint("Neville Previsions");
    BzzPause();
    }
```

It is worth to remark that the `Neville` function returns a `BzzVector`, whereas both the `Newton` and the `Lagrange` functions return a `double`.

To solve this problem, as one knows the point $x = z$ where the prevision is to be evaluated, it is suitable to introduce an ordered series of points by basing on their distance from z. In this way, the round-off errors are minimized.

Many variants of the Neville algorithm were proposed.

1) The first modification was introduced to minimize the round-off errors. It is necessary to operate on the differences between two previsions rather than on the same previsions (Stoer and Bulirsch, 1983).
2) Another implementation type allows to sequentially obtain the previsions of increasing-order polynomials. It allows to stop calculations at any intermediate-order polynomial (Schwarz, 1989).
3) As a prevision in $z = 0$ is often required, it is possible to specialize the algorithm for this specific case.

Neville-type algorithms allow to obtain a prevision without evaluating the polynomial coefficients; unfortunately, this entails the following *disadvantages*.

1) The algorithms cannot be used where the expression of the interpolating polynomial is explicitly required.
2) They are not performing if the same support points are used for more previsions.

Even though it may be curious, any version of this kind of algorithm requires a higher number of calculations than a prevision obtained through the aprioristic evaluation of the coefficients in the Newton form. The computational time is only equivalent when the previsions obtained with intermediate-order polynomials are needed. In such cases, it is, however, possible to implement a special algorithm (Conte and De Boor, 1980), which requires a smaller computational time even evaluating the coefficients of the Newton form.

The advantages of these algorithms are the following.

1) They are very simple to implement and use.
2) It is possible to write versions slightly sensitive to round-off errors.
3) They are a useful introduction to the (similar) algorithms dealing with rational functions (described in the following).

1.9
Hermite Polynomial Interpolation

So far, we have considered the situation with $n+1$ points (x_i, y_i) only.

Knowing also the values of any derivative in some points seems logical to exploit this information to build the polynomial function.

For example, if one knows the values $y_0 = 1, y'_0 = 2, y''_0 = 3$ in correspondence with $x_0 = 0$, the parameters of the polynomial $P_2(x) = a_0 + a_1 x + a_2 x^2$ are immediately obtained by imposing the following conditions:

$$a_0 = 1; \quad a_1 = 2; \quad 2a_2 = 3$$

Although in the exact interpolation there is certainty about the interpolating polynomial existence using $n+1$ points (when all abscissas are different), it is not anymore true in the general case where even the derivatives are assigned.

For example, given the value of a function in x_0 together with the values of its second derivatives in x_0 and x_1, the system

$$a_0 + a_1 x_0 + a_2 x_0^2 = y_0$$
$$2a_2 = y''_0$$
$$2a_2 = y''_1$$

has the matrix with null determinant.

An important case where there is certainty of the interpolating polynomial existence and the uniqueness concerns the development of a polynomial passing through some support points and with the first derivative values assigned in correspondence with the same abscissas.

The polynomial $H_{2n+1}(x)$ that assumes the assigned value y_i and, at the same time, has y'_i as first derivative in correspondence with the abscissas $x_i (i = 0, \ldots, n)$ is called the *Hermite polynomial*.

It is possible to adopt a technique either similar to the Lagrange one (Lagrange-type) or to the Newton one (Newton-type) to evaluate Hermite polynomial.

1.9.1
Lagrange-Type Method

Hermite polynomial can be written as the sum of $2n + 2$ functions (Hamming, 1962):

$$H_{2n+1}(x) = \sum_{i=0}^{n} [y_i g_i(x) + y'_i h_i(x)] \tag{1.48}$$

Functions $g_i(x)$ and $h_i(x)$ are obtained by imposing the following conditions:

$$g_i(x_i) = 1 \tag{1.49}$$

$$h_i(x_i) = 0 \tag{1.50}$$

$$g'_i(x_i) = 0 \tag{1.51}$$

$$h'_i(x_i) = 1 \tag{1.52}$$

$$g_i(x_j) = 0 \quad (i \neq j) \tag{1.53}$$

$$h_i(x_j) = 0 \quad (i \neq j) \tag{1.54}$$

$$g'_i(x_j) = 0 \quad (i \neq j) \tag{1.55}$$

$$h'_i(x_j) = 0 \quad (i \neq j) \tag{1.56}$$

Under these conditions, the following functions are obtained:

$$g_i(x) = \frac{(x-x_0)^2 \cdots (x-x_{i-1})^2 (a_i x + b_i)(x-x_{i+1})^2 \cdots (x-x_n)^2}{(x_i-x_0)^2 \cdots (x_i-x_{i-1})^2 (x_i-x_{i+1})^2 \cdots (x_i-x_n)^2} \tag{1.57}$$

$$a_i = \frac{2}{x_0-x_i} + \cdots + \frac{2}{x_{i-1}-x_i} + \frac{2}{x_{i+1}-x_i} + \cdots + \frac{2}{x_n-x_i} \tag{1.58}$$

$$b_i = 1 - a_i x_i \tag{1.59}$$

$$h_i(x) = \frac{(x-x_0)^2 \cdots (x-x_{i-1})^2 (x-x_i)(x-x_{i+1})^2 \cdots (x-x_n)^2}{(x_i-x_0)^2 \cdots (x_i-x_{i-1})^2 (x_i-x_{i+1})^2 \cdots (x_i-x_n)^2} \tag{1.60}$$

For example, to build a 3-degree Hermite polynomial satisfying the conditions $(0, y_0)$, $(1, y_1)$, $(0, y'_0)$, and $(1, y'_1)$, one has

$$a_0 = 2; \quad b_0 = 1; \quad a_1 = -2; \quad b_1 = 3$$

Hence,

$$H_3 = y_0(x-1)^2(2x+1) + y'_0(x-1)^2 x + y_1 x^2(3-2x) + y'_1 x^2(x-1)$$

If the conditions are (z_0, y_0), (z_1, y_1), (z_0, y'_0), and (z_1, y'_1), it is possible to use the same polynomial after the following scale exchange:

$$x = (z-z_0)/(z_1-z_0)$$

1.9.2
Newton-Type Method

To use the Newton method when the values of ordinates, first, second, and higher derivatives are known, it is sufficient to observe the following rules.

1) Repeat the point as many times as the assigned derivatives.
2) Replace rational differences with the corresponding derivatives divided by $k!$, with k being the derivative order.

To build a 3-degree Hermite polynomial, where the first derivatives are assigned in correspondence with the support points, the procedure is

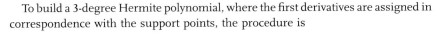

The corresponding polynomial is

$$P_3 = f[x_0] + f[x_0, x_0](x-x_0) + f[x_0, x_0, x_1](x-x_0)(x-x_0) \\ + f[x_0, x_0, x_1, x_1](x-x_0)(x-x_0)(x-x_1) \quad (1.61)$$

where

$$f[x_0] = y_0$$

$$f[x_0, x_0] = y'_0$$

$$f[x_0, x_0, x_1] = \frac{\frac{y_1-y_0}{x_1-x_0} - y'_0}{x_1-x_0}$$

$$f[x_0, x_0, x_1, x_1] = \frac{y'_0 + y'_1 - 2\frac{y_1-y_0}{x_1-x_0}}{(x_1-x_0)^2}$$

As it can be observed, the technique is equal to the one adopted to build the polynomial by the Newton method, with the shrewdness to see the support point where the derivative is known as a distinct point.

For example, to build a 3-degree Hermite polynomial satisfying the conditions $(x_0 = 0, y_0 = 1)$, $(x_1 = 1, y_1 = 0)$, $(x_0 = 0, y'_0 = 0)$, and $(x_1 = 1, y'_1 = -1)$, the following takes place:

$$f[x_0] = y_0 = 1$$
$$f[x_0, x_0] = y'_0 = 0$$
$$f[x_0, x_0, x_1] = -1$$
$$f[x_0, x_0, x_1, x_1] = 1$$

Hence,

$$P_3(x) = 1 - x^2 + x^2(x-1)$$

Through this technique, it is possible to build the polynomial even when in some points the first derivative is unknown.

Given two points $(1, 1)$ and $(2, 2)$ and the first derivative $y'(1) = 0.5$, the following scheme is obtained:

$$\begin{array}{lll} x_0 = 1 & f[x_0] = 1 & \\ x_0 = 1 & f[x_0] = 1 & f[x_0, x_0] = y'_0 = 0.5 \\ x_1 = 2 & f[x_1] = 2 & f[x_0, x_1] = 1 \end{array} \quad f[x_0, x_0, x_1] = 0.5$$

Therefore,

$$P_2(x) = 1 + 0.5(x-1) + 0.5(x-1)^2$$

If the values of the function and its first and second derivatives are known in two points x_0 and x_1, one can write the 5-degree polynomial in the following form:

$$P_5(x) = y_0 + y'_0(x-x_0) + \frac{y''_0}{2}(x-x_0)^2 + f[x_0, x_0, x_0, x_1](x-x_0)^3 \qquad (1.62)$$
$$+ f[x_0, x_0, x_0, x_1, x_1](x-x_0)^3(x-x_1)$$
$$+ f[x_0, x_0, x_0, x_1, x_1, x_1](x-x_0)^3(x-x_1)^2$$

The required scheme to calculate the coefficients is

x_0	y_0						
x_0	y_0	y'_0	$y''_0/2$				
x_0	y_0	y'_0	$f[x_0, x_0, x_1]$	$f[x_0, x_0, x_0, x_1]$			
		$f[x_0, x_1]$	$f[x_0, x_1, x_1]$	$f[x_0, x_0, x_1, x_1]$	$f[x_0, x_0, x_0, x_1, x_1]$		
x_1	y_1	y'_1	$f[x_0, x_1, x_1]$	$f[x_0, x_1, x_1, x_1]$	$f[x_0, x_0, x_1, x_1, x_1]$	$f[x_0, x_0, x_0, x_1, x_1, x_1]$
x_1	y_1	y'_1	$y''_1/2$				
x_1	y_1						

It is possible to solve even intermediate problems where ordinates and derivatives are known in correspondence with some abscissas.

For example, given $x_0 = 1, y_0 = 1, x_1 = 2, y_1 = 3, y_1' = 1, y_1'' = 8$ the following scheme can be developed:

$$
\begin{array}{ll}
x_0 = 1 & y_0 = 1 \\
x_1 = 2 & y_1 = 3 \\
x_1 = 2 & y_1 = 3 \\
x_1 = 2 & y_1 = 3
\end{array}
\quad
\begin{array}{l}
f[x_0, x_1] = 2 \\
f[x_1, x_1] = y_1' = 1 \\
f[x_1, x_1] = y_1' = 1
\end{array}
\quad
\begin{array}{l}
f[x_0, x_1, x_1] = 1 \\
f[x_1, x_1, x_1] = y_1''/2 = 4
\end{array}
\quad
f[x_0, x_1, x_1, x_1] = 3
$$

and we get

$$P_3(x) = 1 + 2(x-1) + (x-1)(x-2) + 3(x-1)(x-2)^2$$

1.10
Interpolation with Rational Functions

A function obtained as ratio between two polynomials is called *rational*:

$$R_{n,m}(x) = \frac{P_n(x)}{P_m(x)} = \frac{a_0 + a_1 x + \cdots + a_n x^n}{b_0 + b_1 x + \cdots + b_m x^m} \tag{1.63}$$

The number of the required parameters to univocally identify the rational function $R_{n,m}$ is equal to $n + m + 1$ (being b_0 arbitrary).

The *standard form for rational functions* is

$$R_{n,m}(x) = \frac{P_n(x)}{P_m(x)} = \frac{a_0 + a_1 x + \cdots + a_n x^n}{1 + b_1 x + \cdots + b_m x^m} \tag{1.64}$$

If the $np = n + m + 1$ support points (x_i, y_i) with $0, \ldots, n+m$ are known, parameters can be evaluated by solving the system

$$R_{n,m}(x_i) = y_i \quad (i = 0, 1, \ldots, n+m) \tag{1.65}$$

This system can be linearized by multiplying both the terms by the denominator of the rational function:

$$a_0 + a_1 x_i + \cdots + a_n x_i^n = (1 + b_1 x_i + \cdots + b_m x_i^m) y_i \\ (i = 0, 1, \ldots, n+m) \tag{1.66}$$

As the condition (1.66) is necessary to solve the system (1.65), one could think that system (1.65) is automatically solved by solving the system (1.66). This should be true if condition (1.66) should be sufficient, besides a necessary condition, but this is not always true. It is worth noting that we moved from the system (1.65) to (1.66) by multiplying the former one by the denominator of the rational function.

Be careful: by multiplying both the right- and the left-hand side of an equation by a given expression, the results become arbitrary if the same expression is equal to zero.

If the denominator of rational function (1.65) is null in one or more points, the left-hand side of system (1.66) also has to be zero. In this case, the system solution does not satisfy the same system (1.65).

In other words, the polynomials $P_n(x)$ and $P_m(x)$ that satisfy the system (1.66) can be written in the roots-product form. If one or more polynomial roots both at the denominator and at the numerator coincide with an abscissa, those terms are removed from the rational function, these being the common terms. In these circumstances, equation (1.65) is unsatisfied in with respect to that specific support point.

For example, given the points $(-1, 1)$, $(1, 2)$, and $(2, 2)$, system (1.66) for the rational function $R_{1,1}$ is

$$a_0 - a_1 = 1 - b_1$$
$$a_0 + a_1 = 2 + 2b_1$$
$$a_0 + 2a_1 = 2 + 4b_1$$

Hence,

$$a_0 = 2; \quad a_1 = 2; \quad b_1 = 1$$

$$R_{1,1} = \frac{2 + 2x}{1 + x} = 2$$

As a result, the rational function $R_{1,1}$ does not pass through the point $(-1, 1)$.

The rational approximation presents another shortcoming when the denominator is equal to zero in the selected interval.

Let us consider the points $(0, 0)$, $(0.5, -1)$, and $(2, 2)$. The rational function

$$R_{1,1} = \frac{x}{x - 1}$$

satisfies the support points but in $x = 1$ (just inside the interval). $R_{1,1} \to \infty$.

Therefore, the use of rational functions may face the following problems.

1) The rational function exactly passing through those specific support points may not exist.
2) The denominator could be zero in the selected interval.
3) Rational functions are more difficult to manipulate in case of integrations or differentiations.

On the other hand, rational functions are considerably better than polynomials in approximating functions, especially for their feature to simulate even situations with asymptotical behaviors.

Two techniques shall be analyzed in the following:

1) A technique to evaluate rational function parameters and, once they are obtained, to provide an estimate in correspondence with an assigned abscissa $x = z$.
2) A technique to directly obtain the prevision without the need to evaluate parameters.

Both the techniques are similar to Newton and Neville methods already explained for polynomials.

1.10 Interpolation with Rational Functions

Only a specific class of rational functions shall be considered here: the one where the numerator and the denominator differ at most by one order.

1.10.1
Thiele's Continuous Fractions

Thiele's continuous fractions allow to sequentially build a rational function with the numerator and the denominator polynomials that differ at most by one order.

The following discussion is valid under the hypothesis that the rational function exactly passes through the given np support points. Usually, this hypothesis is verified, but it will be appropriate to check it in all programs that use rational functions.

The following are called *Thiele's continuous fractions*:

$$R_{0,0} = c_0 \tag{1.67}$$

$$R_{1,0} = c_0 + \frac{x-x_0}{c_1} \tag{1.68}$$

$$R_{1,1} = c_0 + \cfrac{x-x_0}{c_1 + \cfrac{x-x_1}{c_2}} \tag{1.69}$$

$$R_{2,1} = c_0 + \cfrac{x-x_0}{c_1 + \cfrac{x-x_1}{c_2 + \cfrac{x-x_2}{c_3}}} \tag{1.70}$$

$\ldots$

Thiele's continuous fractions are a series of rational functions where both the numerator and the denominator degrees are alternatively increased by one. It is worth noting that Thiele's series represents a particular case of continuous fractions. In general, they are

$$f(x) = b_0 + \cfrac{a_1}{b_1 + \cfrac{a_2}{b_2 + \cfrac{a_3}{b_3 + \cfrac{a_4}{b_4 + \cdots}}}} \tag{1.71}$$

where the coefficients a_i and b_i can be any known function of the variable x.

In these cases, the problem to find out a criterion for detecting which terms are to be introduced in the series can arise. Looking at equation (1.71), one could think it would be necessary to solve the problem by attemps: fixing the amount of terms, solving the problem, increasing the amount of terms, and repeating the procedure. In other words, it would seem impossible to build the series from left to right.

One can avoid trial-and-error method by developing the series from left to right and by using two auxiliary vectors s_k, q_k and the following iterative formulae:

$$s_0 = b_0, \qquad\qquad\qquad q_0 = 1$$
$$s_1 = b_1 \cdot b_0 + a_1, \qquad\quad q_1 = b_1$$
$$s_k = b_k \cdot s_{k-1} + a_k \cdot s_{k-2}, \quad q_k = b_k \cdot q_{k-1} + a_k \cdot q_{k-2}, (k = 2, 3, \ldots)$$

The ratio

$$f_k = \frac{s_k}{q_k}$$

provides the fraction value.

During the sequence, it might happen that the values of s_k and q_k progressively increase or decrease. In these circumstances, there is a risk of *overflow* and *underflow*.

As one is interested in the ratio between s_k and q_k and not in their specific values and as both s_k and q_k are linear combinations of the previous terms, it is enough to divide s_{k-1}, q_{k-1}, s_k, and q_k by q_k to stop any increase or decrease in their values.

In such a specific case, the following algorithm is needed when parameters c_i have already been calculated.

Algorithm 1.12 Previsions with Thiele

Input: number of support points np, abscissas $x_0, x_1, \ldots, x_{np-1}$, abscissa of the prevision $x = z$, and Thiele coefficients $c_0, c_1, \ldots, c_{np-1}$.
Output: previsions $p_0, p_1, \ldots, p_{np-1}$ and prevision differences $dp_0, dp_1, \ldots, dp_{np-2}$.

```
BIG = 1000.      TINY = .001
s₀ = c₀;  q₀ = 1.;  p₀ = s₀
s₁ = c₀c₁ + (z−x₀);  q₁ = c₁
if(q₁ = 0.)quit
p₁ = s₁/q₁
for k = 2(step 1), np−1
   aus = z−x_{k−1}
   s_k = c_k s_{k−1} + aus s_{k−2}
   q_k = c_k q_{k−1} + aus q_{k−2}
   if (q_k = 0.)quit
   p_k = s_k/q_k
   if(|s_k|>BIG and |q_k|>BIG or |s_k| < TINY and |q_k| < TINY)
      s_{k−1} = s_{k−1}/q_k;   q_{k−1} = q_{k−1}/q_k
      s_k = p_k;     q_k = 1.
for k = 1(step 1), np−1
   dp_{k−1} = p_k−p_{k−1}
```

For example, given the points $(1,1)$, $(2,2)$, and $(3,4)$ and the coefficients $c_0 = 1$, $c_1 = 1$, and $c_2 = -3$, the previsions in $z = 1.5$ are

$p_0 = 1$
$s_1 = 1 \cdot 1 + (1.5 - 1) = 1.5$
$q_1 = 1$
$p_1 = 1.5$
$s_2 = -3 \cdot 1.5 + (1.5 - 2) \cdot 1 = -5;$
$q_2 = -3 \cdot 1 + (1.5 - 2) \cdot 1 = -3.5$
$p_2 = 1.4285714$

Suppose to select the abscissas

$$\mathbf{x} = \{0.1; 0.2; 0.4; 0.8; 1.2\}$$

for the function $\cosh(x)$. In correspondence with these points, the following ordinates are obtained:

$$\mathbf{y} = \{1.005004; 1.020067; 1.081072; 1.337435; 1.810656\}$$

The value of the function $\cosh(x)$ in $z = .25$ is $\cosh(.25) = 1.031413$. When we assign the coefficients

$$\mathbf{c} = \{1.005004; 6.638973; -0.074208; -6.879100; -7.636977\}$$

the previsions in $z = .25$ are

$$\mathbf{p} = \{1.005004; 1.027598; 1.030150; 1.031390; 1.031410\}$$

and the error is

$$\mathbf{dp} = \{0.022594; 0.002552; 0.001240; 0.000020\}$$

The coefficients c_i necessary for interpolation with Thiele's rational functions is calculated by the following *inverse rational differences*.

1) Zero-degree inverse rational difference:

$$g_0(x_i) = y_0 \qquad (i = 0, \ldots, np-1) \tag{1.72}$$

2) 1-degree inverse rational difference:

$$g_1(x_i, x_0) = \frac{x_i - x_0}{g_0(x_i) - g_0(x_0)} \qquad (i = 1, \ldots, np-1) \tag{1.73}$$

3) 2-degree inverse rational difference:

$$g_2(x_i, x_1, x_0) = \frac{x_i - x_1}{g_1(x_i, x_0) - g_1(x_1, x_0)} \qquad (i = 2, \ldots, np-1) \tag{1.74}$$

4) k-degree inverse rational difference $(k = 2, \ldots, np-1)$, $(i = k, \ldots, np-1)$:

$$g_k(x_i, x_{k-1}, \ldots, x_1, x_0) = \frac{x_i - x_{k-1}}{g_{k-1}(x_i, x_{k-2}, \ldots, x_0) - g_{k-1}(x_{k-1}, x_{k-2}, \ldots, x_0)} \tag{1.75}$$

1 Interpolation

For example, given the points $(1,1)$, $(2,2)$, and $(3,4)$, the scheme of inverse rational differences is

$$
\begin{array}{llll}
x_0 = 1 & y_0 = g_0(x_0) = 1 & g_1(x_1, x_0) = \dfrac{2-1}{2-1} = 1 & \\
x_1 = 2 & y_1 = g_0(x_1) = 2 & & g_2(x_2, x_1, x_0) = \dfrac{3-2}{\frac{2}{3}-1} = -3 \\
x_2 = 3 & y_2 = g_0(x_2) = 4 & g_1(x_2, x_0) = \dfrac{3-1}{4-1} = \dfrac{2}{3} &
\end{array}
$$

Once the scheme is developed, the values of parameters c_k are on the upper diagonal of the same scheme:

$$c_0 = g_0(x_0) \qquad (1.76)$$

$$c_k = g_k(x_k, x_{k-1}, \ldots, x_1, x_0) \qquad (k = 1, 2, \ldots) \qquad (1.77)$$

As per rational differences in the Newton form, it is not necessary to store the overall scheme of the inverse rational differences: coefficients c_i are enough.

Algorithm 1.13 Coefficients in Thiele's form

Input: number of support points np, abscissas $x_0, x_1, \ldots, x_{np-1}$, and ordinates $y_0, y_1, \ldots, y_{np-1}$.
Output: coefficients in Thiele's form $c_0, c_1, \ldots, c_{np-1}$.

```
for i = 0(step 1), np−1
    aus = y_i
    j = 0
    for k = 1(step 1), k = i
        j = j + 1
        den = aus − c_j
        if (den = 0) quit
        aus = (x_i − x_j)/den
    c_i = aus
```

It is important to prevent any possibility to have two equal values

$$c_{k-1}(x_i, x_{k-2}, \ldots, x_0) = c_{k-1}(x_{k-1}, x_{k-2}, \ldots, x_0) \qquad (1.78)$$

as it would take to a division by zero.
For example, let $\mathbf{x} = \{0.1; 0.2; 0.4; 0.8; 1.2\}$ be the values of abscissas for the function $\cosh(x)$. In these points, the ordinates are

$$\mathbf{y} = \{1.005004; 1.020067; 1.081072; 1.337435; 1.810656\}$$

The coefficients are

$$\mathbf{c} = \{1.005004; 6.638973; -0.074208; -6.879100; -7.636977\}$$

In the `BzzInterpolation` class, the function `Rational` evaluates rational previsions through the Thiele method. This function returns the previsions obtainable with growing-order rational functions.

Example 1.5

Let $\mathbf{x} = \{1., 1.3, 1.6, 1.9, 2.2\}$ be the abscissas for the function $y_i = e^{-x_i^2}$. Evaluate Thiele previsions in $\mathbf{z} = \{1.8, 1.65, 1.35\}$.
The program is

```
#include "BzzMath.hpp"
void main(void)
    {
    BzzPrint("\n\nRational");
    BzzVector x(5,1.,1.3,1.6,1.9,2.2);
    BzzVector y(5);
    for(int i = 1;i <= 5;i++)
        y[i] = exp(-x[i]*x[i]);
    BzzInterpolation p(x,y);
    double prev;
    prev = p.Rational(1.8);
    BzzPrint("\nRational Previsions %e",prev);
    BzzPause();
    prev = p.Rational(1.65);
    BzzPrint("\nRational Previsions %e",prev);
    BzzPause();
    prev = p.Rational(1.35);
    BzzPrint("\nRational Previsions %e",prev);
    BzzPause();
    }
```

Observe that the function `Rational` returns a `double`.

1.10.2 Bulirsch–Stoer Method

Stoer and Bulirsch (1983) proposed an algorithm similar to the Neville procedure, which is valid for a sequence of polynomials and is applicable to a series of rational functions. By increasing the number of points, the polynomial degree of both the denominator and the numerator of the rational function is alternatively increased, too, so as to preserve the denominator degree ever equal or one-order higher than the numerator degree.

In Neville algorithm (1.11), the recursive formula to evaluate the polynomial prevision can be rewritten as follows:

$$k = 1,\ldots,n$$
$$p_i = p_i + \frac{p_i - p_{i-1}}{\frac{z - x_{i-k}}{z - x_i} - 1} \qquad i = n,\ldots,k \qquad (1.79)$$

Bulirsch and Stoer demonstrated that expression (1.79) for a rational function is to be modified in

$$t_i = p_i \tag{1.80}$$

$$p_i = p_i + \frac{p_i - p_{i-1}}{\frac{z - x_{i-k}}{z - x_i}\left[1 - \frac{p_i - p_{i-1}}{p_i - t_{i-1}}\right] - 1} \tag{1.81}$$

where t_i is initialized equal to zero.

Algorithm 1.14 Prevision with Bulirsch–Stoer

Input: number of support points np, abscissas $x_0, x_1, \ldots, x_{np-1}$, ordinates $y_0, y_1, \ldots, y_{np-1}$, and prevision z.
Output: previsions $p_0, p_1, \ldots, p_{np-1}$ and prevision differences $dp_0, dp_1, \ldots, dp_{np-2}$.

$\quad$ for $i = 0(\text{step } 1), np-1$
$\quad\quad t_i = 0.; p_i = y_i$
$\quad$ for $k = 1(\text{step } 1), np-1$
$\quad\quad$ for $i = np-1(\text{step}-1), k$
$\quad\quad\quad t_i = p_i$
$\quad\quad\quad p_i = p_i + \dfrac{p_i - p_{i-1}}{\dfrac{z - x_{i-k}}{z - x_i}\left[1 - \dfrac{p_i - p_{i-1}}{p_i - t_{i-1}}\right] - 1}$
$\quad$ for $i = 0(\text{step } 1), np-2$
$\quad\quad dp_i = p_{i+1} - p_i$

As per the Neville method, some specific variants of the previous algorithm exist and, in particular, an optimized version for round-off errors, another one for the iterative applications, and some others for the case of $z = 0$ are significantly useful.
In the following examples, the Neville algorithm valid for a polynomial prevision is compared to the Bulirsch–Stoer algorithm, which uses a rational function.

Example 1.6

Let $\mathbf{x} = \{1.; 1.3; 1.6; 1.9; 2.2\}$ be abscissas for the function $\exp(-x^2)$. The ordinates $\mathbf{y} = \{0.367879; 0.184520; 0.077305; 0.027052; 0.007907\}$ are obtained in correspondence with these points. Compare Neville and Bulirsch–Stoer algorithms.
The program is

```
#include "BzzMath.hpp"
void main(void)
    {
```

```
BzzPrint("\n\nComparison: Neville and
  BulirschStoer");
BzzVector x(5,1.,1.3,1.6,1.9,2.2);
BzzVector y(5);
for(int i = 1;i <= 5;i++)
    y[i] = exp(-x[i]*x[i]);
BzzInterpolation p(x,y);
BzzVector prev;
prev = p.Neville(1.8);
prev.BzzPrint("Neville Previsions");
prev = p.BulirschStoer(1.8);
prev.BzzPrint("BulirschStoer Previsions");
BzzPause();
prev = p.Neville(2.1);
prev.BzzPrint("Neville Previsions");
prev = p.BulirschStoer(2.1);
prev.BzzPrint("BulirschStoer Previsions");
BzzPause();
prev = p.Neville(1.35);
prev.BzzPrint("Neville Previsions");
prev = p.BulirschStoer(1.35);
prev.BzzPrint("BulirschStoer Previsions");
BzzPause();
}
```

The value of the function $\exp(-x^2)$ in $z = 1.8$ is $f(z) = 0.039164$.
With the Neville algorithm,

$\mathbf{p} = \{0.027052; 0.043803; 0.040346; 0.039070; 0.038932\}$
$\mathbf{dp} = \{0.016751; -0.003456; -0.001277; -0.000137\}$

whereas the Bulirsch–Stoer algorithm takes to

$\mathbf{p} = \{0.027052; 0.034535; 0.037918; 0.038734; 0.039256\}$
$\mathbf{dp} = \{0.007483; 0.003382; 0.000816; 0.000522\}$

The errors are equal to 0.59 and 0.23% for Neville and Bulirsch–Stoer, respectively.
The function value in $z = 2.1$ is $f(z) = 0.012155$.
Using the Neville algorithm,

$\mathbf{p} = \{0.007907; 0.014289; 0.010832; 0.012428; 0.012703\}$
$\mathbf{dp} = \{0.006382; -0.003456; 0.001596; 0.000275\}$

whereas the Bulirsch–Stoer algorithm takes to

$\mathbf{p} = \{0.007907; 0.010348; 0.012820; 0.012446; 0.012017\}$
$\mathbf{dp} = \{0.002441; 0.002472; -0.000374; -0.000429\}$

The errors are equal to 4.5 and 1.1% for Neville and Bulirsch–Stoer, respectively.

Another example was proposed by Schwarz (1989). Let $\mathbf{x} = \{.01; .02; .03; .04; .05\}$ be the abscissas for the function $f(x) = \dfrac{0.1}{x\sqrt{5x+1}}$. The ordinates

$$\mathbf{y} = \{9.759001; 4.767313; 3.108349; 2.282177; 1.788854\}$$

are obtained in correspondence with these points.
The value of the function $f(x)$ in $z = 0.024000$ is $f(z) = 3.937130$.
With the Neville algorithm,

$$\mathbf{p} = \{4.767313; 4.103727; 3.703800; 3.843796; 3.888596\}$$
$$\mathbf{dp} = \{-0.663586; -0.399927; 0.139996; 0.044800\}$$

whereas the Bulirsch–Stoer algorithm takes the form

$$\mathbf{p} = \{4.767313; 3.928613; 3.937524; 3.937132; 3.937130\}$$
$$\mathbf{dp} = \{-0.838700; 0.008910; -0.000391; -0.000002\}$$

The errors are equal to 1.23 and 0% for Neville and Bulirsch–Stoer, respectively.
Finally, Stoer and Bulirsch (1983) proposed the following example: Let $\mathbf{x} = \{1.; 2.; 3.; 4.; 5.\}$ be the abscissas for the function $\cotg(x)$. The ordinates $\mathbf{y} = \{57.289963; 28.636253; 19.081137; 14.300666; 11.430053\}$ are obtained in correspondence with these points.
The value of the function $f(x)$ in $z = 2.5$ is $f(z) = 22.9037655$.
With the Neville algorithm,

$$\mathbf{p} = \{28.636253; 23.858696; 21.471373; 22.366619; 22.635193\}$$
$$\mathbf{dp} = \{-4.777557; -2.387323; 0.895247; 0.268574\}$$

whereas the Bulirsch–Stoer algorithm takes the form

$$\mathbf{p} = \{28.636253; 22.902018; 22.903416; 22.903696; 22.903767\}$$
$$\mathbf{dp} = \{-5.734236; 0.001398; 0.000280; 0.000071\}$$

The errors are equal to 1.17% for the Neville algorithm, whereas only the eighth digit is wrong for the Bulirsch–Stoer algorithm.

Whenever the function has an asymptote, the interpolation through rational functions is better.

1.11
Inverse Interpolation

In some circumstances, it may be appropriate to invert the role of variables, so as to use the variable x as dependent and the variable y as independent. By doing so, an interpolation of the variable x against y could be feasible.

For example, given the points $(1, 1)$, $(2, 2)$, and $(3, 4)$, the 2-degree polynomial in the Newton form, where y is the independent variable and x is the dependent variable, is

$$P_2(y) = 1 + (y-1) - (y-1)(y-2)/6$$

The inverse interpolation is useful particularly when there is the need to estimate the value of the variable x in correspondence with an assigned value of y.

In the previous example, the inverse polynomial interpolation can be adopted to estimate the value of x where $y = 2.1$:

$$P_2(y = 2.1) = 1 + (2.1-1) - (2.1-1)(2.1-2)/6$$

Hence,

$$x = P_2(y = 2.1) = 2.08166667$$

The inverse interpolation is very important to solve the following problems.

1) Function zeroing (see Buzzi-Ferraris and Manenti, 2011a).
2) Extrapolation to zero in iterative processes (see Buzzi-Ferraris and Manenti, 2010a).

In these problems, there is a series of points (x_i, y_i) and we want to know the value of x where $y = 0$. Using a direct interpolation, the problem is not easy to resolve when polynomials have a degree higher than 2 or with rational functions. Conversely, by executing an inverse polynomial, there are no difficulties in evaluating the value of x in correspondence with $y = 0$.

In this case, some specific versions of the Neville algorithm (for the polynomial interpolation) and, *a fortiori*, of the Bulirsch–Stoer algorithm (for the interpolation with rational functions) are useful to make a prevision in $z = 0$.

Example 1.7

Let $x = \{1.3; 1.4; 1.5; 1.6; 1.7\}$ be the abscissas for the function $\sinh(x) - 2$. Evaluate the value of x that zeroes the function.
The program is

```
#include "BzzMath.hpp"
void main(void)
    {
    BzzPrint("\n\nPrevisions in zero");
    BzzVector x(1.3;1.4;1.5;1.6;1.7);
    BzzVector y(5);
    for(int i = 1; i <= 5; i++)
            y[i] = sinh(x[i])-2;
    BzzInterpolation p(y,x);
    BzzVector prev;
```

```
prev = p.Neville(0.);
prev.BzzPrint("Neville Previsions");
prev = p.BulirschStoer(0.);
prev.BzzPrint("BulirschStoer Previsions");
BzzPause();
}
```

1.12
Successive Polynomial Interpolation

As already discussed, it is unseemly to use a unique high-degree polynomial to interpolate numerous points, as the interpolating polynomial usually goes away from the interpolated function when the polynomial degree is increased.

With many support points, it is suitable both to use interpolating polynomials that employ only a portion of the existing data and to employ some strategies to connect them.

For example, let us consider the simplest case of a series of 1-degree polynomials interpolating two adjacent support points.

In this context, the following nomenclature is adopted: the n support points (x_i, y_i) have index $i = 1, \ldots, n$; h_i is the distance between the abscissas x_i and x_{i+1}. Moreover, the interpolating polynomial between the point x_i and x_{i+1} has index i.

The 1-degree polynomial series is

$$L_i(x) = y_{i+1}\frac{x-x_i}{h_i} - y_i\frac{x-x_{i+1}}{h_i} \quad x_i \leq x \leq x_{i+1} \tag{1.82}$$

For example, given the points $(1., 2.)$, $(2., 5.)$, and $(3., 7.)$, the 1-degree polynomials are

$$L_1(x) = 5(x-1) - 2(x-2); \qquad L_2(x) = 7(x-2) - 5(x-3)$$

A series of 1-degree polynomials solve the problem of interpolation divergence while the number of support points increases.

A series of 1-degree polynomials have discontinuous derivatives in correspondence with support points. The function is, therefore, represented by a linear piecewise, and it is not appealing from a graphical point of view, by making it practically useless in all problems requiring a graphical representation of the interpolating function.

With numerous support points, one has to decide how many points should be used to build the interpolating polynomial.

A series of 3-degree polynomials (cubic functions) is a good compromise to represent a function on a large domain, when specific conditions of derivative continuity are imposed in correspondence with support points.

In the case of a series of cubic functions, parameters a_i, b_i, c_i, d_i are to be calculated:

$$P_i(x) = a_i(x-x_i)^3 + b_i(x-x_i)^2 + c_i(x-x_i) + d_i \qquad (1.83)$$
$$(i = 1, \ldots, n-1)$$

Various alternatives exist that shall be discussed in this chapter, such as

1) Hermite cubic polynomials
2) Cubic spline

The cubic polynomial interpolations are particularly important and, therefore, they were implemented in appropriate classes.

In the **BzzMath** library, the classes are called `BzzCubicHermite`, `BzzCubicSpline` and `BzzCubicSmooth`.

The `BzzCubicHermite`, `BzzCubicSpline`, and `BzzCubicSmooth` classes interpolate a function through successive cubic polynomials.

Additional examples of the use of `BzzCubicHermite`, `BzzCubicSpline`, and `BzzCubicSmooth` classes can be found in

`BzzMath/Examples/BzzMathBasic/CubicInterpolation`

either on the enclosed CD-ROM or at the web site:

`www.chem.polimi.it/homes/gbuzzi`.

1.12.1
Hermite Cubic Polynomials

When the first derivatives are known in correspondence with the support points, it is possible to calculate the four parameters of each cubic function: the polynomials have to pass through the two points at the interval boundary and, there, the derivatives have to meet each other.

As already described, it is possible to employ a technique similar to Lagrange or Newton methods.

By using the Newton method, the following polynomials are obtained:

$$\begin{aligned}
h_i(x) = &\, f[x_i] + f[x_i, x_i](x-x_i) \\
&+ f[x_i, x_i, x_{i+1}](x-x_i)(x-x_i) \qquad (i = 1, \ldots, n-1) \\
&+ f[x_i, x_i, x_{i+1}, x_{i+1}](x-x_i)(x-x_i)(x-x_{i+1})
\end{aligned} \qquad (1.84)$$

with

$$f[x_i] = y_i$$
$$f[x_i, x_i] = y'_i$$
$$f[x_i, x_i, x_{i+1}] = \frac{\dfrac{y_{i+1}-y_i}{x_{i+1}-x_i} - y'_i}{x_{i+1}-x_i}$$

$$f[x_i, x_i, x_{i+1}, x_{i+1}] = \frac{y'_i + y'_{i+1} - 2\dfrac{y_{i+1}-y_i}{x_{i+1}-x_i}}{(x_{i+1}-x_i)^2}$$

Rewriting the polynomial in the form (1.83),

$$d_i = y_i$$
$$c_i = y'_i$$
$$b_i = f[x_i, x_i, x_{i+1}] - h_i f[x_i, x_i, x_{i+1}, x_{i+1}]$$
$$a_i = f[x_i, x_i, x_{i+1}, x_{i+1}]$$

If the analytical values of y'_i are unknown, the support points can be used to estimate them. Among all the alternatives, the following is recommended.

Given three adjacent points x_{i-1}, x_i, x_{i+1}, the derivatives in x_i is obtained through the central formula (see Buzzi-Ferraris and Manenti, 2010a) just adapted to the case of variable step h_i:

$$y'_i \approx \frac{\left(\frac{y_{i+1}-y_i}{h_i}\right)h_{i-1} + \left(\frac{y_i-y_{i-1}}{h_{i-1}}\right)h_i}{h_{i-1}+h_i} \tag{1.85}$$

The BzzCubicHermite class has three constructors: the first requires the vector **x** of the abscissas, the corresponding ordinates **y**, and the vector of first derivatives **y'**; the second needs the vectors **x** and **y** only as the object numerically estimates the first derivatives required to get the Hermite cubic functions. The last constructor is the default one.

For example,

```
BzzVector x(...),y(...);
BzzCubicHermite h1(x,y);
BzzVector y1(...);
BzzCubicHermite h2(x,y,y1);
BzzCubicHermite h3;
h3(x,y);
BzzCubicHermite h4;
h4(x,y,y1);
```

Objects are used through the operator (,). To evaluate the prevision obtained in any point belonging to the interval $[x_1, x_n]$, it is sufficient to use the object as a function with the abscissa for the prevision as argument.

For example,

```
BzzVector x(5,1.,2.,3.,4.,5.),y(5,4.,7.,2.,1.,9.);
BzzCubicHermite h(x,y);
double z = 3.123;
BzzPrint("Prevision %e",h(z));
```

One can obtain the first and the second derivatives by adding 1 or 2, respectively, in the previous argument of operator (,).

For example,

```
BzzVector x(5,1.,2.,3.,4.,5.),y(5,4.,7.,2.,1.,9.);
BzzCubicHermite h(x,y);
```

```
double z = 3.123;
BzzPrint("Prevision %e",h(z));
BzzPrint("First derivative %e",h(z,1));
BzzPrint("Second derivative %e",h(z,2));
```

Example 1.8

Introduce new points to improve the interpolation.
The program is

```
#include "BzzMath.hpp"
void main(void)
    {
    BzzVector x(11),y(11);
    double z;
    int i;
    for(z = 1.,i = 1;i <= 11;z += .1,i++)
        {x[i] = z;y[i] = 1./z;}
    BzzCubicHermite h(x,y);
    BzzPrint("\n h(1.76) %e exact %e",h(1.76),1./1.76);
    int j = x.InsertElementInSortedVector(1.76);
    //Element inserted in position j
    double v = 1./x[j];
    y.Insert(j,v);
    h(x,y);
    BzzPrint("\n h(1.76) %e exact %e",h(1.76),1./1.76);
    }
```

It is useful to check the plot in order to validate the curve. If there are some zones with sudden variations or discontinuities, the representation is probably unsatisfactory.

Example 1.9

Create a file for the tool `BzzPlotSparse.exe` to plot the function $\frac{1}{x^2}$ by using the `BzzCubicHermite` objects.
The program `BzzPlotSparse.exe` (Buzzi-Ferraris and Manenti, 2010a) allows one to plot a series of curves with different support points. They should be stored as the rows of two `BzzMatrixSparse` **X** and **Y**. By default, the former trend is plotted with a solid line, whereas the latter one through a dotted line. It is, however, possible to modify the default options.
The program is

```
#include "BzzMath.hpp"
void main(void)
```

```
{
BzzPrint("\n\n\nRunge Example");
int n = 16;
BzzVector x(n,-5.,-4.,-3.,-2.,-1.,-.5,-.3,
    -.1,0.,.1,.3,.5,1.,2.,3.,4.),y(n);
int nz = 50*n - 3;
BzzMatrixSparse Y(2,nz);
BzzMatrixSparse X(2,nz);
double z;
int i;
for(i = 1;i <= n;i++)
    {
    z = x[i];
    y[i] = 1./(1. + z*z);
    X(2,i) = z;
    Y(2,i) = 1./(1. + z*z);
    }
BzzCubicHermite h(x,y);
double dz = (x[n] - x[1])/double(nz-1);
for(z = x[1],i = 1;i <= nz && z <= x[n];z += dz,i++)
    {
    BzzPrint("\nx %e Correct %e",z,1./(1.+z*z));
    BzzPrint("\nx %e Hermite %e",z,h(z));
    X(1,i) = z;
    Y(1,i) = h(z);
    }
BzzSave save("RungeWithHermite.stx");
save << X << Y;
save.End();
}
```

Run the program `BzzPlotSparse.exe`, select the item `File, New` from the menu, and select the file `RungeWithHermite.stx` just created to visualize the trend in Figure 1.1.

The function `Integral` estimates the integral of the function interpolated in the interval $[x_1, x_n]$.

Example 1.10

Evaluate $\int_1^2 \frac{1}{z} dz$.
The program is

```
#include "BzzMath.hpp"
    {
```

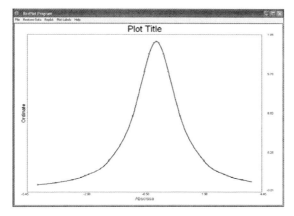

Figure 1.1 Polynomials visualization using the `BzzPlotSparse` toolkit.

```
BzzVector x(11),y(11);
double z;
int i;
for(z = 1.,i = 1;i <= 11;z += .1,i++)
      {x[i] = z; y[i] = 1./z;}
BzzCubicHermite h(x,y);
BzzPrint("\nIntegral %e",h.BzzIntegral());
}
```

In this example, a value of the integral equal to 0.6932331 is obtained, whereas the correct value is $\log(2.) = .6931472$.

The `BzzCubicSmooth` class has a single constructor requiring the vectors **x** and **y** and a parameter in the range $[0, 1]$.

If this parameter is equal to zero, the object simulates a linear piecewise; when it is equal to one, it interpolates with a set of Hermite polynomials. The intermediate values of this parameter give hybrid interpolations with intermediate characteristics between these extreme cases: with small values, the interpolation is less smooth, but the possibility to have undesired minimum or maximum is reduced.

For example,

```
BzzVector x(...),y(...);
BzzCubicSmooth s(x,y,.1);
```

1.12.2
Cubic Spline

Spline indicates the plastic ruler used by designers to draw a curve passing through some assigned points. The aim of spline functions is just to interpolate a certain number of support points.

To obtain a smooth curve, the continuity of derivatives even in correspondence with the support points is required. Specifically, first and second derivatives of two different interpolating pieces have to correspond.

Indicating the generic spline with

$$s_i(x) = a_i(x-x_i)^3 + b_i(x-x_i)^2 + c_i(x-x_i) + d_i \qquad (1.86)$$
$$(i = 1, \ldots, n-1)$$

the following conditions are imposed:

$$s_i(x_i) = y_i \quad (i = 1, \ldots, n-1) \qquad (1.87)$$

$$s_i(x_{i+1}) = y_{i+1} \quad (i = 1, \ldots, n-1) \qquad (1.88)$$

$$s'_i(x_{i+1}) = s'_{i+1}(x_{i+1}) \quad (i = 1, \ldots, n-2) \qquad (1.89)$$

$$s''_i(x_{i+1}) = s''_{i+1}(x_{i+1}) \quad (i = 1, \ldots, n-2) \qquad (1.90)$$

The number of unknown parameters is equal to $4n-4$, whereas the conditions are $4n-6$. Other two relations are required to univocally evaluate parameters.

The second derivatives in the generic point i is indicated with s''_i.

The parameters a_i, b_i, c_i, d_i can be easily obtained by means of ordinates y_i and derivatives s''_i in the support points.

Using relations (1.87), (1.88), and (1.89),

$$a_i = \frac{s''_{i+1} - s''_i}{6h_i} \quad (i = 1, \ldots, n-1) \qquad (1.91)$$

$$b_i = \frac{s''_i}{2} \quad (i = 1, \ldots, n-1) \qquad (1.92)$$

$$c_i = \frac{y_{i+1} - y_i}{h_i} - \frac{h_i(s''_{i+1} + 2s''_i)}{6} \quad (i = 1, \ldots, n-1) \qquad (1.93)$$

$$d_i = y_i \quad (i = 1, \ldots, n-1) \qquad (1.94)$$

The n variables s''_i have to solve the following system, obtained by equation (1.89):

$$h_{i-1}s''_{i-1} + 2(h_{i-1} + h_i)s''_i + h_i s''_{i+1}$$
$$= \frac{6(y_{i+1} - y_i)}{h_i} - \frac{6(y_i - y_{i-1})}{h_{i-1}} \quad (i = 2, \ldots, n-1) \qquad (1.95)$$

Therefore, parameters a_i, b_i, c_i, d_i could be *explicitly* obtained when derivatives s''_i were evaluated. *Tridiagonal system* (1.95), constituted by $n-2$ equations, can be used to calculate the n variables $s''_i (i = 1, \ldots, n)$. To get the n derivative values s''_i is then necessary to add two equations.

Some alternatives were proposed to assign the remaining two conditions:

1) Second derivatives equal to zero on the boundary:
$$s_1'' = s_1''(x_1) = s_{n-1}''(x_n) = s_n'' = 0 \qquad (1.96)$$
In this case, the spline is called *natural*.

2) Second derivatives assigned on the boundary:
$$s_1'' = s_1''(x_1) = d_1'' \qquad (1.97)$$
$$s_n'' = s_{n-1}''(x_n) = d_n'' \qquad (1.98)$$

3) Value of the second derivatives on the boundary has to be proportional to the value of the second derivative in the adjacent point:
$$s_1'' = s_1''(x_1) = \alpha s_1''(x_2) = \alpha s_2'' \qquad (1.99)$$
$$s_n'' = s_{n-1}''(x_n) = \beta s_{n-1}''(x_{n-1}) = \beta s_{n-1}'' \qquad (1.100)$$
Usually, the values for α and β are 1. or 0.5.
If $\alpha = \beta = 1$,
$$s_1''' = 6a_1 = 0 \qquad (1.101)$$
$$s_{n-1}''' = 6a_{n-1} = 0 \qquad (1.102)$$
In this case, both the polynomials s_1 and s_{n-1} become 2-degree polynomials.

The selection of $\alpha = \beta = 1$ is reasonable (and it is a default choice) when one has no information.

4) First derivatives assigned on the boundary:
$$s_1'(x_1) = y_1' \qquad (1.103)$$
$$s_{n-1}'(x_n) = y_n' \qquad (1.104)$$
These two conditions take to the following equations
$$2h_1 s_1'' + h_1 s_2'' = \frac{6(y_2 - y_1)}{h_1} - 6y_1' \qquad (1.105)$$
$$h_{n-1} s_{n-1}'' + 2h_{n-1} s_n'' = -\frac{6(y_n - y_{n-1})}{h_{n-1}} + 6y_n' \qquad (1.106)$$
that have to be added to system (1.95), so as to make it a tridiagonal.
If one does not know the analytical value of y_1' and y_n', it is possible to obtain them numerically. Actually, first four points and last four points can be used to get two 3-degree polynomials that interpolate exactly them; the analytical derivative of such polynomials can be evaluated and, at last, it can be used as an approximation of the real derivative.

5) Parabolic interpolation for the two boundary polynomials:

$$s_1'''(x_1) = 0 \tag{1.107}$$

$$s_{n-1}'''(x_n) = 0 \tag{1.108}$$

This condition is the same as the default one described above.

All the aforementioned conditions introduced in system (1.95) generate a tridiagonal system with a dominant diagonal in the variables s_i''. This system can be solved by adopting the techniques analyzed in Buzzi-Ferraris and Manenti (2010a). As the system has the dominant diagonal, its solution is stable even without pivoting.

6) In case of periodic functions, it may be useful to impose the following conditions. If a periodic function has period T and the support points are disposed so to have x_1 at the beginning and x_n at the end of the period, it is possible to impose that the first and the second derivatives at the initial point have to be equal to the first and the second derivatives, respectively, at the last point.

In this last case, the resulting system has two coefficients out of the tridiagonal structure: the first one is placed on the lower corner at the left of the matrix; the second one on the higher corner at the right of the matrix. Even in this case, the system can be solved without any difficulty by the technique for partially structured systems (see Buzzi-Ferraris and Manenti, 2010a).

As already said in this chapter, to univocally define the cubic spline some additional conditions are required. In the `BzzCubicSpline` class, several possibilities are considered and are discriminated by assigning the following values to a specific parameter:

```
NATURAL
ASSIGNED_SECOND_DERIVATIVE
SECOND_DERIVATIVE_ADJACENT
ASSIGNED_FIRST_DERIVATIVE
PERIODIC
```

The `BzzCubicSpline` class has two constructors. The first one requires the vectors **x** and **y** of the support points, the value of the parameter to select the spline type and two `double`. The meaning of the two `double` changes according to the selected spline type: the boundary values of second derivatives are provided with `ASSIGNED_SECOND_DERIVATIVE`, whereas the values of α and β of equations (1.99) and (1.100) are provided with the selection of
`SECOND_DERIVATIVE_ADJACENT`:

$$s_1'' = s_1''(x_1) = \alpha s_1''(x_2) = \alpha s_2''$$

$$s_n'' = s_{n-1}''(x_n) = \beta s_{n-1}''(x_{n-1}) = \beta s_{n-1}''$$

The boundary values for the first derivatives are provided with the `ASSIGNED_FIRST_DERIVATIVE`.

The latter constructor is used for the NATURAL or PERIODIC spline. This constructor is also used to create the default spline

$$s_1'''(x_1) = 0$$

$$s_{n-1}'''(x_n) = 0$$

which does not require any index for discriminating the spline types.

It is worth remarking that this option is equal to the case SECOND_DERIVATIVE_ADJACENT with $\alpha = \beta = 1$.

For example,

```
BzzVector x(...),y(...);
//First constructor
BzzCubicSpline s1(x,y,ASSIGNED_SECOND_DERIVATIVE,
  .05,-2.);
BzzCubicSpline s2(x,y,
  SECOND_DERIVATIVE_ADJACENT,.5,.5);
BzzCubicSpline s3(x,y,ASSIGNED_FIRST_DERIVATIVE,
  3.,2.);
//Second constructor
BzzCubicSpline s4(x,y,NATURAL);
BzzCubicSpline s5(x,y,PERIODIC);
BzzCubicSpline s6(x,y); // default spline
// or BzzCubicSpline s6(x,y,
  SECOND_DERIVATIVE_ADJACENT);
// or BzzCubicSpline s6(x,y,
  SECOND_DERIVATIVE_ADJACENT,1.,1.);
```

Example 1.11

Use an object of the BzzCubicSpline class to interpolate a periodic function. The program is

```
#include "BzzMath.hpp"
void main(void)
  {
  BzzPrint("\n\nSpline PERIODIC");
  int n = 22;
  BzzVector x(n),y(n);
  double z;
  int i;
  for(z = 0.,i = 1;i <= 22;z += 2.*atan(1)*4./21.,i++)
    {
    x[i] = z;
    y[i] = sin(z);
    }
```

1 Interpolation

```
x.BzzPrint("x");
y[n] = 0.;
BzzCubicSpline s(x,y,PERIODIC);
for(z = 0.;z <= 2.*atan(1)*4.;z +=
   2.*atan(1)*4./100.)
   {
   BzzPrint("\nSpline z %e y %e y1 %e y2 %e",
      z,s(z),s(z,1),s(z,2));
   BzzPrint("\nCorrect z %e y %e y1 %e y2 %e",
      z,sin(z),cos(z),-sin(z));
   BzzPause();
   }
}
```

1.13
Two-Dimensional Curves

An important field for the application of successive interpolation of polynomials is in graphics, where a continuous curve passing through specific points is required.

The argument requires a larger discussion than the one presented in this book. Actually, only a simple application is proposed here.

To draw a curve passing through some known points (x_i, y_i) that cannot be univocally represented as function $y(x)$, it is possible to adopt the following device. Create a new set of points exactly equal to the existing one, with dependent variables x and y and the auxiliary parameter t defined as follows:

$$t_1 = 0 \tag{1.109}$$

$$t_i = t_{i-1} + \sqrt{(x_i - x_{i-1})^2 + (y_i - y_{i-1})^2} \qquad (i = 2, n) \tag{1.110}$$

The parameter t is the abscissa. The function is obtained by varying t from t_1 to t_n and evaluating the corresponding previsions x and y.

It is appropriate to graphically check the curve. If some zones have sudden variations, the representation is unsatisfactory.

1.14
Orthogonal Polynomials

This section deals with orthogonal polynomials, which have a considerable importance in numerical analysis.

1.14 Orthogonal Polynomials

Two vectors **x** and **y** are *orthogonal* if their scalar product is equal to zero:

$$\mathbf{x}^T\mathbf{y} = \sum_{i=1}^{n} x_i y_i = \|\mathbf{x}\|_2 \|\mathbf{y}\|_2 \cos\alpha = 0 \tag{1.111}$$

In other words, two vectors are orthogonal when they generate an angle $\alpha = \pi/2$. This property was extended to the functions (vectors with infinite elements) as follows.

Two functions $g(x)$ and $h(x)$ are *orthogonal* in the interval $[a, b]$ against the weight function $r(x)$ if

$$\int_a^b r(x)g(x)h(x)dx = 0 \tag{1.112}$$

Orthogonal polynomials constitute special families of orthogonal functions consisting of zeroth-, first-, second-, and higher-degree polynomials that are mutually orthogonal. They are characterized by the existence interval $[a, b]$ and the weight $r(x)$ that makes them orthogonal. The main sets are given in Table 1.1.

For example, the polynomials

$$P_2(x) = \frac{3x^2 - 1}{2}$$

$$P_3(x) = \frac{5x^3 - 3x}{2}$$

belong to the Legendre family and the following equation results:

$$\int_{-1}^{1} P_2(x) P_3(x)\, dx = 0$$

Each set of orthogonal polynomials has specific features. One of them correlates three adjacent polynomials. In the following, the recurring relations for the aforementioned polynomials are shown for $n \geq 1$.

- Legendre polynomials:

$$(n+1)P_{n+1}(x) - (2n+1)xP_n(x) + nP_{n-1}(x) = 0 \tag{1.113}$$

Table 1.1 Main sets of orthogonal polynomials.

	a	b	r(x)
Legendre	−1	1	1
Laguerre	0	∞	e^{-x}
Hermite	−∞	∞	e^{-x^2}
Chebyshev	−1	1	$\dfrac{1}{\sqrt{1-x^2}}$

- Laguerre polynomials:

$$(n+1)L_{n+1}(x) - (2n+1-x)xL_n(x) + n^2 L_{n-1}(x) = 0 \tag{1.114}$$

- Hermite polynomials:

$$H_{n+1}(x) - 2xH_n(x) + 2nH_{n-1}(x) = 0 \tag{1.115}$$

- Chebyshev polynomials:

$$T_{n+1}(x) - 2xT_n(x) + T_{n-1}(x) = 0 \tag{1.116}$$

For example, the 4-degree Legendre polynomial can be obtained by knowing 2- and 3-degree polynomials:

$$4P_4(x) = 7xP_3(x) - 3P_2(x) = 7x\frac{5x^3 - 3x}{2} - 3\frac{3x^2 - 1}{2}$$

Hence,

$$P_4(x) = \frac{35x^4 - 30x^2 + 3}{8}$$

These polynomials have numerous features that are not explained here. In the following section, only Chebyshev polynomials are discussed for their relevance.

1.14.1
Chebyshev Polynomials

Let us consider the function

$$T_n(x) = \cos(n(\arccos(x))) \quad (n = 0, 1, \ldots) \tag{1.117}$$

for $x \in [-1, 1]$.
With $n = 0$,

$$T_0(x) = \cos(0) = 1 \tag{1.118}$$

With $n = 1$,

$$T_1(x) = \cos(\arccos(x)) = x \tag{1.119}$$

For the generic n, the following property can be exploited:

$$\cos(nt) = 2\cos(t)\cos((n-1)t) - \cos((n-2)t) \tag{1.120}$$

which gives the recursive formula

$$T_{n+1}(x) = 2xT_n(x) - T_{n-1}(x) \tag{1.121}$$

First terms are

$$T_0 = 1;$$
$$T_1 = x;$$
$$T_2 = 2x^2 - 1$$
$$T_3 = 4x^3 - 3x$$
$$T_4 = 8x^4 - 8x^2 + 1$$
$$T_5 = 16x^5 - 20x^3 + 5x$$
$$T_6 = 32x^6 - 48x^4 + 18x^2 - 1$$
$$T_7 = 64x^7 - 112x^5 + 56x^3 - 7x$$

Functions $T_n(x)$ are called *Chebyshev polynomials*. It is possible to express the powers of x against Chebyshev polynomials by using the previous expressions:

$$1 = T_0$$
$$x = T_1$$
$$x^2 = \frac{T_0 + T_2}{2}$$
$$x^3 = \frac{3T_1 + T_3}{4}$$
$$x^4 = \frac{3T_0 + 4T_2 + T_4}{8}$$
$$x^5 = \frac{10T_1 + 5T_3 + T_5}{16}$$
$$\ldots$$

Chebyshev polynomials are important for some of their properties.

1) Each polynomial $T_n(x)$ in the interval $-1 \leq x \leq 1$ is even in the range $[-1, 1]$. It directly derives from definition (1.117).
2) The n roots of $T_n(x)$ polynomials are real, distinct, and inside the interval $[-1, 1]$; moreover, they can be easily calculated through the formula:

$$\lambda_i = \cos\left(\frac{(2i-1)\pi}{2n}\right) \quad (i = 1, \ldots, n) \quad (1.122)$$

3) Polynomials $T_m(x)$ and $T_n(x)$ with $m \neq n$ are mutually orthogonal in both the continuous

$$\int_{-1}^{1} \frac{1}{\sqrt{1-x^2}} T_m(x) T_n(x) dx = \begin{cases} 0, & m \neq n \\ \frac{\pi}{2}, & m = n \\ \pi, & m = n = 0 \end{cases} \quad (1.123)$$

and against N discrete points x_i

$$\sum_{j=0}^{N-1} T_m(x_j) T_n(x_j) = \begin{cases} 0, & m \neq n \\ \dfrac{N}{2}, & m = n \\ N, & m = n = 0 \end{cases} \quad (1.124)$$

on the condition that abscissas are determined through the relation

$$x_j = \cos\left(\frac{\pi}{N} j\right) \quad (1.125)$$

4) As all orthogonal polynomials, even Chebyshev polynomials, satisfy the three-term relation (1.121).
5) For a large amount of functions, the series expansion of Chebyshev polynomials converges very fast, more than the other expansions. This feature is exploited to represent a function through the economization process.
   For example, the power series expansion

$$\ln(x+1) \approx x - \frac{x^2}{2} + \frac{x^3}{3} - \frac{x^4}{4} + \frac{x^5}{5}$$

has a truncation error on the order of $1./6. = .1666$. This expression can be converted into a Chebyshev polynomial series:

$$\ln(x+1) \approx T_1 - \frac{T_0 + T_2}{4} + \frac{3T_1 + T_3}{12} - \frac{3T_0 + 4T_2 + T_4}{32} + \frac{10T_1 + 5T_3 + T_5}{80}$$

Hence,

$$\ln(x+1) \approx -\frac{11}{32} T_0 + \frac{11}{8} T_1 - \frac{3}{8} T_2 + \frac{7}{48} T_3 - \frac{1}{32} T_4 + \frac{1}{80} T_5$$

In the interval $0 \leq x \leq 1$, this series has the same accuracy as the previous one, even neglecting the last three terms, as $7./48. = 0.146 < 0.166$. Therefore, first three elements of the series expansion are enough:

$$\ln(x+1) \approx -\frac{11}{32} + \frac{11}{8} x - \frac{3}{8}(2x^2 - 1) = -\frac{1}{32} + \frac{11}{8} x - \frac{3}{4} x^2$$

6) Among all the n-degree polynomials with coefficient equal to 1 in correspondence with the term with maximum degree, the polynomial

$$\Phi_n(x) = \frac{T_n(x)}{2^{n-1}} \quad (1.126)$$

has the minimum of the maximum absolute value in the interval $-1 \leq x \leq 1$. This last property allows one to solve a problem that was left in abeyance.

The error in a polynomial interpolation is given by relation (1.12). When it is possible to select the abscissas $x_0, x_1, \ldots, x_n$ in the interval $-1 \leq x \leq 1$, the function

$$\Phi_{n+1}(x) = \Phi_{n+1}(x, x_0, x_1, \ldots, x_n) = (x - x_0)(x - x_1) \cdots (x - x_n) \quad (1.127)$$

can be minimized by selecting the abscissas in correspondence with the roots of the $(n+1)$-degree Chebyshev polynomial.

Since $(n+1)$-degree Chebyshev polynomial has the same roots as the function $\Phi_{n+1}(x)$ and the multiplicative coefficient of its maximum order is equal to 2^n,

$$\frac{T_{n+1}(x)}{2^n} = \Phi_{n+1}(x) = (x-x_0)(x-x_1) \cdots (x-x_n) \tag{1.128}$$

An important consequence of relation (1.128) is related to the fact that Chebyshev polynomials have values less than or equal to 1. and, therefore, the function $\Phi_{n+1}(x)$ is less than or equal to $1/2^n$.

If the interval of interest is $a \leq x \leq b$, it is sufficient to evaluate the zeros of the auxiliary variable $-1 \leq z \leq 1$ and operate a variable transformation:

$$x_i = \frac{z_i(b-a) + (b+a)}{2} \tag{1.129}$$

2
Fundamentals of Statistics

Examples of this chapter can be found in the directory `Vol2_Chapter2` within the enclosed CD-ROM.

2.1
Introduction

The task of statistics is to collect, analyze, and interpret data samples derived from a larger population. Two of the most important branches in statistics deal with the design of experiments and the analysis of experimental data sets. The former one is aimed at optimizing experimentations so as to get the maximum amount of information with the minimum number of experiments. The latter one makes inferences on the population by analyzing the data coming from the population.

It is important to note that inferences deduced from the analysis of data samples are ever based on some hypotheses that cannot be verified. Thus, although an inference is obtained with every possible precaution, it might be incorrect.

Exit polls in the election to the US Presidency have shown many times how previsions can be incorrect.

This warning should be taken seriously as each book on statistics we examined suffers from a critical problem that seems to make statistics stronger than what it really is. Hereinafter, we give a short description of such an error, and it shall be explained in detail later on.

Statistics is based upon two interrelated concepts: statistical tests and confidence limits. Often, both these aspects are improperly used in the literature that deals with statistics (for more details, see also Buzzi-Ferraris, 1999, 2000; Buzzi-Ferraris and Manenti, 2009). In fact, the general approach is based on the fact that if a statistical test satisfies some requirements, it is possible to discard a hypothesis of the test with a predetermined risk α. In addition, the alternative hypothesis can be accepted with a confidence equal to $1-\alpha$.

Interpolation and Regression Models for the Chemical Engineer: Solving Numerical Problems
Guido Buzzi-Ferraris and Flavio Manenti
Copyright © 2010 WILEY-VCH Verlag GmbH & Co. KGaA, Weinheim
ISBN: 978-3-527-32652-5

For example, it is possible to discard the hypothesis that a specific treatment has no positive effect on a product with a risk equal to 5% and it is also possible to say that the same treatment has a positive effect with a probability equal to 95%. This latter assertion shall be demonstrated to be always wrong. Even the former one is wrong when it is literally intended; moreover, it has no practical meaning if the risk is referred to the hypothesis, which the overall test is based on.

It shall be explained how it is never possible to obtain a quantitative value of the risk related to a decision in a statistical test.

It is not possible to take decisions with an absolute certainty. Moreover, it is not possible to properly evaluate the numerical value of the risk involved in the decision.

On the other hand, if nothing is certain, why should the numerical value of the risk related to a decision be without any uncertainty?

Books on statistics state that it is always possible to assign two numbers to the parameter estimation in order to define the confidence limits of the same estimation. In other words, a confidence region is defined by adding and subtracting confidence limits to the parameter estimate. The confidence region is related to the risk assumed in the evaluation of two confidence limits, and the value of the parameter is in the neighborhood of this range.

For example, a Gallup's investigation on the US Presidency election in 1988 (Wonnacott and Wonnacott, 1990) provided the following data: 840 random voters among 1500 were for Bush and only 660 for Dukakis. Probability estimation that the overall population might have voted for Bush was evaluated through the ratio $840/1500 = 0.56$.

To obtain confidence limits of 95%, a value equal to 0.03 (their evaluations shall be explained in the following paragraphs) has to be added and subtracted. As a consequence, there is a confidence of 95% that the value obtained on the overall population is in the range of $0.53-0.59$.

Unfortunately, this assertion is wrong.

It shall be explained that confidence limits of a parameter have a meaning that significantly differs from the one usually defined in books on statistics.

2.2
Fundamentals

This paragraph deals with fundamentals of statistics and it tries to propose them in a very informal way.

Capital letters X, Y, Z shall denote random variables, whereas their values shall be denoted by x, y, z.

A random variable Y is *discrete* when it can assume only discrete values; it is *continuous* otherwise.

For example, the random variable of heads and tails in flipping a coin is a discrete random variable, which can assume only two values.

Let Y be a discrete random variable.

Probability distribution of a discrete variable is the sum of probabilities to get a specific value of y and it is denoted by $P(y)$.

By changing y, different values of P are obtained and they can be either visualized in a plot or considered in a mathematical formulation.

Expected value μ is defined by the relation

$$\mu = E\{Y\} = \sum_y y \cdot P(y) \tag{2.1}$$

If Y is a continuous variable, previous definitions must be revised.

The function $F(y) = P(Y \leq y)$ of *probability distribution* for a continuous random variable is the chance to obtain a value that is not larger than y.

Function $f(y)$ of *probability density* for a continuous random variable is the derivative of function $F(y)$.

For continuous variables, the *expected value* μ is defined as follows:

$$\mu = E\{Y\} = \int_{-\infty}^{\infty} y \cdot f(y) \cdot dy \tag{2.2}$$

The operator *expected value* of continuous random variables has no physical meaning but only a mathematical one.

Let Y be a random variable.

Its *variance* σ^2 is defined as

$$\sigma^2 = V\{Y\} = E\{(Y-\mu)^2\} \tag{2.3}$$

Its *standard deviation* σ is the positive square root of the variance.

To estimate a parameter of a population, that is, μ or σ^2, or, in general, to estimate model parameters, it is necessary to analyze features of the selected estimator.

The estimate b of a parameter β for a population Y obtained with n experimental values $y_i (i = 1, \ldots, n)$ is still a random variable, with a probability distribution depending on the variable Y and on the characteristics of the selected estimator.

Let b be the estimate of a parameter β of a population Y. b is obtained with n experimental values $y_i (i = 1, \ldots, n)$.

The estimate b is *unbiased* if

$$E\{b\} = \beta \tag{2.4}$$

For example, the arithmetic mean

$$\bar{y} = \frac{\sum_{i=1}^{n} y_i}{n} \tag{2.5}$$

is an unbiased estimator only if all experimental values y_i are unbiased. In fact, the following results:

$$E\{\bar{y}\} = E\left\{\frac{\sum_{i=1}^{n} y_i}{n}\right\} = \frac{\sum_{i=1}^{n} E\{y_i\}}{n} = \frac{n\mu}{n} = \mu \tag{2.6}$$

An estimate b of a parameter β is *consistent* when it approaches β by increasing the number of experiments.

Some estimators are consistent even though they are biased. For example, the variance of a population may be estimated by adopting s^2 and v^2, as described in detail in the following paragraphs. Only the former one is unbiased, although they are both consistent.

Since the estimate b is a random variable, it is characterized by a variance denoting the dispersion in the neighborhood of the expected value. A smaller variance of b corresponds to its higher concentration in the neighborhood of the corresponding expected value.

Therefore, an estimator is more *efficient* when its variance is small.

One of the most important probability distributions for continuous random variables is the *normal* (or *Gaussian*) distribution.

A continuous variable Y is normally distributed if

$$F(y) = P(Y \leq y) = \int_{-\infty}^{y} \frac{1}{\sqrt{2\pi}\sigma} \exp\left(\frac{-(x-\mu)^2}{2\sigma^2}\right) dx \tag{2.7}$$

If the population Y is normally distributed and each experiment y_i is unbiased, the variance of the arithmetic mean is

$$V\{\bar{y}\} = E\left\{(\bar{y}-\mu)^2\right\} = \frac{\sigma^2}{n} \tag{2.8}$$

whereas the variance of the median is

$$V\{m_y\} = E\left\{(m_y-\mu)^2\right\} = \frac{\pi\sigma^2}{2n} = \frac{\pi}{2} V\{\bar{y}\} \tag{2.9}$$

As a consequence, the arithmetic mean of a normally distributed population Y is more efficient against the median in estimating μ.

An estimator is *robust* when the parameter estimation is only slightly modified even though some values of the experimental data y_i are biased. An increase in robustness means that the estimator is able to account for an increase in the amount of biased data without any considerable variation in parameter estimation. When one or a few biased experiments take different values, the estimator is *nonrobust*.

The arithmetic mean is a **non**robust estimator as a single error in the experimental data set is enough to significantly change its value.

For example, the arithmetic mean of the following data

$$3.112, 3.115, 3.114, 3.121, 3.112, 3.123, 3.116$$

is equal to 3.116.

Conversely, the arithmetic mean of

$$3.112, 3.115, 31.14^*, 3.121, 3.112, 3.123, 3.116$$

is equal to 7.79.

As a result, a single error is sufficient to dramatically change the value of the arithmetic mean. Conversely, the median is a very robust estimator, which is able to estimate the parameter μ even though almost a half of the experimental data are biased. Referring to data sets mentioned above, values of the median are 3.115 and 3.116, respectively.

Some estimators might require higher computational times, especially when the number of experimental data is large. Sometimes, experimental point values are stored on files, especially with very large data set. This can be a typical case of a large-scale industrial plant, with a lot of measurement to be stored on the historical database system. In such cases, the problem is related to the need of reading data from the file many times, so as to estimate parameters.

For example, it is sufficient to read the data set just once to evaluate the arithmetic mean, whereas the median requires a data reordering and, consequently, many readings.

An experimental point affected by a large error is even called *outlier* or *gross error* (see Chapter 4).

2.3
Estimation of Expected Value

Expected value μ of the population Y is particularly important as it denotes the central value of the random variable. Usually, one does not know what is the value of μ of the population Y, as n experimental points $y_i (i = 1, \ldots, n)$ of only such a population are known. These experimental points are used to estimate the expected value μ.

In the ***BzzMath*** library, the `BzzVector` class allows one to estimate the expected value μ of population Y.

In the ***BzzMath*** library, the value of μ can be estimated by using an object of the `BzzVector` class. This object can be initialized by means of one of the constructors discussed in Buzzi-Ferraris and Manenti (2010a).

For example, to initialize the vector containing the following data

   3.112, 3.115, 3.114, 3.121, 3.123, 3.116

it is possible to adopt the following constructor:

```
BzzVector v(7,3.112,3.115,3.114,3.121,3.112,3.123,3.116);
```

Data may be acquired either from an ASCII file or from a binary file (see again Buzzi-Ferraris and Manenti (2010a) for more details).

2.3.1
Random Selection

Different estimators can be considered for evaluating μ. The most simple is to randomly select a value y_i among the n elements of the overall data set.

2.3.2
Arithmetic Mean

The arithmetic mean can be defined as $\bar{y} = \dfrac{\sum_{i=1}^{n} y_i}{n}$.

 The arithmetic mean is a consistent estimator of the parameter μ.

 The arithmetic mean is an unbiased estimator of μ if all experimental points y_i are unbiased.

 The arithmetic mean is a *nonrobust* estimator. Actually, a single outlier is enough to dramatically change the parameter estimation.

 The arithmetic mean is the most efficient estimator for the parameter μ.

The arithmetic mean requires small computational times. In addition, it is easy to use with large vectors and data files since experimental points are read only once.

The function `Mean` belonging to the **BzzMath** library allows to evaluate the arithmetic mean of a vector. Two functions are implemented: the first requires a `BzzVector` object as argument and the second, the name of the ASCII file, where experimental points are stored.

```
double mean;
mean = Mean(v);
mean = Mean("D:\\Vect.dat");
```

2.3.3
Median

If experimental values y_i are ordered from the smallest one, the median m_y corresponds to the value placed just in the middle of the list. In other words, the median is the value with an equal number of terms smaller and larger of the same median.

Specifically, when the amount of elements n is odd-numbered, the previous definition is right. Conversely, if their amount is even-numbered, the median is the arithmetic mean of the two adjacent values placed in the middle of the list.

The median of a continuous distribution is defined as follows.

The *median of a continuous distribution* X, $\tilde{\mu}$, is a value of the random variable such that the probability is 0.5 that an observed value of X is less than or equal to the median, and the probability is 0.5 that an observed value of X is greater than or equal to the median.

If the probability distribution of the population is *symmetric*, the median is a *consistent* estimator of μ.

If the probability distribution of the population is *symmetric*, the median is an *unbiased* estimator of μ.

The median is a very robust estimator of μ when the probability distribution of the population is *symmetric*. Its estimate is good even if almost half the experimental data are *outliers*.

If the probability is normally distributed, the median is less efficient than the arithmetic mean.

The median may require high computational times when large data sets have to be processed (ordered). Actually, the data reordering is a very expensive operation against the sum in terms of CPU time. Moreover, if the vector has a very large size and it cannot be directly loaded in the memory, some data on a file must be read many times.

The function Median belonging to the ***BzzMath*** library allows to evaluate the median of a vector. It requires an object of the BzzVector class as argument.

```
double med = Median(v);
```

2.3.4
Remedian

When the number n of elements is considerably large, the vector reordering may be computationally time consuming. Specifically, if the vector cannot be loaded in the RAM, some data on a file must be read many times. The remedian overcomes this problem by approximating the median.

Two auxiliary vectors are created: a portion of elements is sequentially loaded in the first vector until it is wholly filled. Subsequently, the median of these elements loaded in the first auxiliary vector is evaluated and stored in the first cell of the second auxiliary vector. Therefore, the first auxiliary vector can be emptied and reloaded with another portion of experimental data and the process is iterated to take into account all the data stored in the original vector.

At this point, the remedian of the original vector is evaluated by calculating the median of the set of submedians stored on the auxiliary vector. This procedure can be expanded to include several auxiliary vectors if the data set is significantly large.

If the probability distribution of the population is *symmetric*, the remedian is a *consistent* estimator of µ.

 If the probability distribution of the population is *symmetric*, the remedian is an *unbiased* estimator of µ.

 The remedian is a very robust estimator of µ when the probability distribution of the population is *symmetric*. The estimation is good even though almost half the data are *outliers*.

 If the probability is normally distributed, the remedian estimator is less efficient than the arithmetic mean.

 The remedian requires short computational times even with very large vectors stored on data files. In fact, elements are read only once for their evaluation.

The function `Remedian` belonging to the ***BzzMath*** library allows to evaluate the remedian of a vector. Two distinct functions are implemented: the first requires an object of the `BzzVector` class as argument; the second, the name of the ASCII file.

```
double remedian;
remedian = Remedian(v);
remedian = Remedian("D:\\Vect.dat");
```

2.3.5
Trimmed Mean

The trimmed mean is a good compromise between the arithmetic mean and the median (or the remedian in case of very large data sets). Elements are still ordered as for the median, but instead of removing all the elements at both the sides of the central value, only a portion of the external values is deleted and the arithmetic mean of remaining central elements is evaluated. As a result, the trimmed mean has some intermediate features between mean and median.

The function `TrimmedMean` within the ***BzzMath*** library allows to evaluate the trimmed mean of a vector. The function requires a `double` and an object of the `BzzVector` class as argument.

```
double trimmedMean, fraction = 0.5;
trimmedMean = TrimmedMean(fraction,v);
```

The variable `fraction` is the amount of the external (left and right) elements to be deleted in the evaluation of the arithmetic mean. If `fraction` is equal to zero, the case is brought back to the arithmetic mean; conversely, when `fraction` is equal to one, the median is evaluated. Accordingly, by selecting a value within the range (0; 1), only the correspondent fractions at both the boundaries of the ordered vector are removed.

For example, by selecting the value 0.5 with a vector of 12 elements, 3 elements are removed at both the sides of the ordered vector, before evaluating the arithmetic mean, which is therefore calculated by using the remaining 6 central elements.

2.3.6
Clever Mean

A shortcoming of the median is, however, present in the trimmed mean: trimmed mean still requires the ordering of the vector of the data set. A valid alternative especially for large-size vectors is the *clever mean* (Buzzi-Ferraris and Manenti, 2010b).

Clever mean consists of removing maximum and minimum values of the vector, without claiming for its ordering. The removal of maxima and/or minima goes on until the arithmetic mean value becomes stable.

The clever mean overcomes the need of defining an appropriate level of robustness against the trimmed mean (trimmed percentage) by self-regulating robustness according to the same set of experimental data one is processing.

Another benefit of clever mean against the trimmed mean is that the former one does not remove the same amount of large and small values. The arithmetic mean is therefore evaluated by excluding only the real outliers. For example, if there were 10 outliers all with large values, the trimmed mean would remove even the 10 smallest values even though they are good observations.

It is possible to implement the function so as to read data set only once. During the reading, the total summation is evaluated and values of an assigned number of minima and maxima are recorded. Such minimum and maximum points are removed once at a time by the summation and their influence is checked on the new estimate of the arithmetic mean.

The function `CleverMean` within the **BzzMath** library allows to evaluate the clever mean of a vector. Two functions are implemented: the first requires an object of the `BzzVector` class as argument; the second, the name of the ASCII file.

```
double cleverMean;
cleverMean = CleverMean(v);
cleverMean = CleverMean ("D:\\Vect.dat");
```

2.3.7
Mode

The mode is the number with the maximum occurrence. This estimator is conceptually important, but it is rarely used, especially for continuous random variables.

2.3.8
Symmetric and Nonsymmetric Distributions

When a discrete random variable is symmetrically distributed, its mean, median, and mode coincide. Conversely, the arithmetic mean, median, and mode are no longer overlapped with a random variable that is nonsymmetrically distributed. As already defined, the mode coincides with the maximum value of the distribution, whereas the arithmetic mean is positioned more or less close to the mode. The median is placed between the mode and the mean and it is closer to the mode when the nonsymmetry is relevant.

When there are few experimental points and some outliers, the probability distribution may appear nonsymmetric even though the population is symmetrically distributed.

As a consequence, it is dangerous to estimate the central value of the population through the arithmetic mean although it has the peculiarity of estimating the expected value of the population independently from symmetry/nonsymmetry of the real distribution.

It is always useful to estimate μ with both the arithmetic mean and the median (or the remedian, if necessary). If these values are not so different, the arithmetic mean is to be selected because of its higher efficiency (smaller variance). Conversely, if their values are different, the median is preferred because of its robustness, so as to detect the possible outliers.

The preferable solution is to always use the *clever mean* as it coincides with the arithmetic mean both when no outliers are present and when all outliers have been removed.

In any case, it is crucial to take care when some outliers are identified: it is essential to realize their origin before removing or correcting them.

2.4
Estimation of Variance

The standard deviation σ and its square value σ^2, that is, the variance of a population Y, are two important indices of the random variable dispersion in the neighborhood of its central value μ. A larger value of σ and σ^2 corresponds to a higher data dispersion. Again, only values of σ and σ^2 related to experimental points $y_i (i = 1, \ldots, n)$ can be evaluated.

In the **BzzMath** library, the `BzzVector` class allows to estimate both σ and σ^2 of the population Y.

Object of the `BzzVector` class can be initialized by means of one of the constructors already described in Buzzi-Ferraris and Manenti (2010a).

2.4.1
Use of Arithmetic Mean

The variance σ^2 can be evaluated through the following relation, by adopting the arithmetic mean $\bar{y}$ of the experimental data set:

$$s^2 = \frac{\sum\limits_{i=1}^{n} (y_i - \bar{y})^2}{n-1} \qquad (2.10)$$

s^2 is an *unbiased* estimator of σ^2.

s^2 is a **non**robust estimator of σ^2. In fact, a single *outlier* is sufficient to significantly change the estimate.

The function `Variance` belonging to the ***BzzMath*** library allows to evaluate s^2. Four functions `Variance` are implemented: the first requires a `BzzVector` object; the second, a `BzzVector` object and the arithmetic mean of the vector elements; the third, the name of the data file containing experimental data; and the last one, the name of the data file and the arithmetic mean.

```
double mean,variance;
variance = Variance(v);
mean = Mean(v);
variance = Variance(v,mean);
variance = Variance("D:\\Vect.dat");
variance = Variance("D:\\Vect.dat",mean);
```

In addition, the following relation can be adopted to estimate the population variance:

$$v^2 = \frac{\sum_{i=1}^{n}(y_i - \bar{y})^2}{n} \qquad (2.11)$$

v^2 is a *biased* estimator of σ^2.

In fact,

$$E\{v^2\} = \sigma^2 \frac{n}{n-1} \qquad (2.12)$$

2.4.2
Using the Median

When the probability is normally distributed, the variance can be estimated through the following relation, which uses the median of the experimental data set:

$$mad2 = (1.253313 \cdot median|y_i - median(y_i)|)^2 \qquad (2.13)$$

If the population probability is *normally* distributed, *mad2* is a *consistent* estimator of σ^2.

If the population probability is *normally* distributed, *mad2* is a very robust estimator.

If the population probability is *normally* distributed, *mad2* is less efficient than s^2.

The function `Mad2` belonging to the ***BzzMath*** library, allows to evaluate the *mad2*. Four functions `Mad2` are implemented: the first requires a `BzzVector` object; the second, a `BzzVector` object and the median (or the remedian) of the experimental points; the third, the name of the data file where the experimental points are collected; and the last, the file name and the median.

```
double median, mad2;
mad2 = Mad2(v);
median = Median(v);
mad2 = Mad2(v, median);
mad2 = Mad2("D:\\Vect.dat");
mad2 = Mad2("D:\\Vect.dat", median);
```

2.4.3
Clever Variance

The variance can be estimated by using the clever mean value rather than the arithmetic mean in equation (2.10) and removing by the summation all elements discarded throughout the estimation of the same clever mean. Of course, even the total amount of observations adopted in estimating the clever variance must also be accordingly modified (Buzzi-Ferraris and Manenti, 2010b).

The variance estimated using this method shall be called *Clever Variance*.

The main advantage of clever mean and clever variance is that their estimations coincide with the ones obtained by traditional estimators once outliers are properly removed.

The use of clever variance is particularly useful when the amount of observations is large, and they must be stored on a file. In fact, contrary to the other alternatives, it is possible to get a robust estimation of mean and variance by a single reading of the file and, at the same time, detecting the presence of outliers.

Actually, it is possible to evaluate the summation of both y_i and their squares y_i^2 and to store an assigned number of maximum and minimum values, while the file containing the data set is read only once. This set of information allows to evaluate the clever mean and the clever variance and simultaneously detect possible outliers.

The function `CleverVariance` belonging to the ***BzzMath*** library allows to evaluate variance estimates. The function can be invoked in two different ways: the first requires a `BzzVector` object; the second, the name of the data file where the experimental points are collected.

```
double cleverVariance;
cleverVariance = CleverVariance(v);
cleverVariance = CleverVariance("D:\\Vect.dat");
```

Example 2.1

Compare estimations of the variance σ^2 in the following cases:

1) The first data set has no outliers
2) The second data set contains five outliers.

2.4 Estimation of Variance

Data can be directly acquired by the following program:

```
#include "BzzMath.hpp"
void main(void)
  {
  int n = 15;
  BzzVector v(n,3.112,3.115,3.121,3.112,3.114,
       3.121,3.112, 3.112,3.115,3.114,3.121,3.112,
       3.123,3.121,3.112);
  double cleverVariance = CleverVariance(v);
  BzzPrint("\ncleverVariance = %e",cleverVariance);
  double variance = Variance(v);
  BzzPrint("\nvariance = %e",variance);
  double mad2 = Mad2(v);
  BzzPrint("\nMad2 = %e",mad2);
  n = 20;
  BzzVector w(n,3.112,3.115,31.15,3.121,3.112,-3.123,
       356.116,3.114,3.121,3.112,3.112,3.115,
       3.114,3.121,3.112,3.123,-31.116,31.14,
       3.121,3.112);
  cleverVariance = CleverVariance(w);
  BzzPrint("\ncleverVariance = %e",cleverVariance);
  variance = Variance(w);
  BzzPrint("\nvariance = %e",variance);
  mad2 = Mad2(w);
  BzzPrint("\nMad2 = %e",mad2);
  }
```

In the former case without any outlier, the following estimations are obtained:

```
cleverVariance = 1.817143e-005
variance = 1.817143e-005
Mad2 = 8.484194e-006
```

whereas the following estimations are obtained in the latter case (with outliers):

```
cleverVariance = 1.817143e-005
variance = 6.347279e+003
Mad2 = 4.335603e-005
```

Note that the clever variance preserves its value in both the cases and it coincides with the traditional variance estimation. The variance estimation obtained by equation (2.10) is erroneous when some outliers are present as it is a nonrobust estimator, whereas *mad2* is an unbiased estimator, but less accurate than the clever variance.

2.5
Estimation of Standard Deviation

2.5.1
Square Root of Variance

Standard deviation s can be evaluated as the square root of variance s^2.

s is a *biased* estimate of σ.

In fact,

$$E\{s\} = \frac{\sigma}{c}, \quad c = \sqrt{\frac{n-1}{2}} \frac{\frac{n-3}{2}}{\frac{n-2}{2}} \tag{2.14}$$

When $n \to \infty$, then $c \to 1$. As a consequence, s is a consistent estimator of σ.

The function StandardDeviation belonging to the ***BzzMath*** library allows to evaluate the standard deviation. Two functions are implemented: the first requires a BzzVector object; the second, a BzzVector object and the arithmetic mean of the experimental data collected into the vector.

```
double mean, stddev;
stddev = StandardDeviation(v);
mean = Mean(v);
stddev = StandardDeviation(v,mean);
```

2.5.2
Unbiased Standard Deviation

An unbiased estimation of the standard deviation can be obtained as follows:

$$usd = c \cdot s \tag{2.15}$$

The function UnbiasedStandardDeviation belonging to the ***BzzMath*** library allows to evaluate the unbiased standard deviation. Two functions are implemented: the first requires a BzzVector object; the second, a BzzVector object and the arithmetic mean of experimental data collected into the vector.

```
double mean, ustddev;
ustddev = UnbiasedStandardDeviation(v);
mean = Mean(v);
ustddev = UnbiasedStandardDeviation(v,mean);
```

2.5.3
Using the Median

When the probability is normally distributed, the standard deviation σ may be estimated through the following relation involving the median of the experimental data set:

$$mad = 1.253313 \cdot median|y_i - median(y_i)| \tag{2.16}$$

where *mad* means *median absolute deviations*.

If the population is normally distributed, *mad* is a *consistent* estimator of σ.

If the population is normally distributed, *mad* is a very robust estimator of σ.

The function Mad belonging to the ***BzzMath*** library allows to evaluate *mad*. Four functions are implemented: the first requires a BzzVector object; the second, a BzzVector object and the median (or the remedian) of the elements of the vector; the third, the name of the data file where experimental points are collected; the last, the name of the data file and the median.

```
double median,mad;
mad = Mad(v);
median = Median(v);
mad = Mad(v, median);
mad = Mad("D:\\Vect.dat");
mad = Mad("D:\\Vect.dat", median);
```

2.5.4
Using the Sum of Absolute Errors

Standard deviation may be evaluated by using the mean of the sum of absolute errors:

$$sa = \frac{\sum_{i=1}^{n}|y_i - \bar{y}|}{n} \tag{2.17}$$

sa is **not** a *consistent* estimator of σ.

If the population is normally distributed, it is possible to make *sa* consistent by multiplying it by 1.253313.

2.5.5
Minimum and Maximum Values

Standard deviation may be estimated through the difference between the maximum and the minimum value of *y*:

$$D = \max y - \min y \tag{2.18}$$

Even though the evaluation of *D* is easy, it is neither robust nor so efficient.

It is worth to estimate σ^2 with both s^2 and *mad2*. If these values are similar, s^2 should be adopted as the estimator because of its higher efficiency. Conversely, if their values are significantly different, the robust estimator has to be used to detect possible outliers.

The preferable solution is to always use the *clever variance* as it coincides with the variance s^2 both when no outliers are present and when all the outliers have been properly removed.

2.6
Outlier Detection

It is easy to make a mistake in valuating aims and features of a robust estimator. In fact, one often thinks a robust estimator neglects outliers because they do not influence it.

A robust method does not neglect outliers, rather it is simply uninfluenced by them. It is just aimed at highlighting outliers that seem neglected by the same method.

A robust estimator should always be used to check the presence of bad experiments; bad experiments should not be simply deleted, rather they should be thoroughly analyzed to understand whether they were generated by an occasional mistake or, conversely, if they are a clear signal either of a shortcoming or of an inadequacy of the method adopted for estimating parameters (see Chapter 4).

For example, in the case of mathematical models, it may denote that the selected model is not completely satisfactory on the overall experimental domain.

Only after this analysis has been done, and on the condition that the existing outliers are really due to simple mistakes, one should proceed to eliminate them to properly estimate parameters.

When the probability is normally distributed, the median is the robust estimator of μ and the *mad* is the robust estimator of σ. On the other hand, the arithmetic mean and the variance s^2 are both nonrobust estimators.

An important consequence of the previous considerations is that the traditional procedure adopted to detect possible outliers is **incorrect** and may be completely unreliable.

Practically, the following procedure is adopted to detect outliers. First, the arithmetic mean $\bar{y}$ and the variance s^2 are evaluated. Then, standardized residuals are calculated:

$$r_i = \frac{y_i - \bar{y}}{s} \tag{2.19}$$

If the absolute value of a standardized residual exceeds a specific threshold value, usually equal to 2.5, the corresponding experimental point is considered as suspicious.

Since both the arithmetic mean and the standard deviation are **non**robust estimators, they are biased even though there is only a single outlier. Generally speaking, it is erroneous to use these estimators to detect possible outliers.

It is necessary to adopt robust estimators to effectively detect outliers; they could be the median and the *mad* in the evaluation of standardized residuals:

$$r_i = \frac{y_i - m_y}{mad} \tag{2.20}$$

Example 2.2

Detect the outlier of the following experimental values, where the third element is erroneously written for this purpose: {3.112, 3.115, 31.14, 3.121, 3.123, 3.116}.
Functions `ResidualsNormalDeviate` and `ResidualsRobustDeviate` both belonging to the ***BzzMath*** library allow to evaluate residuals with equations (2.19) and (2.20), respectively. Both the functions require an object of the `BzzVector` class as argument.
The program is

```
#include "BzzMath.hpp"
void main(void)
  {
  BzzVector v(6,3.112,3.115,3.114,3.121,3.123,3.116);
  double stddev,mean,median,mad;
  BzzPrint("\nMean %e StandardDeviation %e "
    "Median %e Mad %e",
    Mean(v),StandardDeviation(v),Median(v),Mad(v));
  BzzVector r;
  r = ResidualsNormalDeviate(v);
  r.BzzPrint("ResidualsNormalDeviate");
  r = ResidualsRobustDeviate(v);
  r.BzzPrint("ResidualsRobustDeviate");
  BzzVector w(6,3.112,3.115,31.14,3.121,3.123,3.116);
  BzzPrint("\nMean %e StandardDeviation %e "
    "Median %e Mad %e",
    Mean(w),StandardDeviation(w),Median(w),Mad(w));
  r = ResidualsNormalDeviate(w);
  r.BzzPrint("ResidualsNormalDeviate");
  r = ResidualsRobustDeviate(w);
  r.BzzPrint("ResidualsRobustDeviate");
  }
```

Analyzing the correct data (with the value 3.114 against the outlier 31.14), the arithmetic mean and the standard deviation are equal to 3.12 and 0.0043, respectively. By introducing the erroneous value 31.14, the arithmetic mean is equal to 7.79 and the standard deviation is equal to 11.44.
Standardized residuals are

$$\{-0.409, -0.408, 2.04, -0.408, -0.408, -0.408, -0.408\}$$

With the correct data, the median is equal to 3.12, whereas the *mad* is equal to 0.0037. By introducing the outlier, the median is still equal to 3.12 and the *mad* is equal to 0.0059.

Residuals evaluated by robust estimators are

$$\{-1.09, -0.590, 4725., 0.422, .759, -.422\}$$

Therefore, while the traditional procedure is ineffective to detect the presence of possible outliers, robust estimators clearly identify them.

Clever mean and *clever variance* are alternative methods (with respect to the median and the *mad*) in detecting outliers. Besides their robustness, they are even more performing (Buzzi-Ferraris and Manenti, 2010b).

The function `GetCleverMeanVarianceOutliers` belonging to the **BzzMath** library allows to evaluate the clever mean and the clever variance and, at the same time, detecting the outliers. Two versions of the function exist according to the way data are stored (either on a file or in a `BzzVector`).

Example 2.3

Use the function `GetCleverMeanVarianceOutliers` on the data proposed in case no. 2 of Example 2.1.
The program is

```
#include "BzzMath.hpp"
void main(void)
  {
  int n = 20;
  BzzVector v(n,3.112,3.115,31.15,3.121,
      3.112,-3.123,356.116,3.114,3.121,3.112,
      3.112,3.115,3.114,3.121,3.112,3.123,
      -31.116,31.14,3.121,3.112);
  double cleverMean;
  double cleverVariance;
  BzzVectorInt iOutliers;
  BzzVector outliers;
  GetCleverMeanVarianceOutliers(v,&cleverMean,
      &cleverVariance,&iOutliers,&outliers);
  BzzPrint("\ncleverMean = %e",cleverMean);
  BzzPrint("\ncleverVariance=%e",cleverVariance);
  iOutliers.BzzPrint("Outliers Indeces");
  outliers.BzzPrint("Outliers");
  }
```

The following result is obtained:

```
cleverMean = 3.115800e+000
cleverVariance = 1.817143e-005
Outliers Indeces
BzzVectorInt No.4
Size 5
   1  7
   2  3
   3  18
   4  17
   5  6
Outliers
BzzVector No.6
Size 5
   1   3.56116000000000e+002
   2   3.11500000000000e+001
   3   3.11400000000000e+001
   4  -3.11160000000000e+001
   5  -3.12300000000000e+000
```

2.7
Relevant Probability Distributions

Some situations require a probability distribution with special features. Here, the main probability distributions for both discrete and continuous variables are proposed.

2.7.1
Binomial Distribution

The binomial distribution is useful when some specific conditions are detected in the sample of data.

1) The sample consists of n experimental points coming from an infinite population. If the population is finite and limited, experiments have to be reintroduced in the same population.
2) Each experiment may be classified into mutual exclusive categories: either *good* (*successful*) or *bad*.
3) The probability that an experiment is successful is denoted by p and it is constant for each experimental point. Conversely, the probability that an experiment can be *bad* is denoted by $q = 1-p$.
4) All the experimental points are independent.
5) The variable to be evaluated is the probability to obtain k *good* points of the n experiments.

To evaluate the probability of an event (also called either experiment or observation in the following chapters), this is denoted by the term *good* or *successful*, even though this is not necessarily a welcome event.

The random variable is *discrete* as it can assume only two values.

The probability to exactly obtain k successful events with n experiments, with a probability p each, is defined as follows:

$$P(k|n, p) = \frac{n!}{k!(n-k)!} p^k (1-p)^{n-k} \tag{2.21}$$

For example, to evaluate the probability of obtaining three tails on 10 coin flips, under the hypothesis of the perfect coin (equal probability 0.5 to obtain heads or tails), it is possible to use a binomial distribution. In fact, it is easy to verify that all the aforementioned conditions are satisfied.

According to the example, assuming $n = 10$, $k = 3$, and $p = .5$,

$$P(3|10, .5) = \frac{10!}{3!(10-3)!} 0.5^3 (1-0.5)^{10-3} = 0.117$$

On the other hand, the probability that no tails are obtained on 10 attempts is

$$P(0|10, .5) = \frac{10!}{0!(10-0)!} 0.5^0 (1-0.5)^{10-0} = 0.000098$$

The binomial distribution is particularly useful in some circumstances. The following example shows a possible application.

Quality check of a specific industrial commodity is a more complex problem. Suppose the commodity is produced in many elements and it is not possible to operate an adequate control of the quality for each single element. Therefore, a random quality control is adopted.

Suppose a tolerance of 8% on the faulty or damaged products.

How many elements must be analyzed to get a *reasonable* confidence that the percentage of faulty elements is less than 8% when no one of the analyzed elements is faulty?

In this case, n is unknown, whereas $p = 0.08$ and $k = 0$. The probabilities obtained by varying n are reported in Table 2.1.

For example, the probability that no products are faulty is equal to 18.9%, by analyzing 20 elements. On the other hand, by operating a control on 80 elements, the probability that no element is faulty drops to 0.13%. In other words, if no faulty products are identified by analyzing 80 elements, it is *reasonable* to suppose that the overall percentage of faulty products is less than 8%.

If the tolerance of faulty elements is higher than 8% and all the hypotheses are still satisfied, the probability that no faulty elements are detected is significantly lower.

It should be a mistake to affirm that if no faulty elements are detected by analyzing 80 elements, the hypothesis that the percentage of faulty elements is less than 8% is accepted *with a risk* of 0.13% to be itself in fault. In fact, there is **no** certainty that all the hypotheses, which make the distribution *binomial*, are satisfied.

Table 2.1 Product quality control.

n	P(0|n,0.08)
10	0.43389
20	0.18869
30	0.08197
40	0.03561
50	0.01547
60	0.00672
70	0.00292
80	0.00127
90	0.00055

The function `BzzBinomialProbabilityDistribution` belonging to the *BzzMath* library allows to evaluate the probability to exactly obtain k *successful* events with n experiments characterized by a probability p each, for a variable with binomial distribution.

It requires three values as argument: the first is an `int` denoting the value of n; the second is another `int` representing the value of k; and the third is a `double` denoting the value of p.

Example 2.4

Evaluate the probability to obtain 2 good events on 10 experiments when the probability of success is equal to 0.1 and the probability of failure is equal to 0.9. In addition, the random variable is characterized by a binomial distribution.
The program is

```
#include BzzMath.hpp
void main(void)
  {
  int n = 10;
  int k = 2;
  double p = .1;
  BzzPrint("\nThe Binomial Probability Distribution"
      "with n %d k %d p %e is %e", n,k,p,
  BzzBinomialProbabilityDistribution(n,k,p));
  }
```

The binomial probability distribution with $n = 10$, $k = 2$, and $p = 0.1$ is equal to 0.1937102.

Example 2.5

Evaluate the probability to obtain 6 or fewer good events on 20 experiments when the probability of success is equal to 0.5 and the probability of failure is equal to 0.5 when the random variable has a binomial distribution.
The program is

```
#include BzzMath.hpp
void main(void)
   {
   int n = 20;
   int k,m = 6;
   double P = 0.,p = .5;
   for(k = 0;k <= m;k++)
      P += BzzBinomialProbabilityDistribution(n,k,p);
   BzzPrint("\nThe Probability is %e",P);
   }
```

The probability of observing six or fewer good events is equal to 0.0577.

2.7.2
Poisson Distribution

Poisson distribution is useful for events with a known average occurrence. In this case, the objective is to evaluate the probability that a selected number of events occurs in a specific interval. The interval may be a time fraction, a surface, a volume, and so on, according to the nature of the problem.

The following conditions must be satisfied when using Poisson distribution.

1) The mean of the occurrence of events, usually denoted by λ in the literature, should be constant and known a priori.
2) The amount of events occurring in a specific interval should be independent on the amount of events of each other interval not overlapped to the selected one.
3) When the selected interval size is shortened, the probability that an event occurs decreases.

In order to evaluate the probability that k events may occur in a specific interval t, the following can be stated:

$$P(k|\lambda, t) = \frac{(\lambda t)^k e^{-\lambda t}}{k!} \tag{2.22}$$

where λ is the average mean related to the generation of events.

The function `BzzPoissonProbabilityDistribution` belonging to the *BzzMath* library allows to evaluate the probability that k events with average frequency equal to λ and Poisson distribution occur in the time interval t.

It requires three values as argument: the first is a `double` concerning the value of λ; the second is another `double` related to the value of *t*; and the last one is an `int` denoting the value of *k*.

Example 2.6

Suppose an electric engine is characterized by 24 failures per year. Evaluate the probability that more than four failures occur during the first 3 months.
In this case, $\lambda = 24$, $t = 1/4$, and $k = \{5, 6, \ldots, \infty\}$: it is suitable to evaluate the complementary probability, which is characterized by $k = \{0, 1, 2, 3, 4\}$.
One can implement the following program:

```
#include "BzzMath.hpp"
void main(void)
  {
  double lambda = 24.;
  int k;
  double t = .25;
  double prob = 0.;
  for (k = 0; k <= 4; k++)
    prob += BzzPoissonProbabilityDistribution
            (lambda,t,k);
  BzzPrint("\nThe Probability for k>=5 is %e",1. - prob);
  }
```

The probability for $k \geq 5$ is equal to 0.7149435.

2.7.3
Normal (Gaussian) Distribution

One of the most important probability distributions for continuous random variables is the *normal* (or *Gaussian*) distribution.

A continuous variable *Y* is normally distributed if

$$F(y) = P(Y \leq y) = \int_{-\infty}^{y} \frac{1}{\sqrt{2\pi}\sigma} \exp\left(\frac{-(x-\mu)^2}{2\sigma^2}\right) dx \quad (2.23)$$

The function of probability distribution of a normal variable depends on two parameters: the expected value μ and the variance σ^2. As usual, the value of μ is the central value of the distribution, whereas σ^2 is the dispersion of the distribution in the neighborhood of the same μ. Higher σ^2 corresponds to larger dispersions.

An important case of the normal distribution is the *standard normal distribution*. It corresponds to the normal distribution of a random variable Z, with $\mu = 0$ and $\sigma^2 = 1$:

$$F(z) = P(Z \leq z) = \int_{-\infty}^{z} \frac{1}{\sqrt{2\pi}} \exp\left(\frac{-x^2}{2}\right) dx \qquad (2.24)$$

The previous formula allows to evaluate the probability that a normal standard random variable is less than an assigned value z.

Given a generic, normally distributed, random variable with predetermined μ and σ^2, the variable Z can be obtained as follows:

$$z = \frac{y - \mu}{\sigma} \qquad (2.25)$$

Once the value of the standard variable probability is known, it is easy to evaluate the probability of a generic, normal random variable with assigned μ and σ^2.

The function `BzzNormalGreaterThanFixed(z)` belonging to the *BzzMath* library allows to evaluate the probability to obtain a value greater than or equal to z in a population with standard Gaussian distribution.

Example 2.7

Evaluate the probability that a value is greater than or equal to 24.26 in a population with $\mu = 1$, $\sigma = 10$ and normal distribution.
The program is

```
#include "BzzMath.hpp"
void main(void)
   {
   double mu = 1.;
   double sigma = 10.;
   double z = (24.26 - mu)/sigma;
   BzzPrint("\nThe probability that z is greater than %e"
   " is %e",z,BzzNormalGreaterThanFixed(z));
   }
```

The probability that z is greater than $2.326 = \frac{24.26 - 1}{10}$ is equal to 0.01000928.

2.7.4
t-Student Distribution

An important case related to the normal distribution is the so-called *t-Student* distribution.

2.7 Relevant Probability Distributions

The name of this distribution derives from the first work published by its inventor (Gosset *alias* Student, 1908), while he worked at a Guinness brewery in Dublin. He was prohibited from publishing under his own name so the paper was written under the pseudonym *Student*. The *t*-test and the associated theory became well known through the work of Fisher (1925) who called the distribution *Student's distribution*.

Consider a population X with normal distribution, given expected value μ, and a variance not necessarily known. By selecting n points from this population, it is possible to use them for estimating μ by the arithmetic mean $\bar{x}$ and the variance σ^2/n of the random variable $\bar{x}$ by the ratio s^2/n.

The random variable t is defined as

$$t = \frac{\bar{x} - \mu}{\frac{s}{\sqrt{n}}} \qquad (2.26)$$

The distribution of the random variable t is obviously similar to the normal distribution characterizing the arithmetic mean, but it has a higher dispersion and, above all, it depends on the number of degrees of freedom used to evaluate the variable t.

If n represent the amount of the selected points used to evaluate the arithmetic mean, the number of degrees of freedom is equal to $n-1$.

The function `BzzOneWayTest(df,t)` belonging to the ***BzzMath*** library allows to evaluate the probability that a random variable *t*-Student distributed, and with *df* degrees of freedom, is greater than or equal to *t*.

Once this probability is evaluated, it is easy to calculate either the probability to obtain a value less than t or the probability that the value is either in the range or outside the predefined bounds.

Example 2.8

The following 11 experimental points are assigned:
3.15; 3.19; 3.13; 3.18; 3.10; 3.15; 3.21; 3.22; 3.09; 3.12; 3.18.
Evaluate the arithmetic mean and its standard deviation; then, evaluate the probability to obtain a theoretical value of the *t*-Student distribution greater than the value of t calculated with the previous data set and with $\mu = 3.13$.
The program is

```
#include "BzzMath.hpp"
void main(void)
  {
  BzzPrint("\nOne way t test");
  int n = 11;
  BzzVector v(n, 3.15,3.19,3.13,3.18,3.10,3.15,3.21,
      3.22,3.09,3.12,3.18);
```

```
        double mean = Mean(v);
        BzzPrint("\nMean = %e",mean);
        double variance = Variance(v,mean);
        BzzPrint("\nVariance = %e",variance);
        double meanStandardDeviation =
            sqrt(variance/double(n));
        BzzPrint("\nmeanStandardDeviation = %e",
            meanStandardDeviation);
        double t;
        int df = n - 1;
        t = (mean - 3.13)/meanStandardDeviation;
        double probability = BzzOneWayTTest(df,t);
        BzzPrint("\nThe probability that t with %d degrees of"
            " freedom is greater than %e is %e",
            df,t,probability);
        if(probability < .05)
            BzzPrint("\nI accept the hypothesis: mu > 3.13");
        else
            BzzPrint("\nI don't accept the hypothesis:"
                " mu > 3.13");
        BzzPause();
     }
```

One-way *t*-test:

```
    Mean = 3.156364e+000;
    Variance = 1.885455e-003;
    meanStandardDeviation = 1.309217e-002;
    The probability that t with 10 degrees of
    freedom is greater than 2.013695e+000
    is equal to 3.586560e-002
    I accept the hypothesis: mu > 3.13
```

In some cases, it is useful to evaluate the probability that a *t*-Student variable is out of a predefined interval, where higher and lower bounds are the same with opposite sign. This probability may be easily evaluated through the function `BzzOneWayTest(df,t)`: actually, it corresponds to the double of the probability that *t* is higher than the upper bound of the interval.

Example 2.9

Use the function `BzzOneWayTTest(df,t)` to evaluate the probability that a random variable *t*-student distributed and 10 degrees of freedom is out of the interval ±2.7.

The program is

```
#include "BzzMath.hpp"
void main(void)
  {
  BzzPrint("\nTwo way t test");
  int dof = 10;
  double t = 2.7;
  t = fabs(t);
  double probability = BzzOneWayTTest(dof,t);
  probability *= 2.;
  BzzPrint("\nThe probability t-student with %d degrees"
     "of freedom is extern to -%e +%e"
     "is equal to %e",
     dof,t,t,probability);
  BzzPause();
  }
```

Two-way *t*-test:

```
The t-student probability with 10 degrees
of freedom is extern to -2.700000e+000 +2.700000e+000
is equal to 2.231337e-002.
```

2.7.5
χ^2 Distribution

Consider ν independent random variables $X_1, X_2, \ldots, X_\nu$. Suppose they are normally distributed $N(\mu_i, \sigma_i^2)$. Using each of them makes it possible to evaluate

$$U_i^2 = \left(\frac{X_i - \mu_i}{\sigma_i}\right)^2 \tag{2.27}$$

The new random variable χ^2 is defined as

$$\chi^2 = \sum_{i=1}^{\nu} U_i^2 = \sum_{i=1}^{\nu} \left(\frac{X_i - \mu_i}{\sigma_i}\right)^2 = U_1^2 + U_2^2 + \cdots + U_\nu^2 \tag{2.28}$$

The random variable χ^2 has a new kind of distribution, which can be obtained by the normal distribution of X_i.

The value of ν represents the number of degrees of freedom used in the evaluation of χ^2. The distribution of χ^2 depends on the value of ν only, since the variables U are standardized.

If variables used in evaluating χ^2 are independent, ν is equal to their number; otherwise, it is necessary to remove a number of degrees of freedom equal to the number of constraints which variables are subject to.

The probability that χ^2 obtained with ν degrees of freedom is higher or lower than some predefined bounds can be evaluated with theoretical distribution of the variable χ^2.

For example, if $\nu = 8$, the probability that $\chi^2 > 15$ is equal to 5.9%. Conversely, the probability that $\chi^2 < 1.2$, with $\nu = 5$, is equal to 5.5%.

Functions
`BzzChiSquareGreaterThanFixed` and
`BzzChiSquaredLowerThanFixed` both belonging to the *BzzMath* library allow to perform aforementioned calculations.

These two functions require two values as argument: an `int` denoting the number of degrees of freedom and a `double`, which is χ^2 bound.

Example 2.10

Evaluate the probability that χ^2 with 8 degrees of freedom is greater than 15.
The program is

```
#include "BzzMath.hpp"
void main(void)
  {
  double chiSquare = 15.;
  int df = 8;
  BzzPrint("\nThe probability that chi-square with %d"
    "degrees of freedom is greater than %e"
    "is equal to %e",df,chiSquare,
    BzzChiSquareGreaterThanFixed(df,chiSquare));
  }
```

It results in

```
The probability that chi-square with 8
degrees of freedom is greater than 1.500000e+001
is equal to 5.914546e-002
```

Example 2.11

Evaluate the probability that χ^2 with 5 degrees of freedom is lower than 1.2.
The program is

```
#include "BzzMath.hpp"
void main(void)
```

```
{
    double chiSquare = 1.2;
    int df = 5;
    BzzPrint("\nThe probability that chi-square with %d"
        "degrees of freedom is lower than %e"
        "is equal to %e",df,chiSquare,
        BzzChiSquareLowerThanFixed(df,chiSquare));
}
```

It results in

```
The probability that chi-square with 5
degrees of freedom is less than 1.200000e+000
is equal to 5.512263e-002
```

2.7.6
F (Fisher) Distribution

An important distribution is the *F distribution* (Fisher, 1924), which is related to the χ^2 distribution.

Consider a normally distributed population X with variance σ^2. Its expected value is not of interest in this case. Moreover, it is not necessary to know the numerical value of σ^2.

Select a sample of n_1 experimental points from this population, it is possible to estimate the population variance s_1^2. Repeating the calculation by considering another sample n_2, a second population variance s_2^2 can be estimated.

The random variable F is therefore defined as

$$F = \frac{s_1^2}{s_2^2} \tag{2.29}$$

The distribution of the random variable F is evaluated from the χ^2 distribution and it depends on the number of degrees of freedom adopted in estimating both variance s_1^2 and s_2^2. They are $v_1 = n_1 - 1$ and $v_2 = n_2 - 1$, respectively, since 1 degree of freedom is used to evaluate the arithmetic mean.

With the theoretical distribution of the variable F, it is possible to evaluate the probability that F with v_1 and v_2 degrees of freedom is higher than a predefined value.

For example, given $v_1 = 4$ and $v_2 = 9$, the probability that F>3.63 is equal to 0.05. Again, given $v_1 = 12$ and $v_2 = 18$, the probability that F>0.21 is equal to 0.9957.

The function `BzzOneWayFTest(dofNum,dofDen,F)` belonging to the *BzzMath* library allows to evaluate the probability that a random variable with F distribution and `dofNum` and `dofDen` degrees of freedom at numerator and denominator, respectively, is greater or equal to F.

Example 2.12

Evaluate the probability that *F* with 4 and 9 degrees of freedom is greater than 3.63. The program is

```
#include "BzzMath.hpp"
void main(void)
    {
    BzzPrint("\nOne way F test");
    int dfNum = 4;
    int dfDen = 9;
    double F = 3.63; // s1/s2
    BzzPrint("\nThe probability that F"
        "with dfNum %d dfDen"
        " %d \nis greater than %e is equal to %e",
        dfNum,dfDen,F,
        BzzOneWayFTest(dfNum,dfDen,F));
    BzzPause();
    }
```

One-way *F*-test:

```
The probability that F with dfNum 4 dfDen 9
is greater than 3.630000e+000 is equal to 5.010630e-002
```

With the previous function BzzOneWayFTest, the probability that the theoretical *F* is greater than the value inserted in the function argument is evaluated; the degrees of freedom passed in the argument should be for numerator and denominator, respectively.

In some circumstances, it is suitable to calculate the probability that a value of the theoretical *F* is greater than a predefined value F_{ex} with v_1 and v_2 degrees of freedom, when $F_{ex}>1$; otherwise, when $F_{ex}<1$, the probability that $F>1/F_{ex}$ with v_2 and v_1 degrees of freedom.

It is possible to use the function BzzOneWayFTest on this purpose. It is enough to multiply by 2 the probability with the usual degrees of freedom and to use F_{ex} in the function argument when $F_{ex}>1$; on the other side, when $F_{ex}<1$, the probability obtained with the inverted degrees of freedom is to multiply by 2 and $1/F_{ex}$ is to be used as function argument.

The function BzzTwoWayFTest(dofNum,dofDen,F) belonging to the ***BzzMath*** library allows to automatically evaluate the previous calculation.

The function BzzTwoWayFTest requires three values as argument: the first is an int concerning the degrees of freedom of the variance at the numerator; the second is another int concerning the degrees of freedom of the variance at the denominator; and the last one is a double representing the value of *F*.

Example 2.13

Check that the probability evaluated with the function `BzzTwoWayFTest(dofNum,dofDen,F)`, with degrees of freedom $v_1 = 5$ and $v_2 = 12$ and with $F = 9.89$, corresponds to the probability evaluated with the same function by using $v_1 = 12$, $v_2 = 5$, and $F = 1/9.89$.
It should also correspond to the probability obtained with the function `BzzOneWayFTest(5,12,9.89)` by doubling it.
The program is

```
#include "BzzMath.hpp"
void main(void)
 {
 BzzPrint("\nTwo way F test");
 int dfNum = 12;
 int dfDen = 5;
 double F = 9.89; // s1/s2
 BzzPrint("\ndfNum %d dfDen %d F %e Probability %e",
    dfNum,dfDen,F,
    BzzTwoWayFTest(dfNum,dfDen,F));
 BzzPrint("\ndfNum %d dfDen %d F %e Probability %e",
    dfNum,dfDen,F,
    2.*BzzOneWayFTest(dfNum,dfDen,F));
 dfNum = 5;
 dfDen = 12;
 F = 1./9.89;
 BzzPrint("\ndfNum %d dfDen %d F %e Probability %e",
    dfNum,dfDen,F,
    BzzTwoWayFTest(dfNum,dfDen,F));
 }
```

All the three cases return a probability equal to $1.999213 \cdot 10^{-2}$.

2.8
Correct Meaning of Statistical Tests and Confidence Regions

The statistical analysis of a model is based upon two interrelated concepts: statistical tests and confidence limits. Often, both these aspects are incorrectly used in the literature that deals with models as explained elsewhere (Buzzi-Ferraris, 2000; Buzzi-Ferraris and Manenti, 2009). To better understand them, it is useful to consider one of the simplest statistical tests: the two-way t-test.

Let a population x be normal distributed, with expected value $E\{x\} = \mu_0$, n random values x_i, and subject only to random errors. The statistical variable

$$t_{ex} = \frac{\bar{x} - \mu_0}{\frac{s}{\sqrt{n}}} \qquad (2.30)$$

has the well-known t-Student distribution. By assigning a value $\alpha(0<\alpha<1)$, $|t_{ex}|$ value will exceed $t_{\alpha,n-1}$ with a probability α.

t_{ex} has this feature only if the following condition H_0^* is correct: the expected value for x is $E\{x\} = \mu_0$, where variable x has a normal distribution, the sample measures x_i have no outliers, the n values x_i are true random values, there are no errors in the computation of mean and variance values, and so on.

In other words, one can say without mistake that $|t_{ex}|$ becomes greater than a calculable value $t_{\alpha,n-1}$ α times when t_{ex} is a true member of the population of statistic t-Student variable.

When a statistical test is carried out, the following procedure is to be followed. Two complementary hypotheses are proposed: the null hypothesis H_0 and the alternative hypothesis H_a. If one is true, the other one is false and vice versa. For a two-way t-test, H_0 is $\mu = \mu_0$ and H_a is $\mu \neq \mu_0$.

The aforementioned hypotheses are exhaustive and mutually exclusive.

It is important to note that the null hypothesis H_0 is just a part of the whole hypothesis H_0^*.

When a statistical test is carried out, there are two possible types of error (Mendenhall et al., 1990)

- **I-type:** a hypothesis is rejected when it is true. The associated risk is usually denoted by α;
- **II-type:** a hypothesis is accepted when it is false. The associated risk is usually denoted by β;

and there are two possible results for the test: either $|t_{ex}| \leq t_{\alpha,n-1}$ or $|t_{ex}| > t_{\alpha,n-1}$.

If $|t_{ex}| \leq t_{\alpha,n-1}$, the H_0 is accepted, but it is not possible to assign a predetermined risk (it is a well-known mistake to state that the null hypothesis is accepted with a confidence $1-\alpha$).

Indeed, in this case, if H_0 were false, the H_0^* would also be false, so t_{ex} would not belong anymore to the statistical population of t, and the test would lose significance; therefore, no risk can be guaranteed.

If $|t_{ex}| > t_{\alpha,n-1}$, it is a mistake to affirm that the null hypothesis $H_0 : \mu = \mu_0$ can be rejected with a risk α and it is even a mistake to affirm that the risk of a **II-type** error in accepting the alternative hypothesis is $\beta = \alpha$.

Conversely, it is correct to say that it is possible to reject H_0^* (constituted by the hypothesis $\mu = \mu_0$ and by all the conditions that make t_{ex} belonging to t) with a risk α: this is a tautology.

Swapping the previous statements (rejecting H_0 or rejecting H_0^*), the mistake, usually called the *equivocation error* by logicians, is made: the meaning of null hypothesis, which is necessary for the rightness and coherence of reasoning, is changed during the same reasoning.

H_0^* can be rejected with a risk α, not H_0.

Affirming that H_0^* is false, it is not possible to know the reason: H_0^* might be false either because $\mu \neq \mu_0$ or because the distribution is not normal (there are infinite different distributions), or because there are outliers, or for several other reasons.

The null hypothesis $H_0 : \mu = \mu_0$ may be true and, at the same time, one of the other hypotheses, which are a portion of H_0^*, may be false. Under these circumstances, t_{ex} would not belong anymore to the statistical population of t and the test would lose significance; therefore, no risk can be guaranteed.

Since the definition of H_0^* does not require only the hypothesis $\mu = \mu_0$ to make t_{ex} belonging to the theoretical population of t, there is no alternative hypothesis H_a^*, exhaustive and mutually exclusive with H_0^* and it is not possible to assign a value β to the risk of accepting H_a^*. Moreover, since it is not possible to assign a value α to the risk of rejecting H_0, correspondingly, it is not possible to give a value β in order to accept H_a.

Analogous considerations can be done for all the statistical tests, such as F-test and χ^2-test, used in model analysis.

It is important to understand that each test deals with two different null hypotheses: H_0^* and H_0 and that the test allows to discard with a risk α only H_0^* and not H_0, which is the hypothesis of real interest.

What is the real risk in discarding H_0?

It depends on the confidence that one has on the H_0^* and H_0 equivalence, keeping in mind that this confidence has nothing to do with α and that it is not quantifiable.

Certainly, in a simple test like the t-test shown above, the confidence can be quite high: if the number n of experiments, with which the arithmetic mean is evaluated, is large enough (greater than 30–50), the arithmetic mean tends to be normally distributed, even if the original population was not. The calculations necessary to compute mean and variance values are simple and it is easy to detect errors; large outliers can be easily detected with a robust analysis and the minor ones do not represent relevant problems if the number of samples is high.

Nevertheless, a t-test is often performed with few experiments, assured that the test is reliable also in these conditions, since the limit value $t_{\alpha,n-1}$ changes according to the number of experiments.

Once again, this is rigorously true only for hypothesis H_0^*, while this is not the case, in principle, for H_0. The confidence that the two hypotheses are equivalent to a few experiments is very low and this implies that the risk of discarding the null hypothesis H_0 as false when it is true can be very different from α.

It should be reminded and underlined that the following observations hold for any statistical tests:

- There are no cases where the confidence that the hypotheses H_0^* and H_0 coincide can be quantified. As a consequence, the risk in discarding the hypothesis H_0 also cannot be quantified.
- A unique hypothesis H_a^*, which is alternative and exhaustive to hypothesis H_0^*, does not exist; therefore, when H_0^* is discarded with a risk α, an alternative hypothesis that could be accepted with a risk β = α, that is, with a probability 1−α, does not exist.
- An alternative hypothesis H_a, exhaustive and mutually exclusive of the hypothesis H_0, exists, but since the risk of discarding H_0 cannot be quantified, it is never possible to accept the alternative hypothesis H_a with a risk β = α, that is, with a probability 1−α.
- In several situations, such as the test for nonlinear models, the confidence in an equivalence between H_0 and H_0^* is low.

In the following discussion, some considerations are enumerated to bear the last statement. It is quite difficult to think that the expected value of the model is equal to the expected value of dependent variable y, that is, that the model is different from the expected value only due to the experimental error.

Parameters estimation can be very difficult because the minimum search of objective function is not an easy problem. Parameters value can drastically change, according to the design of experiments, and can be different from correct values. In the case of nonlinear models, parameters estimates have a non-Gaussian distribution even if all the other hypotheses are true.

A large part of the statistical analysis of nonlinear models is performed by linearizing the model in the neighborhood of the minimum of parameter values. It is not guaranteed that the ellipsoid, which approximates the region of confidence of the parameters, is similar to the real region of confidence. Specifically, this is true for ill-conditioned models or when experiments have a poor design.

When you have to make difficult measurements (i.e., radical concentrations), outliers are often present. Furthermore, it should be noted that even if measures are usually treated as random variables with normal distribution, they do not have a continuous distribution, they cannot vary in an unconfined range, and they tend to exhibit a non-Gaussian distribution, when the number of observations is limited.

For these reasons, the value of α with which a test is performed, can be different from the theoretical one: it would be more correct to use a test (e.g., the F-test) as follows:

- If $F_{ex} < F_\alpha$, the null hypothesis H_0 is accepted, but it is not possible to assign a predetermined risk.
- If $F_{ex} > F_\alpha$, the null hypothesis H_0 is rejected, but it is not possible to assign a predetermined risk.

These considerations are also very important to explain the true meaning of confidence intervals of a parameter.

Although it would be more correct to use the term regions of confidence since models have usually many parameters, it is worth considering the simplest

2.8 Correct Meaning of Statistical Tests and Confidence Regions

situation of only one parameter, in order to understand the true meaning of the expression

$$\bar{x} - t_\alpha \frac{s}{\sqrt{n}} \leq \mu_0 \leq \bar{x} + t_\alpha \frac{s}{\sqrt{n}} \qquad (2.31)$$

which allows to calculate the confidence limits of the expected value μ_0.

Is it correct to affirm that the parameter μ_0 has a confidence interval $1-\alpha$?

And, if the previous statement is ambiguous, which is the true meaning of relation (2.31)?

Some people (Press et al., 1988) state that one can say there is a 99 percent chance, for example, that the true parameter value falls within the evaluated confidence region.

This statement is wrong not only because it is not possible to speak of chance for the parameter μ_0 to be inside or outside a fixed range (a parameter is not a random variable, so it is not correct to give it a chance); indeed, it is also wrong even though the word chance is replaced with the word confidence.

In statistical books, authors take two different positions, according to the criterion they employ to obtain relation (2.31).

In the first case (Hines and Montgomery, 1990), the relation (2.31) is obtained through a two-way t-test, either when $t_{ex} < -t_\alpha$ or when $t_{ex} > t_\alpha$, the null hypothesis $H_0 : \mu = \mu_0$ can be rejected with a risk $\alpha/2$; conversely, the hypothesis H_0 is accepted when $-t_\alpha < t_{ex} < t_\alpha$.

In order to know the confidence that μ_0 is in the range (2.31), these authors carry out two other one-way t-tests: the first one is required to verify the null hypothesis $H_0 : \mu \leq \mu_0 - \delta$ with the alternative hypothesis $H_a : \mu > \mu_0 - \delta$; the second one verifies the hypothesis $H_0 : \mu \geq \mu_0 + \delta$ with the alternative hypothesis $H_a : \mu < \mu_0 + \delta$. By considering appropriate degrees of freedom, the t distribution is reported in Figure 2.1.

The three curves are plotted by using $\mu = \mu_0 - \delta$, $\mu = \mu_0$, and $\mu = \mu_0 + \delta$, respectively. If we select $\delta = t_\alpha \frac{s}{\sqrt{n}}$, since curves are symmetric, the four colored areas have the same value $\alpha/2$.

Therefore,

- when $t_{ex} > -t_\alpha$ the null hypothesis $H_0 : \mu \leq \mu_0 - \delta$ is rejected with a risk equal to $\alpha/2$ and the alternative hypothesis $H_a : \mu > \mu_0 - \delta$ is accepted with the same risk equal to $\alpha/2$;
- when $t_{ex} < t_\alpha$ the null hypothesis $H_0 : \mu \geq \mu_0 + \delta$ is rejected with a risk equal to $\alpha/2$ and the alternative hypothesis $H_a : \mu < \mu_0 + \delta$ is accepted with the same risk equal to $\alpha/2$.

As a consequence, the first two-way test allows to affirm that μ_0 is out of the range (2.31) only α times, whereas the two one-way tests allow to affirming that μ_0 is in the range (2.31) with a confidence $1-\alpha$.

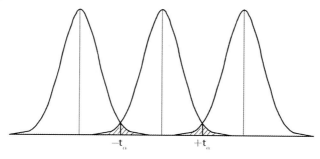

Figure 2.1 Distribution of variable t when $\mu = \mu_0 - \delta$, $\mu = \mu_0$, $\mu = \mu_0 + \delta$, respectively, with $\delta = t_\alpha \frac{s}{\sqrt{n}}$.

This sentence is incorrect because the reasoning is affected by two mistakes:
- the two-way test does not allow to quantify the risk α of rejecting the null hypothesis $H_0 : \mu = \mu_0$, which corresponds to the risk that μ_0 is out of the range (2.31);
- the two one-way tests do not allow to evaluate the risk of rejecting the two respective null hypotheses and *a fortiori* the risk of accepting the alternative hypotheses and, therefore, affirming that μ_0 is in the range (2.31) with a confidence $1-\alpha$.

The approach followed by other authors, such as Berenson *et al.*, (1988), Wonnacott and Wonnacott (1990), and Arnold (1990) is more subtle, but wrong. These authors affirm that either the parameter (for example μ) is in the 95% confidence interval, or it is not. In a particular experiment, we, of course, do not know whether it is in the interval or out of it. However, if we compute 95% confidence intervals many times, about 95% of them will be correct.

Their argument starts from a two-way t-test in the limit condition:

$$|t_{ex}| = \left|\frac{\bar{x} - \mu_0}{\frac{s}{\sqrt{n}}}\right| = t_\alpha \tag{2.32}$$

which can also be written in the form

$$\mu_0 - t_\alpha \frac{s}{\sqrt{n}} \leq \bar{x} \leq \mu_0 + t_\alpha \frac{s}{\sqrt{n}} \tag{2.33}$$

The correct meaning of this relation is the following one: if there is a population that is normal distributed, with expected value μ_0, n drawn values x_i, and subject to only random errors, with which the mean value $\bar{x}$ and the estimate of the variance s^2 are calculated, *there is a probability $1-\alpha$ that the value $\bar{x}$ falls into this interval*.

Expression (2.32) can be algebraically rearranged into the form (2.31), but it is a mistake to believe that what is true for $\bar{x}$ is also true for μ_0, even if it uses the word confidence in place of the word chance.

2.8 Correct Meaning of Statistical Tests and Confidence Regions

It is wrong to affirm that if the procedure were repeated many times with n drawings (n being small), there would be a confidence $1-\alpha$ for μ_0 to fall in the range (2.31).

Indeed, if the hypothesis $H_0 : \mu = \mu_0$ and the hypothesis that changes H_0 into H_0^* were true, the range would be really that one, but if the hypothesis $H_0 : \mu = \mu_0$ were false or if the hypothesis $H_0 : \mu = \mu_0$ were true and, at the same time, the distribution were not normal or if there were outliers, the range would be different, maybe larger, maybe smaller, maybe not symmetric.

In this case, an error similar to the one committed sometimes by formal logicians is made: the scientific propositions are analyzed only by a formal point of view, without taking into account the meaning of the terms in the proposition. While this is true for mathematical logic, this is no longer true in scientific propositions.

μ_0 cannot be exchanged with $\bar{x}$ without taking into account their different meaning in equation (2.32).

In other words, even when equation (2.31)

$$\bar{x} - t_\alpha \frac{s}{\sqrt{n}} \leq \mu_0 \leq \bar{x} + t_\alpha \frac{s}{\sqrt{n}}$$

is considered, it is necessary to read it by referring to equation (2.33)

$$\mu_0 - t_\alpha \frac{s}{\sqrt{n}} \leq \bar{x} \leq \mu_0 + t_\alpha \frac{s}{\sqrt{n}}$$

Actually, confidence limits calculated by using $\bar{x}$ in equation (2.31) include μ_0 with a confidence equal to $1-\alpha$ when μ_0 is known and all conditions that make H_0^* hypothesis true are verified.

It is not an unknown value of μ_0 to be included in two variable limits; rather, it is a known value of μ_0 to be included in.

Another aspect to be considered is the presence of numerical errors in the parameter evaluation.

Although there are no problems in the evaluation of simple parameters, such as the arithmetic mean, some troubles can be quite meaningful in the estimation of model parameters. For linear models (in the absence of experimental errors), the uncertainty on parameters value is proportional to the condition number. If it is high (the model is ill conditioned, the experimental points are not well selected, and so on), the uncertainty on the parameters value can be of the same order or also greater than the region of confidence.

The problem becomes sharper for nonlinear models, also because of the great difficulty in finding the minimum of the objective function (as seen before). Moreover, the distribution in the neighborhood of the solution will be different from the theoretical one: the numerical error will not be quantifiable.

In synthesis, it is still possible to speak about confidence limits or confidence region, but the confidence level α is neither known nor quantifiable.

So, the importance of confidence intervals is weaker than the one highlighted by statistical books.

Anyway, confidence intervals preserve some usefulness, but in a negative sense; a large region of confidence is an index of either a poor model or a bad experimental sample.

2.9
Nonparametric Statistics

Tests of hypotheses and confidence limits considered in the previous paragraph are based on the assumption that one is working with random samples from normal populations. Traditionally, these procedures are called *parametric methods* (or *non-distribution-free* procedures) as they are based on the particular parametric family of normal distribution.

Other procedures called *nonparametric* or *distribution-free* do not make any assumption about the distribution of the underlying population.

One could think that the critique to parametric tests of the previous paragraph cannot be applied to these tests. Unfortunately, this is untrue.

Let us consider the simplest nonparametric test: the sign test (Hines and Montgomery, 1990). The sign test is used to test the hypotheses about the median $\tilde{\mu}$ of a continuous distribution.

Suppose that hypotheses are

$$H_0 : \tilde{\mu} = \tilde{\mu}_0 \tag{2.34}$$

$$H_1 : \tilde{\mu} \neq \tilde{\mu}_0 \tag{2.35}$$

Suppose that $y_1, y_2, \ldots, y_n$ is a random sample from the population of interest. If $H_0 : \tilde{\mu} = \tilde{\mu}_0$ is true, the differences $y_i - \tilde{\mu}_0$ are equally likely to be positive or negative if the experiments are really random variables. Let us denote by H_0^* the combination of $H_0 : \tilde{\mu} = \tilde{\mu}_0$ and the condition of random error. Moreover, let us denote by R^+ the number of these differences with positive sign, by R^- the number of these differences with negative sign, and by $R = \text{Min}(R^+, R^-)$.

If H_0^* were true, R would be characterized by a binomial distribution (see Section 2.7.1). For example, suppose to carry out 20 experiments and that $R = 6$. In Example 2.5, the probability to obtain 6 or fewer good events on 20 experiments was calculated when the probability of success is equal to 0.5 and the probability of failure is equal to 0.5 (where the random variable has binomial distribution), by obtaining a value equal to 0.05766. Such a value is the risk of discarding the hypothesis H_0^* as false, while it is true. It is not possible to evenly quantify the risk of discarding the hypothesis $H_0 : \tilde{\mu} = \tilde{\mu}_0$ as there is no possibility to know when the hypotheses H_0^* and H_0 coincide with each other. In fact, the experiments might be nonrandom for many reasons that cannot to be exhaustively verified.

2.10
Conditional Probability

Let us denote by $P(A)$ the probability that a certain event A occurs and $P(\bar{A}) = 1 - P(A)$ that event A does not. Let us also suppose that a certain event B occurs and it is useful to get additional information on event A. The probability that event A occurs when it is known that event B is yet occurred is denoted by $P(A|B)$.

The probability $P(A|B)$ is called *conditional probability*.

Conditional probability has the following feature, coming from the Bayes theorem:

$$P(A \text{ and } B) = P(A|B) \cdot P(B) = P(B|A) \cdot P(A) \tag{2.36}$$

The probability that both events A and B occur is equal to the product of the two probabilities: the probability that event A occurs by knowing that event B was yet occurred multiplied by the probability that event B occurs or the probability that event B occurs by knowing that event A was yet occurred multiplied by the probability that event A occurs.

From equation (2.36),

$$P(A|B) = \frac{P(B|A) \cdot P(A)}{P(B)}$$
$$= \frac{P(B|A) \cdot P(A)}{P(B|A) \cdot P(A) + P(B|\bar{A}) \cdot P(\bar{A})} \tag{2.37}$$

and

$$P(B|A) = \frac{P(A|B) \cdot P(B)}{P(A)}$$
$$= \frac{P(A|B) \cdot P(B)}{P(A|B) \cdot P(B) + P(A|\bar{B}) \cdot P(\bar{B})} \tag{2.38}$$

Extending the case to more events $E_1, \ldots, E_k$, Bayes theorem becomes

$$P(E_1|B) = \frac{P(B|E_1) \cdot P(E_1)}{P(B)}$$
$$= \frac{P(B|E_1) \cdot P(E_1)}{P(B|E_1) \cdot P(E_1) + \cdots + P(B|E_k) \cdot P(E_k)} \tag{2.39}$$

Calculation of conditional probabilities may take to two kinds of complementary error.

1) Evaluate in a wrong way the conditional probability (the improper use of Bayes theorem).
2) Fully believe in the numerical result just obtained without considering uncertainties related to probabilities involved in calculations.

The first error is highlighted in all books on statistics that deal with conditional probability calculation. It is easy to be wrong in estimating the real conditional probability by following the common sense rather than carrying out the required calculations.

For example, let us suppose that

- the probability that a specific product is faulty is $P(A) = .01$;
- the probability that an *ad hoc* test identifies the product as faulty when it is really faulty is $P(B|A) = .95$;
- the probability that the same test points out a good product as faulty is $P(B|\bar{A}) = .1$.

By analyzing a sample, if the test identifies it as faulty, which is the real probability that the sample is really faulty?

Intuition easily leads to an error in evaluating the probability. Applying the Bayes theorem,

$$P(A|B) = \frac{P(B|A) \cdot P(A)}{P(B|A) \cdot P(A) + P(B|\bar{A}) \cdot P(\bar{A})}$$

$$= \frac{.95 \cdot .01}{.95 \cdot .01 + .1 \cdot .99} = \frac{95}{95 + 990} = 8.8\,\%$$

On the other hand, the second error is often underestimated or neglected in books on statistics.

Remark:
1) In many situations, values of probability involved in previous relations are obtained with poor accuracy.
2) Results dramatically depend on the population adopted to evaluate the probability $P(A)$ and $P(B)$ of events A and B.

3
Linear Regressions

Examples of this chapter can be found in the directory Vol2_Chapter3 within the enclosed CD-ROM.

3.1
Introduction

For the particular case of linear regression problems, the following hypotheses shall be considered in this chapter:

1) There is one dependent variable y subject to experimental error.
2) There are n_X independent variables that are not subject to experimental error: $\mathbf{x}$ are the experimental values and the expected values.
3) The model contains p adaptive parameters β and $\mathbf{b}$ are their estimates.
4) The dependent variable is uniquely determined as follows:

$$y_i = \beta_1 f_1(\mathbf{x}_i) + \beta_2 f_2(\mathbf{x}_i) + \cdots + \beta_p f_p(\mathbf{x}_i) + \varepsilon_i \quad (i = 1, \ldots, n_E) \quad (3.1)$$

where n_E is the total amount of experimental points. The model is linear against parameters β_j whereas the p functions denoted by $f_j(\mathbf{x}_i)$ can be arbitrarily complex.

5) The expected value of y_i is η_i for each $i = 1, \ldots, n_E$.
6) The experimental error ε_i is normally distributed with expected value $E(\varepsilon_i) = 0$ and variance σ_i^2 for each i.
7) The experimental error has constant variance (homoscedasticity condition): $\mathrm{var}(\varepsilon_i) = E(\varepsilon_i - E(\varepsilon_i))^2 = E(\varepsilon_i^2) = \sigma^2$, for each i.
8) There are no correlations between experimental points: $E(\varepsilon_i \varepsilon_j) = 0$, for each $i \neq j$.
9) Functions $f_j(\mathbf{x}_i)$ are linearly independent.
10) There are no gross errors (or outliers) that contaminate model variables. If one or more outliers exist, they must be detected before examining the model. Once identified, it is appropriate to understand their origin before deleting or adjusting them. This topic shall be explained in detail in Chapter 4.

Interpolation and Regression Models for the Chemical Engineer: Solving Numerical Problems
Guido Buzzi-Ferraris and Flavio Manenti
Copyright © 2010 WILEY-VCH Verlag GmbH & Co. KGaA, Weinheim
ISBN: 978-3-527-32652-5

It is worth noting that the model (3.1) is preferable against the alternatives proposed in the literature. Specifically, two formulations are often considered:

$$y_i = \beta_1 + \beta_2 g_1(\mathbf{x}_i) + \cdots + \beta_p g_{p-1}(\mathbf{x}_i) + \varepsilon_i \qquad (i = 1, \ldots, n_E) \qquad (3.2)$$

and

$$y_i = \beta_0 + \beta_1 x_{1i} + \cdots + \beta_p x_{pi} + \varepsilon_i \qquad (i = 1, \ldots, n_E) \qquad (3.3)$$

Formulation (3.2) is a particular case, even though important, of the more general formulation considered here.

As it shall be discussed, a specific technique, which is not valid for the general formulation, is adopted to estimate model parameters in this case; hence, the general case cannot be solved by formulating the problem in this way.

When the first function $f_1(\mathbf{x}_i)$ is identically equal to 1. in all the experimental points, the model (3.1) is reduced to the model (3.2), which is called *model with intercept*.

Formulation (3.3) is unable to enhance the theoretical and practical differences between the independent variables $\mathbf{x}$ and the functions $f_j(\mathbf{x}_i)$ depending on them.

As it shall be discussed later on, neither the best model formulation nor the best experimental points can be found out without accounting for this distinction.

This kind of problem formulation is commonly adopted when independent variables are randomly selected and it is not possible to assign them a specific value. In this case, many authors refer to variables $\mathbf{x}$ of relation (3.3) by calling them *regressors*. The reason that makes such a formulation so spread is the possibility to use a series of packages for statistical analyses without the need of writing any piece of code: it is sufficient to provide the matrix of experimental values and the vector of $\mathbf{y}$. Thus, even those models written in the form (3.1) are reformulated in order to use the form (3.3). For example,

$$y = a + bx + cx^2 + dx^3 \qquad (3.4)$$

or the model

$$y = a + bx_1 + cx_2 + dx_1 x_2 \qquad (3.5)$$

can be both written in the form (3.3):

$$y_i = \beta_0 + \beta_1 x_{1i} + \beta_2 x_{2i} + \beta_3 x_{3i} \qquad (3.6)$$

Reformulation (3.6) should be avoided as it prevents one from using many other possible model formulations that are preferable to get a more accurate analysis.

There is a special and very simple case when the model is linear both in parameters and in its single independent variable.

$$y_i = \beta_1 + \beta_2 x_{1i} + \varepsilon_i \qquad (i = 1, \ldots, n_E) \qquad (3.7)$$

Some authors call *multiple linear regression* or, improperly, *multivariate regression*, the general cases (3.1), (3.2), and (3.3).

The problem can be called *multivariate regression* only when it involves more dependent variables.

Model (3.7) presents two advantages:

- It allows a manual evaluation of parameters.
- It can be easily plotted.

In this chapter, the model (3.7) shall be considered as a particular case of the general model (3.1).

Problems that do not satisfy some of the aforementioned hypotheses shall be discussed in Chapter 6.

3.2
Least Sum of Squares Method

Let us denote by **F** the matrix constituted by p columns $f_j(\mathbf{x}_i)$ for $j = 1, \ldots, p$ and $i = 1, \ldots, n_E$. Let us also denote by **b** estimate of parameters β.

Model with intercept (3.2) can peculiarly calculate the parameter β_1 independent of the other ones. It is even useful in reducing problem size.

Nowadays, it is suitable to keep the distinction between models (3.1) and (3.2) as the matrix **F** is generally better conditioned than the original one if it is obtained by removing the first column and by rewriting the other columns by subtracting their respective mean value.

In general, a vector **b** simultaneously satisfying all equations of an overdimensioned system does not exist and, therefore, it is suitable to write the system in the form

$$\mathbf{Fb} + \mathbf{r} = \mathbf{y} \tag{3.8}$$

where $\mathbf{r} \in \mathbb{R}^{n_E}$.

The vector **r**

$$\mathbf{r} = \mathbf{y} - \mathbf{Fb} \tag{3.9}$$

is called *vector of residuals*. Usually, some of its elements are nonzero for any vector **b**.

It is reasonable to choose the value of **b** that minimizes some norms of **r** as the optimal solution for the overdimensioned system (3.8).

Gauss proposed to minimize the Euclidean norm:

$$S(\mathbf{b}) = \mathbf{r}^T \mathbf{r} = (\mathbf{y} - \mathbf{Fb})^T (\mathbf{y} - \mathbf{Fb}) = \left(\|\mathbf{r}\|_2\right)^2 \tag{3.10}$$

The function

$$S(\mathbf{b}) = \sum_{i=1}^{n_E} \left(y_i - \sum_{j=1}^{p} b_j f_j(\mathbf{x}_i) \right)^2 \qquad (3.11)$$

is called sum of squares (of residuals).

 The method that minimizes the sum of squares (3.11) is called the *least sum of squares method*.

 In the literature, this method is usually called the *sum of least squares method* or the *least squares method*. While the former one is incorrect, the second one is ambiguous as both do not explain what is minimized (the mean or the median).

The selection of the Euclidean norm $\|\mathbf{r}\|_2$ presents some advantages against the other norms for a generic overdimensioned system.

1) The function $S(\mathbf{b})$ is derivable.
2) The function minimum is relatively easy to find.
3) The problem is related to **QR** and **UDV**^{T} factorization methods.

As discussed in Buzzi-Ferraris and Manenti (2010a), which the reader could refer to for more details, the minimum of the function $S(\mathbf{b})$ can be obtained by using two different strategies:

- The first consists of solving the system

$$\mathbf{F}^T \mathbf{F} \mathbf{b} = \mathbf{F}^T \mathbf{y} \qquad (3.12)$$

  obtained by zeroing first derivatives of the function (3.11). Equations in this form are called *normal equations*. The system (3.12) is square, symmetric, and positive definite if **F** is nonsingular; hence, it can be solved with the Cholesky factorization.
- The second strategy is preferable since it directly solves the overdimensioned system (3.8) with either the **QR** or the SVD factorization.

Specifically, the SVD (Singular Value Decomposition) factorization is particularly important for linear regressions.

A matrix $\mathbf{F} \in \mathbb{R}^{n_E \times p}$ with $n_E \geq p$ can always be factorized in three matrices

$$\mathbf{F} = \mathbf{U}\mathbf{D}\mathbf{V}^T \qquad (3.13)$$

where the matrices $\mathbf{U} \in \mathbb{R}^{n_E \times n_E}$ and $\mathbf{V} \in \mathbb{R}^{p \times p}$ are both orthogonal; in other words, $\mathbf{U}^T = \mathbf{U}^{-1}$ and $\mathbf{V}^T = \mathbf{V}^{-1}$. Moreover, $\mathbf{D} \in \mathbb{R}^{n_E \times p}$ is a matrix with the nonzero coefficients d_{ii}, $(i = 1, \ldots, r)$ only, where $r \leq p$ is the matrix rank.

A first relevant feature of this factorization is the following one.

Elements d_{ii} of the matrix **D** are equal to the square roots of eigenvalues of the matrix $\mathbf{F}^T \mathbf{F}$.

In the SVD factorization, coefficients d_{ii} are sorted in decreasing order:

$$d_{11} \geq d_{22} \geq d_{33} \geq \cdots \geq d_{pp} \geq 0 \qquad (3.14)$$

Coefficient d_{11}, the maximum among elements d_{ii} (in the following denoted by a single subscript, i.e., d_i), is the Norm-2 of the matrix **F**.

To realize the other advantages of the SVD factorization, it is useful to look at it from a different point of view.

A rank-p matrix can be seen as the sum of p rank-1 matrices. The SVD factorization allows to find out the p rank-1 matrices that generate the matrix **F** through a summation.

Let $\mathbf{u}_j$ be the jth column of the matrix **U** and $\mathbf{v}_j$ the jth column of the matrix **V**. The outer product $\mathbf{u}_j \mathbf{v}_j^T$ is a rank-1 matrix dimensioned $n_E \times p$. The matrix **F** can be obtained in the following way:

$$\mathbf{F} = \mathbf{U}\mathbf{D}\mathbf{V}^T = \sum_{j=1}^{p} d_j \mathbf{u}_j \mathbf{v}_j^T \qquad (3.15)$$

If the matrix has rank $r < p$, only first r terms of the summation (3.15) contribute to create the matrix **F** since coefficients d_i are positive or null and sorted as follows:

$$d_1 \geq d_2 \geq d_3 \geq \cdots \geq d_r > d_{r+1} = 0 \qquad (3.16)$$

The SVD factorization allows to determine the rank of a matrix in a very simple way: it is enough to count nonzero coefficients d_i.

Some values d_i can be significantly small against the maximum value d_1, but they are not exactly null.

By removing all the terms that can be considered numerically negligible against d_1 (for the selected calculation precision), it is possible to evaluate the so-called *numerical rank* or *pseudorank* of the matrix.

Since the vectors $\mathbf{u}_j$ and $\mathbf{v}_j^T$ are normalized, the relative relevance of rank-1 matrices in the summation (3.15) is given by the decreasing values of d_i. The first matrix is the most important one and the others are progressively less relevant.

The concept of *matrix range* of the matrix **F** becomes important in the case of linear regressions.

The *matrix range* or the *column space* of a matrix is the space described by linearly independent columns of the matrix.

Dimensions of the *matrix range* constitute the matrix rank.
The factorization SVD allows to obtain the *range* of the matrix **F** in a simple way. Let us consider the product:

$$\mathbf{G} = \mathbf{F}\mathbf{V} = \mathbf{U}\mathbf{D}\mathbf{V}^T\mathbf{V} = \mathbf{U}\mathbf{D} \qquad (3.17)$$

The matrix **F** can be seen as a series of p columns $\mathbf{f}_j$. Analogously, the matrix **G**, which is the product of the matrices **F** and **V**, can be considered as the series of the following p column-vectors $\mathbf{g}_j$.

$$\mathbf{g}_j = \mathbf{F}\mathbf{v}_j = \mathbf{f}_1 v_{1j} + \mathbf{f}_2 v_{2j} + \mathbf{f}_3 v_{3j} + \cdots + \mathbf{f}_p v_{pj} \qquad (j = 1, \ldots, p) \tag{3.18}$$

From equation (3.17),

$$\mathbf{g}_j = d_j \mathbf{u}_j \tag{3.19}$$

Since the vector $\mathbf{u}_j$ is normalized, the norm of the vector $\mathbf{g}_j$ is given by the coefficient d_j.

First r columns of the matrix **U** define the *range* of the matrix **F**. Actually, the product

$$\mathbf{g}_j = d_j \mathbf{u}_j = \mathbf{F}\mathbf{v}_j, \qquad (j = 1, \ldots, r) \tag{3.20}$$

is nonzero because of first r nonzero singular values; moreover, the vectors $\mathbf{g}_j$ are all linearly independent as the matrix **U** is orthogonal.

The SVD factorization allows to obtain the range of the matrix **F** without any effort.

It is therefore possible to transform the matrix **F** constituted by p columns in a matrix **G** constituted by r columns.

The matrix **G** is called *principal component decomposition*.

First column $\mathbf{g}_1$ of the matrix **G** is called *principal component*.

Since

$$d_1 \geq d_2 \geq d_3 \geq \cdots \geq d_r > d_{r+1} = 0 \tag{3.21}$$

it is easy to realize the relevance of each column against the others in building the original matrix **F**.

If the values of d_j with $j > k$ are either null or approaching zero against d_1, it is possible to remove $p-k$ linear combinations of columns of the original matrix so as to get a model with k columns only.

For example, when $d_1 = 100.$, $d_2 = 1.$, $d_3 = 10^{-2}$, $d_4 = 10^{-8}$, and $d_5 = 0.$, it is possible to remove last two columns of the matrix **G** to obtain a model with only three parameters but practically equal to the original one and without any correlation among parameters.

In the space generated by the columns of the matrix **G**, note that distances are extended in the direction of the principal component and shortened along the other axes.

It occurs for the different scales proportional to d_j that are adopted in the space directions. This fact shall be useful in Chapter 8 in selecting additional experimental points to improve parameter estimation.

The matrix

$$\mathbf{H} = \mathbf{F}(\mathbf{F}^T\mathbf{F})^{-1}\mathbf{F}^T \qquad (3.22)$$

is called *hat matrix*.

Considering relation (3.12), model estimations in correspondence with experimental points can be obtained by the product $\mathbf{Hy}$.

Model estimations in correspondence with experimental points are commonly denoted by $\hat{\mathbf{y}}$.

The name of the matrix $\mathbf{H}$ comes from this fact. The hat matrix transforms the vector $\mathbf{y}$ in $\hat{\mathbf{y}}$:

$$\hat{\mathbf{y}} = \mathbf{Fb} = \mathbf{F}(\mathbf{F}^T\mathbf{F})^{-1}\mathbf{F}^T\mathbf{y} = \mathbf{Hy} \qquad (3.23)$$

If $\mathbf{F}$ is an object of the `BzzMatrix` class and if it is overdimensioned, it is possible to evaluate the corresponding hat matrix by the following function:

```
BzzMatrix H;
F.GetHatMatrix(&H);
```

Although classical analysis (without any round-off error, see Buzzi-Ferraris and Manenti, 2010a) says that the evaluation of prevision $\hat{\mathbf{y}}$ is equivalent if one uses relation (3.23) or the product $\mathbf{Fb}$, this equivalence is no longer valid in numerical analysis.

Even though the hat matrix is evaluated by using all possible devices,

- without physically inverting the matrix $\mathbf{F}^T\mathbf{F}$;
- without evaluating the product $(\mathbf{F}^T\mathbf{F})^{-1}\mathbf{F}^T$ by solving the corresponding linear system by means of Cholesky algorithm;
- solving the system $\mathbf{F}^{-T}\mathbf{F}^T$ rather than the previous system because of its better conditioning;

it is not possible to get a hat matrix $\mathbf{H}$ with a condition number that is at least the square of the one of the original matrix $\mathbf{F}$.

The calculation of the hat matrix $\mathbf{H}$ can be particularly disadvantageous when there is a large difference between condition number and system conditioning of the matrix $\mathbf{F}$.

As explained in Buzzi-Ferraris and Manenti (2010a) and Buzzi-Ferraris (2010), the system conditioning reveals the accuracy of the system solution, whereas the condition number is related to the product between the matrix and a vector (or another matrix). If the system conditioning is small, the system (3.8) can be solved without any problem to get the vector $\mathbf{b}$. If, at the same time, the condition number of the matrix $\mathbf{F}$ is significantly large, the product to evaluate the matrix $\mathbf{H}$ is inaccurate. This situation shall be considered in Example 5.10.

The hat matrix is to be ever used with care, even if not avoided. Specifically, previsions $\hat{\mathbf{y}}$ should never be evaluated by the product $\mathbf{Hy}$ as such an operation may lead to inaccurate results.

Many authors show the calculation of model parameters **b** and some features of the hat matrix **H** by referring to the particular case of the model (3.7). In this case, the particular structure of the problem can be exploited to manually evaluate coefficients of the matrix **H** without highlighting any risk in using such a matrix in more complex models.

Now let us go back to the advantages in using function (3.11); when the ovedimensioned system (3.8) comes from a problem of parameter estimation for a linear problem, there is an additional advantage.

4) It is often possible to formulate the system in a better way against the general case of overdimensioned systems.

In fact, the only way to improve the conditioning of a generic overdimensioned system is to rewrite it in the standard form. In other words, all the columns must be divided by their maximum absolute value.

As it shall be discussed in Section 3.8, two additional devices can be adopted in the case of parameters estimation of linear models:

- Cleverly plan the design of experiments.
- Select the best model formulation.

In this specific case, if the hypotheses listed in the introduction of the chapter are all verified, there are even some other advantages.

5) Parameter estimates are unbiased: $E\{\mathbf{b}\} = \beta$.
6) They are the most efficient estimates (the ones with minimum variance) among all the possible linear combinations of dependent variables **y**.
7) Parameters variance and covariance matrix is given by $\mathbf{V}(\mathbf{b}) = (\mathbf{F}^T\mathbf{F})^{-1}\sigma^2$.
8) Model estimate in whatever point $\mathbf{x}_0$ far from those adopted in evaluating parameters is

$$y_0 = b_1 f_1(\mathbf{x}_0) + b_2 f_2(\mathbf{x}_0) + \cdots + b_p f_p(\mathbf{x}_0) = \mathbf{f}_0^T \mathbf{b}.$$

9) Variance of this prevision is $V(y_0) = \mathbf{f}_0^T (\mathbf{F}^T\mathbf{F})^{-1} \mathbf{f}_0 \sigma^2$.
10) Variance of the difference between the experimental dependent variable and its prevision is $\mathbf{f}_0^T (\mathbf{F}^T\mathbf{F})^{-1} \mathbf{f}_0 \sigma^2 + \sigma^2$.
11) Expected value of the least sum of squares of $S(\mathbf{b})$ divided by the difference between the number of experimental points and the number of parameters is equal to σ^2.

The ratio between the least sum of squares and $n_E - p$ is denoted by the acronym MSE and it is called *mean square error*, while $n_E - p$ are the degrees of freedom for mean square error.

If all the initial hypotheses are verified, it is possible to both execute some statistical tests and evaluate confidence limits of parameters.

As already shown in Chapter 2, the meaning that many books on statistics attribute to statistical tests and confidence region is not completely correct.

Specifically, it is not possible to make tests and confidence limits quantitative (Chapter 2). It is possible to analyze the main tests and the confidence limits for linear models by keeping this premise in mind.

- Since the mean square error is an estimate of the variance of experimental error, the ratio

$$F = \frac{MSE}{s^2} \tag{3.24}$$

allows to execute an F-test, if an independent estimation of the experimental error variance s^2 with *dof* degrees of freedom is known.

If $F > F_\alpha$, where F_α is the theoretical value evaluated with $n_E - p$, *dof* degrees of freedom, and significance level α, the model is discarded. Traditionally, α was the risk to occur in an *I-type* error: discarding a good model by thinking it to be inadequate. In this circumstance, the model can be discarded; rather, it is not possible to say that α is the risk in affirming that the model is wrong, when it is right.

If $F < F_\alpha$, the model is accepted and even in this case, it is not possible to affirm that $1-\alpha$ is the probability that the model is correct.

- Rather than fixing α and verifying if F is larger or smaller than the theoretical value, it is also possible to invert the process: assuming F as theoretical value, it is possible to get the corresponding α. If the value of α is large, the model is accepted; the model is discarded otherwise.

- Knowing the estimate of the error variance s^2 based on *dof* degrees of freedom, it is possible to check the hypothesis $\beta = \mathbf{b}$ by means of the following F-test based on p, *dof* degrees of freedom:

$$F_{ex} = \frac{(\beta - \mathbf{b})^T (\mathbf{F}^T \mathbf{F})(\beta - \mathbf{b})}{ps^2} \tag{3.25}$$

Previous F-test is useful to evaluate confidence region of parameters. Actually, making such a relation equal to the theoretical value of F with p degrees of freedom at the numerator and *dof* degrees of freedom at the denominator and with a value of α, an ellipsoid equation is obtained (an ellipse for the two-dimensional case) with center $\mathbf{b}$. The ellipsoid identifies the confidence region for the selected value of α.

Be careful: it would be incorrect even in this case to state there is a confidence $1-\alpha$ that the right values of parameters are inside the ellipsoid.

- The SVD factorization allows to evaluate values of ellipsoid diameters: they are the coefficients d_i of the factorization. Hence, different values of d_i unavoidably generate ellipsoids particularly stretched in the direction of the principal component. The corresponding vectors $\mathbf{u}_j$ identify the directions of ellipsoid diameters. Diameters with very different values denote parameter correlations that should be analyzed and removed, when possible.

- It is even possible to carry out a *t*-test to check if a parameter is significantly far from zero.
- As an alternative to the *t*-test, it is possible to calculate the *t*-student probability that corresponds to the experimental *t*. If it is relatively large, such a parameter can be removed by the model.

It is worth underlining the following two points:

1) As usual, a numerical value cannot be assigned to these tests.
2) Figure 3.1 represents elliptical confidence region and limits in the case of two parameters. Confidence limits of the single parameters can be particularly misleading when the ellipse is significantly stretched in the direction of the main diameter.

- A tool that is particularly spread to check whether a linear model is satisfactory is the multiple determination index R^2. Even though it is traditionally evaluated in other ways, it is useful to consider it in a clearer mathematical form. Consider two vectors **v** and **w**; the cosine of the angle between these vectors is

$$\cos\varphi = \frac{\mathbf{v}^T\mathbf{w}}{\|\mathbf{v}\|_2 \|\mathbf{w}\|_2} \tag{3.26}$$

where $\cos(\varphi) \to 0$ when the vectors are perpendicular; whereas $\cos(\varphi) \to \pm 1$ when the vectors are parallel. As a result, when $(\cos(\varphi))^2 \to 0$, the two vectors are linearly independent; conversely, they are dependent as $(\cos(\varphi))^2 \to 1$. Taking experimental values of **y** as the vector **v** and model previsions as **w**, it is possible to evaluate R^2. When $R^2 \to 1$, the model is satisfactory; conversely, the model is not.

R^2 is usually evaluated by one of the following formulae:

$$R^2 = 1 - \frac{\sum_{i=1}^{n_E}(y_i - \hat{y}_i)^2}{\sum_{i=1}^{n_E}(y_i - \bar{y}_i)^2} \tag{3.27}$$

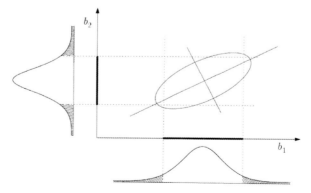

Figure 3.1 Confidence region.

if the model is *with intercept*, otherwise, the index is defined as

$$R^2 = \frac{\sum_{i=1}^{n_E} (y_i \hat{y}_i)^2}{\sum_{i=1}^{n_E} y_i^2 \sum_{i=1}^{n_E} \hat{y}_i^2} \quad (3.28)$$

if the model is without intercept.

Some authors suggest the use of an adjusted R^2:

$$R_a^2 = 1 - \frac{(1-R^2)(n_E-1)}{(n_E-p)} \quad (3.29)$$

since it is statistically more correct; unfortunately, it could sometimes assume negative value.

Contrary to R^2, R_a^2 may decrease as the number of parameters increases.

The multiple determination index is not particularly sensitive and a value larger than .9 or .95 is not enough to ensure a good model. It is ever necessary to support this index by using other information coming from the model analysis.

As per other statistical indices, even R^2 must be considered in rejecting a model: if its value is less than a predetermined threshold (i.e., .9), the model is probably inadequate to entirely represent data. Conversely, it could be incorrect to affirm that the model is reasonably good if R^2 is larger than an assigned threshold (i.e., .95).

3.3
Some Caveat

Before going on in the discussion, it is worth underlining some points that are essential in the analysis of linear models.

Caveat No. 1
It is important that the user of specific software just designed for models analysis has at least a basic knowledge of statistics.

Nevertheless, the basic requirement that the user has a deep knowledge of the physical problem, which is behind the mathematical model he is analyzing, is usually underestimated.

Without a proper understanding of the process, it is often ineffective to adopt sophisticated programs to examine a specific model.

The user should know either an estimate of the experimental error variance or at least the order of magnitude of the error variance. Moreover, he should realize whether it is reasonable to consider the variance constant overall experimental domain.

Caveat No. 2

A model, parameters of which were calculated by methods that shall be described later on in this chapter, should never be used to carry out extrapolations, unless it is supported by a special theory.

In some fields, such as economics, meteorology, and so on, people are often forced to extrapolate. In such cases, one has to be conscious about the risk he is running. In particular, it is worth underlining that the higher the degree of complexity of the model, the higher the risk in extrapolating its behavior.

Actually, using only simple models (i.e., the model (3.7)), the trend outside the experimental domain does not give any surprise.

Accordingly, a model should be ever used to make previsions within the range adopted to evaluate parameters.

Caveat No. 3

One should usually avoid to assign a specific meaning to the parameters obtained with the methods discussed later, except for some special situations.

For example, a special case is represented either by linear models like (3.7) or by polynomial models with a single independent variable x when they are in the Lagrange form.

In most of the other circumstances, one should rely neither on the numerical value of the parameter nor on its sign.

In fact, the numerical value of a parameter can be masked or influenced by the presence (or absence) of other functions involved in the model.

Caveat No. 4

Except some special cases, one should not rely on model plots to deem which new variables or functions are to be introduced in order to improve it.

A special case is given by models with a single independent variable x when the plot is visualized against the same variable x.

With more independent variables, each kind of plot might take erroneous considerations.

Caveat No. 5

One should not completely rely on statistical tests performed by software.

It is worth noting that such tests are much less powerful than what it is usually claimed in books on statistics. Specifically, many tests are based on the very unlikely hypothesis that the model to be analyzed is the model that really describes the phenomenon under study.

Caveat No. 6

One should not completely rely on the reliability of a model that produces results better than other rival models.

This problem is quite important in the case of nonlinear models (Chapter 6), but it can arise even with linear models.

Remember: once a finite amount of experiments are assigned, there are infinite models that fully satisfy the experimental data set.

Some studies (see, for example, Ryan, 2009) demonstrated that often the best model selected among some rival alternatives is not the model adopted to generate the experimental points, even though this model is one of the rival models.

Caveat No. 7
One should not have a kind of *therapeutic obstinacy* against a model.

It may happen that experimental data do not lead to any worthwhile model.
Even though it is always possible to provide a model by joining a dependent variable to one or more independent variables, there is a threshold dictated by common sense in accepting the model. In these cases, two extreme situations should be prevented:

- The experimental error is so large that no reasonable model can find out a real correlation between the dependent variable and the independent ones.
- The model is so complex that it is able to interpolate even the experimental error, by providing an erroneous trend.

The following test named *thumb test* is useful to identify the former situation: it provides the *pollice recto* condition when positive, *pollice verso* otherwise.

Let us denote by $\hat{y}_{max}$ and $\hat{y}_{min}$ maximum and minimum values of model previsions in experimental points used to calculate the same model parameters and by s^2 an estimate of the experimental error variance.

If the condition

$$\frac{\left(\frac{\hat{y}_{max}-\hat{y}_{min}}{2}\right)^2}{s^2} > 1 \qquad (3.30)$$

is verified, the test is said *pollice recto*, *pollice verso* otherwise.

In the *pollice verso* situation, it is reasonable to discard the model as its maximum variation is smaller than the experimental error variance.

An upside-down F-test is useful in detecting the latter situation. In fact, in this circumstance, the mean square error of the model is smaller than the estimate of the experimental error variance.

The F-test must be performed by using the error variance at the numerator and the model mean square error at the denominator.

If the probability to get a theoretical F larger than the experimental F is significantly small, it is appropriate to discard the model as it is probably fitting the experimental error. For example, if the model mean square error is equal to 1337. with 8 degrees of freedom and the experimental error variance is equal to 10000. with 10 degrees of freedom, we get

```
The probability that F with dfNum 10 dfDen 8
is greater than 7.479432e+000 is equal to 4.430662e-003
```

Thus, the mean square error is too small compared to the error variance, and the model is interpolating the experimental errors. The model should be discarded.

3.4
Class for Linear Regressions

Linear regression problems are particularly spread and deserve an independent class.

In the *BzzMath* library, the `BzzLinearRegression` class allows to solve linear regression problems.

The `BzzLinearRegression` class presents a set of constructors. The most common one is shown in the following example, whereas all other constructors and their respective implementation are proposed later.

Example 3.1

The constructor adopted in this example requires the matrix **F** and the vector **y** as argument. If an estimate of the variance is known, it is profitable to provide information to the object through the function `SetVariance`. In this example, the experimental error variance based on 5 degrees of freedom is known, $s2 = 2.5e\text{-}2$. It is enough to use the function `LeastSquaresAnalysis` to estimate parameters and analyze the model with the least sum of squares method. Conversely, the object invokes the function `RobustAnalysis` if a robust analysis is required. A comprehensive report is obtained by the function `BzzPrint`.

```
#include "BzzMath.hpp"
void main(void)
    {
    BzzPrint("\n\nLinearRegression constructor");
    BzzMatrix F(6,2,
         1.,1., 1.,2., 1.,3., 1.,4., 1.,5., 1.,6.);
    BzzVector y(6,12.6225,11.9095,11.4522,
         10.4553,9.8861,9.5247);
    BzzLinearRegression linReg(F,y);
    double s2 = 2.5e-2;
    linReg.SetVariance(s2,5);
    linReg.LeastSquaresAnalysis();
    }
```

Results are printed out on the default file *BzzFile.txt*. One could modify the file name by the following statement, introducing the new file name as argument:

```
bzzFilePrint("RegressionFile.txt");
```

Main information printed for this example is listed hereafter.

- Condition number of the matrix **F**:

  ```
  Condition Number 9.359386e+000
  ```

  If the condition number is large, a **WARNING** is printed for enhancing it.
- System conditioning:

  ```
  System Conditioning 4.784340e+000
  ```

  As already discussed in Buzzi-Ferraris and Manenti (2010a), the system conditioning is preferable over the condition number to deem the conditioning of the system. The difference between these two concepts lies in the fact that the same system (even an overdimensioned system) can be written in many forms all equivalent to each other, rather with different condition number. Conversely, there is a unique system conditioning, representing the conditioning of the system (contrary to the condition number, which represents the conditioning of the matrix **F**). If their values are significantly different, a **WARNING** is printed and it is strongly recommended to reformulate the model to make it better conditioned.

  As it shall be shown in Section 3.8 and in Chapter 5, it is the task of the user to write the system at the best, before evaluating parameters and analyzing the model.
- Optimal values of parameters, their standard error, T-Value for the *t*-test (its null hypothesis is that the corresponding parameter is equal to zero), and the probability that the theoretical *t* is larger in absolute value than the same T-Value.

  ```
  Par.      Value                  Standard Error
  1         1.3230660e+001         1.4719601e-001
  2        -6.4446000e-001         3.7796447e-002
            T-Value                P-Value
            8.9884635e+001         9.1844074e-008
           -1.7050809e+001         6.9386928e-005
  ```

  If either the T-Value is too small or the P-Value is too large, a **WARNING** is printed since the possibility to remove such a parameter should be taken into consideration.
- Confidence region of parameters (95 and 99%):

  ```
  Confidence Interval 95
     Par.         Lower              Upper
     1         1.2822044e+001      1.3639276e+001
     2        -7.4938294e-001     -5.3953706e-001
  Confidence Interval 99
     Par.         Lower              Upper
     1         1.2552970e+001      1.3908350e+001
     2        -8.1847485e-001     -4.7044515e-001
  ```

As discussed in Chapter 2, confidence limits should not be considered quantitatively but only qualitatively.

If the confidence region is significantly large, either the model is ill formulated or it is inadequate to fit experimental points in the overall experimental domain.

- Variance and covariance matrix of parameters:

```
Variance-Covariance Matrix
 2.16666666666667e-002   -5.00000000000000e-003
-5.00000000000000e-003    1.42857142857143e-003
```

- Correlation matrix of parameters:

```
Correlation Matrix
 1.00000000000000e+000   -8.98717034272917e-001
-8.98717034272917e-001    1.00000000000000e+000
```

If nondiagonal values are close to 1. or −1., the corresponding parameters are correlated. In this case, a **WARNING** is printed (see Section 3.9.2).

- Inflation factors (see Section 3.9.2):

```
Variance inflation factor
1    5.2000000e+000
2    5.2000000e+000
```

If inflation factors are large, the corresponding parameters are linearly correlated with the others.

Inflation factors larger than 1000. are considered highly suspicious, even though some authors point out a value of 10. or 5. as critical threshold.

- Tolerance indices (see Section 3.9.2):

```
Columns correlation = Tj Tolerance
1    1.0000000e+000
2    1.0000000e+000
```

If one of these indices is particularly small, the corresponding parameter is linearly correlated with the others.

- A summary of statistical model analysis is then proposed:

```
Total Sum of Squares = 7.3008476e+002
Total Sum of Squares corrected by mean = 7.3744277e+000
Residuals Norm2 = 3.2584599e-001
Sum of Squares = 1.0617561e-001
Standard Deviation = 1.6292300e-001
Mean Square Error = 2.6543903e-002
Coefficient of Determination (R2) = 9.8560219e-001
Adjusted R2 = 9.8200274e-001
Response Variance Assigned = 2.5000000e-002
```

Both the mean square error and the multiple determination index R^2 are particularly important. The former one allows to perform an F-test when an estimate of the variance of the error is known. Conversely, when the latter one approaches 1, it means that the model is reasonably good; the model is inadequate, otherwise.

- If an estimate of the error variance is provided, it is possible to execute an F-test:

  ```
  F-test for the model
  Fexperimental = 1.061756e+000
  The probability that F with dfNum 4 dfDen 5
  is greater than 1.061756e+000 is 4.618463e-001
  ```

  One can check the probability that the theoretical F is larger than the experimental F, which is obtained by the ratio of the mean square error and the estimate of the error variance.

Even in this case, the F-test must be considered only qualitatively: if the probability is large, the model is accepted; the model is discarded when it is small.

- Experimental data, model estimations, residuals, and standard residuals:

  ```
    Observed y      Estimated y        r               rn
  1 1.2622500e+001  1.2586200e+001   3.6300000e-002   0.23
  2 1.1909500e+001  1.1941740e+001  -3.2240000e-002  -0.20
  3 1.1452200e+001  1.1297280e+001   1.5492000e-001   0.98
  4 1.0455300e+001  1.0652820e+001  -1.9752000e-001  -1.25
  5 9.8861000e+000  1.0008360e+001  -1.2226000e-001  -0.77
  6 9.5247000e+000  9.3639000e+000   1.6080000e-001   1.02
  ```

  Many authors use standard residuals to detect outliers.

In Chapter 4, it shall be shown that it is unsuitable to consider these values in identifying outliers.

  On the other hand, they become important to deem whether the model is good, rather only after the outlier detection.
  A more robust and reliable technique must be adopted for their detection.

- At last, confidence limits of the dependent variable (95 and 99%) is printed:

  ```
  Confidence Interval 95% for y
    Exp.     Lower              y              Upper
     1    1.2268530e+001  1.2586200e+001  1.2903870e+001
     2    1.1703247e+001  1.1941740e+001  1.2180233e+001
     3    1.1110568e+001  1.1297280e+001  1.1483992e+001
     4    1.0466108e+001  1.0652820e+001  1.0839532e+001
     5    9.7698670e+000  1.0008360e+001  1.0246853e+001
     6    9.0462300e+000  9.3639000e+000  9.6815700e+000
  ```

```
Confidence Interval 99% for y
 Exp.      Lower               y              Upper
   1   1.2059344e+001    1.2586200e+001   1.3113056e+001
   2   1.1546199e+001    1.1941740e+001   1.2337281e+001
   3   1.0987618e+001    1.1297280e+001   1.1606942e+001
   4   1.0343158e+001    1.0652820e+001   1.0962482e+001
   5   9.6128190e+000    1.0008360e+001   1.0403901e+001
   6   8.8370439e+000    9.3639000e+000   9.8907561e+000
```

Even in this case, it is necessary to look at large confidence regions with care.
- At last, a consideration on the hypothesis of normality condition (4.10) is given:

```
First Index for normality assumption = 9.8732929e-001
The data are consistent with the normality assumption
```

Unfortunately, this index is not so reliable in identifying nonnormality condition (see Section 4.10).

Objects of the `BzzLinearRegression` class can be initialized with the following constructors.

- Default constructor:
    ```
    BzzMatrix F(6,2,
          1.,1., 1.,2., 1.,3.,
          1.,4., 1.,5., 1.,6.);
    BzzVector y(6,12.6225,11.9095,11.4522,
          10.4553,9.8861,9.5247);
    BzzLinearRegression linReg;
    linReg(F,y);
    ```

- Constructor requiring the matrix **F** and the vector **y**:
    ```
    BzzMatrix F(6,2,
          1.,1., 1.,2., 1.,3.,
          1.,4., 1.,5., 1.,6.);
    BzzVector y(6,12.6225,11.9095,11.4522,
          10.4553,9.8861,9.5247);
    BzzLinearRegression linReg(F,y);
    ```

- Using a file with extension *.lrg*, where data are collected:
    ```
    BzzLinearRegression linReg("simple1.lrg");
    ```
    Files with extension *.lrg* shall be described in detail in Section 3.5.1.

- Using a selection of columns of the matrix **F** and of experimental points:
    ```
    BzzMatrix F(8,4,
          3.,1.,1.,3.,
          6.,2.,4.,12.,
          2.,1.,2.,4.,
    ```

3.4 Class for Linear Regressions

```
       1.,1.,3.,5.,
       7.,1.,4.,6.,
       5.,1.,5.,7.,
       4.,1.,6.,8.,
       1.,2.,3.,5.);
    BzzVector y(8,
       12.6225,2.00000,11.9095,11.4522,10.4553,
       9.8861,9.5247,4.0000);
    BzzVectorInt jF(2),iE(5);
    jF(1) = 2; jF(2) = 3; // columns 2 and 3 as matrix F
    //select experiments 1,3,4,5,6
    iE(1) = 1; iE(2) = 3; iE(3) = 4; iE(4) = 5; iE(5) = 6;
    BzzLinearRegression linReg(F,y,jF,iE);
```

Objects `BzzVectorInt jF(2),iE(5)` allow to select two columns of the matrix **F** and five experimental points, respectively.

Objects of the `BzzLinearRegression` class can invoke some useful functions.

- The function `WhoAmI` returns an integer univocally characterizing the object:
  ```
  BzzPrint("\nWhoAmI = %d",linReg.WhoAmI());
  ```

- The function `NumExperiments` returns an integer indicating the amount of experimental points:
  ```
  BzzPrint("\nNumExperiments = %d",
      linReg.NumExperiments());
  ```

- The function `NumParameters` returns an integer indicating the number of model parameters:
  ```
  BzzPrint("\nNumParameters = %d",
      linReg.NumParameters());
  ```

- The function `ObjectCount` returns an integer indicating the total amount of objects of the class used in the program:
  ```
  BzzPrint("\nObjectCount = %d",
      BzzLinearRegression::ObjectCount());
  ```

- The function `ObjectCountInScope` returns an integer indicating the amount of objects still in scope:
  ```
  BzzPrint("\nObjectCountInScope = %d",
      BzzLinearRegression::ObjectCountInScope());
  ```

- The function `DataPrint` prints model data:
  ```
  linReg.DataPrint();
  ```

The model can be analyzed by means of four different techniques.

The first is the classical analysis by means of parameters evaluated with the least sum of squares method:

```
linReg.LeastSquaresAnalysis();
```

The second is the singular value decomposition analysis, which finds out the eigenvalues and eigenvectors of the matrix $\mathbf{F}^T\mathbf{F}$:

```
linReg.SVDAnalysis();
```

The third possibility is the robust analysis, which is suitable to detect outliers (see Chapter 4):

```
linReg.RobustAnalysis();
```

The fourth possibility is to perform an alternative robust analysis, which is, however, suitable to detect outliers (see Chapter 4):

```
linReg.CleverLeastSquaresAnalysis();
```

Some useful functions for the least squares analysis are listed below.

- The function `GetParameters` gets the optimal value of parameters obtained with the least sum of squares method:

    ```
    BzzVector b;
    b = linReg.GetParameters();
    ```

- The function `Get95LowerConfidenceBounds` gets the value of lower confidence bounds of parameters at 95%:

    ```
    BzzVector bcb;
    bcb = linReg.Get95LowerConfidenceBounds();
    ```

- The function `Get95UpperConfidenceBounds` gets the value of upper confidence bounds of parameters at 95%:

    ```
    BzzVector bcb;
    bcb = linReg.Get95UpperConfidenceBounds();
    ```

- The function `Get99LowerConfidenceBounds` gets the value of lower confidence bounds of parameters at 99%:

    ```
    BzzVector bcb;
    bcb = linReg.Get99LowerConfidenceBounds();
    ```

- The function `Get99UpperConfidenceBounds` gets the value of upper confidence bounds of parameters at 99%:

    ```
    BzzVector bcb;
    bcb = linReg.Get99UpperConfidenceBounds();
    ```

- The function `GetResiduals` gets the value of residuals, which are evaluated with the parameters obtained by the least sum of squares method:

    ```
    BzzVector r;
    r = linReg.GetResiduals();
    ```

- The function `GetResidualsStandardized` gets the value of standard residuals, which are evaluated with the parameters obtained by the least sum of squares method:
  ```
  BzzVector rs;
  rs = linReg.GetResidualsStandardized();
  ```
- The function `GetMeanSquareError` provides the value of mean square error:
  ```
  double mse;
  mse = linReg.GetMeanSquareError();
  ```
- The function `GetR2` provides the value of multiple determination index R^2:
  ```
  double R2;
  R2 = linReg.GetR2();
  ```
- The function `GetBTolerance` gets tolerances T_j for parameters **b** that are significantly important to deem possible correlations among parameters (see Section 3.9.2):
  ```
  BzzVector bt = linReg.GetBTolerance();
  ```

Some useful functions for the SVD analysis are listed here.

- Objects d, V, and U contain values obtained by decomposing the matrix **F**.
  ```
  BzzMatrix V,U;
  BzzVector d;
  linReg.GetSortedBzzVectorDAndBzzMatricesVU(&d,&V,
      &U);
  ```
- Object P contains the matrix that allows to transform the matrix **F** into the matrix **G** constituted by principal axes:

$$\mathbf{G} = \mathbf{F}\mathbf{P}^T \qquad (3.31)$$

  ```
  BzzMatrix P;
  linReg.GetPrincipalComponents(&P);
  BzzMatrix G;
  ProductT(F,P,&G);
  ```

As it shall be discussed in Section 3.11, if only three columns from among the five columns constituting the matrix **F** are significant, it is possible to reduce the size of the new matrix **G** by removing last two rows of the matrix **P** before evaluating the product (see Example 3.10).

Some functions useful in the robust analysis are listed below.

- The function `GetCandidateOutliers` gets all possible outliers:
  ```
  BzzVectorInt out;
  out = linReg.GetCandidateOutliers();
  ```

- The function `GetHighlyProbableOutliers` gets only all highly probable outliers:
    ```
    BzzVectorInt out;
    out = linReg.GetHighlyProbableOutliers();
    ```
- The function `GetPossibleOutliers` gets all possible outliers:
    ```
    BzzVectorInt out;
    out = linReg.GetPossibleOutliers();
    ```
- The function `GetRobustParameters` gets the value of parameters evaluated with a robust method:
    ```
    BzzVector br;
    br = linReg.GetRobustParameters();
    ```
- The function `GetRobustResiduals` gets the value of residuals evaluated with a robust method:
    ```
    BzzVector rr;
    rr = linReg.GetRobustResiduals();
    ```
- The function `GetRobustResidualsStandardized` gets the value of standard residuals evaluated with a robust method:
    ```
    BzzVector rrs;
    rrs = linReg.GetRobustResidualsStandardized();
    ```

Example 3.2

Plot a model with independent variables as abscissas and two curves as ordinate: the first contains experimental values indicated by red diamonds, whereas the second is a solid line representing the previsions of the model with parameters obtained by the least sum of squares method. Use the same model and data as given in Example 3.1. The program is

```
#include "BzzMath.hpp"
void main(void)
   {
   BzzPrint("\n\n**** Examples of BzzPlotSparse ****");
   BzzMatrix F(6,2,
         1.,1., 1.,2., 1.,3., 1.,4., 1.,5., 1.,6.);
   BzzVector y(6,12.6225,11.9095,11.4522,10.4553,
         9.8861,9.5247);
   BzzLinearRegression linReg(F,y);
   BzzVector b;
   b = linReg.GetParameters();
   BzzMatrixSparse Y(2,100);
   BzzMatrixSparse X(2,100);
```

```
    double x;
    for(int i = 1; i <= 100;i++)
        {
        x = - double(i - 100)/99. + 6. * double(i - 1)/99.;
        X(1,i) = x;
        Y(1,i) = b[1] + b[2] * x;
        }
    for(i = 1;i <= 6;i++)
        {X(2,i) = F(i,2); Y(2,i) = y[i];}
    BzzSave save("Regression.stx");
    save << X << Y;
    save.End();
    system("BzzPlotSparse.exe");
    BzzPause();
    }
```

To get the plot, it is sufficient to build two objects of the `BzzMatrixSparse` class containing data of abscissas and ordinates of the curves. The first row contains the value of the model previsions and uses the parameters obtained in the regression. The second row contains experimental data. The program `BzzPlotSparse.exe` even gives the opportunity to modify features of the curves (see Buzzi-Ferraris and Manenti, 2010a).

When the program is run, a dialogue window appears. Select the menu item `File`, `New` and, then, select the file where data are collected (in this case, "`Regression.stx`"). The dialogue window of Figure 3.2 appears giving the possibility of modifying the trend style.

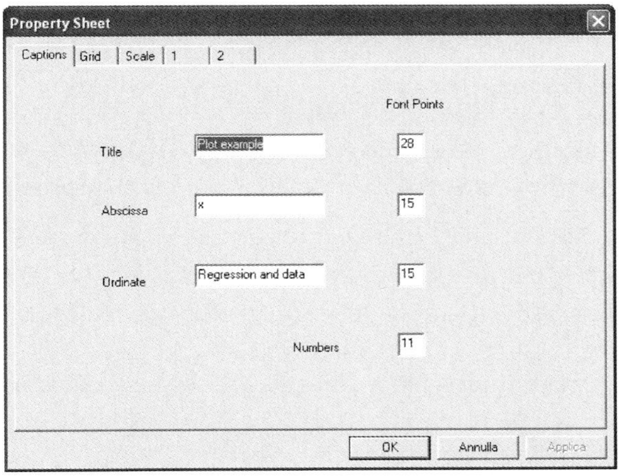

Figure 3.2 Dialogue window to modify plot style.

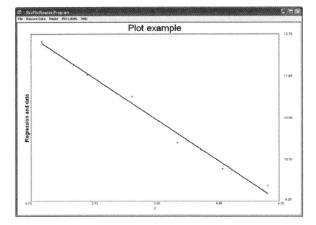

Figure 3.3 Modified plot.

By modifying `Title`, `Abscissa`, and `Ordinate`, the plot of Figure 3.3 is visualized.

Additional examples of the use of `BzzLinearRegression` class can be found in the directory

```
BzzMath/Examples/BzzMathAdvanced/
Regressions/LinearRegressions
```

either on the enclosed CD-ROM or at the web site

```
www.chem.polimi.it/homes/gbuzzi.
```

3.5
Generalized Toolkit for Linear Problems

To solve a linear problem, only the matrix **F** and the vector **y** are required. It was therefore possible to develop a generalized toolkit to face linear regression problems.

In the ***BzzMath*** library, the `BzzLinearRegression.exe` program allows to solve linear regression problems.

When the `BzzLinearRegression` program is run, the dialogue window of Figure 3.4 appears.

Some important pieces of information to properly use the tool are reported in the dialogue window:

- which form of linear model can be analyzed;
- where the program stores results when the solution is reached;
- how to use `Help`.

3.5 *Generalized Toolkit for Linear Problems* | 125

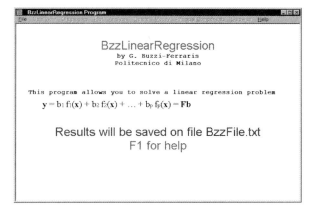

Figure 3.4 Starting dialogue window.

The linear model must comply with the generalized formulation (3.1).

If the function f_1 assumes a value equal to 1 in each experimental point, the model is automatically considered *with intercept*.

It is enough to know the matrix **F** and the vector **y** to analyze the model. Also, for the statistical analysis of the model, it may be useful, although not strictly necessary, to know an estimate of the variance σ^2 based on the specific number of degrees of freedom.

The initialization of a new model is performed by selecting the item File, Open from the main menu. A new dialogue window appears (Figure 3.5) and it allows to choose a file with extension .lrg, where the data concerning the regression problem are collected.

If the item File, Open is newly selected after analyzing a model and if some data were modified, a message box asking for saving modifications appears. If the answer is affirmative, a dialogue window to save the new file automatically opens.

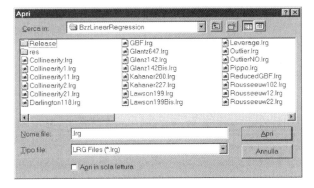

Figure 3.5 Dialogue window to open a predefined regression problem.

3.5.1
Data File Structure

The `BzzLinearRegression.exe` toolkit can be used by writing a priori both the matrix **F** and the vector **y** on an ASCII file with extension `.lrg`.

The file must have the following structure:

- two `int` separated by a blank space in the first row represent the size (number of rows and columns) of the matrix **F**;
- the values of the matrix **F**. They are ordered by row and separated by blank spaces. It is possible, but not necessary, to start a new line for each row;
- data of the vector **y**. An `int` represents the size of the vector (it has to correspond to the number of rows of the matrix **F**) and, subsequently, all its coefficients are reported and separated by blank spaces.

If a variance estimation based on a certain number of degrees of freedom is known, two additional values can be collected in the ASCII file separated by a blank space: the variance and the number of degrees of freedom.

For example, the file `Simple1.lrg` is

```
12 2
1. 110.87
1. 107.14
1. 104.12
1. 101.98
1. 103.01
1. 104.89
1. 106.02
1. 107.96
1. 109.08
1. 110.14
1. 101.12
1. 112.04
12
6.7596 9.0492 10.4553 11.9095 11.4522 9.8861
9.5247 8.1732 7.5921 7.4424 12.6225 6.0732
0.04 5
```

The matrix **F** consists of 12 rows and 2 columns. Since the first column consists of a series of 1., the model is with intercept. After the values of the dependent variable **y**, there is an estimate of the variance σ^2, equal to 0.04, based on 5 degrees of freedom.

3.5.2
Building a Data File

A file `.lrg` can be written by using a generic editing program, such as *Notepad* or *Wordpad*, on the condition that the file is saved as unformatted text, therefore, as an ASCII file.

By programming in C++ and using classes of the ***BzzMath*** library, the file can be generated by the following statements:

```
BzzSave save("FileName.lrg");
save << F << y << s2 << dof;
// save << F << y; // if we don't know s2
save.End();
```

where `F` is a `BzzMatrix`, `y` is a `BzzVector`, `s2` is a `double`, and `dof` is an `int`.

In some circumstances, it is useful to invert the procedure: starting from a file `.lrg`. it is possible to get the matrix **F**, the vector **y**, the estimate of variance s^2 and its degrees of freedom `dof`:

```
BzzMatrix F;
BzzVector y;
double s2;
int dof;
BzzLoad load("FileName.lrg");
load >> F >> y >> s2 >> dof;
load.End();
```

Example 3.3

Build the aforementioned file `Simple1.lrg` by using objects of `BzzMatrix` and `BzzVector` classes.

The program is

```
#include "BzzMath.hpp"
void main(void)
  {
  BzzVector x(12,110.87,107.14,104.12,101.98,103.01,
       104.89,106.02,107.96,109.08,110.14,
       101.12,112.040);
  BzzVector y(12,6.7596,9.0492,10.4553,11.9095,
       11.4522,9.8861,9.5247,8.1732,7.5921,7.4424,
       12.6225,6.0732);
  BzzMatrix F(12,2);
  F.SetColumn(1,1.);
  F.SetColumn(2,x);
  BzzSave save("Simple1.lrg");
  save << F << y << .04 << 5;
  save.End();
  }
```

Files *.lrg* used in this chapter can be found in the directory `Vol2_Chapter3` within the enclosed CD-ROM.

3.5.3
Data Visualization

Once the model is initialized, all the items of the main menu are enabled.

The first item enabled is `DataView`. It allows to check the data of the selected model. It includes three subitems: `Original`, `Current`, and `Standardized`.

By selecting `Original`, it is possible to see the original values of the matrix **F** and the vector **y**, as they were collected in the data file.

By selecting `Current`, the current values adopted in the model analysis are shown. They correspond to the original ones only if no modifications were implemented during the analysis.

Finally, it is possible to see the current standardized values by selecting `Standardized`.

It is possible to print data by using an object of the `BzzLinearRegression` class by means of the function

```
linReg.DataPrint();
```

3.6
Data Modification

By selecting the menu option `Modify`, the popup menu of Figure 3.6 appears.

By selecting the item `Response`, a dialogue window appears, by showing experimental values of **y**; by double clicking on an experimental value, another dialogue window appears and it gives the possibility to modify the selected element. The item `Matrix F` allows to modify an element of the matrix **F**. Again, a dialogue window appears by double clicking on the coefficients of the matrix **F**: the possibility to modify it is then provided. The item `Variance` allows to modify the current variance estimate and its degrees of freedom. `Add Column` allows to add a column to the matrix **F**. The column data is acquired from a `.clf` file that contains the number

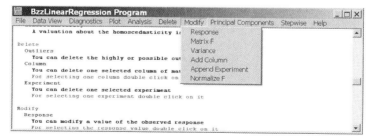

Figure 3.6 Popup menu of the item Modify.

of elements in the column (`int`) and the values of column coefficients (`double`). For example,

```
7
1.2 0.5 6.3 2.1 3.5 2.6 4.7
```

The item `Append Experiment` allows to add a new experiment. The experimental data are acquired from a `.exp` file that contains the number of elements in the matrix row (`int`), the values of row coefficients (`double`), and the new experimental value y (`double`). For example,

```
3
1. 3.5 4.3 0.0241
```

Finally, the item `Normalize F` allows to normalize the columns of the matrix **F**.

It is possible to modify both the matrix **F** and the vector **y** even when the program is running through specific functions of the `BzzLinearRegression` class.

Let us consider a matrix **F** consisting of two columns. It is possible to modify the experimental point no. 3:

```
BzzVector f0(2,1.,70.);
double y0 = 18.;
linReg.ModifyExperiment(3,f0,y0);
```

Let us consider a matrix **F** constituted by two columns. It is possible to insert an experimental point and place it at the position no. 6:

```
BzzVector f0(2,1.,8.);
double y0 = 7.;
linReg.InsertExperiment(6,f0,y0);
```

3.7
Data Deletion

Select the menu option `Delete`, the popup menu of Figure 3.7 appears.

The item `Outliers` allows to delete the highly or the possible outliers. `Column` allows to delete one selected column of the matrix **F**. `Experiment` allows to delete a

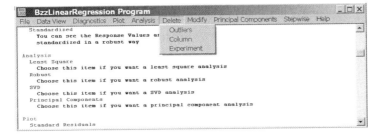

Figure 3.7 Popup menu of the item Delete.

specific experimental point, for example, one specific outlier. To select to remove either the column or the experiment, a double click is enough either on the column or on the row, respectively.

It is possible to use some columns only of the matrix **F** and to use or to remove only some experimental points even when the program is running by means of specific functions of the `BzzLinearRegression` class.

For example, to use columns no. 2 and 3 of the matrix **F** and experimental points no. 1, 3, 4, 5, and 6, it is sufficient to adopt the following constructor:

```
BzzMatrix F(8,4,
    3.,1.,1.,3., 6.,2.,4.,12.,
    2.,1.,2.,4., 1.,1.,3.,5.,
    7.,1.,4.,6., 5.,1.,5.,7.,
    4.,1.,6.,8., 1.,2.,3.,5.);
BzzVector y(8,
    12.6225,2.00000,11.9095,11.4522,10.4553,
    9.8861,9.5247,4.0000);
BzzVectorInt jF(2),iE(5);
jF(1) = 2; jF(2) = 3; // columns 2 and 3 as matrix F
//select experiments 1,3,4,5,6
iE(1) = 1; iE(2) = 3; iE(3) = 4; iE(4) = 5; iE(5) = 6;
BzzLinearRegression linReg(F,y,jF,iE);
```

To remove the experiments no. 6,

```
linReg.DeleteExperiment(6);
```

To remove experiments no. 1 and 4:

```
BzzVectorInt iv(2);
iv[1] = 4;
iv[2] = 1;
linReg.DeleteExperiments(iv);
```

3.8
Preliminary Analysis

As it is highlighted in Buzzi-Ferraris and Manenti (2010a), when a physical phenomenon is to be simulated on a computer, it is necessary to distinguish different levels concerning the problem we are implementing. Specifically, when dealing with a model that represents a certain physical phenomenon, the following points must be analyzed and kept separated:

- The physical phenomenon must be well posed.
- The model formulation must be well conditioned.

3.8 Preliminary Analysis

- Algorithms adopted for estimating parameters must be stable, efficient, and accurate.
- The program that implements such algorithms must be stable, robust, and efficient.

Before calculating parameters and analyzing the model, it is useful to study the physical problem that is behind both the model and the model structure. The physical problem often gives useful information on the model to be analyzed. It is surely true with nonlinear models where the physical phenomenon may suggest the theoretical bind among the variables.

It is essential to formulate the problem at the best. In the case of generic overdimensioned systems, it is preferable to write the system in its standard form, which consists of dividing each column of the matrix **F** by its maximum absolute value. By doing so, the matrix *condition number* coincides with the *system conditioning*, and it gives a reliable estimate of the system solution accuracy.

Overdimensioned systems coming from a linear model afford the possibility to better formulate the problem with respect to the formulation obtained by standardizing the system.

In fact, there are two more advantages in solving this kind of problems against the solution of an overdimensioned system. They both make the system better conditioned.

1) The possibility to properly reformulate (reparameterize) the model so as to improve its structure.
2) The possibility to introduce some clever experimental points.

As it shall be explained in Section 3.9.2, there are various criteria to deem whether model parameters are correlated, rather only the condition number of the matrix **F** is considered in the following example.

Example 3.4

Consider the basic model

$$y_i = \beta_1 + \beta_2 x_{1i} + \varepsilon_i \quad (3.32)$$

and the following experimental values:

$$\mathbf{x} = \{110.87, 107.14, 104.12, 101.98, 103.01, 104.89, \\ 106.02, 107.96, 109.08, 110.14, 101.12, 112.04\} \quad (3.33)$$

$$\mathbf{y} = \{6.7596, 9.0492, 10.4553, 11.9095, 11.4522, 9.8861, \\ 9.5247, 8.1732, 7.5921, 7.4424, 12.6225, 6.0732\} \quad (3.34)$$

The error variance estimate based on 5 *dof* is equal to .04. The second column of the matrix **F** is equivalent to the vector **x** when the model is in the form (3.32).

Using an object of the `BzzLinearRegression` class, the program is

```
#include "BzzMath.hpp"
void main(void)
  {
  BzzVector x(12,110.87,107.14,104.12,101.98,103.01,
        104.89,106.02,107.96,109.08,110.14,
        101.12,112.040);
  BzzVector y(12,6.7596,9.0492,10.4553,11.9095,
        11.4522,9.8861,9.5247,8.1732,7.5921,7.4424,
        12.6225,6.0732);
  BzzMatrix F(12,2);
  F.SetColumn(1,1.);
  F.SetColumn(2,x);
  BzzLinearRegression linReg(F,y);
  linReg.SetVariance(.04,5);
  linReg.LeastSquaresAnalysis();
  }
```

Data of this example are collected in the file `Simple1.lrg`.

It is possible to examine the model even using the `BzzLinearRegression.exe` toolkit.

The matrix condition number is equal to 3300. and the matrix columns become correlated. It can be verified by examining results with the item `Analysis, LeastSquare` (see Section 3.9.2).

In the file `Simple2.lrg`, the model is in the form

$$y_i = \beta_1 + \beta_2 \frac{x_{1i}}{112.04} + \varepsilon_i \tag{3.35}$$

The value 112.04 is used to standardize the matrix **F**. In this case, the condition number is equal to 62.

The model can be modified as

$$y_i = \beta_1 + \beta_2(x_{1i} - \bar{x}_1) + \varepsilon_i \tag{3.36}$$

and data collected in the file `Simple3.lrg` are obtained. The condition number is now equal to 3.44 and each correlation among parameters disappears. Nevertheless, the program points out that the matrix was not standardized; actually, the system conditioning is equal to 1.6.

Example 3.5

Build the aforementioned file `Simple3.lrg` by using a `BzzMatrix` and a `BzzVector`.

The program is

```
#include "BzzMath.hpp"
void main(void)
{
BzzVector x(12,110.87,107.14,104.12,101.98,103.01,
    104.89,106.02,107.96,109.08,110.14,
    101.12,112.040);
BzzVector y(12,6.7596,9.0492,10.4553,11.9095,
    11.4522,9.8861,9.5247,8.1732,7.5921,7.4424,
    12.6225,6.0732);
BzzMatrix F(12,2);
double mean = Mean(x);
F.SetColumn(1,1.);
for(int i = 1;i <= 12;i++)
    F[i][2] = x[i] - mean;
BzzSave save("Simple3.lrg");
save << F << y << .04 << 5;
save.End();
}
```

In the Simple4.lrg file, the model is formulated as follows:

$$y_i = \beta_1 + \beta_2 \frac{(x_{1i}-\bar{x}_1)}{5.509167} \tag{3.37}$$

where 5.509167 is used to standardize the matrix **F**. The condition number is equal to 1.6.

Finally, remarking that Lagrange polynomial form is the best conditioned among all the possible polynomial forms, the model can also be written as

$$y_i = \beta_1 \frac{(x_{1i}-x_{1\,max})}{(x_{1\,min}-x_{1\,max})} + \beta_2 \frac{(x_{1i}-x_{1\,min})}{(x_{1\,max}-x_{1\,min})} + \varepsilon_i \tag{3.38}$$

Data obtained with this model are collected in the file Simple5.lrg. The condition number is now equal to 1.59.

This trivial example shows how important it is to write the model in its best-conditioned form and not in the simplest one.

With the BzzLinearRegression.exe toolkit, it is possible (and strongly recommended) to check whether the model in use is reasonably well formulated or not and/or whether the experimental points are adequate for the selected model.

These checks and advice on the model selection and the experimental points shall be discussed in detail in Chapter 5.

Again, it is essential to start with a good model formulation and an appropriate design of experiments, without claiming that the model analysis points out them as problems.

Another advisable option is to plot the trend of experimental points.
In particular, if there is a single independent variable x, it is quite recommended to graphically see the trend of the dependent variable y against x.

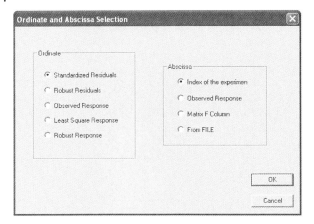

Figure 3.8 Plot dialogue window.

It can be obtained in two ways:

- Using the program `BzzPlotSparse.exe` within the ***BzzMath*** library (see Buzzi-Ferraris and Manenti, 2010a or Example 3.2).
- Exploiting the item `Plot, Generic`.

In the second case, the dialogue window of Figure 3.8 appears.

Select `ObservedResponse` as ordinate and the file name with extension `.clf`, where the values of independent variables are collected. The file requires the following structure: an `int` containing the number of the experimental points; a series of `double` containing the values of the independent variable. If a column of the matrix **F** coincides with independent variable, even this column can be selected as abscissa.

Consider the aforementioned problem of the file `Simple1.lrg`. The second column of the matrix **F** coincides with the independent variable and, therefore, it can be selected as abscissa by obtaining the plot of Figure 3.9.

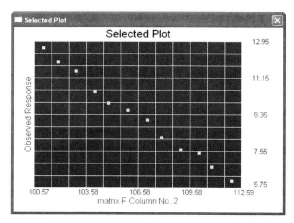

Figure 3.9 Plot example.

Plotting the trend is useful to select a reasonable model according to the existing experimental points. For example, it can be deduced that a simple model $y_i = \beta_1 + \beta_2 x_{1i} + \varepsilon_i$ could be reasonable in this case.

From a statistical point of view, it is incorrect to select the model by exploiting the trend of experimental data since this operation changes the degrees of freedom related to the same model.

Example 3.6

Consider the following data.

```
BzzVector x(11,0.,.1,.2,.3,.4,.5,.6,.7,.8,.9,1.);
BzzVector y(11,2.5002,2.5576,2.5768,2.5672,2.5384,
    2.501,2.4616,2.4328,2.4232,2.4424,2.4999);
```

Analyze the trend of experimental data with `BzzPlotSparse.exe`.
The program is

```
#include "BzzMath.hpp"
void main(void)
  {
  BzzVector x(11,0.,.1,.2,.3,.4,.5,.6,.7,.8,.9,1.);
  BzzVector y(11,2.5002,2.5576,2.5768,2.5672,2.5384,
      2.501,2.4616,2.4328,2.4232,2.4424,2.4999);
  BzzMatrixSparse X(1,11);
  BzzMatrixSparse Y(1,11);
  for(int i = 1;i <= 11;i++)
    {
    X(1,i) = x[i];
    Y(1,i) = y[i];
    }
  BzzSave save("WrongPlotAnalysis.stx");
  save << X << Y;
  save.End();
  system("BzzPlotSparse.exe");
  }
```

The resulting plot is reported in Figure 3.10.

By analyzing this plot, one can assume that the model is $y_i = \beta_1 + \beta_2 x_{1i}(x_{1i} - .5)(x_{1i} - 1.) + \varepsilon_i$.
The amount of degrees of freedom to be assigned to the model would have an offset because three parameters were already selected by using the experimental data set. Therefore, if a statistical test is to be executed, it is necessary to account for this ambiguity in the real number of degrees of freedom of the model.

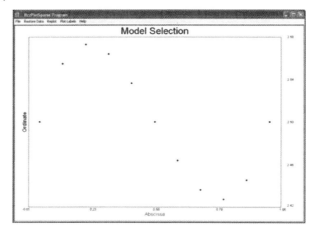

Figure 3.10 Resulting plot.

As already underlined, statistical model analysis is weaker than what people commonly believe (see Chapter 2). Therefore, this ambiguity does not cause any real damage to the future model analysis on the condition that the number of experimental points is satisfactorily large.

When there are more independent variables, this operation can be singularly repeated for each of them.

As underlined by Ryan (2009), Daniel and Wood (1980), and Wood (1973), it could be sometimes misleading to analyze plots against regressors in the case of multiple regressions. Specifically, problems arise if the difference between model (3.1) and model (3.3) is neglected. It is usually preferable to plot points against the real independent variables x_j, by adopting the model (3.1). Conversely, the *regressor* could be a combination of variables by adopting the model (3.3) and it may be misleading.

3.9
Multicollinearity

If one or more columns of the matrix **F** are linear combination of the other ones, the matrix is singular.

When one or more columns are almost linear combinations of the others, the *multicollinearity* (or *collinearity*) condition occurs.

Multicollinearity can seriously perturb the model analysis. Specifically, the multicollinearity occurs when a close dependence between one or more columns of the matrix **F** exists and, in such cases, the solution of the system

(3.8) leads to unreliable parameter estimates due to the quasisingularity of the matrix.

In order to understand the multicollinearity problem, it is important to analyze:

1) When this problem arises?
2) How to detect it?
3) What to do once it is identified?

3.9.1
When Does the Multicollinearity Occur?

Substantially, the multicollinearity problem may arise for three different reasons:

1) The problem is inherently ill conditioned as one of the functions constituting the model is a real linear combination of the other functions. This situation occurs when, for example, one column of the matrix **F** is the sum of other two columns.

   In this circumstance, the only possible remedy is to find out how many columns are linearly independent, which combinations of the original columns generates linear independent vectors, and build a new matrix with a reduced number of columns. This problem shall be discussed in Section 3.11. If the model is explicitly given in the form (3.1), it is often possible to identify linear combinations by simply examining various functions $f_j(\mathbf{x}_i)$.

2) The design of experiment is inadequate for the selected model. For example, consider the trivial model

$$y_i = \beta_1 + \beta_2 x_{1i} + \beta_3 x_{1i}^2 \qquad (3.39)$$

with all the experiments concentrated in two points only. It is obvious that the three parameters of the model cannot be correctly estimated as the columns of the matrix **F** are linearly correlated.

   In this situation, new experiments must be introduced to avoid this form of correlation.

3) The model is ill formulated.

   In this case, one has to modify the structure of the model in order to reduce the ill-conditioning of the matrix **F**. Sometimes, it is not possible to find a model that fits the whole experimental data set, and more models are required each for a specific region of the experimental domain.

3.9.2
How Can Multicollinearity be Detected?

It is worth premising that one or several outliers may spoil the multicollinearity detection by causing a kind of masking effect (see Chapter 4). In such cases, it is first necessary to *find out and reconcile outliers* and to face multicollinearity issue in a subsequent step only.

To detect the multicollinearity, some diagnostics tools have been developed and the most important ones are as follows:

- Since multicollinearity occurs when a column of the matrix **F** is linearly dependent on the others, the condition number of the matrix **F** is a good index to detect this situation. Large values of the matrix condition number denote a probable correlation among parameters.
- A way to point out if the model formulation is inappropriate is by comparing the matrix condition number and the system conditioning. If their values are so far, the model should be formulated in a better way.

If the variance and covariance matrix of parameters is normalized (each row and column is divided by the square root of the corresponding diagonal value), it is called *correlation matrix*.

- As the correlation matrix is conceived, terms on the diagonal are all equal to 1. If a nondiagonal coefficient is close to $\pm 1.$, the corresponding parameters are linearly correlated. This information detects linear correlations between two parameters only.
- Conversely, diagonal coefficients of the inverse correlation matrix allow to identify correlations between a parameter and the others (see Hines and Montgomery, 1990; Ryan, 2009). Actually, if these coefficients are reasonably close to 1., there are no correlations; on the other hand, the corresponding parameter is probably correlated with the others when the diagonal coefficient is significantly large, that is, larger than 1000..

Diagonal coefficients of the inverse correlation matrix are called *variance inflation factors*.

- It is known that the multiple determination index R^2 is a relevant index to check if a linear model is satisfactory (Section 3.2). It is therefore possible to use the following strategy: each jth column of the matrix **F** is considered as the vector of the dependent variable of a linear model; the remaining columns are considered as the reduced matrix **F**' of this linear model; R_j^2 is evaluated for all these pseudomodels; if $R_j^2 \to 1$, the jth column is linearly correlated with the others. For historical reasons, rather than directly considering the R_j^2 value, the variable $T_j = 1 - R_j^2$ is adopted. When $T_j \to 0$, the corresponding column is linearly dependent.

Indices $T_j = 1 - R_j^2$ are called *tolerances* or *tolerance coefficients*. When $T_j \to 1$, the parameter is uncorrelated; when $T_j \to 0$, the parameter is correlated with the others.

Example 3.7

Consider the following program:

```
#include "BzzMath.hpp"
void main(void)
  {
  BzzMatrix F(11,2,
      2.0,4.95, 2.1,5.21, 2.2,5.39, 2.3,5.61,
      2.4,5.79, 2.5,6.01, 2.6,6.19, 2.7,6.41,
      2.8,6.59, 2.9,6.81, 2.0,4.8);
  BzzVector y(11,7.0,7.3,7.6,7.9,58.2,8.5,
      58.8,9.1,59.4,9.7,6.9);
  BzzLinearRegression linReg(F,y);
  linReg.LeastSquaresAnalysis();
  }
```

Main results are reported and discussed below.

- Condition number:

    ```
    Condition Number 1.578000e+002
    ```

    The condition number does not identify serious multicollinearities.
- Correlation matrix:

    ```
    Correlation Matrix
    BzzMatrixSymm No.1
    rows 2 cols 2
    1.00000000000000e+000   -9.99840537592247e-001
    -9.99840537592247e-001   1.00000000000000e+000
    ```

The correlation matrix identifies serious correlations since the nondiagonal coefficient results -9.99840537592247e-001.

- Variance inflation factor:

    ```
    Variance inflation factor
    1   3.1357853e+003    ** WARNING **
    2   3.1357853e+003    ** WARNING **
       ** WARNING ** Correlation between Parameters
    ```

    The variance inflation factor identifies serious multicollinearities.
- T_j tolerance:

    ```
    Columns correlation = Tj Tolerance
    1   3.1889939e-004    ** WARNING **
    2   3.1889939e-004    ** WARNING **
       ** WARNING ** Correlation between Parameters
    ```

Even T_j tolerance identifies serious multicollinearities.

Previous criteria are implemented in the `BzzLinearRegression.exe` toolkit and they were validated by means of many tests.

How can one detect the multicollinearity condition by using the `BzzLinearRegression.exe` toolkit?

1) Adopting the Menu option: `Diagnostics, Multicollinearity`.
2) Adopting the Menu option: `Analysis, LeastSquare`.

When the multicollinearity condition is detected, it is necessary to check whether the model was formulated at the best. If no valid alternative exists, it is necessary to introduce additional experiments, when it is possible to select them, to make parameters uncorrelated. The optimal design of experiments shall be discussed in detail in Chapter 8.

3.10
Best Model Selection

Usually, linear models have no theoretical bases. Only the variables involved in the problem are known even though one often needs to discover them.

In addition, one does not know which variable combination is the most effective to develop a good model; therefore, the problem of selecting the best model among many alternatives is particularly spread.

Once the experimental activity was carried out to obtain values of y_i in correspondence with $\mathbf{x}_i$, the best functions $f_j(\mathbf{x}_i)$ for the model in the form (3.1) must be found. In searching for them, the number and the form of these functions are both unknown: it is necessary to fix a compromise between an easy-to-handle model, consisting of few parameters, and a more accurate model, with many parameters. Unfortunately, even the best functions $f_j(\mathbf{x}_i)$ are unknown in this search.

In such a condition, many functions that can probably meet the model requirements are proposed and the selection the best combination is the task of a calculation program.

Suppose to assign a number N of possible functions $f_j(\mathbf{x})$ that are collected in a matrix $\mathbf{F}$ as for a common linear model:

$$y_i = \beta_1 f_1(\mathbf{x}_i) + \beta_2 f_2(\mathbf{x}_i) + \cdots + \beta_N f_N(\mathbf{x}_i) + \varepsilon_i \qquad (i=1,\ldots,n_E) \qquad (3.40)$$

The calculation program developed to find out the best combination should scan 2^N combinations from a theoretical point of view.

Various models should be selected following some reasonable criteria. Traditionally, the following criteria are adopted:

- The model is selected according to its R^2.
- The model is selected according to its R_a^2.
- The model is selected according to its mean square error.
- The model is selected according to the Mallow index c_p.

Mallow index (Mallow, 1973, 1995; Seber, 1977) is defined as

$$c_p = \frac{MSE_p}{MSE_N} - (n_E - p) \qquad (3.41)$$

In the previous formula, the mean square error of a model with p parameters is denoted by MSE_p and the mean square error obtained with all the possible functions involved in the model is denoted by MSE_N.

In many practical cases, a complete model cannot be calculated because of correlations among its functions. In this circumstance, Mallow index is unavailable.

Within the **BzzMath** library, models are compared with each other on the basis of their mean square error. A best model is selected for each number of parameters p.

To reduce the total amount of calculation, several strategies were proposed:

- **Forward method.** One starts from a model with several assigned parameters and selects the best model with one more parameter. For example, starting from a model without any parameters, one has to search for the best model having a single parameter among the N proposed functions. Once the optimal function is introduced, the search is aimed at the selection of the best combination between one of the remaining functions and the one already selected. The procedure is iterated until no new function generates an improvement in the model mean square error when introduced.
- **Backward method.** One starts from a model with many assigned parameters (e.g., with all the parameters) and selects the function that, when removed, produces the best mean square error. If the new mean square error is better than the existing one, the function is removed. The process is iterated until a worsening in the model mean square error is generated.

Both these strategies present some serious drawbacks.

The Forward strategy is usually unable to find out the best model, or a satisfactory model, especially when one starts from the model without parameters, as the introduction of an important function could be unavoidably prevented by other functions already inserted into the model.

On the other hand, the Backward strategy should start from the model containing all the parameters in order to evenly weight them. Unfortunately, it is often infeasible because of correlations that make the matrix singular.

The strategy commonly adopted is a compromise between the aforementioned ones and it is called *stepwise* strategy. It starts from a model containing only some functions and appropriately selected, and it alternately adopts the previous methods. A check on the possibility to remove a function from the model is carried out: if so, a function is removed. Then, a check on the possibility to introduce one of the remaining functions to significantly improve the model is also carried out: if so, a new function is introduced. The procedure is iterated till the condition becomes steady, where no more introductions or removals are needed.

Following devices are particularly important:

- It is possible to switch from a model with p parameters to another one either with $p-1$ parameters or with $p+1$ by exploiting the existing factorization and, therefore, without having to solve a real linear regression problem every time.
- It is indispensable to use this procedure starting from different models, since there is no guarantee to find out the best model.
- The selection of the function to insert into or remove from the model should be based on a reliable criterion: the one adopted in the **BzzMath** library is to compare the mean square errors of original and new models.
- If N or n_E are not too large, it is possible to select the best model among all 2^N possible combinations.

Example 3.8

Consider the following program, where nine possible functions are proposed and collected in the matrix **F**.

```
#include "BzzMath.hpp"
void main(void)
    {
    int numExperiments = 20;
    BzzMatrix F(numExperiments,9,
      1.,1.,1.,1.,1.,8.415e-001,1.105,0.000,1.000,
      1.,2.,4.,8.,1.600e+001,3.637e+000,1.221,.6931,
      1.414,
      1.,3.,9.,27.,81.,1.27,1.350,1.099,1.732,
      1.,4.,16.,64.1,2.560e+002,-1.211e+001,1.492,
      1.386,2.,
      1.,5.,25.,125.,6.250e+002,-2.397e+001,1.649,
      1.609,2.236,
      1.,6.,36.,216.,1.296e+003,-1.006e+001,1.822,
      1.792,2.449,
      1.,7.,49.,343.,2.401e+003,3.219e+001,2.014,
      1.946,2.646,
      1.,8.,64.,512.,4.096e+003,6.332e+001,2.226,
      2.079,2.828,
      1.,9.,81.,729.,6561.,3.338e+001,2.460,2.197,3.00,
      1.,10.,100.,1000.,1.000e+004,-5.440e+001,2.718,
      2.303,3.162,
      1.,11.,121.,1331.,1.464e+004,-1.210e+002,3.004,
      2.398,3.317,
      1.,12.,144.,1728.,2.074e+004,-7.727e+001,3.320,
      2.485,3.464,
      1.,13.,169.,2197.,2.856e+004,7.101e+001,3.669,
      2.565,3.606,
```

```
    1.,14.,196.,2744.,3.842e+004,1.942e+002,4.055,
    2.639,3.742,
    1.,15.,225.,3375.,5.063e+004,1.463e+002,4.482,
    2.708,3.873,
    1.,16.,256.,4096.,6.554e+004,-7.370e+001,4.953,
    2.773,4.00,
    1.,17.,289.,4913.,8.352e+004,-2.778e+002,5.474,
    2.833,4.123,
    1.,18.,324.,5832.,1.050e+005,-2.433e+002,6.050,
    2.890,4.243,
    1.,19.,361.,6859.,1.303e+005,5.411e+001,6.686,
    2.944,4.359,
    1.,20.,400.,8000.,1.600e+005,3.652e+002,7.389,
    2.996,4.472);
  BzzVector y(numExperiments,
    9.4318e+000,1.1756e+001,1.6766e+001,2.6419e+001,
    4.1333e+001,6.3821e+001,9.4357e+001,1.3550e+002,
    1.8758e+002,2.5240e+002,3.3165e+002,4.2669e+002,
    5.3835e+002,6.6896e+002,8.1900e+002,9.9103e+002,
    1.1854e+003,1.4040e+003,1.6485e+003,1.9200e+003);
  BzzLinearRegression linReg(F,y);
  linReg.SetVariance(1.3e-2,4);
  linReg.StepwiseAnalysis();
}
```

Stepwise analysis leads to the following models (only first four models are printed out):

```
==================================
Best Models with Stepwise Analysis
==================================
Number of Parameter(s) = 1
Mean Square Error = 3.575239e+005

Par.          Value
1        5.3864719e+002
Number of Parameter(s) = 2
Mean Square Error = 2.507465e+000

Par.          Value          t = b/sb
1        1.2302206e+001
4        2.3870521e-001    1.6e+003
```

```
Number of Parameter(s) = 3
Mean Square Error = 1.407025e-002

Par.        Value            t = b/sb
1        3.2793611e+000
4        2.3463297e-001      3.2e+003
7        5.3626472e+000      5.6e+001

Number of Parameter(s) = 4
Mean Square Error = 1.480747e-002
Par.        Value            t = b/sb
1        2.1820558e+000
2       -1.4185128e-001      3.9e-001    ** WARNING **
4        2.3408183e-001      1.7e+002
7        6.4952212e+000      2.2e+000    ** WARNING **
```

The best model selected has three parameters and it is constituted by columns no. 1, 4, and 7 of the original matrix **F**. To analyze this model, it is necessary to add the following statements to the previous program:

```
BzzVectorInt jF(3),iE(numExperiments);
// select columns 1, 4 and 7 as matrix F
jF(1) = 1; jF(2) = 4; jF(3) = 7;
//select all the experiments
for(i = 1;i <= numExperiments;i++)
   iE(i) = i;
BzzLinearRegression lg(F,y,jF,iE);
lg.SetVariance(1.3e-2,4);
lg.LeastSquaresAnalysis();
```

The object `lg` uses the constructor that receives two objects of the `BzzVectorInt` class, besides the matrix **F** and the vector **y**. The first is useful to point out which columns of the original matrix **F** are considered in the object `lg`; the second points out which experiments must be considered. In this specific example, all experiments are taken into account.

The analysis of this model is satisfactory.

The same procedure can be executed by using the `BzzLinearRegression.exe` toolkit through the menu item `Stepwise, Analysis`. Once the best model is identified, it is possible to analyze it through the item `Stepwise, Best Model`. The toolkit proposes the analysis of the best model with the optimal number of parameters by default. One either accepts or modifies this number.

In Chapter 6, other alternatives to the stepwise method shall be considered in order to get a good model even when it is not possible to provide reasonable functions for employing the stepwise approach.

An error to be avoided is to orthogonalize columns before the stepwise analysis.

Vector orthogonalization was performed by Graham-Schmidt method (Golub and Van Loan, 1983); nowadays, the **QR** factorization is preferable for its stability. In the *BzzMath* library, it is possible to get the matrix **Q** that makes orthogonal columns of the matrix **F** by using an object of the `BzzFactorizedQR` class:

```
BzzFactorizedQR W = F;
BzzMatrix Q;
W.GetBzzMatrixQ(&Q);
```

It is unsuitable to transform the matrix **F** into the matrix **Q**, as the *j*th column is now a linear combination of previous *j* columns. Thus, suppose to select a model constituted by columns no. 4 and 9 of the matrix **Q**. The first column of this model is a linear combination of the first four columns of the matrix **F** and the second is a linear combination of the first nine columns.

A proper technique to select the optimal column combinations of the matrix **F** is the principal component (see the next section).

3.11
Principal Components

In some circumstances, it is useful to exploit the SVD factorization for finding out the principal components of the matrix F^TF (see Buzzi-Ferraris and Manenti, 2010a).

Example 3.9

Consider the following program, where the matrix **F** presents strong correlations among columns. First of all, it is useful to see how many columns are independent of the others.

```
#include "BzzMath.hpp"
void main(void)
    {
    BzzMatrix F(7,5,
      1.,2.,3.,4.,5.,
      6.,7.,8.,9.,10.,
      11.,12.,13.,14.,15.,
      16.,17.,18.,19.,20.,
      21.,22.,23.,24.,25.,
      26.,27.,28.,29.,30.,
      31.,32.,33.,34.,35.);
    BzzVector y(7,15.02,39.8,65.03,89.95,
       115.03,140.01,164.95);
    BzzLinearRegression linReg(F,y);
    linReg.SetVariance(1.e-05,4);
    linReg.SVDAnalysis();
    }
```

The analysis carried out with the SVD method leads to the following singular value coefficients:

```
Singular Values D
1  1.2203913e+002
2  4.0558691e+000
3  9.9714322e-015   ** WARNING **
4  2.2535358e-015   ** WARNING **
5  1.8785892e-015   ** WARNING **
```

In other words, only two columns are linearly independent, whereas the remaining ones are correlated. When analyzing results, it is worth noting that parameters are strongly correlated, but, in this case, it is useless to remove a specific column: actually, three *opportune linear combinations* must be removed.

The importance of SVD analysis is that it returns the combination of columns to be removed to prevent any multicollinearity condition.

Note that this is a different problem from the previous ones and it is significantly harder to solve if compared to the direct removal of a single column of the matrix.

Example 3.10

To know which linear combinations are important to prevent multicollinearity condition, principal components of the matrix must be calculated. Example 3.9 showed that three columns are linear combinations, whereas only two columns are independent. Here is the program:

```
#include "BzzMath.hpp"
void main(void)
    {
    BzzMatrix F(7,5,
       1.,2.,3.,4.,5.,
       6.,7.,8.,9.,10.,
       11.,12.,13.,14.,15.,
       16.,17.,18.,19.,20.,
       21.,22.,23.,24.,25.,
       26.,27.,28.,29.,30.,
       31.,32.,33.,34.,35.);
    BzzVector y(7,15.02,39.8,65.03,89.95,
       115.03,140.01,164.95);
    BzzLinearRegression linReg(F,y);
```

3.11 Principal Components

```
    BzzMatrix P;
    linReg.GetPrincipalComponents(&P);
    P.DeleteRow(5);
    P.DeleteRow(4);
    P.DeleteRow(3);
    BzzMatrix newF;
    ProductT(F,P,&newF);
    BzzLinearRegression lrg(newF,y);
    lrg.SetVariance(7.e-3,4);
    lrg.LeastSquaresAnalysis();
}
```

The function `ProductT` makes the product $\mathbf{FP}^T$.

Examining the results, one can see that the new model involves only two parameters. Moreover, it satisfactorily fits experimental data and it is reasonably far from the multicollinearity condition.

```
Mean Square Error = 7.8850000e-003

F-test for the model
Fexperimental = 1.126429e+000
The probability that F with dfNum 5 dfDen 4
is greater than 1.126429e+000 is 4.671295e-001

Observed y          Estimated y          r                   rn
1 1.5020000e+001  1.4947500e+001  7.2500000e-002   0.87
2 3.9800000e+001  3.9955000e+001 -1.5500000e-001  -1.85
3 6.5030000e+001  6.4962500e+001  6.7500000e-002   0.81
4 8.9950000e+001  8.9970000e+001 -2.0000000e-002  -0.24
5 1.1503000e+002  1.1497750e+002  5.2500000e-002   0.63
6 1.4001000e+002  1.3998500e+002  2.5000000e-002   0.30
7 1.6495000e+002  1.6499250e+002 -4.2500000e-002  -0.51
```

The new matrix $\mathbf{F}$ of only two columns, which are linear combination of the previous five columns:

```
-5.64232388758636e-002    -6.79045015003033e-001
-1.47870955289593e-001    -5.13661820944507e-001
-2.39318671703322e-001    -3.48278626885981e-001
-3.30766388117051e-001    -1.82895432827456e-001
-4.22214104530780e-001    -1.75122387689299e-002
-5.13661820944509e-001     1.47870955289596e-001
-6.05109537358238e-001     3.13254149348120e-001
```

Note that these two columns differ from all columns of the original matrix $\mathbf{F}$, as they are the result of linear combination.

Example 3.11

Evaluate the following matrices:

$$\mathbf{B}_1 = d_1 u_1 v_1^T \tag{3.42}$$

$$\mathbf{B}_2 = \mathbf{B}_1 + d_2 u_2 v_2^T \tag{3.43}$$

Since d_3, d_4, and d_5 are practically zero, the matrix $\mathbf{B}_2$ should be evenly equal to the original matrix $\mathbf{F}$.

The program is

```
#include "BzzMath.hpp"
void main(void)
    {
    BzzMatrix F(7,5,
      1.,2.,3.,4.,5.,
      6.,7.,8.,9.,10.,
      11.,12.,13.,14.,15.,
      16.,17.,18.,19.,20.,
      21.,22.,23.,24.,25.,
      26.,27.,28.,29.,30.,
      31.,32.,33.,34.,35.);
    BzzVector y(7,15.02,39.8,65.03,89.95,
      115.03,140.01,164.95);
    BzzLinearRegression linReg(F,y);
    BzzMatrix V,U;
    BzzVector d;
    linReg.GetSortedBzzVectorDAndBzzMatricesVU(&d,&V,&U);
    BzzVector u1,u2,v1,v2;
    u1 = U.GetColumn(1);
    v1 = V.GetColumn(1);
    BzzMatrix B1;
    ProductT(u1,v1,&B1);
    B1 *= d[1];
    B1.BzzPrint("B1");
    u2 = U.GetColumn(2);
    v2 = V.GetColumn(2);
    BzzMatrix B2;
    ProductT(u2,v2,&B2);
    B2 *= d[2];
    B2 += B1;
    B2.BzzPrint("B2");
    }
```

The matrix $\mathbf{B}_1$ is evenly equal to the original matrix $\mathbf{F}$:

```
B1
2.8126 2.9432 3.0738 3.2045 3.3351
7.3711 7.7135 8.0558 8.3982 8.7406
11.929 12.483 13.037 13.592 14.146
16.488 17.254 18.019 18.785 19.551
21.046 22.024 23.001 23.979 24.957
25.605 26.794 27.983 29.173 30.362
30.163 31.564 32.965 34.366 35.768
```

The matrix $\mathbf{B}_2$ is exactly the same as the original matrix $\mathbf{F}$.

4
Robust Linear Regressions

Examples of this chapter can be found in the directory `Vol2_Chapter4` within the enclosed CD-ROM.

4.1
Introduction

Robust methods for regression are not yet widely used. There are several reasons of their unpopularity (Hampel *et al.* 1986, 2005). One possible reason is that computation of robust estimates is much more intensive than the least sum of squares (usually denoted by LSS) estimation; in recent years, however, this reason has become less relevant as computation power has greatly increased.

4.2
Some Caveat

Following points are essential in the analysis of robust linear models.

Caveat No. 1
The most important reason that makes robust methods so unpopular in model analysis is the following one.

Many statisticians believe that classical methods are quite robust.

On the contrary, conventional methods are usually unable to find out outliers: good experiments might be pointed out as outliers and, at the same time, real outliers might remain undetected.

Caveat No. 2
Many people think the hardest task is the model analysis by supposing that the same model they are analyzing is the right (or the true) one.

Interpolation and Regression Models for the Chemical Engineer: Solving Numerical Problems
Guido Buzzi-Ferraris and Flavio Manenti
Copyright © 2010 WILEY-VCH Verlag GmbH & Co. KGaA, Weinheim
ISBN: 978-3-527-32652-5

The hardest task in model analysis is to find out a model that is satisfactory on the overall experimental domain. If there is not a reasonable single model, the experimental domain must be better split in different regions and experimental points must be grouped in clusters, so as to adapt every model to the cluster of points just defined for each region.

The conventional method of examining a model by the least sum of squares is often unable to provide information on how to modify a model to better fit experimental data.

Caveat No. 3

A very frequent equivocation on robust methods is the following one.

Robust methods neglect outliers. This is completely untrue: robust methods allow to evaluate parameters without any perturbation caused by outliers. By doing so, they can detect outliers.

Caveat No. 4

While the previous equivocation was largely underlined by Rousseeuw (1984a, 1990) and Rousseeuw and Leroy (1987), the one that follows has not been highlighted in the literature.

People usually think robust methods deal with the search for gross errors caused only by human factors.

Although this is one of the tasks of robust methods, it is not the only goal and, above all, it is not the most relevant one.

Robust methods are essential to find out drawbacks in the selected model to improve, modify, and replace it by other more performing models, if necessary.

Caveat No. 5

When an outlier is detected by a robust method, it is necessary to know what to do then.

Never delete an outlier when you are not sure that it is a real gross error.

4.3
Outliers and Gross Errors

Outliers have no general definition that all accept. Consequently, equivocations and errors may easily arise when we are speaking about outliers.

The following definition is adopted in this book.

Whatever experimental point that is *unsuitable* for one model is called *outlier for this model*. Thus, any outlier is connected with the specific model one is analyzing. Obviously, one experiment can be considered an outlier for many models.

Some differences of opinions arise when we are dealing with the meaning of *unsuitable* while defining outliers. It is evident that one or more experimental points are *unsuitable* for a model when their presence is dissimilar to the general trend of the same model.

This book shall adopt the following definition to make this concept qualitatively and quantitatively more accurate.

One or more experimental points are unsuitable with respect to a specific model and, therefore, they must be considered outliers for it if their presence generates a significant increase in the mean square error.

Be careful. The previous definition looks like, but it is conceptually and practically different from, the following one: any experimental point that influences the model parameter evaluation is called an outlier.

In Section 4.6, experiments satisfying this last definition are called *influential observations* and *not outliers*.

It could be useful to change the point of view.

A model such that

$$MSE > F_\alpha s^2 \qquad (4.1)$$

contains at least one outlier.

If an experiment is an outlier for some models as it is caused by a human factor, it is not only an outlier for these specific models but also a *gross error*.

Gross errors are a special kind of outliers and they require special operations.

While the robust method has the task to detect possible outliers, the user has the task to check whether outliers are gross errors or not.

Be careful. A gross error is not necessarily an outlier for a specific model.

If one does not take into account this possibility, he can encounter a series of equivocations in testing robust methods. In fact, a common way to test a robust method is as follows: first, a model is adopted to generate experimental points with assigned parameters and experimental error variance; some gross errors are then introduced in the data set; finally, the test checks whether the robust method finds out all and only these bad points (without encountering any *masking* and/or *swamping* problem, both described later on). This procedure may lead to false conclusions when the gross errors are not outliers for the specific model.

A trivial example to explain it is proposed here. Let us consider the model:

$$y = 5(x-2)^2 \qquad (4.2)$$

If an experiment with $x = 1$ is transformed into an experiment with $x = 3$. to introduce a gross error, such a point does not become an outlier for the model, even though it is a gross error.

To set up a problem for checking if a robust method is able to find out all and only the outliers, it is necessary to verify that all the experimental points introduced as gross errors are real outliers for the model one is analyzing.

As it shall be shown later on, it may happen that different combinations of experiments can be pointed out as outliers for the same model since model parameters may significantly vary according to the set of experiments that are excluded in their evaluation.

For example, experiments no. 6 and 7, rather than experiments no. 1, 2, 8, and 9, can be pointed out as outlier for the same model.

In the following discussion, some situations involving outliers that have already been discussed in the scientific literature shall be considered by giving them an appropriate name, as they are not included in the definition of outliers adopted here.

It is important to know the following points, when the problem of outliers arises.

1) When is an outlier generated?
2) How can we detect them?
3) What should be done after their identification?

4.3.1
When is an Outlier Generated?

It is important to note that there are several sources of outliers:

- An outlier can affect an experimental value due to a human factor: it may be located either on dependent or on independent variables and it may be generated either by an experimental problem or by a mistake caused by the operator who acquired that value or by the operator who used it.

In this situation, the outlier is a *gross error* and, once detected, it has to be corrected or removed.

- The model may be unable to explain data in the whole experimental domain.
- The experimental design may be inadequate.
- The error variance is nonconstant in the whole experimental domain (heteroscedasticity condition, see Section 4.11).

Rousseeuw and Leroy (1987) clearly showed that the common technique adopted to detect outliers in linear regression problems was inadequate.

Actually, if parameters of linear models are evaluated by the method of the least sum of squares, when an outlier affects the experimental data, this method tries to reduce the residual of the same outlier and parameters result inevitably biased. This problem enhances when residuals are standardized by using the mean square error of the model.

As the mean square error is based on the model parameters, they are even more biased and the analysis may by completely wrong.

Residuals divided by square root of mean square error are called *standard* or *standardized residuals*.

Standard residuals should not be used to detect outliers.
It shall be shown that

- often, outliers are not detected (*masking*);
- some experiments are frequently pointed out as outliers, although they are good experiments (*swamping*);
- it may happen that a model is discarded as it is considered inadequate, although it is good.

The *masking* occurs when a real outlier is not identified during the model analysis and it is accepted as a good observation. Such a problem usually arises when we are using nonrobust methods.

The *swamping* occurs when the model analysis points out an experiment as outliers even though it is a good observation. This problem may arise with too robust methods.

Let us consider a trivial problem that can be geometrically visualized. The file leverage.lrg contains the same data of the simple3.lrg file (see Example 3.5) with a unique difference: the experiment no. 6 presents an error in the column no. 2 of the matrix **F**. In fact, a misprint affects the experimental value of the variable x in such an experiment: 124.89 rather than 104.89.

This mistake is enough to dramatically change the values of parameters obtained by the method of the least sum of squares. Using the data collected in the file simple3.lrg, we get 8.3202 and $-.59357$. Using the data collected in the file leverage.lrg, we get 9.245 and $-.15811348$.

Plotting standard residuals obtained with data collected in the file leverage.lrg, Figure 4.1 can be obtained by selecting the item Plot, StandardResiduals.

This plot highlights no outliers.

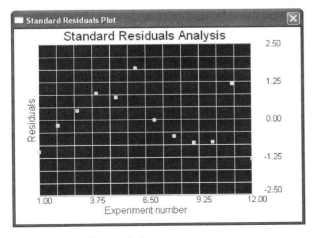

Figure 4.1 Standard residuals.

It is necessary to change the strategy for detecting outliers: it is necessary to use a method that leads to reliable parameter estimation even in the presence of outliers.

4.3.2
How Can We Detect Outliers?

As mentioned in the previous paragraph, an analysis of standard residuals by the least sum of squares method is ineffective in recognizing outliers.

Different alternatives have been proposed to detect outliers.

One of them is the least sum of absolute values; nevertheless, applications pointed out that this method is not enough robust.

Some other approaches shall be considered in Section 4.5.

The robust method proposed by Rousseeuw (1984a) and Rousseeuw and Leroy (1987) is particularly effective in robust parameter estimation of linear models even when several outliers are present. The idea, which this method is based on, is related to the robustness difference between the median and the arithmetic mean.

Instead of evaluating the least sum of squares, the robust method minimizes the median of squares:

$$\min_{\mathbf{b}}(median(r_i^2)), \qquad i = 1, \ldots, n_E \tag{4.3}$$

where r_i is the residual, that is, the difference between the experimental and the calculated values of the variable y at the ith experiment.

The method that minimizes function (4.3) is called *least median of squares* method and it is denoted by acronym LMS.

While the minimization of the sum of squares of a linear model is trivial thanks to the factorization of the matrix **F**, the least median of squares is quite cumbersome even though the model is linear.

One of the main difficulties is that the objective function is neither quadratic nor continuous. Moreover, the objective function is multimodal.

As the aim of the robust method is to detect probable outliers, it is possible to stop the search of the minimum when a reasonable minimum is achieved, without claiming that the global minimum of the function is reached.

The method proposed by Rousseeuw selects different combinations of experiments of p points, where p is the amount of parameters. By using these combinations, the model parameters are evaluated by solving $p \times p$ linear systems. The median of squares is computed for each combination and its value is compared with the best value already obtained by then.

The number of possible combinations rapidly increases both with the number of experiments and with the number of parameters. In general, this procedure is not exhaustive, as it would involve too many combinations.

Each evaluation of the objective function requires the solution of a $p \times p$ linear system.

In both `BzzLinearRegression` class and toolkit, the method proposed by Rousseeuw in minimizing the function (4.3) was improved in two steps.

Device No. 1

The first device deals with the selection and the solution of the linear systems. $p-1$ experimental points are iteratively selected and they are used to set up the $p \times p$ systems, where the remaining points are alternatively introduced one at a time as last experiment. For each selection of $p-1$ experimental points, $n-p+1$ systems are sequentially solved, and each of them is characterized by the same first $p-1$ rows.

Adopting an adequate factorization to solve these systems (either **LQ** or specialized **PLU**), the computational effort is only a few notch higher than the computational time required by the solution of just one $p \times p$ system, as each successive factorization exploits the same factorization carried out for the $p-1$ basic rows of the system.

Through this device, the number of combinations that can be analyzed with the same CPU time is considerably larger and, therefore, there are higher possibilities of detecting a minimum that is reasonably good.

Device No. 2

The second improvement consists of the use of a very robust minimization program, which is based on a variant of the OPTNOV method (Buzzi-Ferraris, 1967; Buzzi-Ferraris and Manenti, 2011a).

The program does not stop the search at the first minimum and, therefore, it is able to solve multimodal problems. Of course, no one can ensure that the global minimum is found, but this is not a serious problem, as it is usually sufficient to significantly reduce the value of function (4.3) for detecting outliers (without claiming that the global minimum is achieved).

With this criterion, parameters are considered as variables. It is not necessary to solve a linear system at each iteration, but one should simply evaluate the product **Fb** to get the value of $\hat{y}$ for estimating residuals.

An advantage of this numerical approach is the possibility of detecting a vector **b**, which is better than the combinations obtained by forcing the model to go through p experimental points.

Here and in the next chapters, we will refer to this improved version of the Rousseeuw method, as this version is implemented in the **BzzMath** library, by simply calling it *robust method*.

Example 4.1

Analyze the data collected into the file `BetterOutlier.lrg` by using an object of the `BzzLinearRegression` class.

The program is
```
#include "BzzMath.hpp"
void main(void)
    {
    BzzLinearRegression linReg("BetterOutlier.lrg");
    linReg.LeastSquaresAnalysis();
    linReg.RobustAnalysis();
    }
```
One could look at the file `BetterOutlier.lrg`:
```
9 2
1. 1. 1. 2. 1. 3. 1. 4. 1. 5.
1. 6. 1. 7. 1. 8. 1. 9.
9
1.8 3.7 4.7 6.8 7.8 9.7 10.9 12.7 15.3
```

This simple example shows that the method proposed by Rousseeuw is sometimes unable to detect an outlier, even considering all the permutations of $p \times p$ systems. The method of the least sum of squares leads to the following values for the parameters: $\beta_1 = 0.13055556$ and $\beta_2 = 1.605$. No outliers are detected by the nonrobust analysis with standard residuals.

By adopting the Rousseeuw method, the median of squares is computed for each combination of experiments and it is compared to the present best value.

In this case, parameters for the least median of squares are $\beta_1 = -0.1$ and $\beta_2 = +1.6$. It is worth noting that this method gives a solution by forcing the model to pass through p experimental points. In this specific case, null robust standard residuals are obtained with respect to experiments no. 3 and no. 8. In fact, the model $y = -.1 + 1.6x$ passes through these points.

No outliers are detected. The highest standardized residual is in correspondence with the experimental point no. 9 and is equal to 1.98.

If the search for the minimum of the function (4.3) is carried out by adopting the robust method just implemented in both the `BzzLinearRegression` class and the toolkit, it results in $\beta_1 = 0.12142857$ and $\beta_2 = 1.5571429$. A highly probable outlier is identified in correspondence with the experimental point no. 9, which has a doubled standard residual (equal to 3.89) against the case of the Rousseeuw method.

The optimal value is then obtained for a combination of β_1 and β_2 that does not solve a $p \times p$ system and allows to identify the presence of an outlier.

Example 4.2

Use an object of the `BzzLinearRegression` class to analyze with a robust method the data recovered in the file `Leverage.lrg`.

The program is

```
#include "BzzMath.hpp"
void main(void)
   {
   BzzLinearRegression linReg("Leverage.lrg");
   linReg.RobustAnalysis();
   }
```

Parameters obtained by the method of the least sum of squares in this example was 9.245 and $-.15811348$, while the values of parameters obtained by the robust method are very far from them: 8.3202339 and $-.59357143$.

Residuals obtained by the method of the least sum of squares do not reveal any problem, whereas residuals of the robust method are

```
     Observed y       Estimated y       Residuals r     Residuals
                                                       Standardized
 1  6.7596000e+000  6.7339143e+000   2.5685713e-002     0.14
 2  9.0492000e+000  8.9479357e+000   1.0126428e-001     0.53
 3  1.0455300e+001  1.0740521e+001  -2.8522143e-001    -1.50
 4  1.1909500e+001  1.2010764e+001  -1.0126429e-001    -0.53
 5  1.1452200e+001  1.1399386e+001   5.2814284e-002     0.28
 6  9.8861000e+000 -1.5879571e+000   1.1474057e+001    60.39*
 7  9.5247000e+000  9.6127357e+000  -8.8035716e-002    -0.46
 8  8.1732000e+000  8.4612071e+000  -2.8800714e-001    -1.52
 9  7.5921000e+000  7.7964071e+000  -2.0430714e-001    -1.08
10  7.4424000e+000  7.1672214e+000   2.7517857e-001     1.45
11  1.2622500e+001  1.2521236e+001   1.0126428e-001     0.53
12  6.0732000e+000  6.0394357e+000   3.3764284e-002     0.18

     These are highly probable Outliers: 6
```

The experimental point no. 6 is clearly an outlier.

It is important to realize the difference between the method of the least sum of squares and a robust method by graphically analyzing this trivial example.

Example 4.3

Plot models of previous Example 4.2 with parameters obtained with the method of the least sum of squares (9.245 and $-.15811348$) and with the robust method (8.3202339 and $-.59357143$).

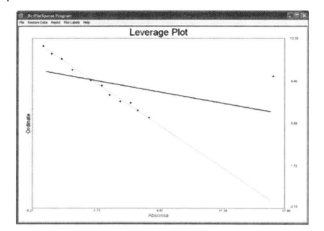

Figure 4.2 Resulting plot.

To get the trends of Figure 4.2, the program is

```
#include "BzzMath.hpp"
void main(void)
    {
    BzzVector x(12,110.87,107.14,104.12,101.98,
            103.01,124.89,106.02, 107.96,109.08,
            110.14,101.12,112.040);
    BzzVector y(12,6.7596,9.0492,10.4553,11.9095,
            11.4522,9.8861,9.5247,8.1732,
             7.5921,7.4424,12.6225,6.0732);
    BzzMatrix F(12,2);
    F.SetColumn(1,1.);
    double mean = Mean(x);
    int i;
    for(i = 1;i <= 12;i++)
        {
        x[i] = (x[i] - mean);
        }
    F.SetColumn(1,1.);
    F.SetColumn(2,x);
    BzzLinearRegression linReg(F,y);
    linReg.LeastSquaresAnalysis();
    linReg.RobustAnalysis();
    BzzVector bl,br;
    bl = linReg.GetParameters();
    br = linReg.GetRobustParameters();
    BzzMatrixSparse X(3,100);
    BzzMatrixSparse Y(3,100);
```

```
for(i = 1;i <= 12;i++)
    {
    X(1,i) = x[i];
    Y(1,i) = y[i];
    }
double xmin = x.Min();
double xmax = x.Max();
double dx = (xmax - xmin) / 101.;
double xx = xmin;
for(i = 1;i <= 100;i++)
    {
    xx += dx;
    X(2,i) = xx;
    Y(2,i) = bl[1] + bl[2] * xx;
    X(3,i) = xx;
    Y(3,i) = br[1] + br[2] * xx;
    }
BzzSave save("LeveragePlot.stx");
save << X << Y;
save.End();
system("BzzPlotSparse.exe");
}
```

Note that the method of the least sum of squares (solid line) is strongly modified by the outlier and it fails in fitting experimental points by making the subsequent model analysis ineffective; on the other hand, the outlier does not affect the robust method (dotted line).

Some people make a mistake that was also underlined by Rousseeuw in deeming the aim of robust methods: they confuse the cause with the effect.

A robust method does not neglect outliers; rather, it is simply uninfluenced by them. It simply aims at highlighting outliers that seem neglected by the same method as they are left out in evaluating parameters.

Be careful. The previous example and other similar problems discussed in the literature could lead to an error, which is particularly spread, thinking that this example shows that an outlier ever leads to very different model parameters when they are evaluated by taking it into account or not.

What significantly changes when parameters are evaluated with and without outliers is the mean square error of the model and not necessarily the model parameters.

Previous criteria are implemented both in the BzzLinearRegression class and in the BzzLinearRegression.exe toolkit and they were validated by many tests.

Another shortcoming of the original method proposed by Rousseeuw arises in standardizing robust residuals. Actually, Rousseeuw does not standardize them by means of the mean square error, as even this value is biased by outliers. Rousseeuw adopts the following value

$$s = 1.483\sqrt{median(r_i^2)} \qquad (4.4)$$

to standardize robust residuals.

As the median is a very robust estimator, sometimes its value is smaller than the real experimental error; consequently, some false outliers can be pointed out for an unrealistic standardization of residuals.

Such a problem is exemplified in Example 4.4. Note that, once again, the selected example is intentionally trivial for enhancing the essence of the problem we are analyzing, as it could be partially masked if complex problems are considered.

Example 4.4

Consider the linear model (3.7). Experimental data can be directly acquired with the following program:

```
#include "BzzMath.hpp"
void main(void)
    {
    BzzVector x(7,3.,5.,6.,8.,12.,15.,18.);
    BzzVector y(7,2.01,1.99,3.99,4.01,8.02,
        7.98,12.03);
    BzzMatrix F(7,2);
    F.SetColumn(1,1.);
    F.SetColumn(2,x);
    BzzLinearRegression linReg(F,y);
    double s2 = 1.5e-1;
    linReg.SetVariance(s2,3);
    linReg.RobustAnalysis();
    BzzVector br;
    br = linReg.GetRobustParameters();
    BzzMatrixSparse X(2,100);
    BzzMatrixSparse Y(2,100);
    int i;
    for(i = 1;i <= 7;i++)
        {
        X(1,i) = x[i];
        Y(1,i) = y[i];
        }
```

```
            double xmin = x.Min();
            double xmax = x.Max();
            double dx = (xmax - xmin) / 15.;
            double xx = 0.;
            for(i = 1;i <= 20;i++)
              {
              xx += dx;
              X(2,i) = xx;
              Y(2,i) = br[1] + br[2] * xx;
              }
            BzzSave save("FalseOutliersPlot.stx");
            save << X << Y;
            save.End();
            system("BzzPlotSparse.exe");
            }
```

If residuals are standardized by adopting the criteria suggested by Rousseeuw,

```
    Observed y      Estimated y      Residuals r           rn
1 2.0100000e+000  1.9980000e+000  1.2000000e-002        0.74
2 1.9900000e+000  3.3340000e+000 -1.3440000e+000      -82.41*
3 3.9900000e+000  4.0020000e+000 -1.2000000e-002       -0.74
4 4.0100000e+000  5.3380000e+000 -1.3280000e+000      -81.42*
5 8.0200000e+000  8.0100000e+000  1.0000000e-002        0.61
6 7.9800000e+000  1.0014000e+001 -2.0340000e+000     -124.71*
7 1.2030000e+001  1.2018000e+001  1.2000000e-002        0.74
```

As shown in Figure 4.3, the model almost exactly passes through some points; the median obtained is therefore excessively small, making the remaining points outliers, as they are standardized by the same median.

Both in the `BzzLinearRegression` class and in the toolkit, robust residuals are standardized by

- square root of the error variance if an estimate is known;
- the same value proposed by Rousseeuw (4.4) if the error variance estimate is unknown and if it is not too small with respect to experimental **y**;
- if none of the previous alternatives is feasible and especially when the minimum of the function (4.3) is considerably small, a threshold value related to the maximum of the experimental **y** is selected. In such a case, a warning is printed for possible inconsistencies that can arise while searching for outliers, as the threshold value is partially arbitrary.

In any case, the problem of an inadequate standardization of residuals disappears either as new experimental points are introduced into the data set or when a reasonable value of the experimental error variance is provided.

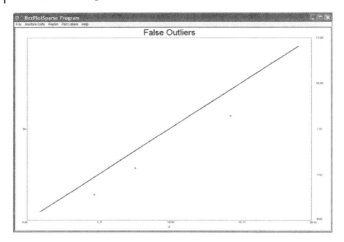

Figure 4.3 Excessive robustness leads to discard good points as outliers.

Rousseeuw (1984b) proposed an alternative method that could be preferred to the least median of squares.

Rather than searching for the minimum of function (4.3), the following objective function is minimized:

$$\min_{\beta} \left(\sum_{i=1}^{h} r_{(i)}^2 \right) \tag{4.5}$$

where $r_{(1)}^2, r_{(2)}^2, r_{(3)}^2, \ldots, r_{(h)}^2$ are the square residuals of the selected experiments; it is necessary to select the best combination of $n_E - h$ experiments, which will not be inserted into function (4.5), for each value of h. The amount of combinations and, therefore, of function (4.5) minima to be examined is equal to $\binom{n_E}{n_E - h}$.

The method that finds out the minimum among all the combinations for an assigned value of h is called *least trimmed sum of squares* and it is denoted by the acronym LTSS; nevertheless, it is usually improperly called *least trimmed squares* and denoted by the acronym LTS in the literature.

The most significant advantage of least trimmed sum of squares method (Ryan, 2009) is that if one is lucky in selecting h, which corresponds to the amount of poor quality experiments, an optimal estimator is obtained as no good points are removed in estimating parameters. As a result, the least trimmed sum of squares is converted into a least sum of squares method applied to only good experiments.

The method of the least trimmed sum of squares also presents some shortcomings.

1) It is hard to select the right value of h (amount of residuals to use in the least sum of squares). If a large value is chosen, the *masking* problem arises and some

outliers remain undetected; if a small value is chosen, the *swamping* problem arises and the method points out some experiments as outliers even though they are good observations.
2) The search for the best selection of the experiments that minimizes function (4.5) may be computationally intensive when the amount of experiments is large and/or the value of h is large.

Rousseeuw and Leroy (1987) proposed a heuristic criteria to assign the value of h. It is related to a percentage α to have outliers against the total amount of experiments:

$$h = (1-\alpha)n_E + 1 \qquad (4.6)$$

Other authors join h to the amount of experiments and to the number of model parameters. For example, the program SYSTAT adopts the following formula:

$$h = \frac{3n_E + p + 1}{4} \qquad (4.7)$$

Ryan (2009) proposed an interesting variant. h is sequentially selected, n_E-1, n_E-2, ..., by avoiding its problematic choice.

This technique for finding out the optimal number of residuals should be employed to calculate the sum of squares is equivalent to the use of the *clever mean* rather than the *trimmed mean* in calculating the mean.

In the case of trimmed mean, the number of trimmed elements for calculating the mean after sorting them is assigned a priori. In the case of clever mean, maximum and minimum values are sequentially removed until the value of the mean becomes stable.

The method that searches for the minimum among all the combinations and, at the same time, changes the value of h to get a satisfactory value of the sum of squares is called *least clever sum of squares* and it is denoted by the acronym LCSS.

The method originally proposed by Ryan (2009) may become prohibitive when the number of combinations is significantly large, that is, when there are many experiments and/or when the number of sequentially selected values of h is large.

Buzzi-Ferraris and Manenti (2010b) recently proposed a novel approach for the outlier detection in linear regression problems. The main idea is based on the use of the function `CleverMean` for the evaluation of the arithmetic mean rather than the median or the trimmed mean.
This technique has been implemented in the function `CleverLeastSquares-Analysis` belonging to the `BzzLinearRegression` class.

The function `CleverLeastSquaresAnalysis` preserves the advantage of the least trimmed sum of squares method of performing the calculation of mean square errors of residuals and, at the same time, prevents the aforementioned shortcomings.

Actually, the selection of the number of experiments to be removed is automatically carried out and this is not done by attempts. From this perspective, the method is similar to Ryan's approach as the search for the best selection of h is a program task.

Contrary to Ryan's approach, which executes the analysis for each possible combination of experiments, the function `CleverLeastSquaresAnalysis` adopts a technique that is dual with respect to the stepwise method in the search for the best model (see Section 3.10) when the number of experimental points is large. Therefore, the minimization of the objective function becomes more performing with a significant number of experimental points.

While in the stepwise method columns of the matrix **F** are either added or removed to find out the smallest mean square error, the function `CleverLeastSquaresAnalysis` manages rows (experiments) in order to find the set of experiments that minimizes the mean square error.

Even starting from the overall matrix **F**, the row to be removed is not the worst one pointed out by the method of the least sum of squares, rather one row at a time is removed and the corresponding mean square error is evaluated without such an experiment. The experimental point that leads to the model with n_E-1 experiments with the best mean square error is then selected and removed.

As per stepwise method, it is suitable to start from different combinations of experimental points. One of these combinations is represented by the whole experimental data set. Adopting the stepwise nomenclature, the so-called *Backward* method is therefore adopted. After removing an experimental point that provides the least value of mean square error, a check on the possible reintroduction of experiments previously deleted is also carried out (*Forward* method).

While the *stepwise method* usually fails when starting with the full model (because of linear combinations among the columns), this problem does not arise anymore in the dual approach of the *least clever sum of squares*.

In the stepwise method, it is opportune to start from different models (different combinations of the columns of the matrix **F**) and alternatively apply *Backward* and *Forward* analyses in searching for the best model. Analogously, it is appropriate to start from different combinations of rows of the matrix **F**.
The function `CleverLeastSquaresAnalysis` can exploit another advantage against *stepwise method* adopted to select the columns and against the successive least trimmed sum of squares proposed by Ryan (2009).

The function `CleverLeastSquaresAnalysis` already knows which experiments are possible outliers through a preventive robust analysis performed by the improved Rousseeuw's method. It significantly simplifies Forward and Backward analyses, as it identifies a series of possible outliers that are independently selected by the Backward analysis.

When the function CleverLeastSquaresAnalysis analyzes robust residuals obtained by minimizing function (4.3), their relative order is important. Hence, there is no (hard) problem in standardizing them for detecting real outliers.

As a result, the function CleverLeastSquaresAnalysis provides the sequence of possible outliers and the corresponding mean square error.
The procedure is stopped when the total amount of experimental points removed is equal to an assigned value; $\frac{n_E}{2}$ is adopted by default.
Even though the function CleverLeastSquaresAnalysis provides a list of possible and probable outliers, it is useful that the user analyze them with care as real outliers are exclusively related to experimental error variance and heteroscedasticity condition.

Example 4.5

Use an object of the BzzLinearRegression class to analyze the data collected in the file Leverage.lrg with the function CleverLeastSquaresAnalysis. The program is

```
#include "BzzMath.hpp"
void main(void)
   {
   BzzLinearRegression linReg("Leverage.lrg");
   linReg.SetVariance(3,2.e-2);
   linReg.CleverLeastSquaresAnalysis();
   }
```

In this example, the object is initialized through the name of the file Leverage.lrg, where data are collected in.
The results are

```
** Iteration 0
numExperiments: 12 Mse: 3.766e+000
** Iteration 1
numExperiments: 11 Mse: 3.396e-002
>>>>>> Highly Probable Outliers: 6 ** WARNING **
** Iteration 2
numExperiments: 10 Mse: 2.577e-002
Possible Outliers: 6 10
```

The outlier is detected in correspondence with the experimental point no. 6. Actually, the mean square error drops from 3.766 to $3.396 \cdot 10^{-2}$ by removing this point.

How can an outlier be identified through a `BzzLinearRegression` class object?

1) One can check messages at the end of the robust analysis. If the object detects some outliers, it separately lists only highly probable outliers and possible outliers.
2) One can examine residuals evaluated in the robust analysis: outliers are highlighted by large residuals.
3) One can use the function `CleverLeastSquaresAnalysis`.

If the previous robust analysis has highlighted some outliers and if parameter values are different when they are calculated adopting the *least sum of squares* method or the *least median of squares* method, the outliers are also *influential observations* (see Section 4.6).

How can an outlier be identified through the `BzzLinearRegression.exe` toolkit?

1) Adopt the `Menu` option: `Diagnostics, Outliers`.
2) Adopt the `Menu` option: `Plot, RobustResiduals`.
3) Adopt the `Menu` option: `Plot, yRobust/y`.
4) Analyze results by adopting the `Menu` option: `Analysis, Robust`. In particular, it is important to examine residuals.

Problems involving outliers shall be proposed in the next chapter.

4.3.3
What Should be Done When Outliers are Detected?

It is *necessary to find and reconcile the outliers*, so as to avoid large mistakes in the model parameter evaluation.

When an outlier is detected, it is important to understand why it exists and what has generated it.

Remember: the outliers can occur for the following reasons:
1) Errors in the data set.
2) Model inadequacy to fit all the experimental points. The model should be modified or its validity range should be reduced.
3) Inadequacy of the current design of experiments. Additional points should be introduced.
4) Heteroscedasticity condition.

Example 4.6

Consider the case proposed by Ryan (2009) to check whether a program is able to detect outliers.

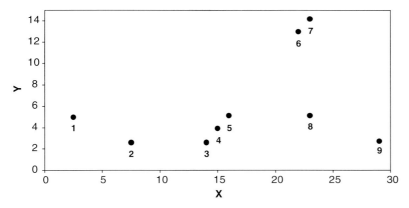

Figure 4.4 Original data set.

The selected example is intentionally trivial for enhancing the essence of the problem we are analyzing, as it could be partially masked if complex problems would be considered.

Experimental data can be directly obtained with the following program, but it is interesting to graphically visualize the experimental points of this example (see Figure 4.4).

```
#include "BzzMath.hpp"
void main(void)
    {
    int numExperiments = 9;
    BzzVector x1(numExperiments,
                 2.5,7.5,14.,15.,16.,22.,23.,23.,29.);
    BzzMatrix F(numExperiments,2);
    BzzVector y(numExperiments,
                 5.,2.6,2.6,3.9,5.1,13.,14.2,5.1,2.7);
    F.SetColumn(1,1.);
    F.SetColumn(2,x1);
    BzzLinearRegression linReg(F,y);
    linReg.LeastSquaresAnalysis();
    linReg.RobustAnalysis();
    linReg.CleverLeastSquaresAnalysis();
    }
```

Analysis of residuals performed by the method of the least sum of squares does not identify any outliers.

According to Ryan (2009) and the least trimmed sum of squares method, there are two evident outliers: experiments no. 6 and 7.

Results of `RobustAnalysis` vary according to the value assigned to the experimental error variance. As mentioned above, one of the main difficulties of the method that adopts the residuals evaluated by minimizing function (4.3) is to choose the basis of their standardization before deeming if there are outliers.

By standardizing residuals by the weight (4.4), as it was proposed by Rousseeuw, the problem of *swamping* may arise.

The median is so robust an estimator that it might point out too many outliers. Without an estimate of the experimental error variance, it is hard to assign it a reasonable value.

If no error variance estimates are assigned before invoking the function `RobustAnalysis`, no probable outliers are detected. Conversely, if a value (even significantly approximate) is provided, such as

```
linReg.SetVariance(10.,1);
```

the function `RobustAnalysis` identifies the following experiments as outliers:

```
Outliers sorted by importance:
9 1 8 2
These are highly probable Outliers: 1 2 8 9
```

Experiments no. 9, 1, 8, and 2 are highlighted by the robust method for their bad residual. Labeling them or not as outliers is just a problem of weights.

Results of `CleverLeastSquaresAnalysis` are

```
** Iteration 0
numExperiments: 9 Mse: 1.983e+001
** Iteration 1
numExperiments: 8 Mse: 1.301e+001
>>> Probable Outliers: 7 ** WARNING **
** Iteration 2
numExperiments: 7 Mse: 1.748e+000
>>> Probable Outliers: 7 6 ** WARNING **
** Iteration 3
numExperiments: 6 Mse: 1.514e+000
Possible Outliers: 7 6 2
** Iteration 4
numExperiments: 5 Mse: 3.571e-003
>>>>>> Highly Probable Outliers: 9 1 8 2 ** WARNING **
```

The function `CleverLeastSquaresAnalysis` identifies two possibilities: either experiments no. 6 and 7 or experiments no. 9, 1, 8, and 2 could be alternatively considered outliers.

What should be done in such a situation?

When outliers are detected, it is crucial to realize if they were generated by a gross error due to a human factor (mistyping error, transcription, misprint, etc.).

In any case, if an outlier is caused by a human factor (if it is a gross error), the remedy is always the same: *errata corrige*; bad points must be corrected or deleted.

Never delete an outlier without the certainty that it is a real gross error.

If no human factors generated the outlier, there are two possible approaches:

- Find out an alternative model.
- Introduce additional experimental points (if possible).

The problem of adding new experiments involves both linear and nonlinear models; it shall be discussed in Chapter 8.

In the case under study, there is not a reasonable alternative model that seems able to satisfy the data set.

It is sure that experiments no. 7 and 8 are incompatible as, otherwise, experiments were carried out either with a very large variance or under the condition of heteroscedasticity.

Suppose to have the possibility to get new experimental points. They should dispel any doubt on possible outliers detected and provides new elements to deem if it is necessary either to modify the model or to remove some points as they are real outliers or to modify some hypotheses adopted in evaluating parameters or to give up having a reasonable model joining variables y and x.

Following scenarios may take place.

Scenario No. 1

By examining the existing experimental data, one can realize that the experiment no. 8 of Figure 4.4 is a gross error and therefore it can be removed. After generating new experimental points, data set reported in Figure 4.5 is obtained.

Additional experiments confirm that experiment no. 8 was a gross error. Moreover, it is clear that the variable y is joined to the independent variable x by a more complex relation rather than the one proposed at the beginning. If the theory is able to provide the model characterizing the physical phenomenon, this new model can be analyzed by new. On the other hand, if there are no possibilities to obtain the proper model, one can adopt the technique explained in Section 7.3 and applied in Example 7.18.

In this scenario, an outlier was removed as it was a gross error, whereas all the remaining experiments pointed out as outliers in the original model forced us to change the model.

Scenario No. 2

Experiments no. 6 and 7 are pointed out as gross errors by an accurate analysis and they can be removed.

After generating new experimental points, data set reported in Figure 4.6 is obtained. New observations enhance the incompatibility of the deleted experiments against the other experiments.

4 Robust Linear Regressions

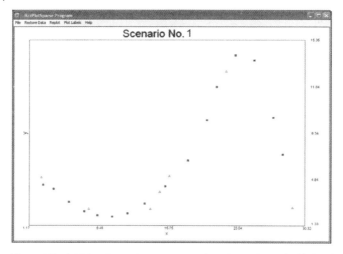

Figure 4.5 Additional experiments: a complex relationship is highlighted.

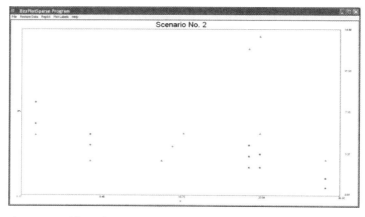

Figure 4.6 Additional experiments confirm that experiments no. 6 and 7 were gross errors.

Example 4.7

Analyze the data set obtained in scenario no. 2 once experiments no. 6 and 7 are removed. Data can be directly acquired by the following program:

```
#include "BzzMath.hpp"
void main(void)
    {
//int numExperiments = 20;
```

```
    int numExperiments = 18;
    BzzVector x1(numExperiments,
//      2.5,7.5,14.,15.,16.,22.,23.,23.,29.,2.5,7.5,
        14.,15.,16.,23.,29.,2.5,2.5,7.5,7.5,23.,23.,
        29.,29.,22.,22.,22.);
    BzzMatrix F(numExperiments,2);
    BzzVector y(numExperiments,
//      5.,2.6,2.6,3.9,5.1,13.,14.2,5.1, 2.7,5.,2.6,
        2.6,3.9,5.1,5.1,2.7,6.,8.,4.,5.,3.2,2.,1.,
        .1,3.,2.,4.);
    F.SetColumn(1,1.);
    F.SetColumn(2,x1);
    BzzLinearRegression linReg(F,y);
    linReg.SetVariance(12,2.5);
    linReg.LeastSquaresAnalysis();
    linReg.RobustAnalysis();
    linReg.CleverLeastSquaresAnalysis();
    BzzVector b;
    b = linReg.GetParameters();
    BzzMatrixSparse Y(3,100);
    BzzMatrixSparse X(3,100);
    double x;
    for(int i = 1; i <= 100;i++)
      {
      x = - 2.5 * double(i - 100)/99. +
         29. * double(i - 1)/99.;
      X(1,i) = x;
      Y(1,i) = b[1] + b[2] * x;
      }
    for(i = 1;i <= 7;i++)
      {
      X(2,i) = F(i,2);Y(2,i) = y[i];
      }
    for(i = 8;i <= numExperiments;i++)
      {
      X(3,i) = F(i,2);Y(3,i) = y[i];
      }
    BzzSave save("Scenario2.stx");
    save << X << Y;
    save.End();
    system("BzzPlotSparse.exe");
    }
```

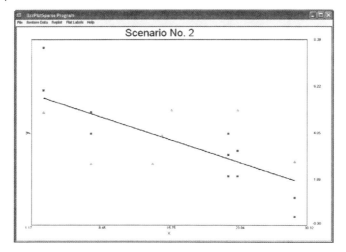

Figure 4.7 Additional experiments show a linear trend.

The model is satisfactory and no outliers are detected (Figure 4.7). Conversely, by analyzing this data set by accounting even for the original experiments no. 6 and 7, they should be identified as outliers.

Scenario No. 3

Experiments no. 8 and 9 can be considered gross errors and, therefore, they can be removed. The initial model is inadequate, as all possible outliers have not been removed. Consequently, either the model or some hypotheses on the experimental error or both of them must be modified. After generating new experimental points, data set reported in Figure 4.8 is obtained.

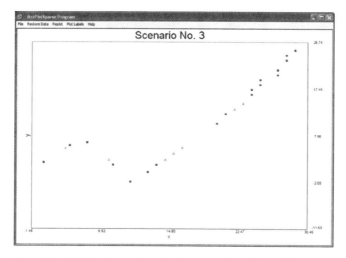

Figure 4.8 Additional experiments show a complex relationship.

Example 4.8

Analyze data set obtained in scenario no. 3 once the experiments no 8 and 9 are excluded. Data can be directly acquired with the following program:

```
#include "BzzMath.hpp"
void main(void)
   {
   int i;
   int numExperiments = 25;
   BzzVector x1(numExperiments,
         2.5,7.5,14.,15.,16.,22.,23.,0.,3.,5.,8.,10.,
         12.,13.,20.,21.,24.,24.,25.,25.,27.,27.,28.,
         28.,29.);
   BzzMatrix F(numExperiments,3);
   BzzVector y(numExperiments,
         5.,2.6,2.6,3.9,5.1,13.,14.2,2.,
         5.5,6.1,1.5,-2.,0.,1.5,10.,12.,16.,
         17.,19.,18.,20.,21.,24.,23.,25.);
   F.SetColumn(1,1.);
   F.SetColumn(2,x1);
   for(i = 1;i <= numExperiments;i++)
         F[i][3] = BzzPow2(x1[i]);
   BzzLinearRegression linReg(F,y);
   linReg.SetVariance(12,2.5);
   linReg.LeastSquaresAnalysis();
   linReg.RobustAnalysis();
   linReg.CleverLeastSquaresAnalysis();
   BzzVector b;
   b = linReg.GetRobustParameters();
   BzzMatrixSparse Y(3,100);
   BzzMatrixSparse X(3,100);
   double x;
   for(i = 1; i <= 100;i++)
      {
      x = 29.* double(i - 1)/99.;
      X(1,i) = x;
      Y(1,i) = b[1] + x * (b[2] + b[3] * x);
      }
   for(i = 1;i <= 7;i++)
      {
      X(2,i) = x1[i];Y(2,i) = y[i];
      }
   for(i = 8;i <= numExperiments;i++)
```

4 Robust Linear Regressions

```
    {
      X(3,i) = x1[i];Y(3,i) = y[i];
    }
    BzzSave save("Scenario3.stx");
    save << X << Y;
    save.End();
    system("BzzPlotSparse.exe");
    BzzPause();
  }
```

Robust analysis points out the following outliers:

```
Outliers sorted by importance:
 9 1 10 8 2 11
These are highly probable Outliers: 1 2 8 9 10
These are possible Outliers: 11
```

Results of `CleverLeastSquaresAnalysis` are

```
** Iteration 0
numExperiments: 25 Mse: 3.160e+000
** Iteration 1
numExperiments: 24 Mse: 2.321e+000
Possible Outliers: 8
** Iteration 2
numExperiments: 23 Mse: 1.606e+000
>>> Probable Outliers: 8 12 ** WARNING **
** Iteration 3
numExperiments: 22 Mse: 1.276e+000
Possible Outliers: 8 12 13
** Iteration 4
numExperiments: 21 Mse: 9.757e-001
Possible Outliers: 8 12 13 10
** Iteration 5
numExperiments: 20 Mse: 8.352e-001
Possible Outliers: 8 12 13 10 14
** Iteration 6
numExperiments: 19 Mse: 3.182e-001
>>>>> Highly Probable Outliers: 9 1 10 8 2 11 **WARNING**
** Iteration 7
numExperiments: 18 Mse: 2.041e-001
>>> Probable Outliers: 9 1 10 8 2 11 21 ** WARNING **
```

If the experiments no 1, 2, 8, 9, 10, and 11 are removed, the following regression with quadratic model is obtained (Figure 4.9):

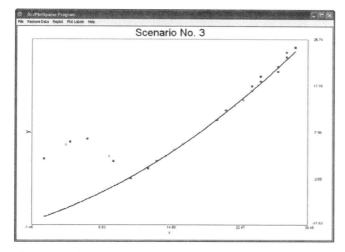

Figure 4.9 Additional experiments show the need of piecewise models.

The need of piecewise models is evident. In this specific case, a first model should fit experiments in the range $[0, 10]$ of independent variable x, whereas the second model should fix experiments in the range $[10, 29]$. Both the models look like a parabola.

It is possible to use a single model divided into two submodels (with experiments not necessarily divided into two mutually exclusive data sets) by inserting a (Boolean) dummy variable (Draper and Smith, 1998).

The dummy variable assumes value 1 for a subset of experiments and value 0 for the other one. The model should be written so as to evaluate parameters fitting the first data subset when the dummy variable is equal to 1 and to fit the other data subset when the dummy variable is zero.

Example 4.9

Analyze data set obtained in scenario no. 3 once the experiments no. 8 and 9 are excluded.
Experimental data set is divided in two subsets: the first contains experimental points with $x_{1i} \leq 10.$; the second contains all the experiments with $x_{1i} \geq 10$. Data can be directly acquired by the following program (Figure 4.10).

```
#include "BzzMath.hpp"
void main(void)
   //Ryan 433 Scenario No. 3
   {
   int i;
   int numExperiments = 26;
```

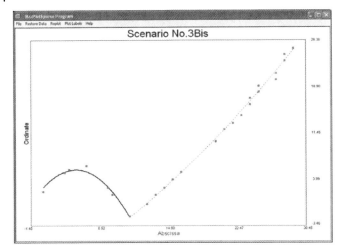

Figure 4.10 Use of submodels.

```
BzzVector x1(numExperiments,
    2.5,7.5,0.,3.,5.,8.,10.,14.,15.,16.,
    22.,23.,10.,12.,13.,20.,21.,24.,
    24.,25.,25.,27.,27.,28.,28.,29.);
BzzVector x2(numExperiments,
    1.,1.,1.,1.,1.,1.,1.,0.,0.,0.,0.,0.,
    0.,0.,0.,0.,0.,0.,0.,0.,0.,0.,0.,0.,0.);
BzzMatrix F(numExperiments,6);
BzzVector y(numExperiments,
    5.,2.6,2.,5.5,6.1,1.5,-2.,2.6,3.9,5.1,
    13.,14.2,-2.,0.,1.5,10.,12.,16.,
    17.,19.,18.,20.,21.,24.,23.,25.);
for(i = 1;i <= numExperiments;i++)
    {
    F[i][1] = x2[i];
    F[i][2] = x2[i] * x1[i];
    F[i][3] = x2[i] * BzzPow2(x1[i]);
    F[i][4] = 1. - x2[i];
    F[i][5] = (1. - x2[i]) * x1[i];
    F[i][6] = (1. - x2[i]) * BzzPow2(x1[i]);
    }
BzzLinearRegression linReg(F,y);
linReg.SetVariance(12,2.5);
linReg.LeastSquaresAnalysis();
linReg.RobustAnalysis();
linReg.CleverLeastSquaresAnalysis();
}
```

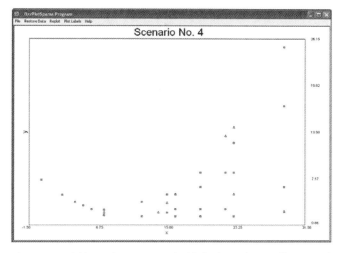

Figure 4.11 Additional experiments highlight the violation of homoscedasticity condition.

Unfortunately, this technique unavoidably perturbs the analysis of model collinearities by offsetting the columns of the matrix **F** through the same dummy variable.

Scenario No. 4
None of the possible outliers can be considered a gross error in this scenario. Even in this case, it is necessary to modify either the model or some hypotheses on the experimental error or both of them. After generating new experimental points, data set reported in Figure 4.11 is obtained.

In this case, a reasonable model seems to contain a quadratic term; moreover, heteroscedasticity condition appears evident when we look at Figure 4.11.

Objects of the `BzzLinearRegression` class cannot examine this model, as the variance is nonconstant; an object of the `BzzNonLinearRegression` class is required (see Chapter 6 and 7; see also Example 7.21).

Scenario No. 5
As in the previous scenario, no outliers are gross errors. After generating new experimental points, data set reported in Figure 4.12 is obtained.

Figure 4.12 shows that no reasonable model can properly fit the experimental points. Actually, a simple model should be almost surely rejected by the thumb test, by obtaining a *pollice verso*; conversely, a complex model would probably interpolate the experimental error and it should be discarded as its mean square error would be too small compared to the experimental error variance.

4.4
Studentized Residuals

As already explained, residuals (even standard residuals) are ineffective in detecting outliers. A spread and preferable technique is the following one.

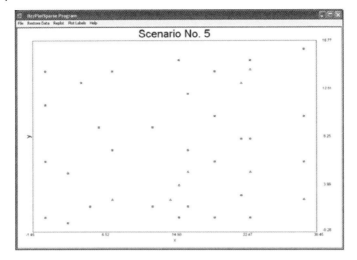

Figure 4.12 No reasonable models can fit the experimental data set.

Be careful: although it is preferable to conventional standard residual analysis, even this technique should be avoided.

It could be demonstrated (see Draper and Smith, 1998) that the mean square error of the model estimated by removing the *i*th experiment can be obtained as follows:

$$s_i^2 = \frac{(n_E-p)s^2 - \frac{r_i^2}{1-h_{ii}}}{n_E-p-1} \tag{4.8}$$

where the mean square error obtained with all the experiments is denoted by s^2, the residual of the experimental point to be removed is denoted by r_i, and the coefficient on the main diagonal of the hat matrix is denoted by h_{ii}.

Be careful: the equivalence between s_i^2 evaluated by using equation (4.8) and the one obtained after removing *i*th experiment is valid only for classical analysis. As coefficients h_{ii} are easily and significantly perturbed by numerical errors, the equivalence is no longer valid in numerical analysis.

Once estimation s_i^2 is known, it is possible to evaluate studentized residuals.

Coefficients

$$t_i = \frac{r_i}{s_i\sqrt{1-h_{ii}}} \tag{4.9}$$

are called studentized residuals.

From certain aspects, these coefficients look like the initial search carried out by `CleverLeastSquaresAnalysis` as, even in this case, the equivalent value of s_i^2 is evaluated to check which experiment provides the most significant decrease in the mean square error. Notwithstanding, the following differences have to be underlined:

- In the function `CleverLeastSquaresAnalysis`, s_i^2 is not estimated through the hat matrix, which can be ill conditioned and, therefore, unreliable.
- The same hat matrix is not used to build an index for deeming whether an experimental point is an outlier or not. The value of t_i could be strongly influenced by inaccuracies in evaluating h_{ii}.
- The procedure of the least clever sum of squares is iterated in a stepwise-like process that allows to find out all real outliers. Masking and swamping phenomena may arise when analyzing studentized residuals. The masking problem could occur even though the hat matrix is reliable.

In the `BzzLinearRegression` class, it is possible to get an estimation of the vector t_i by means of the function `GetStudentizedResiduals`. The function has a pointer to a `BzzVector` as argument, containing the vector of studentized residuals. Hence, the required statements are

```
BzzVector str;
linReg.GetStudentizedResiduals(&str);
str.BzzPrint("str");
```

The next chapter shall propose some examples showing that even though this analysis is superior to the classical standard residuals analysis, it is not ever adequate in finding out all and only the real outliers.

4.5
M-Estimators

Huber (1981) introduced *M-estimators* for regression. The M in M-estimators stands for *maximum likelihood type*. In subsequent years, various alternatives were proposed (see Rousseeuw and Leroy, 1987; Draper and Smith, 1998).

The idea the M-estimators are based on is an extension of the method of the least sum of squares. The method of the least sum of squares searches for the minimum of the objective function:

$$\sum_{i=1}^{n_E} \left(\frac{y_i - \mathbf{f}_i^T \boldsymbol{\beta}}{s} \right)^2 \qquad (4.10)$$

M-estimators adopt a different objective function, such as the abovementioned absolute value. In the general case, one can write

$$\sum_{i=1}^{n_E} \varrho \left(\frac{y_i - \mathbf{f}_i^T \boldsymbol{\beta}}{s} \right) \qquad (4.11)$$

where ϱ is a specific function characterizing the M-estimator method.

Huber (1981) proposed one of the most common functions:

$$\begin{aligned} \varrho(t) &= t^2 & |t| \leq A \\ \varrho(t) &= 2A|t| - A^2 & |t| > A \end{aligned} \quad (4.12)$$

where A is a constant that is selected in accordance with the problem.

Many alternatives were proposed in the literature (see Draper and Smith, 1998; Hines and Montgomery, 1990; Ryan, 2009; Seber and Wild, 2003; Bates and Watts, 2007).

M-estimators have to tackle three problems (Draper and Smith, 1998):

1) If the real experimental error variance is unknown, it is not easy to choose the most adequate function ϱ.
2) It is usually suitable to weight the single residuals appropriately; rather the selection of weights may be hard.
3) The selection of the order of magnitude to balance residuals is not trivial and it may lead to very different results according to the selection.

   Two additional issues may be quoted:
4) The minimization of function (4.11) may be hard from a numerical point of view as discontinuities are present.
5) In a general program, it is not trivial to foresee which alternatives have to be inserted for all future regressions and especially to automatically select optimal parameters involved in these functions.

Ryan (2009) and Rousseeuw (in Wadsworth, 1989) consider these alternatives obsolete.

In the `BzzLinearRegression` class, M-estimators are not implemented because of the efficiency of the previous two methods in identifying outliers.

4.6
Influential Observations

Any experimental point that significantly influences model parameters evaluation is called *influential observation*.

Cook (1977) proposed the following criterion to evaluate influential observations. Given n_E experimental points, model parameters are evaluated by leaving out one experiment at a time. Denoting by **b** the vector of parameters obtained by wholly considering the data set and by $\mathbf{b}_i$ the ones obtained without the ith experiment, the following calculation can be performed for each i:

$$D_i = \frac{(\mathbf{b} - \mathbf{b}_i)^T \mathbf{F}^T \mathbf{F} (\mathbf{b} - \mathbf{b}_i)}{ps^2} \quad (4.13)$$

The higher the value of D_i, the larger the relevance of the experiment (influential observation).

Criterion to identify influential experiments by the value of function (4.13) is called *Cook statistics*.

In the `BzzLinearRegression` class, the function `InfluentialObservations` allows to identify influential observations by Cook statistics. Two versions of this function are provided: the first has `void` argument and prints results on file; the second

```
BzzVectorInt influentialEx;
BzzVector normalizedCook,cook;
linReg.InfluentialObservations(&influentialEx,
        &normalizedCook,&cook);
```

allows to recover influential observations ordered by a decreasing relevance in the `BzzVectorInt influentialEx`, the value of standardized D_i in the vector `BzzVector normalizedCook`, and the value of D_i in the `BzzVector cook`.

The Jackknife approach is related to the Cook statistics, as it is based on the same principle of deleting one experimental point at a time and of checking the gap between the vectors **b**$_i$ and **b** (see Draper and Smith, 1998; Seber and Wild, 2003).

It is important to fully realize the difference between an *influential observation* and an *outlier*.

- An outlier significantly modifies the mean square error of the model; an influential observation significantly modifies model parameters. These two aspects are very far from each other!
- The search for outliers *must* always be performed, as it is essential to identify data that can perturb the model analysis. Conversely, even though it could be useful, it is not necessary to carry out the search for influential observations.
- If any outlier is detected, model analysis *must* be stopped until each outlier has been properly recovered, by either removing or correcting them, if due to gross errors; by either revising the model or adding new experimental points, otherwise. On the other hand, even though any influential observation is identified, it could indicate shortages in experimental design; rather, there is no need to stop model analysis.
- An outlier can be even an influential observation and vice versa.
- The presence of one or more outliers usually generates influential observations; conversely, the presence of one or more influential observations does not necessarily generate outliers.
- Techniques for outlier detection do not provide useful information on influential observations; techniques to identify influential observations must not be used to detect outliers.

It is a serious mistake to use techniques for influential observations for detecting outliers.

- Even though the function `CleverLeastSquaresAnalysis` seems to correspond to Cook statistics, at least in its starting phase (*Backward*), it is completely different as it is conceived: it points out real outliers, not influential observations.

First experimental point indicated as outlier by the function `CleverLeastSquaresAnalysis` is the one minimizing the model mean square error when removed.

First experimental point indicated as influential observation by Cook statistics is the one causing the maximum variation in model parameters when removed.

These two criteria usually point out different experiments; the only way to get the same result is given by outliers that are, at the same time, even influential observations. Criteria are compared through the next example, proposed by Draper and Smith (1998).

Example 4.10

Use an object of the `BzzLinearRegression` class to analyze data using the functions `RobustAnalysis, CleverLeastSquaresAnalysis,` and `InfluentialObservations`.
The program is

```
#include "BzzMath.hpp"
void main(void)
   {
   BzzVector x(21,15.,26.,10.,9.,15.,20.,18.,11.,8.,
         20.,7.,9.,10.,11.,11.,10.,12.,42.,17.,
         11.,10.);
   BzzVector y(21,95.,71.,83.,91.,102.,87.,93.,100.,
         104.,94.,113.,96.,83.,84.,102.,100.,105.,57.,
         121.,85.,100.);
   BzzMatrix F(21,2);
   F.SetColumn(1,1.);
   F.SetColumn(2,x);
   BzzLinearRegression linReg(F,y);
   linReg.LeastSquaresAnalysis();
   linReg.RobustAnalysis();
   linReg.CleverLeastSquaresAnalysis();
   linReg.InfluentialObservations();
   }
```

The function `RobustAnalysis` leads to the following results:
`Outliers sorted by importance:`
    `19 13 3`

The function `CleverLeastSquaresAnalysis` leads to the following results:

```
=========================================
Clever Least Squares Regression Analysis
=========================================
** Iteration 0
numExperiments: 21 Mse: 1.228e+002
** Iteration 1
numExperiments: 20 Mse: 7.563e+001
>>> Probable Outliers: 19 ** WARNING **
** Iteration 2
numExperiments: 19 Mse: 6.720e+001
>>> Probable Outliers: 19 13 ** WARNING **
** Iteration 3
numExperiments: 18 Mse: 5.570e+001
Possible Outliers: 19 13 3
** Iteration 4
numExperiments: 17 Mse: 4.516e+001
Possible Outliers: 19 13 3 14
** Iteration 5
numExperiments: 16 Mse: 3.301e+001
Possible Outliers: 19 13 3 14 20
** Iteration 6
numExperiments: 15 Mse: 2.325e+001
Possible Outliers: 19 13 3 14 20 4
** Iteration 7
numExperiments: 14 Mse: 1.829e+001
Possible Outliers: 19 13 3 14 20 4 2
** Iteration 8
numExperiments: 13 Mse: 1.286e+001
Possible Outliers: 19 13 3 14 20 4 2 12
** Iteration 9
numExperiments: 12 Mse: 1.116e+001
Possible Outliers: 19 13 3 14 20 4 2 12 5
```

According to the experimental error variance, the analysis identifies the following experiments as outliers: 19, 13, and 3.
The function `InfluentialObservations` leads to the following results:

```
=========================
Influential Observations
=========================
 18 1.00e+000 6.45e+001
 19 5.72e-001 3.69e+001
```

```
 2 3.44e-001 2.22e+001
13 3.22e-001 2.08e+001
 3 3.22e-001 2.08e+001
11 2.85e-001 1.84e+001
14 2.63e-001 1.69e+001
20 2.43e-001 1.57e+001
 4 1.92e-001 1.24e+001
17 1.63e-001 1.05e+001
 5 1.62e-001 1.04e+001
10 1.51e-001 9.73e+000
15 8.96e-002 5.78e+000
12 8.13e-002 5.24e+000
 9 7.64e-002 4.92e+000
 7 6.84e-002 4.41e+000
 8 5.05e-002 3.26e+000
 1 3.70e-002 2.39e+000
21 3.02e-002 1.95e+000
16 3.02e-002 1.95e+000
 6 6.79e-003 4.38e-001
```

Note that the sequence of possible outliers come out with the function Clever-LeastSquaresAnalysis does not include the experimental point no. 18, which is instead the most influential observation according to Cook statistics.

Cook method identifies experiment no. 19 as second influential observation; rather, it is only a coincidence as Cook statistics is not aimed at identifying outliers, contrary to the functions RobustAnalysis and CleverLeastSquaresAnalysis.

4.7
y-Outliers, X-Outliers, and F-Outliers

By considering the vector of experimental **y** as a statistical variable, it is possible to identify its outliers by the technique described in Chapter 2, which consists of adopting either the median and the *mad* or the clever mean and clever variance to evaluate standardized robust residuals.

Outliers detected by the analysis of standardized robust residuals of the vector **y** are called *y-outliers*.

y-outliers point out which experimental points have different values of *y* against the other experiments.

It is a serious mistake to consider these outliers as real outliers for a given model.

It is even possible to consider each column of the matrix **F** as a vector and to get outliers from them by the same procedure.

Outliers obtained by the analysis of standardized robust residuals of the columns of the matrix **F** are called *F-outliers*.

F-outliers point out which experimental points have different values in the columns of the matrix **F** against the other experiments.

It is a serious mistake to consider these outliers as real outliers for a given model.

During the robust analysis carried out with an object of the `BzzLinearRegression` class, standardized robust residuals are calculated and, if necessary, highlighted for both the vector **y** and the columns of the matrix **F**.

Finally, if support abscissas **x** are known for each experimental point, it is possible to create the matrix **X** and adopt the same procedure as used in the case of the matrix **F**.

Outliers obtained by the analysis of standardized robust residuals of the various columns of the matrix **X** are called *X-outliers*.

X-outliers point out which experimental points have different values in the columns of the matrix **X** against the other experiments.

It is a serious mistake to consider these outliers as real outliers for a given model.

It is worth remarking that once an object of the `BzzVector` class is assigned, it is possible to calculate its robust residuals by the function
```
BzzVector rn;
    rn = ResidualsRobustDeviate(y);
```

Moreover, each column of a `BzzMatrix` may be obtained by the function
```
    BzzVector c;
    c = F.GetColumn(i);
```

4.8
Secluded Observations

Any experimental point that is isolated with respect to other points is called *secluded observation*.

Consider the generic linear model (3.1) constituted by p functions and n_X independent variables **x**.

An observation may be secluded in the following distinct spaces:

- In the normal space of independent variables x_i.
- In the space of principal components of the matrix **X**.
- In the space of columns of the matrix **F**.
- In the space of principal components of the matrix **F**.
- In the space of dependent variable y.

For the sake of simplicity, let us consider a problem with two independent variables x_1 and x_2 (problems with a single independent variable are an atypical case; it shall be discussed later).

In such a space, the reciprocal distance among experimental points is trivial to calculate. The minimum distance between a point and all the other ones is to be found; the experiment that presents the maximum of this minimum distance is the secluded point in this space.

On the other hand, consider the space of principal components of the matrix **X** consisting of all experimental points. Here, axes are orthogonal and their directions can be easily obtained by exploiting SVD factorization of the matrix **X**. Moreover, each axis has a relevance factor just proportional to the corresponding coefficient of the SVD factorization. Thus, two experiments placed on the principal axis are far c in the normal space, whereas they are far c/d_1 in the space of principal components. Analogously, two points placed on the second axis are far c in the normal space, whereas they are far c/d_2 in the other space. As $d_1 \geq d_2$, the distance along the second axis is usually significantly enlarged against the main axis in the space of principal component.

This is the reason that makes mainly secluded all the experiments placed on directions that are orthogonal to the principal components.

When experimental points are aligned, the principal axis is oriented in the direction of the experiments, and the secondary axis becomes orthogonal.

What is mentioned for the **x**-space is also valid for the space of columns of the matrix **F**. Obviously, if **F** and **X** are the same matrix, even the two spaces coincide.

In the one-dimensional case, there is no difference between normal and principal component spaces.

Contrary to influential observations, note that outliers have no effects on the evaluation of secluded observations unless gross errors affect **x** or the matrix **F**. In the case of secluded observations investigated in the space of **X**, errors only on **x** could perturb their evaluation.

Some authors call *leverage* those outliers coming from an error in building the matrix **F**.

If X is an object of the `BzzMatrix` class, the function `X.GetSecludedObservations()` allows to obtain both secluded observations and X-outliers.

Example 4.11

Use an object X of the `BzzMatrix` class to get secluded observations and X-outliers. The program is

```
#include "BzzMath.hpp"
void main(void)
  {
  BzzMatrix X(7,2,
    0.,0., 2.,2., 4.,4., 6.,
```

```
            6.,7.,7., 10.,10., 4.,6.);
    X.GetSecludedObservations();
}
```

While the experiment (10., 10.) is secluded from the remaining ones in the *x*-space (it is far 4.24 from the experiment (7., 7.)), the farthest point in the space of principal components X is (4., 6.), which is far 1. from the experiment (0., 0.). In this latter space, previous points are distant .21.

4.9
Robust Indices

Some indices such as R^2 and R_a^2 were already introduced for the least sum of squares method, in order to give information on the correctness of the linear regression. Since these indices are based on the use of nonrobust estimators, such as the arithmetic mean, they are also subject to all those abovementioned problems related to the high sensitivity to outliers.

In this context, other indices must replace the others that were introduced in the previous paragraph:

$$R^2 = 1 - \left(\frac{median|y_i - \hat{y}_i|}{mad(y_i)}\right)^2 \tag{4.14}$$

for models with intercept, and

$$R^2 = 1 - \left(\frac{median|y_i - \hat{y}_i|}{median|y_i|}\right)^2 \tag{4.15}$$

for models without intercept. In the `BzzLinearRegression` class, such indices are evaluated during the robust analysis by the function `RobustAnalysis` and are printed on the item `Coefficient of Determination`

4.10
Normality Condition

It is hard to check whether the experimental error is normally distributed as required in the basic hypotheses.

The technique adopted in the ***BzzMath*** library is based on the following procedure. Standardized residuals **r** are calculated and sorted by value. The vector:

$$f_i = \frac{i - .5}{n_E}, \quad i = 1, ..., n_E \tag{4.16}$$

is then calculated. Thus, a test to verify whether vectors **r** and **f** are linearly dependent is carried out

$$\cos \varphi = \frac{\mathbf{r}^T\mathbf{f}}{\|\mathbf{r}\|_2 \|\mathbf{f}\|_2} \tag{4.17}$$

If $\cos \varphi > .95$, the normality condition seems to be verified; the condition could be violated, otherwise.

This test is not so reliable. The user should consider with care its problem to realize whether the experimental error variance is constant and if the error is normally distributed.

A check on the normality condition is performed through the index (4.17) in the function `LeastSquaresAnalysis`.

4.11
Heteroscedasticity Condition

In the ***BzzMath*** library, two indices are adopted to detect a possible violation of homoscedasticity condition.

Both the indices require the calculation of standard robust residuals and the median *mr* of their absolute values.

The first index requires the calculation of the maximum absolute value of robust residuals. If the ratio between *mr* and this maximum value is smaller than .2, the homoscedasticity condition is probably violated.

The second index requires the arithmetic mean *ma* of the absolute values of robust residuals.

The homoscedasticity condition is probably violated when

$$\frac{|mr - ma|}{ma} > .3 \tag{4.18}$$

An object of the `BzzLinearRegression` class can check the possible violation of homoscedasticity condition by the function `Homoscedasticity-Analysis()`.

Example 4.12

Use an object of the `BzzLinearRegression` class to analyze the data collected into the file `Leverage.lrg` by the function `HomoscedasticityAnalysis`.

The program is

```
#include "BzzMath.hpp"
void main(void)
   {
```

4.11 Heteroscedasticity Condition

```
BzzLinearRegression linReg("Leverage.lrg");
linReg.HomoscedasticityAnalysis();
}
```

The following warnings are printed out:

```
First index 8.825500e-003 ** WARNING **
Possible violation of homoscedasticity hypothesis

Second index 9.067467e-001 ** WARNING **
Possible violation of homoscedasticity hypothesis
```

5
Linear Regression Case Studies

Examples of this chapter can be found in the directory `Vol2_Chapter5` within the enclosed CD-ROM.

5.1
Introduction

This chapter proposes some typical regression problems that are linear in parameters with a single dependent variable and different degrees of complexity.

5.2
Ferrari F1's Test

The first trivial example is proposed to underline two caveats of Chapter 3: the importance of a deep understanding of the physical phenomena that are behind the model and of the risk involved in assigning a certain relevance to the numerical value of a specific parameter when one is not sure whether the same model is good or not.

Example 5.1

Let us consider lap times of a portion of a Formula 1 Grand Prix as experimental data. A parameter indicating tire consumption is adopted as an independent variable. Such a parameter has an initial value equal to 5. and a final value equal to 1.4.

The proposed model is

$$y_i = \beta_1 + \beta_2 x_{1i} + \beta_3 x_{1i}^2 + \varepsilon_i \qquad (5.1)$$

Experimental data can be directly acquired with the following program:

Interpolation and Regression Models for the Chemical Engineer: Solving Numerical Problems
Guido Buzzi-Ferraris and Flavio Manenti
Copyright © 2010 WILEY-VCH Verlag GmbH & Co. KGaA, Weinheim
ISBN: 978-3-527-32652-5

```
#include "BzzMath.hpp"
void main(void)
  {
  int i,numExperiments = 19;
  BzzMatrix F(numExperiments,3);
  double gx,gStart = 5.;
  double gEnd = 1.4;
  BzzVector y(numExperiments,
    7.414000e+001,7.391600e+001,7.371400e+001,
    7.350400e+001,7.334600e+001,7.316000e+001,
    7.341600e+001,7.288400e+001,7.273400e+001,
    7.262500e+001,7.253000e+001,7.243600e+001,
    7.234300e+001,7.226400e+001,7.223600e+001,
    7.218000e+001,7.212600e+001,7.212400e+001,
    7.211400e+001);
  for(i = 1;i <= numExperiments;i++)
    {
    gx = - gStart * double(i - 19)/18. +
       gEnd * double(i - 1)/18.;
    F[i][1] = 1.;
    F[i][2] = gx;
    F[i][3] = gx * gx;
    }
  BzzLinearRegression linReg(F,y);
  linReg.LeastSquaresAnalysis();
  }
```

Analyzing results, the model is

$$y_i = 72.25 - .312 x_{1i} + .138 x_{1i}^2 + \varepsilon_i \tag{5.2}$$

According to the second parameter, it seems that tire consumption leads to a decrease in lap times.

Example 5.2

The model of Example 5.1 neglects an important aspect: gasoline load is the real factor responsible for lap time reduction. The proper model selected according to the physical phenomenon is

$$y_i = \beta_1 + \beta_2 x_{2i} + \beta_3 x_{1i}^2 + \varepsilon_i \tag{5.3}$$

where the variable x_2 is the gasoline load; it changes from the initial 100 kg to the final value of 10 kg after 19 laps.

```
#include "BzzMath.hpp"
void main(void)
  {
  int i,numExperiments = 19;
  BzzMatrix F(numExperiments,3);
  double gx,gStart = 5.;
  double gEnd = 1.4;
  double bx,bStart = 100.;
  double bEnd = 10.;
  BzzVector y(numExperiments,
    7.414000e+001,7.391600e+001,7.371400e+001,
    7.350400e+001,7.334600e+001,7.316000e+001,
    7.341600e+001,7.288400e+001,7.273400e+001,
    7.262500e+001,7.253000e+001,7.243600e+001,
    7.234300e+001,7.226400e+001,7.223600e+001,
    7.218000e+001,7.212600e+001,7.212400e+001,
    7.211400e+001);
  for(i = 1;i <= numExperiments;i++)
    {
    bx = - bStart * double(i - 19)/18. +
    bEnd * double(i - 1)/18.;
    gx = - gStart * double(i - 19)/18. +
      gEnd * double(i - 1)/18.;
    F[i][1] = 1.;
    F[i][2] = bx;
    F[i][3] = gx * gx;
    }
  BzzLinearRegression linReg(F,y);
  linReg.LeastSquaresAnalysis();
  linReg.RobustAnalysis();
  linReg.CleverLeastSquaresAnalysis();
  }
```

The model results

$$y_i = 71.94 - .0125 x_{2i} + .138 x_{1i}^2 + \varepsilon_i \tag{5.4}$$

Therefore, tire contribution is defined by only the third term and it shows that after an initial improvement, tire consumption unavoidably worsens the performance.

Examining data by functions RobustAnalysis and CleverLeastSquaresAnalysis, the experimental point no. 7 is pointed out as an outlier. In correspondence with this lap, a car was lapped.

5.3
Best Model Formulation

Model formulation is an essential point in model analysis, even though the model is linear. As already highlighted in previous chapters, there are two more advantages in solving this kind of problems against the solution of an over-dimensioned system: the possibility to properly reformulate (reparameterize) the model and to introduce some additional experimental points. They both make the system better conditioned.

Example 5.3

Consider the model

$$y_i = \beta_1 + \beta_2 x_{1i} + \beta_3 x_{1i}^2 + \varepsilon_i \tag{5.5}$$

Experimental data can be directly acquired with the following program:

```
#include "BzzMath.hpp"
void main(void)
  {
  BzzMatrix F(5,3,
    1.,1.e-5,1.e-10,
    1.,1.0002e-5,1.00040004e-10,
    1.,1.0005e-5,1.00100025e-10,
    1.,1.0008e-5,1.00160064e-10,
    1.,1.001e-5,1.002001e-10);
  BzzVector y(5,
    7.009012e+005,7.01181408e+005,7.01601825e+005,
    7.02022368e+005,7.023028e+005);
  BzzLinearRegression linReg(F,y);
  linReg.LeastSquaresAnalysis();
  }
```

The resulting system is surely ill conditioned as columns no. 2 and 3 have small values compared to the first column.

Actually, the condition number is very large, `1.013051e+017`, whereas the system conditioning is significantly smaller: `6.073711e+003`.

The correlation matrix, inflation factors, and tolerances point out strong correlations among parameters.

It unequivocally shows that the model must be reformulated: if the system were a generic overdimensioned system, the only possibility to improve it would be to write it in the standard form, that is, matrix columns must be divided by their corresponding maximum value.

Example 5.4

Transform the previous system by dividing the second column by 10^{-5} and the third column by 10^{-10}.

The program is

```
#include "BzzMath.hpp"
void main(void)
  {
  BzzMatrix F(5,3,
    1.,1.,1., 1.,1  .0002,1.00040004,
    1.,1.0005,1.00100025, 1.,1.0008,1.00160064,
    1.,1.001,1.002001);
  BzzVector y(5,
    7.009012e+005,7.01181408e+005,7.01601825e+005,
    7.02022368e+005,7.023028e+005);
  BzzLinearRegression linReg(F,y);
  linReg.LeastSquaresAnalysis();
  }
```

The condition number is still large: $4.302313e + 007$. The correlation matrix, inflation factors, and tolerances point out strong correlations among parameters.

Therefore, this device is not enough to remove correlations among the columns of the system.

Example 5.5

As the previous system was generated by the search for parameters of the model

$$y_i = \beta_1 + \beta_2 x_{1i} + \beta_3 x_{1i}^2 + \varepsilon_i \tag{5.6}$$

it is possible to reformulate the model so as to obtain a better conditioned system. For this purpose, it is important to remark that the Lagrange form is always well conditioned:

$$\begin{aligned} y_i &= \beta_1 \frac{(x_{1i}-\bar{x}_1)(x_{1i}-x_{1\max})}{(x_{1\min}-\bar{x}_1)(x_{1\min}-x_{1\max})} + \beta_2 \frac{(x_{1i}-x_{1\min})(x_{1i}-x_{1\max})}{(\bar{x}_1-x_{1\min})(\bar{x}_1-x_{1\max})} \\ &+ \beta_3 \frac{(x_{1i}-x_{1\min})(x_{1i}-\bar{x}_1)}{(x_{1\max}-x_{1\min})(x_{1\max}-\bar{x}_1)} + \varepsilon_i \end{aligned} \tag{5.7}$$

The program is

```
#include "BzzMath.hpp"
void main(void)
  {
  BzzMatrix F(5,3);
```

```
    BzzVector y(5,
      7.009012e+005,7.01181408e+005,7.01601825e+005,
      7.02022368e+005,7.023028e+005);
    int i;
    BzzVector t(5,1000.,1000.2,1000.5,1000.8,1001.);
    for(i = 1;i <= 5;i++)
      {
      F[i][1] = (t[i] - 1000.5)*(t[i] - 1001.)/(.5);
      F[i][2] = (t[i] - 1000.)*(t[i] - 1001.)/
                ((.5)*(-.5));
      F[i][3] = (t[i] - 1000.)*(t[i] - 1000.5)/(.5);
      }
    BzzLinearRegression linReg(F,y);
    linReg.LeastSquaresAnalysis();
    }
```

The condition number is good, $1.395994e+000$, and neither the correlation matrix nor the inflation factors identify any correlation among parameters. In addition, even tolerances are significantly good.

As a result, this device is sufficient to remove model parameter correlations.

Example 5.6

Consider the model

$$y_i = \beta_1 + \beta_2 x_{1i} + \beta_3 x_{2i} + \beta_4 x_{1i} x_{2i} + \beta_5 x_{1i}^2 + \beta_6 x_{2i}^2 + \varepsilon_i \tag{5.8}$$

Experimental data can be directly acquired with the following program:

```
#include "BzzMath.hpp"
void main(void)
  {
  BzzMatrix F(17,6);
  BzzVector y(17,
2.923e+006,3.327e+006,3.766e+006,2.957e+006,3.332e+006,
3.777e+006,2.945e+006,3.342e+006,3.799e+006,3.116e+006,
3.324e+006,3.553e+006,3.128e+006,3.561e+006,3.131e+006,
  3.359e+006,3.569e+006);
  BzzMatrix X(17,2,
      750.,10.,  800.,10., 850.,10., 750.,15.,
      800.,15.,  850.,15., 750.,20., 800.,20.,
      850.,20.,  775.,12.5, 800.,12.5, 825.,12.5,
      775.,15.,  825.,15., 775.,17.5, 800.,17.5,
      825.,17.5);
  for(int i = 1;i <= 17;i++)
```

```
{
F[i][1] = 1.;
F[i][2] = X[i][1];
F[i][3] = X[i][2];
F[i][4] = X[i][1] * X[i][2];
F[i][5] = X[i][1] * X[i][1];
F[i][6] = X[i][2] * X[i][2];
}
BzzLinearRegression linReg(F,y);
linReg.SetVariance(8.2e7,4);
linReg.LeastSquaresAnalysis();
}
```

The condition number is significantly large: $4.078560e+008$.
Inflation factors point out strong parameter correlations: the maximum value is $1.6171883e+006$. Even tolerances show correlations among parameters: the minimum value is $3.5943041e\text{-}004$.

Example 5.7

If the variables of previous example are normalized as follows

$$y_i = \beta_1 + \beta_2 t_{1i} + \beta_3 t_{2i} + \beta_4 t_{1i} t_{2i} + \beta_5 t_{1i}^2 + \beta_6 t_{2i}^2 + \varepsilon_i$$

$$t_{1i} = \frac{x_{1i} - 800.}{50.}$$

$$t_{2i} = \frac{x_{2i} - 15.}{5.}$$

(5.9)

the condition number shrinks to $3.422260e+000$; inflation factors do not identify any correlation among parameters: the maximum value is $2.6513761e+000$; and tolerances are good: the minimum value is $9.0577897e\text{-}001$.
The mean square error is satisfactory:

```
Mean Square Error = 9.2692581e+007
F-test for the model
Fexperimental = 1.130397e+000
The probability that F with dfNum 11 dfDen 4
is greater than 1.130397e+000 is 4.956225e-001

Examining t-tests, parameters β4 and β6 seem to be
irrelevant:

Par.    T-Value           P-Value
1       9.3353682e+002    2.6765343e-028
```

```
2    1.2786706e+002  8.3795015e-019
3    4.1533609e+000  1.6072904e-003
4    6.0263053e-001  5.5897321e-001 ** WARNING **
5    4.7780630e+000  5.7319676e-004
6   -9.8118098e-001  3.4759133e-001 ** WARNING **
```

Actually, either a small value of the corresponding T-Value or a high value of the corresponding P-Value shows the possibility that the parameter could be removed.

Example 5.8

By removing irrelevant parameters of Example 5.7, the following model is obtained:

$$t_{1i} = \frac{x_{1i} - 800.}{50.}$$

$$t_{2i} = \frac{x_{2i} - 15.}{5.} \qquad (5.10)$$

$$y_i = \beta_1 + \beta_2 t_{1i} + \beta_3 t_{2i} + \beta_4 t_{1i}^2 + \varepsilon_i$$

The model is satisfactory:

```
Mean Square Error = 8.6795425e+007
F-test for the model
Fexperimental = 1.058481e+000
The probability that F with dfNum 13 dfDen 4
is greater than 1.058481e+000 is 5.308812e-001
```

and even the robust analysis does not point out any outlier.

5.4
Outliers

As mentioned in the previous chapter, outliers can be generated by

- Poor quality data (gross errors)
- Model inadequacy
- Experimental drawbacks
- Heteroscedasticity condition

Following examples shall consider all these possibilities.

5.4.1
Outliers Generated by Poor Quality Data

One important case leading to the presence of outliers is the poor quality of a single experimental point or, generally speaking, of the experimental data set. It might occur for several reasons, such as bad experimentation, transcription error, misprint, and so on.

In this case, the total amount of outliers is rarely larger than few experiments.

Example 5.9

Let us insert two outliers in the experimental data set of a model. This example is aimed at checking whether the program can detect them.

For this purpose, data of Example 5.6 were modified as follows:

- $y_{17} = 3.869 \cdot 10^6$, whereas the original value was $y_{17} = 3.569 \cdot 10^6$;
- $x_{4,1} = 760.$, whereas the original value was $x_{4,1} = 750.$

Experimental data can be directly acquired with the following program. The experimental error variance obtained with 4 degrees of freedom is equal to $8.2 \cdot 10^7$.

The program is

```
#include "BzzMath.hpp"
void main(void)
  {
  BzzMatrix F(17,4);
  BzzVector y(17,
      2.923e+006,3.327e+006,3.766e+006,2.957e+006,
      3.332e+006,3.777e+006,2.945e+006,3.342e+006,
      3.799e+006,3.116e+006,3.324e+006,3.553e+006,
      3.128e+006,3.561e+006,3.131e+006,3.359e+006,
//    3.569e+006);
      3.869e+006);
  BzzMatrix X(17,2,
      750.,10.,   800.,10.,   850.,10.,
//    750.,15.,
      760.,15.,
      800.,15.,   850.,15.,   750.,20.,   800.,20.,
      850.,20.,   775.,12.5,  800.,12.5,  825.,12.5,
      775.,15.,   825.,15.,   775.,17.5,  800.,17.5,
      825.,17.5);
  double x1,x2;
  int i;
  for(i = 1;i <= 17;i++)
      {
```

```
            x1 = (X[i][1] - 800.) / 50.;
            x2 = (X[i][2] - 15.) / 5.;
            F[i][1] = 1.;
            F[i][2] = x1;
            F[i][3] = x2;
            F[i][4] = x1 * x1;
        }
    BzzLinearRegression linReg(F,y);
    linReg.SetVariance(8.2e7,4);
    linReg.LeastSquaresAnalysis();
    linReg.RobustAnalysis();
    linReg.CleverLeastSquaresAnalysis();
    BzzVector str;
    linReg.GetStudentizedResiduals(&str);
    str.BzzPrint("str");
    }
```

Residuals of the robust analysis are

```
 1  2.9230000e+006  2.9242467e+006 -1.2467077e+003 -0.17
 2  3.3270000e+006  3.3197498e+006  7.2502421e+003  0.98
 3  3.7660000e+006  3.7652564e+006  7.4363909e+002  0.10
 4  2.9570000e+006  3.0103492e+006 -5.3349195e+004 -7.23*
 5  3.3320000e+006  3.3307519e+006  1.2480802e+003  0.17
 6  3.7770000e+006  3.7762585e+006  7.4147717e+002  0.10
 7  2.9450000e+006  2.9462510e+006 -1.2510316e+003 -0.17
 8  3.3420000e+006  3.3417541e+006  2.4591829e+002  0.03
 9  3.7990000e+006  3.7872607e+006  1.1739315e+004  1.59
10  3.1160000e+006  3.1212489e+006 -5.2488696e+003 -0.71
11  3.3240000e+006  3.3252508e+006 -1.2508388e+003 -0.17
12  3.5530000e+006  3.5417537e+006  1.1246304e+004  1.52
13  3.1280000e+006  3.1267500e+006  1.2500494e+003  0.17
14  3.5610000e+006  3.5472548e+006  1.3745223e+004  1.86
15  3.1310000e+006  3.1322510e+006 -1.2510316e+003 -0.17
16  3.3590000e+006  3.3362530e+006  2.2746999e+004  3.08*
17  3.8690000e+006  3.5527559e+006  3.1624414e+005 42.88*

These are highly probable Outliers: 17
These are possible Outliers: 4 16
```

The resulting model with parameters evaluated by the method of the least sum of squares is

$$y_i = 3.36 \cdot 10^6 + 4.54 \cdot 10^5 f_{2i} + 3.37 \cdot 10^4 f_{3i} - 6.93 \cdot 10^3 f_{4i} \qquad (5.11)$$

Conversely, the robust method leads to

$$y_i = 3.33 \cdot 10^6 + 4.205 \cdot 10^5 f_{2i} + 1.1 \cdot 10^4 f_{3i} + 2.5 \cdot 10^4 f_{4i} \tag{5.12}$$

Since these methods bring about different model parameter estimates, the outliers are even *influential observations* (see Section 4.6).

The analysis performed by the function `CleverLeastSquaresAnalysis` leads to the following results:

```
=========================================
Clever Least Squares Regression Analysis
=========================================

** Iteration 0
numExperiments: 17 Mse: 6.446e+009
** Iteration 1
numExperiments: 16 Mse: 2.343e+008
>>> Probable Outliers: 17 ** WARNING **
** Iteration 2
numExperiments: 15 Mse: 5.324e+007
>>>>>> Highly Probable Outliers: 17 4 ** WARNING **
** Iteration 3
numExperiments: 14 Mse: 2.895e+007
>>> Probable Outliers: 17 4 16 ** WARNING **
** Iteration 4
numExperiments: 13 Mse: 2.333e+007
Possible Outliers: 17 4 16 14
```

Therefore, the function `CleverLeastSquaresAnalysis` detects the real outliers.

The experiment no. 17 only looks like an outlier by the studentized residuals analysis, while the experiment no. 4 remains undetected.

Example 5.10

This example shows how the analysis of studentized residuals may be erroneous in detecting outliers when the matrix **F** has strong correlations. If the condition number of the matrix **F** is large, the hat matrix, on which studentized residuals are based, is evaluated in an inaccurate way.

Introduce an outlier in the experimental of Example 5.6, where the matrix is ill conditioned, by changing the 11th coefficient of **y** from the original value $3.324e+006$ to the new one $3.356e+006$.

The program is

```
#include "BzzMath.hpp"
void main(void)
  {
  BzzMatrix F(17,6);
  BzzVector y(17,
2.923e+006,3.327e+006,3.766e+006,2.957e+006,3.332e+006,
3.777e+006,2.945e+006,3.342e+006,3.799e+006,3.116e+006,
   // 3.324e+006,
  3.356e+006,
  3.553e+006,3.128e+006,3.561e+006,3.131e+006,
  3.569e+006);
  BzzMatrix X(17,2,
     750.,10.,   800.,10.,   850.,10.,   750.,15.,
     800.,15.,   850.,15.,   750.,20.,   800.,20.,
     850.,20.,   775.,12.5,  800.,12.5,  825.,12.5,
     775.,15.,   825.,15.,   775.,17.5,  800.,17.5,
     825.,17.5);
  for(int i = 1;i <= 17;i++)
    {
    F[i][1] = 1.;
    F[i][2] = X[i][1];
    F[i][3] = X[i][2];
    F[i][4] = X[i][1] * X[i][2];
    F[i][5] = X[i][1] * X[i][1];
    F[i][6] = X[i][2] * X[i][2];
    }
  BzzLinearRegression linReg(F,y);
  linReg.SetVariance(8.2e7,4);
  linReg.RobustAnalysis();
  linReg.CleverLeastSquaresAnalysis();
  BzzVector str;
  linReg.GetStudentizedResiduals(&str);
  str.BzzPrint("str");
  }
```

Residuals evaluated by the least sum of squares method do not highlight any outlier. Conversely, the robust method does it:

```
11 3.3560000e+006 3.3193877e+006 3.6612338e+004 2.55**
```

Even the function `CleverLeastSquaresAnalysis` points out the same experiment as the most probable outlier:

```
** Iteration 0
numExperiments: 17 Mse: 1.346e+008
** Iteration 1
numExperiments: 16 Mse: 9.727e+007
```

```
>>> Probable Outliers: 11 ** WARNING **
** Iteration 2
numExperiments: 15 Mse: 6.179e+007
>>> Probable Outliers: 11 4 ** WARNING **
** Iteration 3
numExperiments: 14 Mse: 3.999e+007
>>> Probable Outliers: 11 4 16 ** WARNING **
```

Conversely, studentized residuals detect the experiment no. 9 as the most probable outlier.

Example 5.11

Hawkins, Bradu, and Kass (1984) originally proposed this example to test robust methods. It consists of 75 experimental points and 3 independent variables. The model is with intercept and was used to generate the experimental data set. First 10 experiments were intentionally modified and, as they are gross errors, they should be pointed out as outliers. Experimental data can be directly acquired with the following program:

```
#include "BzzMath.hpp"
void main(void)
   {
   int numExperiments = 75;
   BzzVector x1(numExperiments,
       10.1,9.5,10.7,9.9,10.3,10.8,10.5,9.9,9.7,9.3,
       11.,12.,12.,11.,3.4,3.1,0.,2.3,0.8,3.1,2.6,.4,
       2.,1.3,1.,.9,3.3,1.8,1.2,1.2,3.1,.5,1.5,.4,3.1,
       1.1,.1,1.5,2.1,.5,3.4,.3,.1,1.8,1.9,1.8,3.,3.1,
       3.1,2.1,2.3,3.3,.3,1.1,.5,1.8,1.8,2.4,1.6,.3,
       .4,.8,1.1,2.8,2.,.2,1.6,.1,2.,1.,2.2,.6,.3,0.,.3);
   BzzVector x2(numExperiments,
       19.6,20.5,20.2,21.5,21.1,20.4,20.9,19.6,20.7,19.7,
       24.,23.,26.,34.,2.9,2.2,1.6,1.6,2.9,3.4,2.2,3.2,
       2.3,2.3,0.,3.3,2.5,.8,.9,.7,1.4,2.4,3.1,0.,2.4,
       2.2,3.,1.2,0.,2.,1.6,1.,3.3,.5,.1,.5,.1,1.6,2.5,
       2.8,1.5,.6,.4,3.,2.4,3.2,.7,3.4,2.1,1.5,3.4,.1,
       2.7,3.,.7,1.8,2.,0.,.6,2.2,2.5,2.,1.7,2.2,.4);
   BzzVector x3(numExperiments,
       28.3,28.9,31.,31.7,31.1,29.2,29.1,28.8,31.,30.3,
       35.,37.,34.,34.,2.1,.3,.2,2.,1.6,2.2,1.9,1.9,.8,
       .5,.4,2.5,2.9,2.,.8,3.4,1.,.3,1.5,.7,3.,2.7,2.6,
       .2,1.2,1.2,2.9,2.7,.9,3.2,.6,3.,.8,3.,1.9,2.9,
       .4,1.2,3.3,.3,.9,.9,.7,1.5,3.,3.3,3.,.3,.2,2.9,
       2.7,.8,1.2,1.1,.3,2.9,2.3,1.5,2.2,1.6,2.6);
```

```
    BzzMatrix F(numExperiments,4);
    BzzVector y(numExperiments,
        9.7,10.1,10.3,9.5,10.,10.,10.8,10.3,9.6,9.9,-.2,
        -.4,.7,.1,-.4,.6,-.2,0.,.1,.4,.9,.3,-.8,.7,-.3,
        -.8,-.7,.3,.3,-.3,0.,-.4,-.6,-.7,.3,-1.,-.6,.9,
        -.7,-.5,-.1,-.7,.6,-.7,-.5,-.4,-.9,.1,.9,-.4,
        .7,-.5,.7,.7,0.,.1,.7,-.1,-.3,-.9,-.3,.6,-.3,
        -.5,.6,-.9,-.7,.6,.2,.7,.2,-.2,.4,-.9,.2);
    F.SetColumn(1,1.);
    F.SetColumn(2,x1);
    F.SetColumn(3,x2);
    F.SetColumn(4,x3);
    BzzLinearRegression linReg(F,y);
//  linReg.SetVariance(1.e-1,1);
    linReg.LeastSquaresAnalysis();
    linReg.RobustAnalysis();
    linReg.CleverLeastSquaresAnalysis();
    BzzVector str;
    linReg.GetStudentizedResiduals(&str);
    str.BzzPrint("str");
    BzzVectorInt jF(4),iE(numExperiments - 10);
    int i;
    //select all columns
    for(i = 1;i <= 4;i++)
      jF(i) = i;
    for(i = 11;i <= numExperiments;i++)
      iE[i - 10] = i;
    BzzLinearRegression lg(F,y,jF,iE);
    lg.LeastSquaresAnalysis();
    }
```

The function `RobustAnalysis` detects these outliers as the most probable ones:

```
    Outliers sorted by importance:
    7 3 8 2 10 5 6 9 1 4
```

Moreover, it detects experiments 1–10 as y-outliers and experiments 1–14 as F-outliers.

Conversely, the function `CleverLeastSquaresAnalysis` detects this series:

```
    ** Iteration 0
    numExperiments: 75 Mse: 5.063e+000
    ** Iteration 1
    numExperiments: 74 Mse: 3.670e+000
    Possible Outliers: 12
    ** Iteration 2
    numExperiments: 73 Mse: 2.418e+000
```

```
>>> Probable Outliers: 12 11 ** WARNING **
** Iteration 3
numExperiments: 72 Mse: 1.477e+000
>>> Probable Outliers: 12 11 13 ** WARNING **
** Iteration 4
numExperiments: 71 Mse: 4.542e-001
>>> Probable Outliers: 12 11 13 14 ** WARNING **
** Iteration 5
numExperiments: 70 Mse: 4.329e-001
Possible Outliers: 12 11 13 14 38
** Iteration 6
numExperiments: 69 Mse: 4.109e-001
Possible Outliers: 12 11 13 14 38 62
** Iteration 7
numExperiments: 68 Mse: 3.864e-001
Possible Outliers: 12 11 13 14 38 62 68
** Iteration 8
numExperiments: 67 Mse: 3.684e-001
Possible Outliers: 12 11 13 14 38 62 68 27
** Iteration 9
numExperiments: 66 Mse: 3.523e-001
Possible Outliers: 12 11 13 14 38 62 68 27 57
** Iteration 10
numExperiments: 65 Mse: 3.105e-001
>>> Probable Outliers: 7 3 8 2 10 5 6 9 1 4 ** WARNING **
```

The 10 outliers are properly identified, even though they do not appear so significant as they reduce the model mean square error only slightly compared to other families of outliers.

If experiments no. 11, 12, 13, 14, 27, 38, 57, 62, and 68 were considered as outliers, the mean square error would be `3.523e-001`, whereas experiments no. 1–10 inserted as outliers lead to a mean square error equal to `3.105e-001`. There is no significant difference between them.

Even though this is a much-referenced artificial data set, largely adopted to test robust methods in finding out known outliers, it should not be used as the problem is ill posed.

By removing the 10 probable outliers and carrying out the thumb test, we get

$$\frac{\left(\frac{\hat{Y}_{max}-\hat{Y}_{min}}{2}\right)^2}{s^2} = \frac{\left(\frac{.315+.311}{2}\right)^2}{.31} = .33 < 1 \qquad (5.13)$$

with the obvious result of *pollice verso*! Experimental points have a variance that is significantly larger than the model variation: it is senseless to use such a model to match these data.

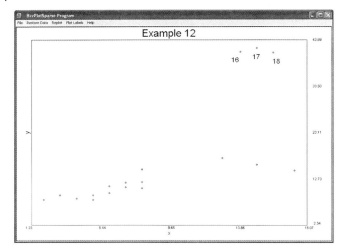

Figure 5.1 Original experimental data.

Moreover, this is again the problem already underlined in Chapter 4, where even though experiments are generated and some gross errors are introduced, they do not necessarily result outliers: if gross errors are, however, within the range of the experimental error, they cannot be considered outliers.

Even other authors (i.e., Ryan, 2009) criticized this example.

Example 5.12

This problem was originally proposed by Ryan (2009) to test robust methods. It consists of 18 experimental points and a single independent variable. Experimental points are visualized in Figure 5.1.

The examined model is linear. It is evident that the six points with the largest x can generate problems for the model.

Experimental data can be directly acquired with the following program:

```
#include "BzzMath.hpp"
void main(void)
  {
  int numExperiments = 18;
  BzzVector x1(numExperiments,
    2.,3.,4.,5.,5.,6.,6.,7.,7.,8.,8.,8.,
    12.9,15.,17.3,14.,15.,16.);
  BzzMatrix F(numExperiments,2);
  BzzVector y(numExperiments,
    8.,9.,8.3,8.,9.,9.5,11.,10.8,11.8,12.,
    10.6,14.8,17.3,15.9,14.6,41.1,42.,41.);
```

5.4 Outliers

```
     F.SetColumn(1,1.);
     F.SetColumn(2,x1);
     BzzLinearRegression linReg(F,y);
     linReg.LeastSquaresAnalysis();
     linReg.RobustAnalysis();
     linReg.CleverLeastSquaresAnalysis();
     BzzVector b,br;
     b = linReg.GetParameters();
     br = linReg.GetRobustParameters();
     BzzMatrixSparse Y(3,100);
     BzzMatrixSparse X(3,100);
     double x;
     for(i = 1; i <= 100;i++)
       {
       x = - 2. * double(i - 100)/99. +
           18. * double(i - 1)/99.;
       X(1,i) = x;
       Y(1,i) = b[1] + b[2] * x;
       X(2,i) = x;
       Y(2,i) = br[1] + br[2] * x;
       }
     for(i = 1;i <= numExperiments;i++)
       {
       X(3,i) = x1[i]; Y(3,i) = y[i];
       }
     BzzSave save("OulierEx10.stx");
     save << X << Y;
     save.End();
     system("BzzPlotSparse.exe");
     BzzPause();
     }
```

Analysis of the standardized residuals does not detect any outlier.

Robust analysis highlights three outliers: experiments no. 16, 17, and 18. As shown in Figure 5.2, the two models are very far from each other: the solid line is the model obtained by the method of least sum of squares, whereas the dotted line is the model obtained by robust analysis.

The function `CleverLeastSquaresAnalysis` identifies the following series of possible outliers:

```
    ** Iteration 0
    numExperiments: 18 Mse: 6.969e+001
    ** Iteration 1
    numExperiments: 17 Mse: 4.985e+001
    Possible Outliers: 15
    ** Iteration 2
```

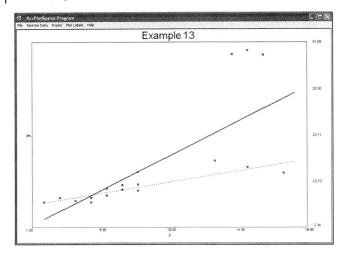

Figure 5.2 Possible linear models fitting data at the best.

```
numExperiments: 16 Mse: 3.222e+001
>>> Probable Outliers: 15 14 ** WARNING **
** Iteration 3
numExperiments: 15 Mse: 2.491e+000
>>>>>> Highly Probable Outliers: 17 16 18 ** WARNING **
** Iteration 4
numExperiments: 14 Mse: 1.740e+000
>>> Probable Outliers: 17 16 18 15 ** WARNING **
** Iteration 5
numExperiments: 13 Mse: 9.411e-001
>>> Probable Outliers: 17 16 18 12 13 ** WARNING **
```

Assuming only two outliers are present, experiments no. 14 and 15 are denoted as bad points. Conversely, assuming three outliers are present, the same points of the robust analysis are selected as bad points. Assuming five outliers are present, bad points are the experiments no. 17, 16, 18, 12, and 13.

It is evident that if experiments no. 16, 17, and 18 are not real gross errors, the homoscedasticity condition is violated.

 Be careful: **never delete** an outlier without being sure that it is a **real gross error**.

Example 5.13

This problem was originally proposed by Ryan (2009) to test robust methods. Three gross errors (experiments no. 28, 29, and 30) were introduced in the experimental data set.

5.4 Outliers

Experimental data can be directly acquired with the following program:

```
#include "BzzMath.hpp"
void main(void)
  {
  int numExperiments = 30;
  BzzVector x1(numExperiments,
    11.,14.,16.,18.,23.,22.,21.,20.,16.,12.,19.,17.,
    15.,13.,12.,24.,25.,20.,15.,10.,13.,15.,22.,24.,
    31.,32.,34.,31.,33.,35.);
  BzzVector x2(numExperiments,
    32.,28.,39.,35.,36.,42.,40.,41.,35.,33.,29.,46.,
    28.,31.,38.,41.,38.,41.,45.,44.,35.,26.,31.,48.,
    42.,58.,60.,63.,59.,66.);
  BzzVector x3(numExperiments,
    68.,50.,49.,61.,63.,66.,48.,64.,65.,53.,50.,59.,
    68.,52.,67.,62.,65.,53.,59.,61.,58.,50.,52.,68.,
    79.,78.,81.,82.,80.,85.);
  BzzMatrix F(numExperiments,4);
  BzzVector y(numExperiments,
    192.453,140.125,131.522,167.656,181.396,181.191,
    131.443,169.829,182.263,137.33,153.592,137.975,
    200.989,142.088,163.871,162.01,182.666,139.104,
    137.298,131.868,152.65,138.864,139.007,180.265,
    232.376,194.843,203.432,239.322,230.985,247.94);
  F.SetColumn(1,1.);
  F.SetColumn(2,x1);
  F.SetColumn(3,x2);
  F.SetColumn(4,x3);
  BzzLinearRegression linReg(F,y);
  linReg.LeastSquaresAnalysis();
  linReg.RobustAnalysis();
  linReg.CleverLeastSquaresAnalysis();
  BzzVector str;
  linReg.GetStudentizedResiduals(&str);
  str.BzzPrint("str");
  }
```

The robust method detects the following outliers sorted by their relevance:

28 30 29 1 9 3 24

As usual, the break point depends on the value adopted in standardizing robust residuals. In any case, the gross errors are the first three experiments pointed out by the analysis.

The function `CleverLeastSquaresAnalysis` detects the following series of possible outliers:

```
** Iteration 0
numExperiments: 30 Mse: 1.061e+002
** Iteration 1
numExperiments: 29 Mse: 8.836e+001
>>> Probable Outliers: 28 ** WARNING **
** Iteration 2
numExperiments: 28 Mse: 6.159e+001
>>> Probable Outliers: 28 30 ** WARNING **
** Iteration 3
numExperiments: 27 Mse: 3.866e+001
>>> Probable Outliers: 28 30 29 ** WARNING **
** Iteration 4
numExperiments: 26 Mse: 2.757e+001
Possible Outliers: 28 30 29 23
```

Therefore, the three outliers are detected by both functions `RobustAnalysis` and `CleverLeastSquaresAnalysis`.

Conversely, studentized residuals detect the experiments no. 28, 27, and 26 as probable outliers.

Example 5.14

Rousseeuw in Wadsworth's handbook (1990) proposed the present example related to Hertzsprung–Russell diagram for star cluster CYG OB1 to test robust methods. Experimental data can be directly acquired with the following program:

```
#include "BzzMath.hpp"
void main(void)
  {
  int numExperiments = 47;
  BzzVector x1(numExperiments,
    4.37,4.56,4.26,4.56,4.3,4.46,3.84,4.57,4.26,
    4.37,3.49,4.43,4.48,4.01,4.29,4.42,4.23,4.42,
    4.23,3.49,4.29,4.29,4.42,4.49,4.38,4.42,4.29,
    4.38,4.22,3.48,4.38,4.56,4.45,3.49,4.23,4.62,
    4.53,4.45,4.53,4.43,4.38,4.45,4.5,4.45,4.55,
    4.45,4.42);
  BzzMatrix F(numExperiments,2);
  BzzVector y(numExperiments,
    5.23,5.74,4.93,5.74,5.19,5.46,4.65,5.27,5.57,
    5.12,5.73,5.45,5.42,4.05,4.26,4.58,3.94,4.18,
    4.18,5.89,4.38,4.22,4.42,4.85,5.02,4.66,4.66,
```

```
    4.9,4.39,6.05,4.42,5.1,5.22,6.29,4.34,5.62,
    5.1,5.22,5.18,5.57,4.62,5.06,5.34,5.34,5.54,
    4.98,4.5);
F.SetColumn(1,1.);
F.SetColumn(2,x1);
BzzLinearRegression linReg(F,y);
linReg.LeastSquaresAnalysis();
linReg.RobustAnalysis();
linReg.CleverLeastSquaresAnalysis();
BzzVector str;
linReg.GetStudentizedResiduals(&str);
str.BzzPrint("str");
BzzVector b,br;
b = linReg.GetParameters();
br = linReg.GetRobustParameters();
BzzMatrixSparse Y(3,100);
BzzMatrixSparse X(3,100);
double x;
int i;
for(i = 1; i <= 100;i++)
  {
  x = - 3.4 * double(i - 100)/99. +
     4.8 * double(i - 1)/99.;
  X(1,i) = x;
  Y(1,i) = b[1] + b[2] * x;
  X(2,i) = x;
  Y(2,i) = br[1] + br[2] * x;
  }
for(i = 1;i <= numExperiments;i++)
  {
  X(3,i) = x1[i];   Y(3,i) = y[i];
  }
BzzSave save("StarCluster.stx");
save << X << Y;
save.End();
system("BzzPlotSparse.exe");
BzzPause();
}
```

It is interesting to see the difference between the model obtained by the least sum of squares method (solid line in Figure 5.3) and the model obtained by the robust method (dotted line).

As it can be noted that experiments no. 34, 30, 20, and 11 (experiments with small abscissas) attract the model obtained by the least sum of squares method, whereas these outliers do not influence the robust method.

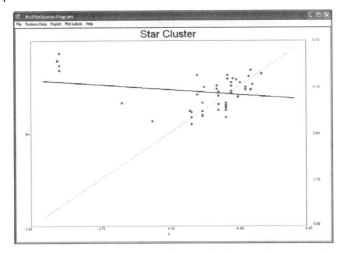

Figure 5.3 Comparison between robust method and the least sum of squares method.

The function `RobustAnalysis` detects the following outliers:

```
Outliers sorted by importance:
34 30 20 11 7 9
These are highly probable Outliers: 11 20 30 34
These are possible Outliers: 7 9
```

The function `CleverLeastSquaresAnalysis` detects the following outliers:

```
** Iteration 0
numExperiments: 47 Mse: 3.188e-001
** Iteration 1
numExperiments: 46 Mse: 2.976e-001
Possible Outliers: 17
** Iteration 2
numExperiments: 45 Mse: 2.742e-001
Possible Outliers: 17 14
** Iteration 3
numExperiments: 44 Mse: 2.490e-001
>>> Probable Outliers: 34 30 20 ** WARNING **
** Iteration 4
numExperiments: 43 Mse: 1.647e-001
>>> Probable Outliers: 34 30 20 11 ** WARNING **
```

Example 5.15

Rousseeuw in Wadsworth's handbook (1990) and Ryan (2009) proposed even the present example to test robust methods. Experimental data can be directly acquired with the following program:

```
#include "BzzMath.hpp"
void main(void)
  {
  int numExperiments = 21;
  BzzVector x1(numExperiments,
    80.,80.,75.,62.,62.,62.,62.,62.,58.,58.,58.,
    58.,58.,58.,50.,50.,50.,50.,50.,56.,70.);
  BzzVector x2(numExperiments,
    27.,27.,25.,24.,22.,23.,24.,24.,23.,18.,18.,
    17.,18.,19.,18.,18.,19.,19.,20.,20.,20.);
  BzzVector x3(numExperiments,
    89.,88.,90.,87.,87.,87.,93.,93.,87.,80.,89.,
    88.,82.,93.,89.,86.,72.,79.,80.,82.,91.);
  BzzMatrix F(numExperiments,4);
  BzzVector y(numExperiments,
    42.,37.,37.,28.,18.,18.,19.,20.,15.,14.,14.,
    13.,11.,12.,8.,7.,8.,8.,9.,15.,15.);
  F.SetColumn(1,1.);
  F.SetColumn(2,x1);
  F.SetColumn(3,x2);
  F.SetColumn(4,x3);
  BzzLinearRegression linReg(F,y);
// linReg.SetVariance(1.e-1,1);
  linReg.LeastSquaresAnalysis();
  linReg.RobustAnalysis();
  linReg.CleverLeastSquaresAnalysis();
  BzzVector str;
  linReg.GetStudentizedResiduals(&str);
  str.BzzPrint("str");
  }
```

The robust method identifies the experiments no. 1, 4, 3, and 21 as highly probable outliers sorted by relevance.

The function `CleverLeastSquaresAnalysis` detects the following series of possible outliers:

```
** Iteration 0
numExperiments: 21 Mse: 1.052e+001
** Iteration 1
numExperiments: 20 Mse: 6.601e+000
>>> Probable Outliers: 21 ** WARNING **
** Iteration 2
numExperiments: 19 Mse: 3.986e+000
>>> Probable Outliers: 21 4 ** WARNING **
** Iteration 3
numExperiments: 18 Mse: 3.107e+000
```

```
        Possible Outliers: 21 4 3
        ** Iteration 4
        numExperiments: 17 Mse: 1.569e+000
        >>> Probable Outliers: 21 4 3 1 ** WARNING **
        ** Iteration 5
        numExperiments: 16 Mse: 1.050e+000
        >>> Probable Outliers: 21 4 3 1 13 ** WARNING **
```

Results coincide with the ones obtained by Rousseeuw.

5.4.2
Outliers Originated by Inadequate Models

Previous examples are important to check potentialities of robust methods in detecting gross errors. Even though such an analysis is essential, robust methods go beyond this basic feature. In fact, if one who wants to examine a model takes care of all the required operations to face this problem, he can prevent any kind of gross error.

The main goal of robust methods is to support one in the best model selection.

When the model cannot fit experimental data, some experiments are pointed out as outliers. In these cases, it is necessary to modify the model:

- making it more complex through the introduction of additional terms;
- using two or more models according to the region of the experimental domain (piecewise approach).

Example 5.16

Consider data collected in the file `FalseLeverage1.lrg`. The model is

$$y_i = \beta_1 + \beta_2 x_{1i} + \varepsilon_i \tag{5.14}$$

Note that, once again, the selected example is intentionally trivial for enhancing the essence of the problem we are analyzing, as some of its features could be partially camouflaged if complex problems would be considered.
Experimental data can be also directly acquired with the following program:

```
        #include "BzzMath.hpp"
        void main(void)
          {
          BzzMatrix F(11,2,
            1.,110.87, 1.,107.14, 1.,104.12, 1.,101.98,
            1.,103.01, 1.,124.89, 1.,106.02, 1.,107.96,
            1.,109.08, 1.,110.14, 1.,101.12);
          BzzVector y(11,
```

```
      6.9596,9.0492,10.4553,11.9095,11.4522,
      9.8861,9.5247,8.1732,7.5921,7.4424,12.6225);
   BzzLinearRegression linReg(F,y);
   linReg.SetVariance(.05,3);
   linReg.LeastSquaresAnalysis();
   linReg.RobustAnalysis();
   linReg.CleverLeastSquaresAnalysis();
   BzzVector str;
   linReg.GetStudentizedResiduals(&str);
   str.BzzPrint("str");
   }
```

Standard residual analysis performed by the least sum of squares method does not detect any outlier, whereas the robust analysis highlights a highly probable outlier in correspondence with the experiment no. 6 because of its large standard residual: 45.35.

Parameters obtained by these two methods are significantly different. The method of least sum of squares leads to

$$y_i = 23.737 - 1.3154 \cdot 10^{-1} x_{1i} + \varepsilon_i \qquad (5.15)$$

whereas the robust method leads to

$$y_i = 70.585 - 5.7429 \cdot 10^{-1} x_{1i} + \varepsilon_i \qquad (5.16)$$

Since these methods bring about different model parameter estimates, the outliers are even *influential observations* (see Section 4.6).

Even the analysis performed by the function `CleverLeastSquaresAnalysis` identifies the experiment no. 6 as a probable outlier.

Therefore, robust analyses lead to conclude that the experiment no. 6 is an outlier for this model.

Let us suppose that this experiment is not a gross error. In this situation, either the model or some hypotheses have to be modified. The first thing to do is to check whether the experiment no. 6 has some features that make it different from the other points (beyond the feature of being an outlier for the model).

In these circumstances, it is important to check y-outliers, X-outliers, F-outliers, and secluded observations.

To do so, it is enough to add the following statement:

```
   F.GetSecludedObservations();
```

The experiment no. 6 is an F-outlier, and it is a secluded observation in the normal space and in the space of principal components.

It is therefore appropriate to perform new experiments, if possible, in the experimental region bounded by the same experiment no. 6 ($x = 124.89$) and the experiment no. 1, which is the closest point ($x = 110.87$).

Example 5.17

According to Example 5.16, two additional experimental points are introduced in the experimental range (110.87 < x < 124.89) and the resulting experimental data can be directly acquired either by the file FalseLeverage2.lrg or by the following program:

```
#include "BzzMath.hpp"
void main(void)
  {
  BzzMatrix F(13,2,
    1.,110.87, 1.,107.14, 1.,104.12, 1.,101.98,
    1.,103.01, 1.,124.89, 1.,106.02, 1.,107.96,
    1.,109.08, 1.,110.14, 1.,101.12,
    1.,117.89, 1.,120.51);
  BzzVector y(13,
    6.9596,9.0492,10.4553,11.9095,11.4522,
    9.8861,9.5247,8.1732,7.5921,7.4424,12.6225,
    6.7853,7.6012);
  BzzLinearRegression linReg(F,y);
  linReg.SetVariance(.05,3);
  linReg.LeastSquaresAnalysis();
  linReg.RobustAnalysis();
  linReg.CleverLeastSquaresAnalysis();
  BzzVector str;
  linReg.GetStudentizedResiduals(&str);
  str.BzzPrint("str");
  }
```

The robust analysis and the function CleverLeastSquaresAnalysis both show the presence of three highly probable outliers: the previous point no. 6 and the additional points (no. 12 and 13).

Conversely, the function GetStudentizedResiduals identifies the experiment no. 6 as an outlier, by showing to be less effective than the previous techniques even in this case.

By examining this file with the BzzLinearRegression.exe toolkit and by plotting robust residuals against the second column of the matrix **F**, which corresponds to the independent variable **x**, the trend of Figure 5.4 is obtained. It shows a nonlinear relation against **x**.

As already underlined, plots could be misleading in the selection of the additional functions for the model. This is a special case and, unfortunately, we are not always so lucky.

This is a special case for two reasons: first, there is a single independent variable x and, second, it is possible to write the model in the form (3.1), which highlights possible relationships between y and the real variable x.

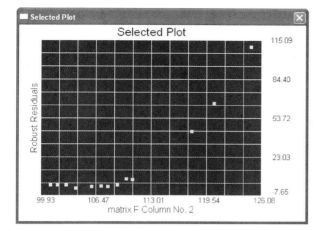

Figure 5.4 Nonlinear dependence in experimental data.

Example 5.18

Introduce an additional quadratic term and analyze data for the new model:

$$y_i = \beta_1 + \beta_2 x_{1i} + \beta_3 x_{1i}^2 + \varepsilon_i \tag{5.17}$$

The program is

```
#include "BzzMath.hpp"
void main(void)
  {
  BzzLinearRegression linReg("FalseLeverage3.lrg");
  linReg.LeastSquaresAnalysis();
  linReg.RobustAnalysis();
  linReg.CleverLeastSquaresAnalysis();
  BzzVector str;
  linReg.GetStudentizedResiduals(&str);
  str.BzzPrint("str");
  }
```

The new model satisfactorily fits experimental data and outliers are detected neither by `RobustAnalysis` nor by `CleverLeastSquaresAnalysis` functions, even though it would be suitable to normalize matrix columns as explained in Example 5.3 to avoid multicollinearities.

Conversely, the function `GetStudentizedResiduals` points out the experiment no. 11 as probable outlier, but it is due to the ill conditioning of the matrix **F**, which induces more ill conditioning in the hat matrix **H**.

Example 5.19

Consider the model

$$y_i = \beta_1 + \beta_2 x_{1i} + \varepsilon_i \qquad (5.18)$$

Data are collected in the file `PiecewiseA1.lrg`. Also, data can be directly acquired with the following program.

The experimental error variance obtained with 3 degrees of freedom is equal to 10^{-3}. The program is

```
#include "BzzMath.hpp"
void main(void)
  {
  BzzMatrix F(21,2);
  BzzVector x(21,100.,105.,110.,115.,120.,
    125.,130.,135.,140.,145.,150.,155.,160.,
    165.,170.,175.,180.,185.,190.,195.,200.);
  BzzVector y(21,
    12.01,10.52,8.99,7.53,5.98,7.05125,7.87667,
    8.68625,9.26,9.6779167,9.99,10.18625,10.1467,
    10.05125,9.71,9.352917,8.76,8.01125,7.17667,
    6.17625,4.99);
  F.SetColumn(1,1.);
  F.SetColumn(2,x);
  BzzLinearRegression linReg(F,y);
  linReg.SetVariance(1.e-3,3);
  linReg.LeastSquaresAnalysis();
  linReg.RobustAnalysis();
  linReg.CleverLeastSquaresAnalysis();
  }
```

The model is clearly inadequate to represent experimental data. In fact, we get

```
Mean Square Error = 2.7332341
F-test for the model
Fexperimental = 2.733234e+003
The probability that F with dfNum 19 dfDen 3
is greater than 2.733234e+003 is 1.004349e-005 *WARNING*
```

Example 5.20

One can think to introduce even the quadratic term:

$$y_i = \beta_1 + \beta_2 x_{1i} + \beta_3 x_{1i}^2 + \varepsilon_i \qquad (5.19)$$

5.4 Outliers

Data of this problem are collected in the file `PiecewiseA2.lrg`, obtained by inserting a new column containing the values of x_{1i}^2 into the matrix **F** of Example 5.19.

The program becomes

```
#include "BzzMath.hpp"
void main(void)
    {
    BzzLinearRegression linReg(PicewiseA2.lrg);
    linReg.LeastSquaresAnalysis();
    linReg.RobustAnalysis();
    linReg.CleverLeastSquaresAnalysis();
    }
```

It is interesting to examine the differences between the least sum of squares method and the robust analysis.

The model with parameters estimated by the least sum of squares method is

$$y_i = -1.405 + .1622x_{1i} - .000609x_{1i}^2 \qquad (5.20)$$

whereas the model obtained by the robust method takes completely different parameters:

$$y_i = -63.19 + .929x_{1i} - .00293x_{1i}^2 \qquad (5.21)$$

Since these methods bring about different model parameter estimates, the outliers are even *influential observations*.

The model obtained by the least sum of squares method is completely wrong. Conversely, the robust method and the function `CleverLeastSquaresAnalysis` both point out first four experiments as highly probable outliers, whereas the remaining points are all satisfactory.

Example 5.21

Data of the Example 5.20 are split into two subsets: one contains the first five experimental points, whereas the other one involves experimental points from the fifth to the last one. These two sets are then fitted separately.

A model satisfactorily fitting the former data subset is

$$y_i = \beta_1 + \beta_2 x_{1i} + \varepsilon_i \qquad (5.22)$$

The program is

```
#include "BzzMath.hpp"
void main(void)
    {
    BzzLinearRegression linReg("PicewiseA3.lrg");
    linReg.LeastSquaresAnalysis();
    linReg.RobustAnalysis();
```

```
linReg.CleverLeastSquaresAnalysis();
}
```
The model fits experimental data subset satisfactorily.

Example 5.22

The selected model for the latter data subset of Example 5.20 (specifically experimental points from 5 to 21) is

$$y_i = \beta_1 + \beta_2 x_{1i} + \beta_3 x_{1i}^2 + \varepsilon_i \tag{5.23}$$

The program is
```
#include "BzzMath.hpp"
void main(void)
  {
  BzzLinearRegression linReg("PicewiseA4.lrg");
  linReg.LeastSquaresAnalysis();
  linReg.RobustAnalysis();
  }
```
An accurate analysis shows that both the models should be reparameterized as explained in Example 5.3 and in Chapter 3, so as to reduce multicollinearities.

Example 5.23

The matrix **F** consists of 55 rows and 6 columns. Data are collected in the file `PiecewiseB1.lrg`. In this case, only the matrix **F** is known, whereas dependences $f_j(\mathbf{x}_i)$ are unavailable. This example shows that the formulation (3.1) is preferable to (3.3) as the former one makes the model analysis easier.

The program is
```
#include "BzzMath.hpp"
void main(void)
  {
  BzzLinearRegression linReg("PicewiseB1.lrg");
  linReg.LeastSquaresAnalysis();
  linReg.RobustAnalysis();
  linReg.CleverLeastSquaresAnalysis();
  }
```
The least sum of squares method shows that the model is inadequate to fit all experimental points. Conversely, the robust analysis and the function `CleverLeastSquaresAnalysis` both point out 10 highly probable outliers. Even in this

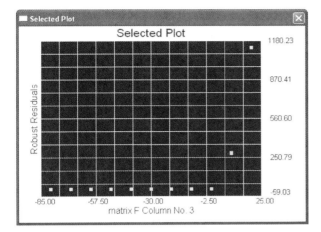

Figure 5.5 Robust residuals.

case, it is suitable to plot the situation. As the dependence of functions $f_j(\mathbf{x}_i)$ against independent variables is unavailable, trends are generated against the columns of the matrix **F**.

Among all the possibilities, the most significant one concerns robust residuals against the third column of the matrix **F** (see Figure 5.5).

Figure 5.5 shows that residuals are good for negative values of the column, whereas they are unsatisfactory for positive values.

It is then natural to split data into two distinct subsets: one containing negative values of the third column of the matrix **F** and another one containing positive values. Points with null values in the third column of the matrix **F** are included in both the subsets. The former subset is collected in the file `PiecewiseB2.lrg` and consists of 46 experimental points, whereas the latter subset is collected in the file `PiecewiseB3.lrg` and consists of 15 experimental points.

When both models are separately analyzed, no outliers are detected.

Note that these models have very different values for the parameter β_6, motivating incompatibility and, hence, the presence of outliers in the model involving the whole data set.

Parameter estimates for the first model are

$$y_i = 74.998 + 15.00 f_{2i} + 2.00 f_{3i} + 7.00 \cdot 10^{-1} f_{4i} \\ + 5.00 \cdot 10^{-1} f_{5i} - 5.476 \cdot 10^{-6} f_{6i} + \varepsilon_i \tag{5.24}$$

Parameter estimates for the second model are

$$y_i = 75.015 + 15.00 f_{2i} + 2.00 f_{3i} + 7.00 \cdot 10^{-1} f_{4i} \\ + 4.99 \cdot 10^{-1} f_{5i} + 10^{-1} f_{6i} + \varepsilon_i \tag{5.25}$$

5.4.3
Outliers Generated by Inadequate Design of Experiments

A poor design of experiments may make hard the model parameter estimation. In addition, the robust method may fail in considering some experiments as outliers if they are placed far from the majority of the existing points. In these cases, a check on the experimental design is often sufficient to identify such a problem and, if so, additional experiments are needed.

The function `GetSecludedObservations` applied to the matrices **F** or **X** highlights whether F-outliers and/or X-outliers or secluded experiments are present.

Example 5.24

Data for a linear model with 5 parameters and 21 experimental points are collected in the file `AmbiguousOutliers21.lrg`. It is interesting to look at the differences between the least sum of squares method and the robust method.

The program is

```
#include "BzzMath.hpp"
void main(void)
{
  BzzLinearRegression linReg("AmbiguousOutliers21.lrg");
  linReg.DataPrint();
  linReg.LeastSquaresAnalysis();
  linReg.RobustAnalysis();
  CleverLeastSquaresAnalysis();
  BzzMatrix F;
  BzzLoad load("AmbiguousOutliers21.lrg");
  load >> F;
  load.End();
  F.GetSecludedObservations();
}
```

The condition number is reasonable: `2.768604e+000`; inflation factors and tolerances do not detect any multicollinearity among parameters.

Analysis of residuals with the robust method leads to several outliers:

```
    These are highly probable Outliers: 17 18 19 20
    These are possible Outliers: 2 7 8 15
```

However, outliers are detected neither by the method of the least sum of squares nor by the function `CleverLeastSquaresAnalysis`.

The method of the least sum of squares leads to the following parameter estimates

$$y_i = -5 \cdot 10^{-1} - 4.913 \cdot 10^{-1} f_{2i} + 2.476 f_{3i} + \\ -2.016 \cdot 10^{-1} f_{4i} + 1.451 \cdot 10^{-1} f_{5i} + \varepsilon_i \tag{5.26}$$

whereas the robust method leads to very different values

$$y_i = 2.388 \cdot 10^3 - 7.589 \cdot 10^3 f_{2i} + 1.309 \cdot 10^3 f_{3i}$$
$$+ 8.115 \cdot 10^3 f_{4i} - 3.169 \cdot 10^3 f_{5i} + \varepsilon_i \tag{5.27}$$

by underlining that there are some problems apparently due to the presence of outliers. Using the `BzzLinearRegression.exe` toolkit for analyzing the data collected into the file `AmbiguousOutliers21.lrg`, it is possible to plot robust residuals against columns of the matrix **F**. By doing so, one can realize that outliers are concentrated only in some regions of the experimental domain. By examining the data of the matrix **F**, one can see that the design of experiments is particularly unbalanced: there are two groups of experimental points and the outliers are concentrated in only one of them.

Even the statement `F.GetSecludedObservations();` detects experiments no. 16–21 as F-outliers and, therefore, they are unbalanced in the experimentation against the others. It is appropriate to acquire new experimental data.

Example 5.25

An additional experimental point was introduced in the data set of previous Example 5.24. The overall data is collected in the file `AmbiguousOutliers22.lrg`.

The program is

```
#include "BzzMath.hpp"
void main(void)
{
// AmbiguousOutliers22.lrg
BzzLinearRegression linReg("AmbiguousOutliers22.lrg");
linReg.LeastSquaresAnalysis();
linReg.RobustAnalysis();
}
```

A single additional experiment was sufficient to completely change results of the robust analysis (a series of additional experiments are commonly necessary to get an analogous result and, even in this case, it would be wise to introduce further experimental points). The robust method does no longer identify the outlier.

Moreover, the method of the least sum of squares leads to the following parameter estimates:

$$y_i = -5.096 \cdot 10^{-1} - 4.849 \cdot 10^{-1} f_{2i} + 2.491 f_{3i} +$$
$$- 1.951 \cdot 10^{-1} f_{4i} + 1.598 \cdot 10^{-1} f_{5i} + \varepsilon_i \tag{5.28}$$

which are reasonably close to the estimates of the robust method:

$$y_i = -5.179 \cdot 10^{-1} - 4.803 \cdot 10^{-1} f_{2i} + 2.502 f_{3i} +$$
$$- 1.876 \cdot 10^{-1} f_{4i} + 1.827 \cdot 10^{-1} f_{5i} + \varepsilon_i \tag{5.29}$$

5.4.4
Outliers Generated by Heteroscedasticity Condition

Sometimes, outliers are generated when the homoscedasticity condition is violated.

Example 5.26

In the file `Heteroscedasticity1.lrg`, an experimental data set consisting of 44 points is provided for the model analysis.
The program is

```
#include "BzzMath.hpp"
void main(void)
  {
  BzzLinearRegression linReg("Heteroscedasticity1.lrg");
  linReg.LeastSquaresAnalysis();
  linReg.RobustAnalysis();
  linReg.CleverLeastSquaresAnalysis();
  linReg.HomoscedasticityAnalysis();
  }
```

The robust analysis highlights the presence of possible outliers.

```
Outliers sorted by importance:
37 44 33 43 38 32
```

The function

```
linReg.HomoscedasticityAnalysis();
```

shows possible heteroscedasticity condition in both the indices (Section 4.11).

```
First index 1.374225e-001 ** WARNING **
Possible violation of homoscedasticity hypothesis
Second index 4.954976e-001 ** WARNING **
Possible violation of homoscedasticity hypothesis
```

Using the toolkit `BzzLinearRegression.exe` to visualize robust residuals against experimental points, the heteroscedasticity condition appears evident, as the variance is nonconstant in the experiments (Figure 5.6).

It is necessary to use an object of the `BzzNonLinearRegression` class to tackle problems with nonconstant variance (see Chapters 6 and 7).

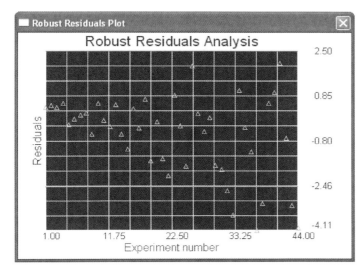

Figure 5.6 Heteroscedasticity condition; the variance is nonconstant on the experimental domain.

5.5
Best Model Selection

Sometimes, especially in the case of linear models, there are no theories providing the model structure. In such cases, it is necessary to perform a series of attempts. Nevertheless, some techniques allow to select the functions among a series of possibilities to get a reasonable model. These techniques are explained in the next examples.

Example 5.27

Consider the model

$$\begin{aligned} y_i &= \beta_1 \exp(-x_{1i}) + \beta_2 \exp(-1.5x_{1i}) + \beta_3 \exp(-2x_{1i}) \\ &+ \beta_4 \exp(-2.5x_{1i}) + \beta_5 \exp(-3x_{1i}) + \beta_6 \exp(-3.5x_{1i}) \\ &+ \beta_7 \exp(-4x_{1i}) + \beta_8 \exp(-4.5x_{1i}) + \beta_9 \exp(-5x_{1i}) \\ &+ \beta_{10} \exp(-5.5x_{1i}) + \varepsilon_i \end{aligned} \quad (5.30)$$

Experimental data can be directly acquired with the following program. Also, data are collected in the file `exp30.lrg`. The experimental error variance obtained with 4 degrees of freedom is equal to $1.7 \cdot 10^{-5}$.

The program is

```
#include "BzzMath.hpp"
void main(void)
    {
    int numExperiments = 30;
```

```
int i,j;
BzzVector x(numExperiments,
  0.0,.1,.2,.3,.4,.5,.6,.7,.8,.9,
  1.0,1.1,1.2,1.3,1.4,1.5,1.6,1.7,1.8,1.9,
  2.0,2.1,2.2,2.3,2.4,2.5,2.6,2.7,2.8,2.9);
BzzMatrix F(numExperiments,10);
for(i = 1;i <= numExperiments;i++)
  {
  F[i][1] = exp(-x[i]);
  F[i][2] = exp(-1.5*x[i]);
  F[i][3] = exp(-2*x[i]);
  F[i][4] = exp(-2.5*x[i]);
  F[i][5] = exp(-3.*x[i]);
  F[i][6] = exp(-3.5*x[i]);
  F[i][7] = exp(-4.*x[i]);
  F[i][8] = exp(-4.5*x[i]);
  F[i][9] = exp(-5.*x[i]);
  F[i][10] = exp(-5.5*x[i]);
  }
BzzVector y(numExperiments,
  3.9000e+000,2.7845e+000,2.0198e+000,1.4883e+000,
  1.1134e+000,8.4508e-001,6.5030e-001,5.0686e-001,
  3.9975e-001,3.1871e-001,2.5663e-001,2.0851e-001,
  1.7078e-001,1.4092e-001,1.1704e-001,9.7809e-002,
  8.2172e-002,6.9373e-002,5.8833e-002,5.0096e-002,
  4.2810e-002,3.6709e-002,3.1578e-002,2.7234e-002,
  2.3551e-002,2.0419e-002,1.7734e-002,1.5445e-002,
  1.3470e-002,1.1767e-002);
BzzLinearRegression linReg(F,y);
  linReg.SetVariance(1.7e-5,4);
  linReg.LeastSquaresAnalysis();
}
```

As it was predictable, the model analysis shows strong correlations among parameters. No improvements are obtained by increasing the number of experiments. To check it, one can use data collected in the file exp55.lrg and adopt the BzzLinearRegression.exe toolkit. Alternatively, one can analyze results of the following program:

```
#include "BzzMath.hpp"
void main(void)
  {
  BzzLinearRegression linReg("exp55.lrg");
  linReg.SetVariance(1.7e-5,4);
  linReg.LeastSquaresAnalysis();
  }
```

5.5 Best Model Selection

In such cases, the function `StepwiseAnalysis` allows to examine the best models according to the amount of parameters involved in.

For this purpose, it is sufficient to replace the function `LeastSquaresAnalysis` with

```
linReg.StepwiseAnalysis();
```

One can also select the menu item `Stepwise, Analysis` in the `BzzLinearRegression.exe` toolkit. Only first three models are reported here.

```
====================================
Best Models with Stepwise Analysis
====================================
Number of Parameter(s) = 1
Mean Square Error = 2.246729e-003

Par.         Value
 5      3.8171457e+000      1.2e+002

Number of Parameter(s) = 2
Mean Square Error = 1.977809e-005

Par.         Value              t = b/sb
 2      9.2107115e-001      1.8e+002
 7      2.9788705e+000      4.1e+002

Number of Parameter(s) = 3
Mean Square Error = 9.688560e-006

Par.         Valu               t = b/sb
 2      8.4535126e-001      5.9e+001
 4      1.9087131e-001      5.5e+000
 7      2.8575219e+000      1.3e+002
```

As the experimental error variance is equal to $1.7 \cdot 10^{-5}$, the model with two parameters is already satisfactory. Conversely, the model with three parameters is characterized by strong correlations among them.

If one would analyze the model with two parameters, the following statements should be added to the program:

```
BzzVectorInt jF(2),iE(numExperiments);
jF(1) = 2; jF(2) = 7; // select F columns 2 and 7
//select all experiments
for(i = 1;i <= numExperiments;i++)
      iE(i) = i;
BzzLinearRegression lg(F,y,jF,iE);
lg.SetVariance(1.7e-5,10);
lg.LeastSquaresAnalysis();
```

The object `lg` uses the constructor:

```
BzzLinearRegression lg(F,y,jF,iE);
```

requiring two objects of the `BzzVectorInt` class besides the matrix **F** and the vector **y**. An object includes the list of indices of the columns to be used in the model; the other one contains the list of experimental points to be used in the model analysis. All the experiments were selected in this specific case.

The analysis of the model with two parameters is fully satisfactory.

It is possible to use the `BzzLinearRegression.exe` toolkit by selecting the menu item `Stepwise, Best Model` and inserting the number 2 when the specific dialogue window opens.

Example 5.28

Consider the data set collected in the file `StepwiseGBF.lrg`.
The model analysis can be performed either using the toolkit or by using the following program:

```
#include "BzzMath.hpp"
void main(void)
  {
  BzzLinearRegression linReg("StepwiseGBF.lrg");
  linReg.StepwiseAnalysis();
  }
```

Only first five models are reported here:

```
==================================
Best Models with Stepwise Analysis
==================================

Number of Parameter(s) = 1
Mean Square Error = 9.965639e+002

   Par.     Value
    1    1.0353963e+002

Number of Parameter(s) = 2
Mean Square Error = 4.179827e+001

   Par.     Value         t = b/sb
    1    3.1879034e+001
    5    9.4015358e-001   2.4e+001

Number of Parameter(s) = 3
Mean Square Error = 1.037638e+001
```

```
   Par.     Value          t = b/sb
    1    2.7253326e+001
    4    1.0752462e+000    8.8e+000
    5    8.6002422e-001    4.0e+001
```

Number of Parameter(s) = 4
Mean Square Error = 2.830216e+000

```
   Par.     Value          t = b/sb
    1    2.2355884e+001
    2    4.8519193e+000    1.2e+001
    5    7.9558099e-001    5.5e+001
    7    3.8142671e-001    1.3e+001
```

Number of Parameter(s) = 5
Mean Square Error = 2.903052e+000

```
   Par.     Value          t = b/sb
    1    2.2080824e+001
    2    4.8290992e+000    1.2e+001
    5    7.7177900e-001    2.0e+001
    6    4.6400539e-003    6.5e-001 ** WARNING **
    7    4.1666568e-001    6.8e+000
```

As one can verify, the model with four parameters is the best choice. Actually, it has the minimum mean square error, which is equal to 2.830216 and it is the last one without any correlation among parameters. This model uses the columns no. 1, 2, 5, and 7. To get the new model, it is sufficient to implement the following program:

```cpp
#include "BzzMath.hpp"
void main(void)
  {
  BzzMatrix F;
  BzzVector y;
  double s2;
  int dof;
  BzzLoad load("StepwiseGBF.lrg");
  load >> F >> y >> s2 >> dof;
  load.End();
  int numExperiments = y.Size();
  BzzVectorInt jF(4,1,2,5,7); // select 1,2,5,7 columns
  BzzVectorInt iE(numExperiments);
  //select all experiments
  for(int i = 1; i <= numExperiments; i++)
     iE(i) = i;
```

```
BzzLinearRegression linReg(F,y,jF,iE);
linReg.SetVariance(s2,dof);
linReg.LeastSquaresAnalysis();
linReg.RobustAnalysis();
}
```

The selected model is fully satisfactory and the robust analysis does not point out any outlier.

Example 5.29

A typical theoretical model for mechanical engineering is

$$y_i = \beta_1 \exp(-\beta_2 x_{1i}) + \beta_3 + \beta_4 x_{1i} - \exp(\beta_5 x_{1i} + \beta_6 (20. - x_{1i})) \tag{5.31}$$

Actually, the experimental points show that central experimental values are characterized by a linear trend, whereas the external experimental values collapse, and this is confirmed by theory.

As the model is nonlinear, if one wants to use an object of the `BzzLinearRegression` class, it is necessary to find out a group of functions that correctly approximate the nonlinear model. It is possible to use the function `StepwiseAnalysis` to select the most adequate functions to build the model.

Before using such a function, it is, however, reasonable to look out for experiments pointed as outliers for the linear model, so to have more information on the function to be added to the linear model.

The same information could be obtained even with a simple plot of the experimental points or by looking at the values of **y**. As already underlined, some examples are intentionally trivial, just to propose a demonstrative use of some specific functions as their features could be masked in solving complex problems.

```
#include "BzzMath.hpp"
void main(void)
  {
  int numExperiments = 35;
  int i,j;
  BzzVector x(numExperiments,
    0.0,.1,.2,.3,.4,.5,.6,.7,.8,.9,
    1.,2.,3.,4.,5.,6.,7.,8.,9.,10.,
    11.,12.,13.,14.,15.,16.,17.,18.,19.,20.,
    20.1,20.2,20.3,20.4,20.5);
  BzzMatrix F(numExperiments,2);
  for(i = 1;i <= numExperiments;i++)
    {
    F[i][1] = 1.;
    F[i][2] = x[i];
```

```
        }
    BzzVector y(numExperiments,
        9.750,8.75,8.12,7.881,7.657,7.466,7.425,7.326,
        7.316,7.287,7.246,7.125,7.103,6.941,6.818,
        6.716,6.634,6.531,6.409,6.337,6.224,6.102,
        6.005,5.927,5.815,5.711,5.567,5.379,4.517,
        -1.966,-3.673,-5.776,-8.368,-11.56,-15.50);
    BzzLinearRegression linReg(F,y);
    linReg.CleverLeastSquaresAnalysis();
    }
```

The function `CleverLeastSquaresAnalysis` highlights the experiments no. 1–7 and 28–35 as outliers.

Therefore, the initial collapse is important until $x \leq 0.6$ and the second collapse becomes significant for $x \geq 18$.

Example 5.30

The function `StepwiseAnalysis` is adopted to select the most adequate functions for the model of previous example.

The program is

```
    #include "BzzMath.hpp"
    void main(void)
      {
      int numExperiments = 35;
      int i,j;
      BzzVector x(numExperiments,
        0.0,.1,.2,.3,.4,.5,.6,.7,.8,.9,
        1.,2.,3.,4.,5.,6.,7.,8.,9.,10.,
        11.,12.,13.,14.,15.,16.,17.,18.,19.,20.,
        20.1,20.2,20.3,20.4,20.5);
      BzzMatrix F(numExperiments,18);
      for(i = 1;i <= numExperiments;i++)
        {
        F[i][1] = 1.;
        F[i][2] = x[i];
        F[i][3] = exp(-x[i]);
        F[i][4] = exp(-1.5*x[i]);
        F[i][5] = exp(-2*x[i]);
        F[i][6] = exp(-2.5*x[i]);
        F[i][7] = exp(-3.*x[i]);
        F[i][8] = exp(-3.5*x[i]);
        F[i][9] = exp(-4.*x[i]);
```

```
        F[i][10] = exp(-4.5*x[i]);
        F[i][11] = exp(-5.*x[i]);
        F[i][12] = exp(-5.5*x[i]);
        F[i][13] = exp(-18. + x[i]);
        F[i][14] = exp(-36. + 2. * x[i]);
        F[i][15] = exp(-20. + x[i]);
        F[i][16] = exp(-40. + 2. * x[i]);
        F[i][17] = exp(-22. + x[i]);
        F[i][18] = exp(-44. + 2. * x[i]);
    }
    BzzVector y(numExperiments,
        9.750,8.75,8.12,7.881,7.657,7.466,7.425,7.326,
        7.316,7.287,7.246,7.125,7.103,6.941,6.818,
        6.716,6.634,6.531,6.409,6.337,6.224,6.102,
        6.005,5.927,5.815,5.711,5.567,5.379,4.517,
        -1.966,-3.673,-5.776,-8.368,-11.56,-15.50);
    BzzLinearRegression linReg(F,y);
    linReg.StepwiseAnalysis();
    }
```

The first five best models selected are as follows:

```
Number of Parameter(s) = 1
Mean Square Error = 3.605443e+001

Par.      Value
 1    4.3212000e+000

Number of Parameter(s) = 2
Mean Square Error = 8.417293e-001

Par.      Value           t = b/sb
  1    6.8598394e+000
 14   -1.5301204e-001    3.8e+001

Number of Parameter(s) = 3
Mean Square Error = 1.662576e-001

Par.      Value           t = b/sb
  1    6.2690935e+000
  4    2.9670333e+000    1.2e+001
 14   -1.4737052e-001    7.9e+001

Number of Parameter(s) = 4
Mean Square Error = 8.180460e-003
```

```
Par.      Value       t = b/sb
 1     7.3456453e+000
 2    -9.8527856e-002   3.5e+001
12     2.4348808e+000   2.8e+001
16    -7.5653593e+000   2.7e+002

Number of Parameter(s) = 5
Mean Square Error = 1.231824e-003

Par.   Value t = b/sb
 1     7.3813153e+000
 2    -1.0703116e-001   8.5e+001
12     2.3805528e+000   7.1e+001
13     1.2924578e-001   1.3e+001
18    -4.4618781e+002   1.7e+002
```

Therefore, the best linear model with five parameters is

$$y_i = 2.38 \exp(-5.5 x_{1i}) + 7.38 - .107 x_{1i} \\ + 12. \exp(-18. + x_{1i}) - 446.\exp(-44. + 2 x_{1i}) \tag{5.32}$$

From a statistical point of view, one should take care in examining the model obtained in this way. In fact, even though the model has only five parameters, it really has more than five, as previous parameters were selected from among many combinations.

It is the same discussion as the one on the model selection based on the data plot proposed in Section 3.8.

Even in this case, the following consideration is valid.

It is worth noting that statistical model analysis is weaker than what people commonly believe (see Chapter 2). Therefore, this preventive analysis does not generate any real damage to the future model analysis provided the number of experimental points is satisfactorily large.

Example 5.31

A further application of the function `StepwiseAnalysis` is proposed here. Experimental data was originally proposed by Draper and Smith (1998).

The program is

```
#include "BzzMath.hpp"
void main(void)
  {
  BzzMatrix F(13,5,
    1.,7.,26.,6.,60.,   1.,1.,29.,15.,52.,
    1.,11.,56.,8.,20.,  1.,11.,31.,8.,47.,
```

```
       1.,7.,52.,6.,33.,    1.,11.,55.,9.,22.,
       1.,3.,71.,17.,6.,    1.,1.,31.,22.,44.,
       1.,2.,54.,18.,22.,   1.,21.,47.,4.,26.,
       1.,1.,40.,23.,34.,   1.,11.,66.,9.,12.,
       1.,10.,68.,8.,12.);
    BzzVector y(13, 78.5,74.3,104.3,87.6,95.9,109.2,102.7,
       72.5,93.1,115.9,83.8,113.3,109.4);
    BzzLinearRegression linReg(F,y);
    linReg.StepwiseAnalysis();
    F.DeleteColumn(4);
    linReg(F,y);
    linReg.SetVariance(5.,3);
    linReg.LeastSquaresAnalysis();
    linReg.RobustAnalysis();
    linReg.CleverLeastSquaresAnalysis();
    }
```

The function finds out columns no. 1, 2, 3, and 5 as the best model. It is possible to analyze the best model by adopting the usual functions by removing the column no. 4 from the matrix.

Example 5.32

Use the function `StepwiseAnalysis` to analyze the data proposed by Wood (1973). Data were artificially created by the following model:

$$y_i = 20 + 20x_{1i} - 3x_{2i} - x_{1i}^2 + \varepsilon_i \qquad (5.33)$$

The experimental error variance is constant on the whole experimental domain. Data can be directly acquired with the following program:

```
#include "BzzMath.hpp"
void main(void)
  {
  // Wood 1973
  int numExperiments = 40;
  BzzMatrix F(numExperiments,6);
  BzzVector y(numExperiments,
     20.164,18.847,6.678,8.709,36.934,8.397,-1.778,
     53.136,51.883,31.564,5.739,-6.466,56.494,28.523,
     47.498,-4.575,10.73,8.214,23.79,-3.518,20.283,
     16.97,8.379,9.876,37.719,8.445,-1.841,54.339,
     51.646,30.738,5.373,-7.537,53.974,28.636,46.065,
     -6.327,13.001,7.855,26.869,-3.659);
  BzzVector x1(numExperiments,0.,.2,.5,1.,1.5,2.,2.5,
```

```
      3.,3.5,4.,4.5,5.,5.3,5.5,6.,6.5,7.,7.5,7.8,8.,
      0.,.2,.5,1.,1.5,2.,2.5,3.,3.5,4.,4.5,5.,5.3,
      5.5,6.,6.5,7.,7.5,7.8,8.);
    BzzVector x2(numExperiments,0.,2.,7.,10.,4.,16.,
      22.,6.,9.,18.,28.,34.,14.,24.,19.,38.,33.,
      35.,30.,40.,0.,2.,7.,10.,4.,16.,22.,6.,9.,
      18.,28.,34.,14.,24.,19.,38.,33.,35.,30.,40.);
    double xx1,xx2;
    int i;
    for(i = 1;i <= 17;i++)
      {
      xx1 = (x1[i] - 4.) / 4.;
      xx2 = (x2[i] - 20.) / 20.;
//    xx1 = x1[i];
//    xx2 = x2[i];
      F[i][1] = 1.;
      F[i][2] = xx1;
      F[i][3] = xx2;
      F[i][4] = xx1 * xx2;
      F[i][5] = xx1 * xx1;
      F[i][6] = xx2 * xx2;
      }
    BzzLinearRegression linReg(F,y);
    linReg.StepwiseAnalysis();
    }
```

The best model involves four parameters (1, 2, 3, and 5) that coincide with the ones adopted in generating the experimental data set.

Example 5.33

Ryan (2009) proposed another application of the function `StepwiseAnalysis`. Five functions are proposed to find out the best model. The program is

```
#include "BzzMath.hpp"
void main(void)
  {
  int numExperiments = 16;
  int i,j;
  BzzVector x(numExperiments,
    1.7,2.9,3.,3.2,3.6,3.8,4.2,4.3,4.8,
    5.4,6.,6.8,7.4,8.5,9.3,10.2);
  BzzMatrix F(numExperiments,5);
  for(i = 1;i <= numExperiments;i++)
```

```
    {
    F[i][1] = 1.;
    F[i][2] = x[i];
    F[i][3] = BzzPow2(x[i]);
    F[i][4] = BzzPow3(x[i]);
    F[i][5] = BzzPow4(x[i]);
    }
  BzzVector y(numExperiments,
    -125.35,218.83,205.78,244.82,92.31,192.02,
    220.39,152.93,115.18,291.37,502.64,836.76,
    1128.26,1710.14,2434.10,2996.33);
  BzzLinearRegression linReg(F,y);
  linReg.SetVariance(1.e4,5);
  linReg.StepwiseAnalysis();
  BzzVector b(4,6.,2.,-2.,3.);
  BzzMatrixSparse Y(4,100);
  BzzMatrixSparse X(4,100);
  double xx;
  for(i = 1; i <= 100;i++)
    {
    xx = - 1.7*double(i-100)/99. + 10.2*double(i-1)/99.;
    X(1,i) = xx;
    X(2,i) = xx;
    X(3,i) = xx;
    Y(1,i) = b[1] + b[2]*xx + b[3]*xx*xx + b[4]*xx*xx*xx;
    Y(2,i) = -1.7583076e+003 + 1.6983554e+003 * xx +
      -5.3025338e+002 * xx*xx + 6.7565598e+001 *
      xx*xx*xx -2.6893571e+000 * xx*xx*xx*xx;
    Y(3,i) = -2.1576794e+001 + 2.8706309e+000 * xx*xx*xx;
    }
  for(i = 1;i <= numExperiments;i++)
    {
    X(4,i) = x[i];
    Y(4,i) = y[i];
    }
  BzzSave save("StepwiseRyan300.stx");
  save << X << Y;
  save.End();
  system("BzzPlotSparse.exe");
  }
```

The data for this example were artificially generated by the model

$$y_i = 6 + 2x_{1i} - 2x_{1i}^2 + 3x_{1i}^3 + \varepsilon_i \qquad (5.34)$$

while the best model obtained by stepwise function is the full model, containing all five proposed functions:

$$y_i = -1.758 \cdot 10^3 + 1.698 \cdot 10^3 x_{1i} - 5.303 \cdot 10^2 x_{1i}^2 \\ + 67.57 x_{1i}^3 - 2.689 x_{1i}^4 + \varepsilon_i \tag{5.35}$$

Note that the numerical values of parameters of this specific model are completely different from those of the model adopted to generate the experimental data set.

The experimental error chosen for generating experimental data is large; in addition, it does not seem to be normally distributed. As a result, the discrimination is particularly hard and the model only containing constant and cubic terms:

$$y_i = -21.58 + 2.871 x_{1i}^3 + \varepsilon_i \tag{5.36}$$

is better than the model that really generated the data set. In fact, these two models are practically overlapped, but the model (5.36) has a smaller mean square error because of its larger amount of degrees of freedom.

The model with five parameters (5.35) is the best one, but it interpolates the experimental error as shown in Figure 5.7.

The model (5.35) has a mean square error equal to $4.967 \cdot 10^3$, whereas the variance is 10000. The upside-down F-test (see Chapter 3, caveat no. 7) leads to $10000./4967. = 2.01$.

As a result, the probability that the theoretical F is greater than 2.01 is equal to $9.39 \cdot 10^{-2}$.

Hence, it is reasonable to discard the model (5.35) as it interpolates the experimental error. To select the best model, it is necessary to insert new experimental points (Chapter 8).

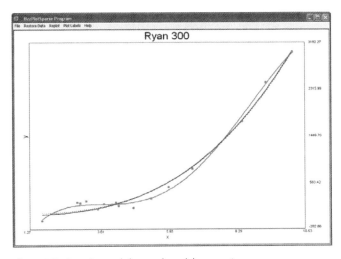

Figure 5.7 Experimental data and model comparison.

Example 5.34

Ryan (2009) proposed even the following application. The experimental data were artificially generated by the model:

$$y_i = \beta_1 + \beta_2 x_{1i} + \frac{\beta_3}{x_{2i}} + \varepsilon_i \qquad (5.37)$$

Possible functions for the model are 1., x_{1i}, x_{2i}, and $1./x_{2i}$.

The program is

```
#include "BzzMath.hpp"
void main(void)
  {
  // Ryan pag.196
  int i,numExperiments = 20;
  BzzMatrix F(numExperiments,4);
  BzzVector x1(numExperiments,1.35,2.34,2.85,
    1.55,2.5,1.48,1.79,1.84,3.5,1.67,1.99,
    2.25,3.04,2.59,3.56,3.87,2.05,1.68,1.45,2.12);
  BzzVector x2(numExperiments,
    .16,.1,.09,.15,.1,.15,.14,.14,.08,.19,.1,.11,
    .08,.08,.07,.06,.11,.16,.14,.13);
  BzzVector y(numExperiments,11.31,12.06,10.25,
    10.36,7.51,10.67,7.15,4.52,3.47,-1.5,18.37,
    8.08,15.6,20.,14.56,13.4,14.35,5.27,16.67,4.48);
  F.SetColumn(1,1.);
  F.SetColumn(2,x1);
  F.SetColumn(3,x2);
  for(i = 1;i <= numExperiments;i++)
    F[i][4] = 1. / x2[i];
  BzzLinearRegression linReg(F,y);
  linReg.StepwiseAnalysis();
  F.DeleteColumn(3);
  linReg(F,y);
  linReg.SetVariance(5.,3);
  linReg.LeastSquaresAnalysis();
  linReg.RobustAnalysis();
  linReg.CleverLeastSquaresAnalysis();
  linReg.HomoscedasticityAnalysis();
  }
```

The best model is constituted by parameters 1, 2, and 4 and it corresponds to the original model (5.37), as some problems arise for the column no. 3 while using the complete model.

The resulting model is satisfactory by removing the column no. 3, unless there is a possible violation of homoscedasticity condition.

```
First index 1.585065e-001 ** WARNING **
Possible violation of homoscedasticity hypothesis

Second index 5.114607e-001 ** WARNING **
Possible violation of homoscedasticity hypothesis
```

5.6 Principal Components

As already underlined in previous chapters, when the model is unknown, but only the matrix **F** and the vector **y** are given, two important tools to improve model analysis are missing: the possibility to reparameterize the model and the selection of new experimental points to improve parameter estimation.

This situation occurs when the model is formulated by a nongeneral form (3.3) and the independent variables $x_{i,j}$ depend on each other.

Principal component analysis of the matrix $\mathbf{F}^T\mathbf{F}$ becomes particularly important both in identifying the best combinations of columns and in removing some other pointless combinations.

This kind of analysis should be exploited even in the case of known model structure in the form (3.1). Knowing the best linear combinations among the columns could indicate how to reparameterize the model to make it better.

As already shown in Example 3.10, principal component can be found by using either the `BzzLinearRegression` class or the `BzzLinearRegression.exe` toolkit.

Example 5.35

Experimental data collected in the file `Principal1.lrg` are associated with a linear model with multicollinearity problems, as some columns of the matrix **F** are linear dependent on the others. Find how many and which columns are really independent.

The program is

```
#include "BzzMath.hpp"
void main(void)
  {
  BzzLinearRegression linReg("Principal1.lrg");
  linReg.SVDAnalysis();
  }
```

It is easy to note that four components are significantly larger than the remaining ones:

```
======================================
Singular Value Decomposition Analysis
======================================
Singular Values D
1   1.6636682e+006
2   8.3899578e+004
3   3.4071974e+003
4   1.5826437e+003
5   4.1693601e+001   ** WARNING **
6   3.6480938e+000   ** WARNING **
7   3.4237091e-004   ** WARNING **
```

Therefore, it is possible to remove three combinations of the original columns and, by exploiting information contained in the principal components, it is possible to get a new model constituted by four correct combinations only of the original columns.

Example 5.36

Exploit principal components to obtain columns for a new model by starting from experimental data of previous Example 5.35.

The program is

```
#include "BzzMath.hpp"
void main(void)
  {
  BzzLinearRegression linReg("Principal1.lrg");
  BzzMatrix P;
  linReg.GetPrincipalComponents(&P);
  P.DeleteRow(7);
  P.DeleteRow(6);
  P.DeleteRow(5);
  BzzMatrix newF;
  ProductT(F,P,&newF);
  BzzLinearRegression lrg(newF,y);
  lrg.LeastSquaresAnalysis();
  }
```

The analysis shows that the new model is satisfactory.

Example 5.37

Experimental data collected in the file `Principal2.lrg` is associated with a linear model with multicollinearity problems, as some columns of the matrix **F** are linear dependent on the others. Find how many and which columns are really independent.

The program is

```
#include "BzzMath.hpp"
void main(void)
    {
    BzzLinearRegression linReg("Principal2.lrg");
    linReg.SVDAnalysis();
    }
```

The analysis shows that three components are more important than the remaining ones:

```
======================================
Singular Value Decomposition Analysis
======================================
Singular Values D
1    9.9999996e-001
2    9.9999996e-002
3    1.0000003e-002
4    9.9976502e-006    ** WARNING **
5    9.7598293e-008    ** WARNING **
```

Example 5.38

Use principal components analysis to get a new model by starting from the data of Example 5.37.

The program is

```
#include "BzzMath.hpp"
void main(void)
    {
    BzzLinearRegression linReg("Principal2.lrg");
    BzzMatrix P;
    linReg.GetPrincipalComponents(&P);
    P.DeleteRow(5);
    P.DeleteRow(4);
    BzzMatrix newF;
```

```
            ProductT(F,P,&newF);
            BzzLinearRegression lrg(newF,y);
            lrg.LeastSquaresAnalysis();
        }
```

The analysis shows that the new model is satisfactory.

6
Nonlinear Regressions

Examples of this chapter can be found in the directory `Vol2_Chapter6` within the enclosed CD-ROM.

6.1
Nonlinear Regression Problems

A series of hypotheses should be discussed before giving a general description of nonlinear regression problems.

1) There are n_Y dependent variables **y** subject to experimental error, with expected value **η**.
2) There are n_X independent variables that can be subject to experimental error: **z** is the experimental value, **x** is the estimated value, and **ξ** is the expected value.
3) The model contains p adaptive parameters, **β** and **b** are their estimates.
4) Dependent variables are uniquely determined by n_Y relations.
5) There are no gross errors (or outliers) that contaminate model variables. If any outlier exists, it must be detected before examining the model. Once identified, it is appropriate to understand their origin before deleting or adjusting them. This task shall be explained with more details in Section 6.6.
6) There are no correlations among experimental points.
7) Experimental errors for **y** vector components are not correlated.
8) Experimental errors for **x** vector components are not correlated.

The most general case, involving correlations among components of the vector **y**, shall not be considered in this book since it would require variance and covariance matrix for each y_i at each experimental point and it becomes practically infeasible to achieve. If anyone could be interested in this topic, we suggest them to refer to Box and Draper (1965) and Bates and Watts (2007).

Relations among variables can be written as

$$\begin{cases} \mathbf{y}_i = \mathbf{g}(\boldsymbol{\xi}_i, \boldsymbol{\beta}) + \boldsymbol{\varepsilon}_{\mathbf{y}_i} \\ \mathbf{z}_i = \boldsymbol{\xi}_i + \boldsymbol{\varepsilon}_{\mathbf{x}_i} \end{cases} \quad i = 1, \ldots, n_E \tag{6.1}$$

where n_E is the number of experimental points and $\boldsymbol{\varepsilon}_{\mathbf{y}_i}$ and $\boldsymbol{\varepsilon}_{\mathbf{x}_i}$ are random variables with normal distribution, null expected value, and known diagonal variance matrices. n_Y functions denoted by $\mathbf{g}$ can be arbitrarily complex, but they univocally determine an estimate of $\mathbf{y}$.

Parameters $\mathbf{b}$ (estimates of $\boldsymbol{\beta}$) and values $\mathbf{x}$ (estimates of $\boldsymbol{\xi}$) are calculated by minimizing the function:

$$S(\mathbf{x}_1, \ldots, \mathbf{x}_{n_E}, \mathbf{b}) = \sum_{i=1}^{n_E} \left\{ \sum_{k=1}^{n_Y} [\omega_{i,k}(y_{i,k} - g_k(\mathbf{x}_i, \mathbf{b}))]^2 + \sum_{l=1}^{n_X} [\omega_{i,l}(z_{i,l} - x_{i,l})]^2 \right\} \tag{6.2}$$

where

- $\omega_{i,k} = \frac{1}{\sigma_{i,k}}$ and $\sigma_{i,k}^2$ denote the variance of the kth dependent variable in the ith experiment.
- $\omega_{i,l} = \frac{1}{\sigma_{i,l}}$ and $\sigma_{i,l}^2$ is the variance of the lth independent variable in the ith experiment.

When variances of all the variables subject to experimental error are constant in the overall experimental space, the function to be minimized is

$$S(\mathbf{x}_1, \ldots, \mathbf{x}_{n_E}, \mathbf{b}) = \sum_{k=1}^{n_Y} \frac{\sum_{i=1}^{n_E}(y_{i,k} - g_k(\mathbf{x}_i, \mathbf{b}))^2}{\sigma_k^2} + \sum_{l=1}^{n_X} \frac{\sum_{i=1}^{n_E}(z_{i,l} - x_{i,l})^2}{\sigma_l^2} \tag{6.3}$$

Usually, the hypothesis of deterministic independent variables is assumed, leading to the following formulation:

$$S(\mathbf{b}) = \sum_{i=1}^{n_E} \sum_{k=1}^{n_Y} [\omega_{i,k}(y_{i,k} - g_k(\mathbf{x}_i, \mathbf{b}))]^2 \tag{6.4}$$
$$\text{with} \quad \mathbf{z} = \boldsymbol{\xi} = \mathbf{x}$$

which should not be employed uncritically. If the errors on independent variables are relevant, disregarding the second term of (6.2) might lead to an incorrect estimation of parameters, as the model is nonlinear.

In addition, it is advisable to consider some other important and useful simplifications.

If the error variance is constant for each $\mathbf{y}$ vector component, previous relation (6.4) becomes

$$S(\mathbf{b}) = \sum_{k=1}^{n_Y} \frac{\sum_{i=1}^{n_E}(y_{i,k} - g_k(\mathbf{x}_i, \mathbf{b}))^2}{\sigma_k^2} \tag{6.5}$$

Quite often, there is only one dependent variable y: if the variance is known in each experimental point, the function to be minimized is

$$S(\mathbf{b}) = \sum_{i=1}^{n_E} \frac{(y_i - g(\mathbf{x}_i, \mathbf{b}))^2}{\sigma_i^2} \tag{6.6}$$

or

$$S(\mathbf{b}) = \sum_{i=1}^{n_E} (y_i - g(\mathbf{x}_i, \mathbf{b}))^2 \qquad (6.7)$$

if the variance is constant on the whole experimental domain.

In the ***BzzMath*** library, the class for solving nonlinear regression problems is called `BzzNonLinearRegression`.

Steps required to analyze nonlinear models coincide with the one explained for linear models (see Chapter 3), even though more problems and difficulties arise in this case.

These difficulties are briefly discussed below, whereas each of them shall be discussed in detail in the next chapter through the introduction of specific case studies.

When investigating the nonlinear models, the following steps should be taken:

1) **Preventative analysis of the problem**. The user that proposes the model (or models) must carefully study the physical phenomenon he wants to describe. This analysis should answer the following questions:
   (a) Which is a good design of experiments?
   (b) Which are the rival models?
   (c) Which is their best formulation?
   (d) According to the problem, which is the preferable objective function to be selected among equations (6.2)–(6.7)?

2) **Selection of the ad hoc constructor of the** `BzzNonLinearRegression` **class and program development**. After choosing the function to be minimized and the optimal model formulation, the most suitable constructor of the `BzzNonLinearRegression` class is to be selected and, then, the program to analyze the model is to be developed. This point shall be described by a simple example in Section 6.4.

3) **Outlier detection**. It is essential to check whether any outlier is present for each model, so as to prevent any incorrect result in examining the same models. If an outlier is detected, it is crucial to realize why it was generated and, therefore, it is essential to take care of it. This topic shall be discussed in detail in Section 6.6.

4) **Identification of correlations among parameters**. Once outliers were identified and revised and/or removed, it is fundamental to check whether both the model formulation and the experimental design are adequate. In fact, bad experiment designs and improper model formulations lead to parameters correlations, by generating difficulties in parameter estimation and ill-conditioning problems. Such a problem corresponds to the multicollinearity (or collinearity) problem of linear regression problems. Actually, a technique to highlight this phenomenon is based on the model linearization in the neighborhood of the optimal value of the parameters and on the analysis of the linearized model. Section 6.7 deals with this topic. In any case, when this kind of problem arises, it is often necessary to reanalyze and reformulate the model. Alternatively, some additional experimental points could be inserted into the existing data set.

5) **Checking the hypotheses** . It is particularly hard to check some of the hypotheses adopted in selecting the objective function. The hypothesis of assuming that the selected model is reasonable for the available data set is verified by an *F*-test or χ^2-test, by remarking that such tests are qualitative only. The preventative analysis is essential for the other hypotheses. This topic is discussed in detail in Section 6.8.
6) **Analysis of results** . The program provides several indices to deem if the model is satisfactory or not. As general rule, it is essential to accomplish the following tasks:
   (a) Repeat calculations by starting from different guesses.
   (b) Repeat calculations by modifying the model even though the same model seems to be reasonably good.

   Such repetitions are useful to tackle local minima for multimodal problems, even if there is no certainty of identifying the global minimum.
7) **Additional experimental points** . With a single model, the new experiments have to improve parameter estimation and fill up the experimental domain at the best. With many rival models, beyond the previous task, the additional experiments should drive the selection of the best model among all the possibilities. The selection of additional experiments to improve the parameter estimation and model discrimination are both closely related and are discussed in Chapter 8.

6.2
Some Caveat

Before moving forward on the discussion, it is worth to underline some points that are essential to the analysis of nonlinear models.

Caveat No. 1

It is important that the user of specific software designed for model analysis has at least a basic knowledge on statistics.

But the basic requirement, which is usually underestimated, is the need that the user has a thorough knowledge of the physical problem that is behind the mathematical model he is analyzing.

It is not only important in the case of linear models but also essential for nonlinear models as they are often proposed on the basis of specific theoretical requirements. Without a proper understanding of the process, it is often ineffective to adopt sophisticated programs to examine a specific model.

The user should know either an estimate of the experimental error variance or at least the order of magnitude of the error variance. Moreover, he should realize whether it is reasonable to consider the variance constant in the whole experimental domain.

Caveat No. 2

It is an error to think the model selected is the *right one* (or the *true one*) among a set of rival alternatives.

Chapter 8 shall explain how to reasonably select experimental points so as to make easier the model discrimination. Nevertheless, it is worth remarking that once a finite number of experiments are assigned, there are infinite models that could satisfactorily describe them. Therefore, it is never possible to state that a specific model is the *true model* that originated them.

Caveat No. 3
It is an error to think the theory that generates the best model from among different alternatives is right (or *true*).

This is a typical error of logic called *fallacy in affirming the consequent*. It could be resumed by the following reasoning: if the theory is true, the model originated must be the best one; thus, if the model is the best one among a series of rival models, the theory behind the best model is true.

Analogously, the following example is structurally equal to the previous one: every man is a mortal; Socrates is dead, then Socrates is a man. Unfortunately, Socrates that we are speaking about was a dog.

Even though the model is the best among all the proposed alternatives, one cannot say the theory behind it is the *right one*.

Caveat No. 4
Another serious error related to the previous one is to attribute physical meaning to the numerical value of model parameters.

Many industrial chemists and chemical engineers think it is possible to ponder over the theory that generated the model based on the numerical values of the calculated parameters. Beyond previous issues of logic, it is worth considering that the value of parameters may radically change according to different factors, such as the presence of other variables, other terms in the model, the selected experiments, efficiency and robustness of the optimization algorithm, and so on.

Caveat No. 5
It is an error to think that the true model (supposing that it is rational to speak about the true model) is included in the arena of rival models one is analyzing; *a fortiori*, it is wrong to think that the specific model one is examining is the true one.

This kind of error may lead to the illusion that the selected model can be preferred to generate experimental points. This topic shall be discussed in detail in Chapter 8.

Caveat No. 6
It is an error to think it is always possible to find out a single model that is significantly better than all other alternatives.

Contrary to what someone thinks and each one hopes, the solution with a single model and with a possibility to reasonably discard all others obtained by starting from an arena of rival models is an extraordinary event. An important application is provided in Section 6.10.

Caveat No. 7

It is an error to manipulate the model to make the parameter evaluation easier when such a reformulation leads to an incorrect use of the functions involved in the minimization.

This error was particularly spread when computers and programs were not so performing. For example, it was a common procedure to linearize, when possible, the model as parameters were easier to be evaluated. It shall be detailed in Section 6.8.

6.3
Parameter Evaluation

In order to estimate parameters for nonlinear regressions, it is necessary to find out the minimum of an adequate objective function by requiring a specific program that meets peculiarities of the problem:

1) The number of parameters involved in the model is limited. This allows to employ robust methods that could not be used if the number of variables was high since they would become computationally too expensive.
2) The objective function is a sum of squares: it is useful to adopt the Newton method applied to the linearized model; the method is also necessary for an approximated statistical analysis.
3) Very often, the problem is ill conditioned for the parameter correlations and the objective function has extremely narrow valleys. In this case, it is quite easy to find out the bottom of the valley, but it is very hard to go down along it to achieve the minimum.
4) Sometimes, one cannot write constraints on parameters in an analytical form. For some values of parameters, the model either could be indeterminable or may have physical meaning. In these situations, the value of the objective function for that set of parameters may be unknown. For example, for some values of parameters, a differential equation system could be impossible to integrate and, therefore, the objective function value would be unknown.
5) Assigning a first reasonable guess could be problematic.
6) The objective function may present many minima. It can be useful to adopt algorithms that do not stop the search after the first minimum detection, and it is also recommended to adopt different starting points for the minimum search.

In `BzzNonLinearRegression` class, many kinds of algorithms are implemented to minimize the objective function. One of them is based on the Newton method and it is just designed for the minimization of a sum of squares and for statistical analysis: it requires a local linearization of the model in the neighborhood of the best parameter values.

When converging, the Newton method is very efficient as it has a quadratic convergence.

The other methods are selected from among those that are able to both follow the direction of narrow valleys and manage nonanalytical constraints (see Buzzi-Ferraris and Manenti, 2011a).

Among all methods inserted in the `BzzNonLinearRegression` class, the improved version of the *OPTNOV* method (Buzzi-Ferraris, 1967) is significantly robust and adequate to solve this specific problem.

Basic ideas underlying this method are the following ones:

- The search for a point on the bottom of the valley is easy; unfortunately, this point is usually different from the absolute minimum.
- The line connecting two distinct points on the bottom of the valley is a good approximation of the direction of the valley.
- Once a good direction of the valley is known, rather than carrying out a one-dimensional search in that direction, which usually does not give any significant improvement, a point can be projected along the direction of the valley. Starting from the projected point, a short search is performed in the subspace perpendicular to the same projection in order to find out a new point on the bottom of the valley. Now, by connecting this new point to the previous one, a new valley direction is identified, and the procedure can be iterated.
- One-dimensional searches do not stop at the first minimum found, but they carry out a thorough search along their direction to find out more local minima. Obviously, there is no certainty of the detection of the global minimum except for a few specific problems.

As mentioned above, the Newton method is one of the methods that should be included in a program just developed for solving nonlinear regression problems. Really, the Newton method is to be rearranged for matching the best with the objective function to be minimized, which consists of the least sum of squares originated by the difference between the experimental value and the model estimate. For the sake of simplicity, let us suppose to have one dependent variable only $y = g(\mathbf{x}, \mathbf{b})$; moreover, the objective function is equation (6.7). Let $\mathbf{F}_n$ be the matrix of linearized model:

$$\mathbf{F}_n = \begin{bmatrix} f_1(\mathbf{x}_1, \mathbf{b}) & f_2(\mathbf{x}_1, \mathbf{b}) & \ldots & f_p(\mathbf{x}_1, \mathbf{b}) \\ f_1(\mathbf{x}_2, \mathbf{b}) & f_2(\mathbf{x}_2, \mathbf{b}) & \ldots & f_p(\mathbf{x}_2, \mathbf{b}) \\ \ldots & \ldots & \ldots & \ldots \\ f_1(\mathbf{x}_n, \mathbf{b}) & f_2(\mathbf{x}_n, \mathbf{b}) & \ldots & f_p(\mathbf{x}_n, \mathbf{b}) \end{bmatrix} \tag{6.8}$$

where the coefficients $f_k(\mathbf{x}_i, \mathbf{b})$ are the first derivatives of the function g against parameters b_k calculated in correspondence with $\mathbf{x}_i$ and for the optimal value $\mathbf{b}$.

In the neighborhood of the optimal value **b**, it is possible to write the following Taylor expansion:

$$\mathbf{y} \simeq \mathbf{g} + \mathbf{F} \cdot \mathbf{db} \qquad (6.9)$$

In other words, a linear model against the correction **db** is obtained.

With many dependent variables, a matrix such as $\mathbf{F}_n$ is to be provided for each of them.

Newton method can be iteratively used to evaluate the correction **db** for the parameters **b** through relation (6.9). The minimum of the objective function is achieved when the correction **db** is considerably small.

Objects of the `BzzNonLinearRegression` class account even for this information to check the achievement of the minimum condition. Besides a significant improvement in efficiency in searching for the minimum, the introduction of the Newton method in the minimization program allows to conduct a statistical analysis, even though approximated, by using the linearized model.

6.3.1
Test to Check the Robustness of a Minimization Program

There are many tests proposed in the literature to validate minimization algorithms. Since regression problems present specific features, it is useful to adopt even very specific tests. For this purpose, two specific problems are proposed for nonlinear regressions (Buzzi-Ferraris and Manenti, 2009).

The first test consists of the following function, reported in Figure 6.1:

$$\Psi_1 = [x_2 - 10000(x_1-1)(x_1-3)(x_1-5)(x_1-7)(x_1-9)]^2 + (x_1-8)^2 \qquad (6.10)$$

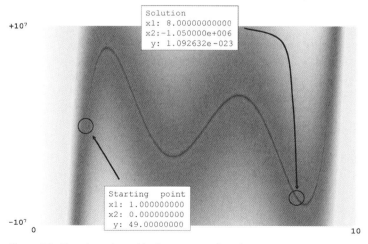

Figure 6.1 Function adopted in the test no. 1 for robust minimization (Buzzi-Ferraris and Manenti, 2009).

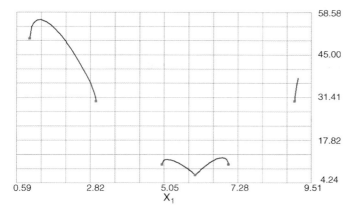

Figure 6.2 Function adopted in the test no. 2 for robust minimization (Buzzi-Ferraris and Manenti, 2009).

Isolines of Ψ_1 show a very narrow valley with steep walls; since the two variables x_1 and x_2 are very unbalanced, $x_1 \in [0;9]$, whereas $x_2 \in [-1.1 \cdot 10^6; 1.1 \cdot 10^6]$. Darker colors of Figure 6.1 correspond to smaller values of the function (the minimum value is $1.1 \cdot 10^{-23}$), whereas lighter colors correspond to higher values of the function (the maximum value is $4.81 \cdot 10^{19}$). The function presents only one minimum, which is particularly far from the starting point.

The second test requires the minimization of the function:

$$\Psi_2 = \sqrt{-945 + x_1[1689 + x_1(-950 + x_1(230 + x_1(-25 + x_1)))] + e^{-x_1}} + 10|x_2 - 10x_1| + 10|x_1 - 6| \qquad (6.11)$$

Figure 6.2 shows a slice of Ψ_2, which is a function of x_1, for the optimal value x_2. Ψ_2 shows many minima and the function has some ranges (not known a priori) where it is undefined. Indeed, the square root applied to a transcendental function introduces some nonanalytical constraints.

6.4
BzzNonLinearRegression Class

In the *BzzMath* library, the class for solving nonlinear regression problems is called `BzzNonLinearRegression`.

The class has several constructors that allow to select the most appropriate function in accordance with the problem.

All the constructors present the following common portions:

```
int numModels;
```

where the variable `numModels` is to be initialized with the number of models that the user wants to adopt simultaneously.

```
int numX;
```

The variable `numX` is to be initialized with the number of independent variables **x**.

```
int numY;
```

The variable `numY` is to be initialized with the number of dependent variables **y**.

```
int numExperiments;
```

The variable `numExperiments` is to be initialized with the number of the existing experimental points.

```
BzzMatrix X(numExperiments,numX);
```

The matrix `X` is to be initialized with the values of variables **x** in each experimental point. Each row contains the vector of **x** in that specific experimental point.

```
BzzMatrix Y(numExperiments,numY);
```

The matrix `Y` is to be initialized with the values of variables **y** in each experimental point. Each row contains the vector of **y** in that specific experimental point.

The function, where the model estimate is evaluated, should have the following prototype:

```
void ModelName(int model,int ex,BzzVector &b,
        BzzVector &x,BzzVector &y);
```

where `ModelName` is arbitrary and is used inside the constructor.

The variable `model` is used when more rival models are adopted. This point shall be discussed in detail later.

The variable `ex` indicates that experimental point is adopted in a specific function call, with the main aim to prevent pointless operations and, consequently, to optimize the code. Its use shall be shown in some examples of next chapter.

The function is called with specific values of parameters `b` and variables `x`, corresponding to the experimental point `ex`. Variables `y` have to be evaluated in the function, in correspondence with `b` and `x`.

Once all the aforementioned variables and objects are defined, the appropriate constructor is selected, according to the problem one has to solve. All the possibilities are proposed in case studies in Chapter 7.

In the demonstrative Example 6.1, relation (6.7) is selected as an objective function and the following constructor is adopted:

```
BzzNonLinearRegression nonLinReg(numModels,X,Y,
        FirstExample1);
```

Once the object of the `BzzNonLinearRegression` class is defined, it is possible to assign the variance to dependent variables, if known.

6.4 BzzNonLinearRegression Class

```
BzzVector s2(1,.075);
int dof = 6;
nonLinReg.SetVariance(dof,s2);
```

Therefore, both model and parameters must be initialized.

```
BzzVector b1(2,1.,1.);
nonLinReg.InitializeModel(1,b1);
```

With many rival models, it is necessary to repeat this operation for each model one wants to examine. Uninitialized models will not be considered in the subsequent analysis.

It is sometimes useful to assign lower and upper bounds for parameters in order to prevent possible calculation errors. For example,

```
BzzVector b(2,1.,1.);
BzzVector bMin(2,-5.,10.);
BzzVector bMax(2,100.,1000.);
nonLinReg.InitializeModel(1,b,bMin,bMax);
```

Finally, it is possible to invoke one of the functions that allow to analyze models that were initialized. To carry out a common analysis that evaluates parameters with the least sum of squares method of the function selected by the constructor, the following statement can be introduced in the code:

```
nonLinReg.LeastSquaresAnalysis();
```

Conversely, if a robust method is needed to detect possible outliers, the following statement should be adopted:

```
nonLinReg.RobustAnalysis();
```

Other specific functions, such as

```
LeastSquaresAnalysisAndExperimentsSearch
```

which is useful to search for new experimental points, shall be detailed in the case studies in Chapter 8.

The objects of the `BzzNonLinearRegression` class can be exploited to get some useful pieces of information for each analyzed model. For example,

```
BzzVector b = nonLinReg.GetParameters(3);
```

collects the values of parameters of the model no. 3 in the `BzzVector b`.

```
BzzVector r = nonLinReg.GetResiduals(3);
```

collects the values of residuals obtained with the model no. 3 in the `BzzVector r`. If the model has many dependent variables, residuals are sequentially stored for each dependent variable.

```
BzzVector s = nonLinReg.GetResidualsStandardized(3);
```

collects the values of standardized residuals obtained with the model no. 3 in the `BzzVector s`.

```
            double mse = nonLinReg.GetMeanSquareError(3);
```
collects the mean square error of the model no. 3 in `mse`.

Example 6.1

Let us consider a regression problem with a single model, one dependent variable, one independent variable, and two parameters:

$$y_{1i} = \beta_1\, e^{\beta_2/x_{1i}} + \varepsilon_{1i} \tag{6.12}$$

Let us also suppose that only the dependent variable is subject to experimental error with constant variance and its estimate based on 6 degrees of freedom is equal to .075. Moreover, theoretical considerations ensure that the parameter β_1 is positive.
Using the following experimental data set, evaluate the model parameters and analyze the model:

$$\mathbf{x} = \{273., 283., 293., 303., 313., 323., 333., 343., 353., 363., 373.\}$$
$$\mathbf{y} = \{191.67, 264.88, 357.60, 474.21, 616.19, 789.61, 995.68, 1239.71,$$
$$1523.46, 1850.92, 2226.47\}$$

The program is

```
    #include "BzzMath.hpp"
    void FirstExample(int model,int ex,BzzVector &b,
            BzzVector &x,BzzVector &y);
    void main(void)
      {
      BzzPrint("\n\nFirstExample");
      int numModels = 1;
      int numX = 1;
      int numY = 1;
      int numExperiments = 11;
      BzzMatrix X(numExperiments,numX,
           273.,283.,293.,303.,313.,323.,
           333.,343.,353.,363.,373.);
      BzzMatrix Y(numExperiments,numY,
             191.67,264.88,357.60,474.21,616.19,789.61,
             995.68,1239.71,1523.46,1850.92,2226.47);
      BzzNonLinearRegression nonLinReg(numModels,X,Y,
             FirstExample);
      BzzVector s2(1,.075);
      int df = 6;
      nonLinReg.SetVariance(df,s2);
      BzzVector b1(2,1.,1.);
      nonLinReg.InitializeModel(1,b1);
      nonLinReg.LeastSquaresAnalysis();
      }
```

```
void FirstExample(int model,int ex,BzzVector &b,
    BzzVector &x,BzzVector &y)
    {
    y[1] = b[1] * exp(b[2] / x[1]);
    }
```

The constructor adopted here requires the number of models to be analyzed, the matrix X containing the experimental values of the independent variables **x**, the matrix Y containing the experimental values of the dependent variables **y**, and the name of the function `FirstExample` where the model is evaluated:

```
BzzNonLinearRegression nonLinReg(numModels,X,Y,
        FirstExample);
```

If the error variances of the dependent variables are known, the following statements should be added:

```
BzzVector s2(1,.075);
int df = 6;
nonLinReg.SetVariance(df,s2);
```

A value should be provided to the error variance when it is constant in the experimental domain. If its real estimate is unavailable, even an order of magnitude can be provided.

The object initializes parameters of the models (in this specific case, it initializes only the parameters of the model no. 1) through the following function:

```
nonLinReg.InitializeModel(1,b1);
```

At last, the object calls the function:

```
nonLinReg.LeastSquaresAnalysis();
```

which evaluates the model (or models) parameters and analyzes them.

Results are printed out on the default file *BzzFile.txt* and the most significant ones are discussed here.

- First of all, the model is reasonably good. In fact, the mean square error is $8.2950454 \cdot 10^{-2}$, whereas the estimate of the variance of the experimental error is equal to .075. Therefore, we get

```
F-test for the model
Fexperimental = 1.106006e+000
The probability that F with dfNum 9 dfDen 6
is greater than 1.106006e+000 is 4.682340e-001
```

The value `Fexperimental` is the ratio between the mean square error of the model and the estimate of the error variance, .075. The probability that the theoretical F is higher than such a value is equal to 46.8%. It is reasonable to accept the model.

- The value of parameters evaluated by minimizing the function with the criteria implemented in the regression program practically coincides with the estimate of the Newton method: it is a reasonable assurance on the optimal value of parameters.

  ```
       Parameters obtained           Parameters obtained
       by minimization with          Newton method
  1    1.80280143228136e+006         1.80279636993964e+006
  2   -2.49788940333422e+003        -2.49788844296985e+003
  ```

- The experimental `T-Value` to check whether a parameter can be erased and the respective probability `P-Value` that the operation is necessary are

  ```
  Par.      T-Value            P-Value
  1       8.6728369e+002    1.8339984e-023
  2       6.3464404e+003    3.0485870e-031
  ```

  The `T-Value` is to be compared with a theoretical t-student value in a t-test to check if the selected parameter is zero. The `P-Value` indicates the probability related to the same hypothesis to have a theoretical t higher than the experimental one. The parameters are both important since the `T-Value` is particularly high and the `P-Value` is significantly small for each of them.

- The condition number of the model is

  ```
  Condition Number 8.523894e+004 ** WARNING **
  ```

  Large values of the condition number denotes correlations among parameters.

- The correlation matrix is

  ```
  Correlation Matrix
  BzzMatrixSymm No.2
  rows 2 cols 2
   1.00000000000000e+000 -9.98078683841010e-001
  -9.98078683841010e-001  1.00000000000000e+000
  ```

  Nondiagonal coefficients close to ± 1 denote correlations among parameters.

- Inflation factors are

  ```
  Variance inflation factor
  1 2.6048851e+002
  2 2.6048851e+002
  ** WARNING ** Correlation between Parameters
  ```

  Large values of the inflation factor means that the corresponding parameter is probably correlated with the others.

- T_j tolerances are

  ```
  Columns correlation = Tj Tolerance
  1 3.8389409e-003 ** WARNING **
  2 3.8389409e-003 ** WARNING **
  ```

```
** WARNING ** Correlation between Parameters
The Tj Tolerance identifies serious multicollinearities
```

Small T_j values indicate that the corresponding parameter is probably correlated with the others.

- Diameters of the ellipsoid of the matrix $\mathbf{F}^T\mathbf{F}$ are

```
===============================
Singular Value Analysis
===============================
Singular Values D
1   1.1230056e+001
2   1.3174796e-004 ** WARNING **
```

A small ratio between a secondary diameter and the main one highlights a parameter correlation. In the case of many parameters, the amount of small ratios indicates the number of correlations in the model parameters.

All the aforementioned results show that a strong parameter correlation exists; moreover, a robust analysis (discussed later) shows that no outliers affect the raw data set. Since the design of experiment is reasonable and the model adequately fits the experimental points, the parameter correlation points out that the model is ill formulated (see Section 6.8 and Chapter 7).

6.5
Nonalgebraic Constraints

In some circumstances, the model cannot be calculated for certain values of parameters. This occurs when parameters do not satisfy a constraint that cannot be analytically formulated.

In these cases, it could be suitable to avoid any model evaluation when it becomes infeasible and, at the same time, to send a warning about it to the program that is searching for the best model parameters. In the `BzzNonLinearRegression` class, when the model cannot be evaluated for a certain set of parameter values and for a specific experimental point, it is sufficient to assign value of 1 to the global variable `bzzUnfeasible`.

Example 6.2

Let us consider a regression problem with a single model, with one dependent variable, two independent variables, and three parameters:

$$y_{1i} = \frac{x_{2i}}{\sqrt{\exp(-\beta_1(x_{1i}-373.)+\beta_2(x_{1i}-273.))-\beta_3 x_{2i}}} + \varepsilon_{1i} \qquad (6.13)$$

Let us also suppose that only the dependent variable is subject to experimental error with constant variance and its estimate based on 3 degrees of freedom is equal to

$2 \cdot 10^{-6}$. The square root argument must always be positive to avoid any numerical issue. It is sufficient to insert a check on the argument value in the function that evaluates the model: if it should become *nonpositive* for any reason, it is enough to assign `bzzUnfeasible = 1` and to exit the function without evaluating any model estimate.

The program is

```
#include "BzzMath.hpp"
void ConstraintsExample(int model,int ex,BzzVector &b,
        BzzVector &x,BzzVector &y);
void main(void)
    {
    BzzPrint("\n\nConstraintsExample");
    int numModels = 1;
    int numX = 2;
    int numY = 1;
    int numExperiments = 11;
    BzzVector x1(numExperiments,
        273.,283.,293.,303.,313.,323.,
        333.,343.,353.,363.,373.);
    BzzVector x2(numExperiments,
        .12,.34,.18,.22,.32,.31,
        .64,.32,.18,.33,.21);
    BzzMatrix X(numExperiments,numX);
    X.SetColumn(1,x1);
    X.SetColumn(2,x2);
    BzzMatrix Y(numExperiments,numY,
        .0736,.225,.114,.148,.223,.223,.526,
        .238,.132,.260,.164);
    BzzNonLinearRegression nonLinReg(numModels,X,Y,
        ConstraintsExample);
    BzzVector s2(1,2.e-6);
    int df = 3;
    nonLinReg.SetVariance(df,s2);
    BzzVector b(3,.05,.05,3.);
    nonLinReg.InitializeModel(1,b);
    nonLinReg.LeastSquaresAnalysis();
    }
void ConstraintsExample(int model,int ex,BzzVector &b,
        BzzVector &x,BzzVector &y)
    {
    double h;
    h = exp(-b[1] * (x[1] - 373.) +
        b[2] * (x[1] - 273.)) - b[3] *x[2];
    if(h < 0.)
```

```
    {
      bzzUnfeasible = 1;
      return;
    }
    y[1] = x[2] / sqrt(h);
    }
```

The model is satisfactory and there is no numerical error throughout the parameter evaluation. Note that some points become unfeasible during the parameter estimation.

6.6
Algorithms for Outlier Detection

Before calculating model parameters, it is necessary to find out and reconcile possible outliers of the raw data set, so as to prevent possible large mistakes in the parameter evaluation. As already discussed in the case of linear regressions (Chapter 4), there are many sources of outliers:

1) A gross error affecting an experimental value: it may be located on dependent or independent variables and it may derive either from a experimental problem or from a mistake of the operator who acquired that value.
2) The experimental design may be inadequate.
3) The model may be unable to explain the data in the whole experimental domain.
4) The condition of homoscedasticity may be violated.

With nonlinear models, it is still necessary to minimize the function

$$\min_{\beta}(median(r_i^2)), \quad i = 1, \ldots, n_E \tag{6.14}$$

The minimum search is, however, significantly harder than the linear case.

Some methods that do not stop the search at the detection of the first minimum are implemented in the `BzzNonLinearRegression` class.

Obviously, no one can generally ensure that the global minimum is found, but this is not a serious problem, as it is usually sufficient to significantly reduce the value of function (6.14) for detecting outliers.

When outliers have been identified, it is worth to know what originated them and why they exist before they are deleted. Actually, they can be a symptom of drawbacks that a model suffers from while interpreting experimental data and, therefore, the model has to be appropriately revised.

Example 6.3

This example presents a comparison between the least sum of squares method and the robust method implemented in the `BzzNonLinearRegression` class when the data set contains some outliers. The data set is generated by using the model:

$$y_{1i} = \beta_1 \cdot \exp\left[-\beta_2 \cdot \left(\frac{1}{x_{1i}} - 0.003\right)\right] + e_{1i} \tag{6.15}$$

with $\beta_1 = 1000.$, $\beta_2 = 2500.$

where e_i are the random errors of dependent variables with known variance. Experimental data can be easily acquired with the following program.

Parameters estimated by the least sum of squares method are equal to $1.0034 \cdot 10^3$ and $2.4979 \cdot 10^3$. Then, an outlier is introduced by changing the last value of the independent variable x from its original value 373. into 383.. Model parameters b_1 and b_2 are calculated by using both the least sum of squares method and the robust method. To detect the outliers, it is sufficient that the object of the BzzNonLinearRegression class invokes the function nonLinReg.RobustAnalysis(). By comparing the robust analysis with the least sum of squares analysis, it is possible to check the presence of outliers.

Possible outliers are identified above all by the following tests:

1) Residuals evaluated by the robust method.
2) If the mean square error is larger than the value of the least median of squares, it is probable that at least an outlier is perturbing the data set.

If the parameter values obtained with the two methods are significantly different, at least an influential observation is present (Section 4.6).

The program is

```
#include "BzzMath.hpp"
void Outlier(int model,int ex,BzzVector &b,
      BzzVector &x,BzzVector &y);
void main(void)
    {
    BzzPrint("\n\nOutlier");
    int numModels = 1;
    int numX = 1;
    int numY = 1;
    int numExperiments = 11;
    BzzMatrix X(numExperiments,numX,
        273.,283.,293.,303.,313.,323.,
//      333.,343.,353.,363.,373.);
        333.,343.,353.,363.,383.);
    BzzMatrix Y(numExperiments,numY,
        191.67,264.88,357.60,474.21,616.19,789.61,
        995.68,1239.71,1523.46,1850.92,2226.47);
    BzzNonLinearRegression nonLinReg(numModels,X,Y,
```

```
    Outlier);
      BzzVector b1(2,1.,1.);
    nonLinReg.InitializeModel(1,b1);
    nonLinReg.LeastSquaresAnalysis();
    nonLinReg.RobustAnalysis();
    }
```

While the robust method is able to identify the outlier (this is clearly visible by its large residual):

```
Response Variable 1
     Observed y       Estimated y      Residuals r    Residuals W
 1 1.9167000e+002  1.9179911e+002  -1.2910794e-001   -0.13
 2 2.6488000e+002  2.6495254e+002  -7.2541039e-002   -0.07
 3 3.5760000e+002  3.5802334e+002  -4.2333627e-001   -0.42
 4 4.7421000e+002  4.7426892e+002  -5.8918977e-002   -0.06
 5 6.1619000e+002  6.1707112e+002  -8.8112498e-001   -0.88
 6 7.8961000e+002  7.8989203e+002  -2.8202992e-001   -0.28
 7 9.9568000e+002  9.9623053e+002  -5.5053297e-001   -0.55
 8 1.2397100e+003  1.2395809e+003   1.2910793e-001    0.13
 9 1.5234600e+003  1.5233941e+003   6.5875686e-002    0.07
10 1.8509200e+003  1.8510429e+003  -1.2292117e-001   -0.12
11 2.2264700e+003  2.6507636e+003  -4.2429356e+002 -424.29*
```

the least sum of squares method cannot do it. As a result, some serious effects can be underlined: in fact, the mean square error evaluated by the least sum of squares method is significantly large ($5.6912772 \cdot 10^3$) and it would cause to discard the model. On the other hand, the robust method gives a least median of squares significantly smaller: $1.6668860 \cdot 10^{-2}$. Moreover, the least sum of squares method fails to estimate parameters: the second parameter passes from a value of 2497.9 estimated without the outlier to a value of 2198.8, whereas the parameter estimates do not change in the robust analysis, whether the outlier is considered or not.

It is important to note that the presence of outliers also affects the model discrimination: a valid model might be discarded or, conversely, a bad model might be erroneously accepted.

In this simple example, an analysis of the experiment no. 11 would show that the value of x_{11} was badly written.

6.7
Correlations Among Model Parameters

As mentioned above, once the model parameters are evaluated by all methods implemented within the `BzzNonLinearRegression` class, the model is linearized by checking that the correction foreseen by the Newton method is small. In such a case, the linearized model can be used to provide approximate information on the corresponding nonlinear model. Some of the most important pieces of information deal with correlation indices for linear models, in order to identify possible correlations among parameters.

They are

- The Jacobian matrix condition number.
- The correlation matrix.
- Inflation factors.
- Tolerance indices.

These indices will be adopted in the next section to check if a model is well or ill formulated.

6.8
Preventative Model Analysis

Before examining a specific model, the user has to accomplish some essential tasks for a good outcome of the preventative analysis.

1) The experimentation must be reasonably good to provide reliable values of the dependent variables **y** in correspondence with the dependent variables **x**.
2) Basing on theoretical considerations on the physical phenomenon under study, one or more models must be suggested. Sometimes, the model can be suggested by plotting the trend of experimental points when a theoretical model cannot be proposed.
3) Once the model (or models) is selected, the design of experiments must be analyzed to check whether it is adequate for such a model. As a trivial example, if a model contains three parameters and the experimental points are concentrated in two points, there will certainly be problems in their evaluation.
4) By assuming a good design of experiments, the model formulation is a crucial point. The model must be written so as to reduce the parameter correlations as much as possible.

The analysis of the model of the previous Example 6.1 written in the form:

$$y_{1i} = \beta_1 \exp(\beta_2/x_{1i}) + \varepsilon_{1i} \tag{6.16}$$

showed a strong correlation between parameters b_1 and b_2.

Consider the following formulation of the same model:

$$y_{1i} = \beta_1 \exp\left(\beta_2 \left(\frac{1}{x_{1i}} - \frac{1}{300}\right)\right) + \varepsilon_{1i} \tag{6.17}$$

Even this model can be examined with the same program as in Example 6.1; it is enough to replace the definition of the function `FirstExample`:

```
void FirstExample(int model, int ex, BzzVector &b,
     BzzVector &x, BzzVector &y)
```

```
{
y[1] = b[1] * exp(b[2] * ( 1./ x[1] - 1./ 300.));
}
```

With this new formulation, there is a slight correlation between parameters; as an example, T_j tolerances are

```
Columns correlation = Tj Tolerance
1 9.7524484e-002
2 9.7524484e-002
```

Another possible formulation of the same model is

$$y_i = \exp\left(\beta_1 + \beta_2 \left(\frac{1}{x_i} - \frac{1}{300}\right)\right) + \varepsilon_i \tag{6.18}$$

Again, the model can be examined with the same program as in Example 6.1; it is enough to replace the definition of the function `FirstExample`:

```
void FirstExample(int model, int ex,
        BzzVector &b, BzzVector &x, BzzVector &y)
{
y[1] = exp(b[1] + b[2] * ( 1./ x[1] - 1./ 300.));
}
```

This mathematical formulation presents correlation indices that are practically equal to the previous case. In other words, even though the formulation is better than the first one, the parameters estimation is still influenced by correlations among parameters.

Therefore, the model can be reformulated as follows:

$$c = \frac{1}{\frac{1}{323} - \frac{1}{373}}$$

$$y_{1i} = \exp\left(\beta_1 + c\beta_2 \left(\frac{1}{x_{1i}} - \frac{1}{300}\right)\right) + \varepsilon_{1i} \tag{6.19}$$

To analyze this form with the same program as in Example 6.1, the definition of the function `FirstExample` is

```
void FirstExample(int model, int ex,
        BzzVector &b, BzzVector &x, BzzVector &y)
{
double c = 1. / (1./323. - 1./373.);
y[1] = exp(b[1] + c * b[2] * ( 1./ x[1] - 1./ 300.));
}
```

In this formulation, the second term at the exponent is multiplied by a coefficient to normalize it. As a result, the condition number is largely improved, even though the other correlation indices are quite equal to the previous formulation:

```
Condition Number 6.407599e+000
```

At last, the model can also be formulated as follows:

$$c = \frac{1}{\frac{1}{373} - \frac{1}{273}}$$

$$y_{1i} = e^{c\beta_1 \left(\frac{1}{x_{1i}} - \frac{1}{273}\right) - c\beta_2 \left(\frac{1}{x_{1i}} - \frac{1}{373}\right)} + \varepsilon_{1i}$$

(6.20)

To examine it, the function `FirstExample` definition is to be replaced:

```
void FirstExample(int model,int ex,
        BzzVector &b,BzzVector &x,BzzVector &y)
{
double c = 1. / (1./373. - 1./273.);
double f1 = 1./x[1] - 1./273.;
double f2 = 1./x[1] - 1./373.;
y[1] = exp(c*(b[1]*f1 - b[2] * f2));
}
```

This formulation adopts a polynomial in the Lagrange form at the exponent. As already discussed in Chapter 1, it is largely better than the other standard forms.

The condition number here is further smaller:

```
Condition Number 4.599046e+000
```

and even the correlation indices are significantly improved compared to all the above formulations, that is, the values of the T_j tolerance are

```
Columns correlation = Tj Tolerance
1 7.7775150e-001
2 7.7775150e-001
```

In every formulation, the model is rearranged so as to preserve the dependent variable, which is the only one to be subject to experimental error as in hypotheses (with null expected value and constant variance for the error).

In previous formulations, parameters were denoted by the same symbols even though they have different numerical values. In this case, it is necessary that the model parameters of the original formulation are obtained by parameters of other formulations.

5) The most appropriate function is to be selected; there is the need to check which variables are subject to experimental error, which features characterize the error, and so on.

6.9 Model Discrimination

It is worth remarking that a common error is to linearize the model to make the calculation easier.

Let us take, for example, the hydrodealkylation kinetic model for the toluene and hydrogen reaction to benzene and methane, respectively (Fogler, 1992):

$$-r_T = \frac{kK_T p_{H_2} p_T}{1 + K_B p_B + K_T p_T} \tag{6.21}$$

Linearizing the model in order to evaluate the parameters is a spread error:

$$y = \frac{p_{H_2} p_T}{-r_T} = \frac{1}{kK_T} + \frac{K_B}{K_T p_T} p_B + \frac{p_T}{k} = \beta_1 + \beta_2 p_B + \beta_3 p_T \tag{6.22}$$

Such a linearizing procedure must be repeated at each temperature because parameters k, K_T, and K_B are Arrhenius-like functions:

$$k_1 \cdot \exp\left(\frac{E_1}{RT}\right) \tag{6.23}$$

and another linearization is required to get two parameters for each kinetic constant as a function of the inverse of the absolute temperature.

Clearly, with this *modus operandi*, a function different from the theoretical one is minimized and the parameter evaluation may be quite different (possibly, also with an opposite sign) from the right one.

In the past, this technique was adopted, as there were no performing programs to solve nonlinear regression problems and computational times were prohibitive on old computers, and this approach is generally avoided nowadays.

6) Finally, the program for determining the parameters and for analyzing the models can be written.

6.9
Model Discrimination

A frequent problem concerns the selection of the best model among various alternatives.

Objects of the `BzzNonLinearRegression` class can simultaneously examine more models and provide an accurate analysis for each of them by both the method of the least sum of squares and the method of the least median of squares. Moreover, a comparative result is provided at the end of the single-model analyses.

Example 6.4

Analyze the following seven models:

$$y_{1i} = \beta_1 + \beta_2(1-\exp(-\beta_3 x_{1i})) + \varepsilon_{1i} \tag{6.24}$$

$$y_{1i} = \beta_1 + \beta_2 \left(\frac{\beta_3 x_{1i}}{1 + \beta_3 x_{1i}} \right) + \varepsilon_{1i} \qquad (6.25)$$

$$y_{1i} = \beta_1 + \beta_2 \operatorname{atan}(\beta_3 x_{1i}) + \varepsilon_{1i} \qquad (6.26)$$

$$y_{1i} = \beta_1 + \beta_2 \tanh(\beta_3 x_{1i}) + \varepsilon_{1i} \qquad (6.27)$$

$$y_{1i} = \beta_1 + \beta_2 \exp\left(\frac{-\beta_3}{x_{1i}} \right) + \varepsilon_{1i} \qquad (6.28)$$

$$y_{1i} = \frac{\beta_1 + \beta_2 x_{1i} + \beta_3 x_{1i}^2}{1 + \beta_4 x_{1i} + \beta_5 x_{1i}^2} + \varepsilon_{1i} \qquad (6.29)$$

$$y_{1i} = \frac{\beta_1 + \beta_2 x_{1i} + \beta_3 x_{1i}^2 + \beta_4 x_{1i}^3}{1 + \beta_5 x_{1i} + \beta_6 x_{1i}^2 + \beta_7 x_{1i}^3} + \varepsilon_{1i} \qquad (6.30)$$

Models (6.24)–(6.28) were proposed by (Wilcoxson, 1965; Himmelblau, 1970), whereas models (6.29) and (6.30) were just added for this specific example. If the experimental error is larger than a certain value, it may be hard not only to reject all the rival models, except the only one able to properly fit experimental data, but also to select the model even when it is known to be the true one.

In this example, experiments were generated by the model (6.24) by assuming the following parameters:

$$y_{1i} = 10 + 100(1 - \exp(-.115 x_{1i})) \qquad (6.31)$$

By generating the data set in the range $0. \leq x_{1i} \leq 100.$ without experimental errors, the following mean square errors are obtained for each model:

```
1 3.624513e-018
2 1.350316e+001
3 3.305766e+000
4 4.207274e+000
5 1.096260e+001
6 4.706260e-002
7 8.809647e-005
```

It is evident that if the experimental error variance is larger than $4. \div 5.$, models (6.24), (6.26), (6.27), (6.29), and (6.30) have not so large a mean square error to reject them even though many experimental points are generated. Specifically, models (6.29) and (6.30) are almost the same as the true model adopted in generating the data set. Actually, models (6.24), (6.29), and (6.30) are practically overlapped in the selected range.

As shown by Himmelblau (1970), by generating the experimental points with an assigned variance $s^2 > 4.$, the model (6.24) is not ever pointed out as the best one (even without accounting for models (6.29) and (6.30) inserted here).

Caveat no. 6 is then confirmed.
To analyze all the models, the program is

```cpp
#include "BzzMath.hpp"
void MultiModelEx1(int model,int ex,BzzVector &b,
    BzzVector &x,BzzVector &y);
void main(void)
    {
    BzzPrint("\n\nMultiModelEx1");
    int numModels = 7;
    int numX = 1;
    int numY = 1;
    int numExperiments = 16;
    BzzMatrix X(numExperiments,numX,
        0.0001,0.001,0.01,.1,1.,2.,4.,6.,9.,
        12.,16.,18.,20.,40.,70.,100.);
    BzzMatrix Y(numExperiments,numY,
        1.122e+001,1.245e+001,8.895e+000,1.480e+001,
        1.476e+001,3.177e+001,4.443e+001,6.472e+001,
        7.692e+001,8.240e+001,9.778e+001,9.616e+001,
        9.509e+001,1.102e+002,1.124e+002,1.051e+002);
//  BzzMatrix Y(numExperiments,numY,
//      1.122e+001,7.571e+000,1.499e+001,1.358e+001,
//      1.842e+001,3.421e+001,4.565e+001,5.496e+001,
//      7.570e+001,8.728e+001,9.046e+001,1.010e+002,
//      9.509e+001,1.066e+002,1.124e+002,1.100e+002);
//BzzMatrix Y(numExperiments,numY,
//      3.901e+000,1.123e+001,7.675e+000,1.602e+001,
//      2.330e+001,2.811e+001,5.053e+001,5.862e+001,
//      6.960e+001,8.606e+001,9.656e+001,9.372e+001,
//      1.036e+002,1.041e+002,1.075e+002,1.185e+002);
    BzzNonLinearRegression nonLinReg(numModels,X,Y,
        MultiModelEx1);
    BzzVector s2(1,Variance(e));
    int df = 5;
    nonLinReg.SetVariance(df,s2);
    BzzVector b1(3,1.,1.,1.);
    BzzVector bMin(3),bMax(3);
    nonLinReg.InitializeModel(1,b1);
    BzzVector b2(3,1.,100.,1.);
    nonLinReg.InitializeModel(2,b2);
    BzzVector b3(3,1.,1.,1.);
    nonLinReg.InitializeModel(3,b3);
    BzzVector b4(3,1.,1.,1.);
    nonLinReg.InitializeModel(4,b4);
```

```
    BzzVector b5(3,1.,1.,1.);
    nonLinReg.InitializeModel(5,b5);
    BzzVector b6(5,1.,1.,1.,1.,1.);
    nonLinReg.InitializeModel(6,b6);
    BzzVector b7(7,1.,1.,1.,1.,1.,1.,1.);
    nonLinReg.InitializeModel(7,b7);
    nonLinReg.LeastSquaresAnalysis();
    }
void MultiModelEx1(int model,int ex,BzzVector &b,
        BzzVector &x,BzzVector &y)
    {
    switch(model)
        {
        case 1:
            y[1] = b[1] + b[2] * (1. - exp(-b[3] * x[1]));
            break;
        case 2:
            y[1] = b[1] + b[2] * (b[3] * x[1] /
                (1. + b[3] * x[1]));
            break;
        case 3:
            y[1] = b[1] + b[2] * (atan(b[3] * x[1]));
            break;
        case 4:
            y[1] = b[1] + b[2] * (tanh(b[3] * x[1]));
             break;
        case 5:
            y[1] = b[1] + b[2] * exp(-b[3] / x[1]);
            break;
        case 6:
            y[1] = (b[1] + x[1] * ( b[2] + b[3] * x[1])) /
                 (1. + x[1] * (b[4] + b[5] * x[1]));
            break;
        case 7:
            y[1] = (b[1] + x[1] * ( b[2] + x[1] *
                (b[3] + b[4] * x[1]))) /
                (1. + x[1] * (b[5] + x[1] * (b[6] +
                b[7] * x[1])));
            break;
        }
    }
```

Each model uses the function `InitializeModel` to initialize parameters. Such a function requires the specific model number one wants to initialize and an initial guess of parameters as argument. If needed, upper and lower bounds

6.9 Model Discrimination

can be assigned to parameters. If a model is not initialized, its analysis is not performed.

Three different sets of data, all generated with an experimental error variance equal to 8.6, and the respective comparative results are reported here.

Data set no. 1 and comparative results .

```
BzzMatrix Y(numExperiments,numY,
 1.122e+001,1.245e+001,8.895e+000,1.480e+001,
 1.476e+001,3.177e+001,4.443e+001,6.472e+001,
 7.692e+001,8.240e+001,9.778e+001,9.616e+001,
 9.509e+001,1.102e+002,1.124e+002,1.051e+002);
```

```
    MSE   MSE/Best   Fexp      P-Value     Pseudo P-Value
1 12.947 1.1858 1.508693e+000 3.419468e-001 8.161700e-001
2 31.125 2.8508 3.627025e+000 8.168890e-002 1.209606e-001
3 15.978 1.4634 1.861896e+000 2.549656e-001 5.749847e-001
4 16.964 1.5538 1.976844e+000 2.330327e-001 5.137542e-001
5 15.190 1.3913 1.770136e+000 2.744784e-001 6.294936e-001
6 13.725 1.2572 1.599418e+000 3.156215e-001 7.429350e-001
7 10.917 1.0000 1.272256e+000 4.152022e-001 1.000000e+000
```

Model no. 7 (model (6.30)) is the best one.

Data set no. 2 and comparative results .

```
BzzMatrix Y(numExperiments,numY,
 1.122e+001,7.571e+000,1.499e+001,1.358e+001,
 1.842e+001,3.421e+001,4.565e+001,5.496e+001,
 7.570e+001,8.728e+001,9.046e+001,1.010e+002,
 9.509e+001,1.066e+002,1.124e+002,1.100e+002);
```

```
    MSE   MSE/Best   Fexp      P-Value     PseudoP-Value
1 10.772 1.0000 1.255266e+000 4.288532e-001 1.000000e+000
2 24.338 2.2590 2.836109e+000 1.284343e-001 1.548524e-001
3 12.998 1.2066 1.514633e+000 3.401893e-001 7.399455e-001
4 14.298 1.3273 1.666117e+000 2.990444e-001 6.171289e-001
5 21.210 1.9690 2.471648e+000 1.628433e-001 2.351268e-001
6 12.118 1.1249 1.412096e+000 3.703988e-001 8.293431e-001
7 13.575 1.2602 1.581871e+000 3.191115e-001 6.830343e-001
```

Contrary to previous results, the best model is now the model no. 1 (model (6.24)).

Data set no. 3 and comparative results .

```
BzzMatrix Y(numExperiments,numY,
 3.901e+000,1.123e+001,7.675e+000,1.602e+001,
 2.330e+001,2.811e+001,5.053e+001,5.862e+001,
 6.960e+001,8.606e+001,9.656e+001,9.372e+001,
 1.036e+002,1.041e+002,1.075e+002,1.185e+002);
```

```
     MSE   MSE/Best     Fexp           P-Value        PseudoP-Value
1 19.422   1.0027 1.805344e+000 2.667657e-001 9.962167e-001
2 26.292   1.3574 2.443981e+000 1.659480e-001 5.896478e-001
3 19.370   1.0000 1.800510e+000 2.678076e-001 1.000000e+000
4 25.429   1.3128 2.363769e+000 1.754168e-001 6.307791e-001
5 31.796   1.6415 2.955592e+000 1.193328e-001 3.831162e-001
6 22.039   1.1378 2.048600e+000 2.213669e-001 8.143693e-001
7 21.570   1.1136 2.005081e+000 2.295459e-001 8.339591e-001
```

Model no. 3 (model (6.26)) is pointed out as the best one even with this data set.

When the experimental error variance is larger than the mean square errors obtained without any experimental error, the best model selected may arbitrarily differ from the one that generated the same experimental data set. Furthermore, none of the seven rival models can be reasonably discarded.

Chapter 8 shall explain methods to select new experimental points in order to improve the model discrimination. It should be evident that even by adopting the best experimental design, it could be impossible to get a single satisfactory model from among rival alternatives.

6.10
Model Collection and Model Selection

Users of toolkits developed to examine models have the important task to provide the model, or more frequently the models, that can reasonably characterize the physical phenomenon one is analyzing.

These models can be dictated by some theories especially in the case of nonlinear models; but theories usually cannot provide a single specific model, rather they can lead to a family of models having a particular structure.

Model collection can be defined as the task of collecting reasonable models.

A relevant case is given by heterogeneous reactions, where, according to Hougen–Watson kinetics, the reaction rate can be expressed as follows:

$$r = \frac{num}{\left(\sum_{i=1}^{n} k_i \varphi_i\right)^\alpha} \quad (6.32)$$

where n denotes the amount of terms in the expression at the denominator. The numerator *num* is a known function, whereas neither the most adequate functions φ_i to characterize the phenomenon nor their total amount are known. The model contains adaptive parameters α and k_i that should be evaluated for each model in order to fit the assigned experimental data set.

Buzzi-Ferraris *et al.* (1974a) proposed a method that allows to generate the functions φ_i automatically in such situations. By doing so, it is possible to examine a large amount of rival models and look at the ones that better fit experimental points. Moreover, it is possible to assign physical meaning for each of them by adopting some specific devices.

The proposed technique is similar to the stepwise method adopted for linear models, but in this specific case, the problem is to select the best combinations of functions at the denominator of equation (6.32) by using forward and backward procedures.

Buzzi-Ferraris et al. (1974b) applied this procedure to the ammonia kinetic. φ_i and the exponent α depend on the chosen assumptions on the reaction mechanism and on the rate-controlling step. The kinetic constants k_i are exponentials in the reciprocal of temperature:

$$k_i = K_i \exp\left(-\frac{E_i}{T}\right) \tag{6.33}$$

where K_i and E_i are parameters. When α is an integer, the expression at the denominator can be expanded and the following equation is derived:

$$r = \frac{num}{\sum_{i=1}^{N} \varkappa_i \phi_i} \tag{6.34}$$

where $N \geq n$ is the number of terms in the denominator; $\phi_i = \varphi_i$ and $\varkappa_i = k_i$ for $\alpha = 1$ only. As a result, rate expression (6.34) is more complex than (6.32) and includes it as a particular case.

It is worth remarking that the amount of terms φ_i (or ϕ_i) in equations (6.32) and (6.34) is often excessively large even for simple reactions. Moreover, some of the constants k_i (or $\varkappa_i$) may be equal to zero and the corresponding parameters of equation (6.33) can be correlated with other parameters in the denominator.

More than a million of possible rate expressions are examined for each numerator if $N \simeq 20$.

This application confirms caveat no. 6: in fact, 23 models are satisfactory among all the rival models that were automatically generated and it is not possible to affirm that only one of them is significantly better than the others.

Model selection can be defined as the task of selecting the best performing model from a set of adequate models on the basis of the available data and the features of model structure.

Spriet (1985) argued that the best model is selected as a trade-off between model fit, model parsimony, and balanced accuracy. So far, the comparison among models was exclusively based on the model ability of matching experimental data.

Model parsimony is related to the complexity of the model.

Some authors associate model parsimony with the number of model parameters (Donckels, 2009). For example, Akaike information criterion (AIC) adopts the following function:

$$AIC = n_E \cdot \log\left(\frac{SSE}{n_E}\right) + 2 \cdot p \qquad (6.35)$$

whereas de Brauwere *et al.* (2005) and Spriet (1985) use Bayesian information criterion (BIC):

$$BIC = n_E \cdot \log\left(\frac{SSE}{n_E}\right) + p \cdot \log(n_E) \qquad (6.36)$$

If the two models present the same least sum of squares, the simplest one, which has a smaller amount of parameters, is selected.

It is evident that models with the same number of parameters cannot be effectively selected by both the previous functions if they are already satisfactory for their mean square error.

Therefore, it can be concluded that the best model selection is an infeasible problem in many practical cases when the selection is based on the model ability only of fitting experimental data.

Moreover, it is worth reminding caveat no. 5: it is an error to think the true model (supposing that it is rational to speak about the true model) is included in the arena of rival models one is analyzing.

The knowledge of the physical problem, which the model is searched for, and its final use can often support us in a reasonable selection of the most appropriate model.

7
Nonlinear Regression Case Studies

Examples of this chapter can be found in the directory Vol2_Chapter7 within the enclosed CD-ROM.

7.1
Introduction

This chapter proposes some typical problems with different degrees of complexity. It shows how to solve main issues that one can encounter while developing a program and analyzing results for nonlinear regression problems.

It is worth remarking that when a model with an only dependent variable is reformulated to prevent any correlation among parameters, two rules are ever valid:

If more parameters are grouped in a product, it is profitable to consider such a product as a single parameter, when possible.

For example, if the model has the form

$$y_{1i} = \frac{\beta_1 \beta_2 \beta_3 x_{1i} x_{2i}}{(1. + \beta_2 x_{1i} + \beta_3 x_{2i})^\alpha} + \varepsilon_{1i} \tag{7.1}$$

it is suitable to reformulate it either as

$$y_{1i} = \frac{\beta_1 x_{1i} x_{2i}}{(1 + \beta_2 x_{1i} + \beta_3 x_{2i})^\alpha} + \varepsilon_{1i} \tag{7.2}$$

or as

$$y_{1i} = \frac{x_{1i} x_{2i}}{(\beta_1 + \beta_2 x_{1i} + \beta_3 x_{2i})^\alpha} + \varepsilon_{1i} \tag{7.3}$$

when the new parameter β_1 is surely positive.

When two parameters are in the following form

$$\beta_i \exp(\beta_j x) \tag{7.4}$$

Interpolation and Regression Models for the Chemical Engineer: Solving Numerical Problems
Guido Buzzi-Ferraris and Flavio Manenti
Copyright © 2010 WILEY-VCH Verlag GmbH & Co. KGaA, Weinheim
ISBN: 978-3-527-32652-5

and the parameter β_i is surely positive, it is useful to reparameterize them as

$$c = \frac{\exp(c[\beta_i(x-x_{\max})-\beta_j(x-x_{\min})])}{x_{\min}-x_{\max}} \tag{7.5}$$

On the other hand, if one is not sure that β_i is positive, it is suitable to transform (7.4) into

$$\beta_i \exp\left(\beta_j \frac{x-\bar{x}}{.5(x_{\max}-x_{\min})}\right) \tag{7.6}$$

Both these two reparameterizations (7.5) and (7.6) are better than the usual reparameterization

$$\beta_i \exp(\beta_j(x-\bar{x})) \tag{7.7}$$

Besides aforementioned rules, other devices should be taken into account, even though they can sometimes be ineffective. For example, the following two points usually improve the model formulation:

When a parameter is at the numerator and, at the same time, the denominator consists of a summation where one of its terms is constant, one can try to move the parameter from the numerator to the denominator. To clarify it, the model

$$y_{1i} = \frac{\beta_1 x_{1i} x_{2i}}{(1+\beta_2 x_{1i}+\beta_3 x_{2i})^\alpha} + \varepsilon_{1i} \tag{7.8}$$

can be transformed into

$$y_{1i} = \frac{x_{1i} x_{2i}}{(\beta_1+\beta_2 x_{1i}+\beta_3 x_{2i})^\alpha} + \varepsilon_{1i} \tag{7.9}$$

when β_1 is surely positive.

When there is a summation, it is suitable to normalize the functions that multiply the parameters. For example, by taking into account the previous case, it could be interesting to examine even the model

$$y_{1i} = \frac{\beta_1 x_{1i} x_{2i}}{\left(1+\beta_2 \frac{x_{1i}}{x_{1\max}}+\beta_3 \frac{x_{2i}}{x_{2\max}}\right)^\alpha} + \varepsilon_{1i} \tag{7.10}$$

and, when β_1 is surely positive, the model

$$y_{1i} = \frac{x_{1i} x_{2i}}{\left(\beta_1+\beta_2 \frac{x_{1i}}{x_{1\max}}+\beta_3 \frac{x_{2i}}{x_{2\max}}\right)^\alpha} + \varepsilon_{1i} \tag{7.11}$$

Finally, when there is a product such as

$$y_{1i} = \beta_1 f_1(x_i)^{\beta_2} f_2(x_i)^{\beta_3} + \varepsilon_{1i} \tag{7.12}$$

it is suitable to try the model

$$y_{1i} = \beta_1 \left[\frac{f_1(\mathbf{x}_i)}{f_{1\max}}\right]^{\beta_2} \left[\frac{f_2(\mathbf{x}_i)}{f_{2\max}}\right]^{\beta_3} + \varepsilon_{1i} \tag{7.13}$$

It is important to underline that it is essential to follow three rules while analyzing a model.

Rule No. 1

Calculations must be repeated by starting from different initial guesses.

Rule No. 2

Calculations must be repeated by modifying the model even though the same model seems reasonably good.

These repetitions are needed as the objective function may present many local minima; actually, the program could identify one of them and not necessarily the global minimum.

Example 7.1

Consider the model (Watts, 1981; Seber and Wild, 2003) with one dependent variable, one independent variable, and two parameters

$$y_{1i} = \beta_1 \exp(-\beta_2 x_{1i}) + \varepsilon_{1i} \tag{7.14}$$

Parameter β_1 can be even negative in this specific case. Experimental data can be directly acquired by the following program:

```
#include "BzzMath.hpp"
void MultimodalExample(int model, int ex, BzzVector &b,
        BzzVector &x, BzzVector &y);
void main(void)
    {
    int numModels = 1;
    int numX = 1;
    int numY = 1;
    int numExperiments = 4;
    BzzMatrix X(numExperiments, numX,
            -2.,-1.,1.,2.);
    BzzMatrix Y(numExperiments, numY,
            0.,1.,-.9,0.);
    BzzNonLinearRegression nonLinReg(numModels, X, Y,
            MultimodalExample);
    BzzVector b1(2,1.,1.);
// BzzVector b1(2,.087,.62);
// BzzVector b1(2,-.063,-.699);
```

```
            nonLinReg.InitializeModel(1,b1);
            nonLinReg.LeastSquaresAnalysis();
        }

        void MultimodalExample(int model,int ex,BzzVector &b,
                BzzVector &x,BzzVector &y)
        {
        y[1] = b[1] * exp(-b[2] * x[1]);
        }
```

Two minima exist: one in correspondence with the following values of parameters:

```
    1    8.71907092587850e-002
    2    6.19906183662809e-001
```

and the other one with

```
    1    -6.33648206431802e-002
    2    -6.98853731263718e-001
```

According to the initial guess, the program may reach one of these minima.

Rule No. 3

Model analysis cannot be focused on a specific feature (i.e., a specific correlation index), rather it must be the most general as much as possible.

Before accepting or discarding a model, it must be thoroughly examined by taking care of each warning that highlights any unsatisfactory feature of the analysis.

The third rule shall be often neglected in the examples of this book as they are proposed to simply enhance one special feature of a model analysis. In addition, some problems could be trivially solved by adopting other techniques.

Previous example is a clear demonstration of our approach: it is evident that the experimental design is inadequate to seriously analyze the model, rather the example is prepared to show without any ambiguity that the objective function of nonlinear models might be multimodal.

It is not a case that some of the following examples were already proposed in the scientific literature (Seber and Wild, 2003; Bates and Watts, 2007; Ryan, 2009; Himmelblau, 1970), but often different data sets are adopted in examining them in order to highlight some specific aspects of model analysis.

7.2
One Dependent Variable with Constant Variance

The following examples refer to problems where it is essential to reformulate the model in order to properly analyze the model.

Example 7.2

Consider the following theoretical model with one dependent variable, one independent variable, and five parameters:

$$y_{1i} = \beta_5 \frac{\beta_1 x_{1i} + 2.\beta_1\beta_2 x_{1i}^2 + 3.\beta_1\beta_2\beta_3 x_{1i}^3 + 4.\beta_1\beta_2\beta_3\beta_4 x_{1i}^4}{1. + \beta_1 x_{1i} + \beta_1\beta_2 x_{1i}^2 + \beta_1\beta_2\beta_3 x_{1i}^3 + \beta_1\beta_2\beta_3\beta_4 x_{1i}^4} + \varepsilon_{1i} \quad (7.15)$$

Let us also suppose that only the dependent variable is subject to experimental error with constant variance, the estimation of which based on 4 degrees of freedom is equal to $7.5 \cdot 10^{-4}$.

Experimental values can be directly acquired by the following program.

The model in its original form is surely ill conditioned: products $\beta_1\beta_2$, $\beta_1\beta_2\beta_3$, and $\beta_1\beta_2\beta_3\beta_4$ make parameters correlated. In fact, the analysis of the model in this form leads to the following results:

```
Condition Number 6.405454e+015 ** WARNING **
Columns correlation = Tj Tolerance
1    3.0807301e-003      ** WARNING **
2    1.0886689e-001
3    1.7783183e-003      ** WARNING **
4    6.3793370e-003      ** WARNING **
5    2.3823624e-003      ** WARNING **


      ** WARNING ** Correlation between Parameters
  The Tj Tolerance identifies serious multicollinearities
```

Therefore, the model is to be reformulated. A possible alternative is

$$y_{1i} = \beta_5 \frac{\beta_1 x_{1i} + .02\beta_2 x_{1i}^2 + .003\beta_3 x_{1i}^3 + .0004\beta_4 x_{1i}^4}{1 + \beta_1 x_{1i} + .01\beta_2 x_{1i}^2 + .001\beta_3 x_{1i}^3 + .0001\beta_4 x_{1i}^4} + \varepsilon_{1i} \quad (7.16)$$

The program is

```
#include "BzzMath.hpp"
void ModelEx1(int model,int ex,BzzVector &b,
        BzzVector &x,BzzVector &y);
void main(void)
    {
    int numModels = 1;
    int numX = 1;
    int numY = 1;
    int numExperiments = 31;
    BzzMatrix X(numExperiments,numX,
         0.,1.,2.,3.,4.,5.,6.,7.,8.,9.,
         10.,11.,12.,13.,14.,15.,16.,17.,18.,19.,
         20.,21.,22.,23.,24.,25.,26.,27.,28.,29.,30.);
```

7 Nonlinear Regression Case Studies

```
    BzzMatrix Y(numExperiments,numY,
        .05,.0857,.20119,.2940,.3806,.550,.7073,.9536,
        1.211,1.471,1.799,2.09,2.316,2.588,2.834,3.071,
        3.131,3.317,3.431,3.606,3.675,3.701,3.785,
        3.86,3.948,3.988,3.961,4.016,4.04,4.037,4.112);
    BzzVector s2(1,7.5e-4);
    BzzNonLinearRegression nonLinReg(numModels,X,Y,
        ModelEx1);
    nonLinReg.SetVariance(4,s2);
    BzzVector b(5,1.,1.,1.,1.,1.); // Original
//  BzzVector b(4,1.,1.,1.,1.); // k2 = 0.
//  BzzVector b(3,1.,1.,1.); // k2 = 0. k3 = 0.
    nonLinReg.InitializeModel(1,b);
    nonLinReg.LeastSquaresAnalysis();
//  nonLinReg.RobustAnalysis();
    BzzPause();
    }

void ModelEx1(int model,int ex,BzzVector &b,
        BzzVector &x,BzzVector &y)
    {
    double k1,k2,k3,k4,vmax;
    k1 = b[1];   k2 = b[2];   k3 = b[3];   k4 = b[4];
    vmax = b[5];
    double wn = x[1] * (k1 + x[1] * (2.*k2*.01 + x[1] *
        (3.*k3*.001 + x[1] * 4.*k4*.0001)));
    double wd = 1. + x[1] * (k1 + x[1] * (k2*.01 + x[1] *
        (k3*.001 + x[1] * k4*.0001)));
    y[1] = vmax * wn / wd;
    }
```

In this case, the constructor

```
    BzzNonLinearRegression nonLinReg(numModels,X,Y,
        ModelEx1);
```

requires the number of rival models, the matrix X containing the experimental values of the independent variables **x**, the matrix Y containing the experimental values of the dependent variables **y** and the name of the function `ModelEx1` where the model is evaluated.

Since the experimental error variance is known, the following instructions are added to the program:

```
    BzzVector s2(1,7.5e-4);
    int dof = 4;
    nonLinReg.SetVariance(dof,s2);
```

7.2 One Dependent Variable with Constant Variance

The object initializes parameters of all the rival models (in this case, only the model no. 1):

```
BzzVector b(5,1.,1.,1.,1.,1.);
nonLinReg.InitializeModel(1,b1);
```

Finally, the object invokes the function

```
nonLinReg.LeastSquaresAnalysis();
```

that evaluates the model (or models) parameters and analyzes them.
Results are printed out on the default file `BzzFile.txt`.
Main results are reported and discussed here.
First of all, the model can be considered reasonably good since the mean square error is small: `8.2783666e-004`. Therefore, knowing the error variance,

```
F-test for the model
Fexperimental = 1.103782e+000
The probability that F with dfNum 26 dfDen 4
is greater than 1.103782e+000 is 5.250443e-001
```

The value `Fexperimental` is the ratio between the mean square error of the model and the estimate of the error variance (0.075). The probability that the theoretical F is higher than such a value is equal to 52.5%. Thus, it is reasonable to accept the model.

Values of parameters evaluated by minimizing the function with criteria implemented in the regression program are quite close to estimates of the Newton method: it is a reasonable assurance on the optimal value of parameters.

```
        Parameters obtained        Parameters obtained
        by minimization            with Newton method
   1    1.00875531532904e-001      1.00862728065602e-001
   2   -4.43975576967639e-002     -4.37120441716498e-002
   3    2.41604012877922e-001      2.40802116750217e-001
   4    8.30860055171348e-001      8.31286979432577e-001
   5    1.08936047263191e+000      1.08930012274018e+000
```

The condition number of the model is equal to `6.036847e+002` and it seems to be good.

The correlation matrix does not identify any serious correlation among parameters. Inflation factors are

```
Variance inflation factor
   1    1.4133238e+002
   2    8.2503739e+002
   3    1.0200690e+003    ** WARNING **
   4    1.0059625e+003    ** WARNING **
   5    4.3188336e+002

** WARNING ** Correlation between Parameters
```

Large values of inflation factors indicate that the corresponding parameters are probably correlated with the others.

7 Nonlinear Regression Case Studies

T_j tolerances are

```
Columns correlation = Tj Tolerance
1    7.0755194e-003   ** WARNING **
2    1.2120663e-003   ** WARNING **
3    9.8032586e-004   ** WARNING **
4    9.9407281e-004   ** WARNING **
5    2.3154400e-003   ** WARNING **

** WARNING ** Correlation between Parameters
The Tj Tolerance identifies serious multicollinearities
```

Small tolerances indicate that the corresponding parameter is probably correlated with the others.

Previous results show that there is a strong correlation among parameters. Since the experimental design is assumed to be good, the model satisfactorily fits experimental points, and no outliers are detected (as it shall be discussed later); the presence of a parameter correlation unavoidably means that the model is not well-formulated.

Since only a few alternative formulations are available, one can consider some parameters as pointless.

Such information is provided by T-Value of parameters. In fact, the experimental T-Value (to check if a parameter can be removed) and the corresponding probability P-Value (which gives an order of magnitude of the parameter relevance) are

```
Par.    T-Value              P-Value

1     4.1240406e+000      3.3807651e-004
2    -7.6565123e-002      9.3955565e-001   ** WARNING **
3     4.1521668e-001      6.8138989e-001   ** WARNING **
4     3.1311619e+000      4.2706326e-003
5     2.8199382e+001      5.0529001e-021
```

The T-Value is to be compared to the theoretical t-student value in a t-test to check the hypothesis that the analyzed parameter is equal to zero. The P-Value indicates the probability related to the same hypothesis to have a theoretical t larger than the experimental one. Since the T-Value is particularly small for two parameters and, consequently, the P-Value is enough large, it should be reasonable to remove the second parameter. To do so, it is sufficient to adopt the following definition

```
//  BzzVector b(5,1.,1.,1.,1.,1.); // Original
    BzzVector b(4,1.,1.,1.,1.); // Without b2: k2 = 0.
```

and to modify the function

```
void ModelEx1(int model, int ex, BzzVector &b,
        BzzVector &x, BzzVector &y)
    {
    double k1, k2, k3, k4, vmax;
    k1 = b[1];
```

```
    k2 = 0.;
    k3 = b[2];
    k4 = b[3];
    vmax = b[4];
    double wn = x[1] * (k1 + x[1] * (2.*k2*.01 + x[1] *
            (3.*k3*.001 + x[1] * 4.*k4*.0001)));
    double wd = 1. + x[1] * (k1 + x[1] * (k2*.01 + x[1] *
            (k3*.001 + x[1] * k4*.0001)));
    y[1] = vmax * wn / wd;
    }
```

By examining the function, it is possible to see that the amount of parameters is now equal to 4 and k_2 is zeroed. Of course, the code is no longer optimal as some operations have become ineffective; rather, it is not a problem in this case.

By analyzing the results, one can see that the new model is better than the previous one. In fact, the mean square error is `7.9734261e-004`. Therefore,

```
F-test for the model
Fexperimental = 1.063123e+000
The probability that F with dfNum 27 dfDen 4
is greater than 1.063123e+000 is 5.444304e-001
```

and the condition number of the model becomes $8.817070e + 001$, which was significantly improved.

Inflation factors do not detect any collinearity, whereas tolerance indices are

```
Columns correlation = Tj Tolerance
1      4.5457791e-002
2      4.4189141e-002
3      8.7176382e-003    ** WARNING **
4      2.1905221e-002
```

showing that the third parameter is still correlated with the others.

Neither the experimental `T-Value` nor the related probability gives a clear indication about a possible parameter removal.

One could try to remove even the parameter k_3. To do so, the old definition of b is to be replaced with the new one

```
//   BzzVector b(5,1.,1.,1.,1.,1.); // Original
//   BzzVector b(4,1.,1.,1.,1.); // With k2 = 0.
     BzzVector b(3,1.,1.,1.); // With k2 = k3 = 0.
```

and, accordingly, the function becomes

```
    void ModelEx1(int model,int ex,BzzVector &b,
            BzzVector &x,BzzVector &y)
    {
    double k1,k2,k3,k4,vmax;
    k1 = b[1];
    k2 = 0.;
```

```
            k3 = 0.;
            k4 = b[2];
            vmax = b[3];
            double wn = x[1] * (k1 + x[1] * (2.*k2*.01 + x[1] *
                    (3.*k3*.001 + x[1] * 4.*k4*.0001)));
            double wd = 1. + x[1] * (k1 + x[1] * (k2*.01 + x[1] *
                    (k3*.001 + x[1] * k4*.0001)));
            y[1] = vmax * wn / wd;
            }
```

Analyzing the new function, it is possible to see that the total amount of parameters is now equal to 3, as $k_2 = k_3 = 0$.

The analysis of the new model leads to the following considerations.

First of all, the model is still very good. In fact, the value of mean square error is particularly small: 8.9538039e-004. Therefore,

```
        F-test for the model
        Fexperimental = 1.193841e+000
        The probability that F with dfNum 28 dfDen 4
        is greater than 1.193841e+000 is 4.870590e-001
```

and the condition number of the model becomes 1.518590e+001, by showing that a further improvement is obtained through the last reparameterization.

Inflation factors and tolerances do not detect any collinearity:

```
        Columns correlation = Tj Tolerance
        1      1.8395823e-001
        2      2.1180377e-001
        3      3.1137888e-001
```

Hence, this last formulation seems to be preferable rather than the previous ones.

It is also necessary to check that no outliers are present. On this subject, it is sufficient to substitute the least sum of squares method with a robust analysis, by replacing the statement

```
        nonLinReg.LeastSquaresAnalysis();
```

with

```
        nonLinReg.RobustAnalysis();
```

No probable outliers are identified.

Example 7.3

Consider the following theoretical model with one dependent variable, one independent variable, and five parameters:

$$y_{1i} = \beta_1 \exp(\beta_2 x_{1i}) + \beta_3 \exp(\beta_4 [x_{1i} - \beta_5]^2) + \varepsilon_{1i} \tag{7.17}$$

7.2 One Dependent Variable with Constant Variance

Only the dependent variable is subject to experimental error with constant variance and its estimate based on 4 degrees of freedom is equal to $9.8 \cdot 10^{-4}$. Parameters β_1 and β_3 are surely positive for theoretical reasons.

Experimental values can be directly acquired by the following program. Evaluate model parameters and analyze the model.

The program is

```
#include "BzzMath.hpp"
void ModelEx2(int model,int ex,BzzVector &b,
         BzzVector &x,BzzVector &y);
void main(void)
   {
   int numModels = 1;
   int numX = 1;
   int numY = 1;
   int numExperiments = 23;
   BzzMatrix X(numExperiments,1,
       0.,.5,1.,1.5,2.,2.5,3.,3.5,4.,4.5,5.,5.5,
       6.,6.5,7.,7.5,8.,8.5,9.,9.5,10.,10.5,11.);
   BzzMatrix Y(numExperiments,numY,
       25.318,21.538,18.275,15.586,13.152,11.249,
       9.526,8.172,6.929,5.843,5.028,4.228,3.554,
       4.634,31.801,5.668,1.925,1.549,1.335,
       1.183,.997,.875,.685);
   BzzVector s2(1,9.8e-4);
   BzzNonLinearRegression nonLinReg(numModels,
       X,Y,ModelEx2);
   nonLinReg.SetVariance(4,s2);
   BzzVector b(5,1.,1.,1.,1.,1.);
   nonLinReg.InitializeModel(1,b);
   nonLinReg.LeastSquaresAnalysis();
   }

void ModelEx2(int model,int ex,BzzVector &b,
         BzzVector &x,BzzVector &y)
   {
   y[1] = b[1] * exp(b[2] * (x[1] - 5.5)) +
          b[3] * exp(b[4] * BzzPow2(x[1] - b[5]));
   }
```

Main results are reported and discussed here.

The condition number is equal to `9.978499e+002`. The Jacobian matrix is well conditioned.

	Parameters obtained by minimization	Parameters obtained with Newton method
1	6.55516116507940e+000	6.56188144556826e+000

```
    2  -1.46324529410255e-001   -1.47198643386633e-001
    3   1.20184668071665e+001    1.17615270618419e+001
    4  -2.43458805958322e-001   -2.53245332726533e-001
    5  -7.47160518186305e-001   -6.98210334060464e-001
```

Since the estimate of the Newton method practically coincides with the one obtained through the implemented minimization criteria, one can assume that the minimum is achieved.

The mean square error is equal to $4.2805368e+001$ and since the estimate of the variance of the error is equal to $9.8 \cdot 10^{-4}$,

```
F-test for the model
Fexperimental = 4.367895e+004
The probability that F with dfNum 18 dfDen 4
is greater than 4.367895e+004 is 1.164735e-009 *** WARNING
```

The model could seem inadequate to represent the experimental points on the whole domain, but it is suitable to make an attempt using another initial guess and a model reformulation before discarding the existing model.

By replacing the initial guess with

```
BzzVector b(5,1.,-1.,1.,-1.,1.);
```

the same outcome is obtained, by further verifying the hypothesis that the objective function is at the minimum condition.

Conversely, if the model is reformulated as follows

$$y_{1i} = \exp\left(\frac{\beta_1(x_{1i}-11) + \beta_2 x_{1i}}{-11}\right) + \exp\left(\beta_3 + \beta_4[x_{1i}-\beta_5]^2\right) + \varepsilon_{1i} \qquad (7.18)$$

by means of the following code

```
void ModelEx2(int model, int ex, BzzVector &b,
              BzzVector &x, BzzVector &y)
{
    double c = 1./(-11.);
    y[1] = exp(c * (b[1] * (x[1] - 11.) + b[2] * x[1])) +
           exp(b[3] + b[4] * BzzPow2(x[1] - b[5]));
}
```

using the following initial guess

```
BzzVector b(5,1.,1.,1.,1.,1.);
```

the condition number is equal to $1.077853e+002$. The Jacobian matrix is well conditioned.

As the estimate of the Newton method practically coincides with the one obtained through the implemented minimization criteria, one can assume that the minimum is achieved.

The mean square error is equal to $1.3078117e-003$ and since the estimate of the variance of the error is equal to $9.8 \cdot 10^{-4}$,

```
F-test for the model
Fexperimental = 1.334502e+000
The probability that F with dfNum 18 dfDen 4
is greater than 1.334502e+000 is 4.287761e-001
```

In other words, the model is adequate to represent the experimental points. Considering again the original model and adopting the following initial guesses:

```
BzzVector b(5,1.,1.,30.,-10.,7.);
```

It leads to

```
Condition Number 4.551936e+002
Mean Square Error = 1.3078117e-003
```

Hence, the previous solution was an only local minimum.

Since the condition number of the reformulated model is smaller than the previous one and even indices indicating parameter correlations are better, this latter formulation is preferable.

A further improvement is obtained with the following formulation:

$$y_{1i} = \exp\left(\frac{\beta_1(x_{1i}-11)+\beta_2 x_{1i}}{-11}\right) + \exp(\beta_3 + 5 \cdot \beta_4[x_{1i}-\beta_5]^2) + \varepsilon_{1i} \quad (7.19)$$

implemented through these statements:

```
void ModelEx2(int model,int ex,BzzVector &b,
       BzzVector &x,BzzVector &y)
   {
   double e1 = c * (b[1] * (x[1] - 11.) + b[2] * x[1]);
   double e2 = b[3] + 5. * b[4] * BzzPow2(x[1] - b[5]);
   if(e1 > 100.)e1 = 100;
   else if(e1 < -100.) e1 = -100.;
   if(e2 > 100.)e2 = 100;
   else if(e2 < -100.) e2 = -100.;
   y[1] = exp(e1) + exp(e2);
   }
```

and with

```
BzzVector b(5,1.,1.,log(30.),-10.,7.);
```

as initial guess. The condition number is equal to $2.184103e+001$. Hence, this last formulation seems the best one.

It is also necessary to check that no outliers are present. On this subject, it is sufficient to substitute the least sum of squares method with a robust analysis, by replacing the statement

```
nonLinReg.LeastSquaresAnalysis();
```

with

```
nonLinReg.RobustAnalysis();
```

No outliers are detected through a robust analysis.

Example 7.4

Consider the following theoretical model with one dependent variable, one independent variable, and five parameters:

$$y_{1i} = \frac{\beta_1 + \beta_2 x_i + \beta_3 x_{1i}^2}{1 + \beta_4 x_{1i}} + \varepsilon_{1i} \qquad (7.20)$$

Only the dependent variable is subject to experimental error with constant variance and its estimate based on 5 degrees of freedom is equal to $5.8 \cdot 10^{-2}$.

Experimental values can be directly acquired with the following program. Evaluate the model parameters and analyze the model.

The program is

```
#include "BzzMath.hpp"
  void ModelEx3(int model,int ex,BzzVector &b,
          BzzVector &x,BzzVector &y);
  void main(void)
    {
    int numModels = 1;
    int numX = 1;
    int numY = 1;
    int numExperiments = 14;
    BzzMatrix X(numExperiments,numX,
          10.,12.,14.,16.,18.,20.,22.,24.,26.,
          28.,30.,50.,100.,200.);
    BzzMatrix Y(numExperiments,numY,
          -3.022,-2.89,-3.14,-2.67,-3.40,-2.72,
          -2.94,-2.25,-2.37,-2.68,-2.09,
          -1.54,.628,6.12);
    BzzVector s2(1,5.8e-2);
    BzzNonLinearRegression nonLinReg(numModels,X,Y,
          ModelEx3);
    nonLinReg.SetVariance(5,s2);
    BzzVector b(4,1.,1.,1.,1.);
// BzzVector b(3,1.,1.,1.);
    nonLinReg.InitializeModel(1,b);
    nonLinReg.LeastSquaresAnalysis();
// nonLinReg.RobustAnalysis();
    }

  void ModelEx3(int model,int ex,BzzVector &b,
          BzzVector &x,BzzVector &y)
    {
    y[1] = (b[1] + x[1] * (b[2] + b[3] * x[1])) /
          (1. + x[1] * b[4]);
    }
```

Main results are reported and discussed here.
The condition number is

```
Condition Number 1.033140e+005 ** WARNING **
```

The Jacobian matrix is ill conditioned.

As the estimate of the Newton method practically coincides with the one obtained through the implemented minimization criteria, one can assume that the minimum is achieved.

The mean square error is equal to `7.9110546e-002`. Since the estimate of the error variance is equal to $5.8 \cdot 10^{-2}$,

```
F-test for the model
Fexperimental = 1.363975e+000
The probability that F with dfNum 10 dfDen 5
is greater than 1.363975e+000 is 3.849943e-001
```

In other words, the model seems adequate to represent the experimental points. Actually, a strong correlation among parameters exists and it is underlined by inflation factors

```
Variance inflation factor
1    2.1505142e+001
2    1.4293240e+004    ** WARNING **
3    7.7252860e+004    ** WARNING **
4    2.5846351e+004    ** WARNING **
```

and tolerances

```
Columns correlation = Tj Tolerance
1    4.6500507e-002
2    6.9963143e-005    ** WARNING **
3    1.2944505e-005    ** WARNING **
4    3.8690181e-005    ** WARNING **
```

It is therefore appropriate to reformulate the model. By using the following reformulation:

$$y_{1i} = \left(\frac{(\beta_1(x_{1i}-100.)(x_{1i}-200.))}{((10.-100.)(10.-200.))} + \frac{(\beta_2(x_{1i}-10.)(x_{1i}-200.))}{((100.-10.)(100.-200.))} \right.$$
$$\left. + \frac{(\beta_3(x_{1i}-10.)(x_{1i}-100.))}{((200.-10.)(200.-100.))} \right) / (1. + \beta_4 x_{1i}) + \varepsilon_{1i} \quad (7.21)$$

which can be implemented in the program by replacing the previous function with

```
void ModelEx3(int model, int ex, BzzVector &b,
        BzzVector &x, BzzVector &y)
{
    double x1 = 10.;
    double x2 = 100.;
    double x3 = 200.;
```

```
y[1] = (b[1] * ((x[1] - x2) * (x[1] - x3)) /
       ((x1 - x2) * (x1 - x3)) +
       b[2] * ((x[1] - x1) * (x[1] - x3)) /
       ((x2 - x1) * (x2 - x3)) +
       b[3] * ((x[1] - x1) * (x[1] - x2)) /
       ((x3 - x1) * (x3 - x2))) /
       (1.+ x[1] * b[4]);
}
```

the following results are obtained.

```
Condition Number 1.291342e+005 ** WARNING **
```

The Jacobian matrix is ill conditioned and even the other indices show that there are strong correlations among parameters.

Analyzing the T-Value for eliminating some parameters results in

```
Par.        T-Value            P-Value
 1    -4.5229472e+000     1.1033203e-003
 2     4.5707390e-001     6.5738631e-001 ** WARNING **
 3     1.5894026e-001     8.7688007e-001 ** WARNING **
 4    -1.6284803e-001     8.7388191e-001 ** WARNING **
```

Consequently, there are significant indications saying that a parameter can be neglected. Removing the third parameter, the following model formulation is obtained:

$$y_{1i} = \frac{(\beta_1(x_{1i}-200.)-\beta_2(x_{1i}-10.))}{(10.-200.)(1.+\beta_3 x_{1i})} + \varepsilon_{1i} \qquad (7.22)$$

In the program, it is sufficient to reinitialize the remaining three parameters

```
//   BzzVector b(4,1.,1.,1.,1.);
BzzVector b(3,1.,1.,1.);
```

and replace the old model by introducing the following statements:

```
void ModelEx3(int model,int ex,BzzVector &b,
       BzzVector &x,BzzVector &y)
{
  double x1 = 10.;
  double x2 = 200.;
  double c = 1. / (x1 - x2);
  y[1] = c * (b[1] * (x[1] - x2) - b[2] * (x[1] - x1))
       / (1. + b[3] * x[1]);
}
```

Main results are reported and discussed here:

```
Condition Number 2.783576e+003 ** WARNING **
```

The Jacobian matrix is still ill conditioned, even though it has been significantly improved.

```
        Parameters obtained        Parameters obtained
          by minimization           with Newton method
1   -3.08735805854853e+000      -3.08783476649398e+000
2    4.64961882629136e+000       4.65268337768344e+000
3   -1.19926640499357e-003      -1.19565622904018e-003
```

Since the estimate of Newton method practically coincides with the one obtained through the implemented minimization criteria, one can assume that the minimum is achieved.

The mean square error is equal to 7.2100040e-002 as the estimate of the variance of error is equal to $5.8 \cdot 10^{-2}$

```
F-test for the model
Fexperimental = 1.243104e+000
The probability that F with dfNum 11 dfDen 5
is greater than 1.243104e+000 is 4.304620e-001
```

In other words, the model is adequate to represent the experimental data. Actually, inflation factors are

```
Variance inflation factor
1    2.1761955e+000
2    9.6623441e+000
3    9.3720301e+000
```

and tolerances are

```
Columns correlation = Tj Tolerance
1    4.5951754e-001
2    1.0349455e-001
3    1.0670047e-001
```

As a result, the model has uncorrelated parameters in this last formulation, making it preferable against the previous one.

No outliers are detected through a robust analysis.

Example 7.5

Consider the following theoretical model with one dependent variable, one independent variable, and five parameters:

$$y_{1i} = \beta_1 \exp(\beta_2 x_{1i}) + \beta_3 \exp(\beta_4 x_{1i}) + \beta_5 \exp(\beta_6 x_{1i}) + \varepsilon_{1i} \tag{7.23}$$

Only the dependent variable is subject to experimental error with constant variance and its estimate based on 6 degrees of freedom is equal to $5.6 \cdot 10^{-2}$. Parameters β_1, β_3, and β_5 are surely positive for theoretical reasons.

Experimental values can be directly acquired by the following program. Evaluate the model parameters and analyze the model.

7 Nonlinear Regression Case Studies

The program is

```
#include "BzzMath.hpp"
void ModelEx4(int model,int ex,BzzVector &b,
       BzzVector &x,BzzVector &y);
void main(void)
    {
    BzzPrint("\n\nModelEx4");
    int numModels = 1;
    int numX = 1;
    int numY = 1;
    int numExperiments = 30;
    BzzMatrix X(numExperiments,numX,
        1.,2.,3.,4.,5.,6.,7.,8.,9.,10.,
        11.,12.,13.,14.,15.,16.,17.,18.,19.,20.,
        21.,22.,23.,24.,25.,26.,27.,28.,29.,30.);
    BzzMatrix Y(numExperiments,numY,
        1.04406164843470e+001,8.12684606807341e+000,
        6.82234358142487e+000,5.96850353739722e+000,
        5.18800135716795e+000,4.66993299705158e+000,
        4.14870359128013e+000,3.78312218229980e+000,
        3.38942295296424e+000,3.01817344443933e+000,
        2.77262067534577e+000,2.46772456895745e+000,
        2.19957171320495e+000,2.03501312760196e+000,
        1.85143718340168e+000,1.62662492800586e+000,
        1.52865599602141e+000,1.31584579479173e+000,
        1.20670220348158e+000,1.12989460231553e+000,
        1.01423082831238e+000,9.38639344013669e-001,
        8.02154934826507e-001,7.33906878452713e-001,
        6.93108914006121e-001,5.99050574411640e-001,
        5.61089591535024e-001,4.88645174418688e-001,
         4.71192018375059e-001,3.98254939503910e-001);
    BzzNonLinearRegression nonLinReg(numModels,X,Y,
        ModelEx4);
    BzzVector s2(1,5.6e-4);
    int df = 5;
    nonLinReg.SetVariance(df,s2);
    BzzVector b1(6,.1,.1,.1,.1,.1,.1); // 1,2
//  BzzVector b1(4,.1,.1,.1,.1); // 3, 4
    nonLinReg.InitializeModel(1,b1);
    nonLinReg.LeastSquaresAnalysis();
    }

void ModelEx4(int model,int ex,BzzVector &b,
       BzzVector &x,BzzVector &y)
    {
```

```
y[1] = b[1] * exp(b[2] * x[1]) + b[3] *
       exp(b[4] * x[1]) + b[5] * exp(b[6] * x[1]);
}
```

Main results are reported and discussed here:

```
Condition Number 9.978322e+003 ** WARNING **
```

The Jacobian matrix is slightly ill conditioned.

As the estimate of Newton method practically coincides with the one obtained through the minimization criteria implemented in the `BzzNonLinearRegression` class, one can assume that the minimum is achieved.

The mean square error is equal to `6.8137447e-004` as the estimate of the variance of the error is equal to $5.6 \cdot 10^{-4}$,

```
F-test for the model
Fexperimental = 1.216740e+000
The probability that F with dfNum 24 dfDen 5
is greater than 1.216740e+000 is 4.537009e-001
```

In other words, the model is adequate to represent the whole experimental data set. Inflation factors are

```
Variance inflation factor
1    2.8062083e+003    ** WARNING **
2    7.3592006e+002
3    7.7636750e+001
4    3.4701489e+001
5    3.1764763e+002
6    3.0000687e+002
```

and tolerances are

```
Columns correlation = Tj Tolerance
1    3.5635274e-004    ** WARNING **
2    1.3588432e-003    ** WARNING **
3    4.7860707e-003    ** WARNING **
4    2.8817207e-002
5    9.9710269e-003    ** WARNING **
6    9.3115649e-004    ** WARNING **
```

It might be suitable to reformulate the model by using the following form:

$$y_{1i} = \exp\left(\frac{\beta_1(x_{1i}-30.)-\beta_2(x_{2i}-1.)}{29.}\right)$$
$$+ \exp\left(\frac{\beta_3(x_{1i}-30.)-\beta_4(x_{2i}-1.)}{29.}\right) \quad (7.24)$$
$$+ \exp\left(\frac{\beta_5(x_{1i}-30.)-\beta_6(x_{2i}-1.)}{29.}\right) + \varepsilon_{1i}$$

which can be implemented through the following statements:

```
void ModelEx4(int model,int ex,BzzVector &b,
        BzzVector &x,BzzVector &y)
{
double c = 1./29.;
double f1 = x[1] - 30.;
double f2 = x[1] - 1.;
y[1] = exp(c*(b[1]*f1 - b[2] * f2)) +
        exp(c*(b[3]*f1 - b[4] * f2))
        + exp(c*(b[5]*f1 - b[6] * f2));
}
```

The condition number is

```
Condition Number 1.099799e+004 ** WARNING **
```

The conditioning of Jacobian matrix is slightly worsened. As the estimate of the Newton method practically coincides with the one obtained through the implemented minimization criteria, one can assume that the minimum is achieved. Inflation factors and tolerances highlight the presence of parameter correlations.

When analyzing the *t*-test for parameters, note that the parameter no. 3 can be removed. Experience with this kind of models showed that two terms as $\beta_i \exp(\beta_j x_{1i})$ are often enough to appropriately represent experimental points of an exponential decay. Hence, it could be useful to try with the following model of 4 parameters:

$$y_{1i} = \beta_1 \exp(\beta_2 x_{1i}) + \beta_3 \exp(\beta_4 x_{1i}) + \varepsilon_{1i} \qquad (7.25)$$

Parameters definition is to be revised in the program

```
BzzVector b1(4,.1,.1,.1,.1);  // 3, 4
```

together with the function of the model

```
void ModelEx4(int model,int ex,BzzVector &b,
        BzzVector &x,BzzVector &y)
{
y[1] = b[1] * exp(b[2] * x[1]) +
        b[3] * exp(b[4] * x[1]);
}
```

Main results are reported and discussed here:

```
Condition Number 6.510115e+002
```

The conditioning of Jacobian matrix is significantly improved. Since the estimate of the Newton method practically coincides with the one obtained through the implemented minimization criteria, one can assume that the minimum is achieved. Inflation factors and tolerances are good and they do not detect any correlation among parameters.

The mean square error is still good compared to the estimate of the error variance, even though it is slightly worsened against the previous one.

In fact, we have:

```
F-test for the model
Fexperimental = 1.612382e+000
The probability that F with dfNum 26 dfDen 5
is greater than 1.612382e+000 is 3.144138e-001
```

Finally, it is appropriate to check even the following formulation:

$$y_{1i} = \exp\left(\frac{\beta_1(x_{1i}-30.)-\beta_2(x_{1i}-1.)}{29.}\right) + \exp\left(\frac{\beta_3(x_{1i}-30.)-\beta_4(x_{1i}-1.)}{29.}\right) + \varepsilon_{1i} \quad (7.26)$$

The model is implemented through the following code:

```
void ModelEx4(int model, int ex, BzzVector &b,
        BzzVector &x, BzzVector &y)
{
    double c = 1./29.;
    double f1 = x[1] - 30.;
    double f2 = x[1] - 1.;
    y[1] = exp(c*(b[1]*f1 - b[2] * f2)) +
        exp(c*(b[3]*f1 - b[4] * f2));
}
```

Main results are reported and discussed here. The condition number is equal to 4.590649e+002.

The conditioning of Jacobian matrix and correlation indices are both slightly improved. As a result, the model seems the best one among all the proposed formulations.

Example 7.6

Kinetic models are an important source of nonlinear regressions. In addition, they are even an example of how a model reformulation could be essential for successful nonlinear regression problems.

Specifically, the kinetic model proposed by Kittrell, Hunter, and Watson (1966) shows how a correct model formulation can significantly improve the results, by avoiding the problem of ill conditioning. The kinetic model is

$$r = \frac{k K_{NO} K_{H_2} p_{NO} p_{H_2}}{(1 + K_{NO} p_{NO} + K_{H_2} p_{H_2})^2} \quad (7.27)$$

where r is subject to experimental error, while p_{NO} and p_{H_2} are two deterministic variables.

Kinetic model (7.27) is reproposed in (7.28) by the notation adopted in this book:

$$y_{1i} = \frac{\beta_1 \beta_2 \beta_3 x_{1i} x_{2i}}{(1+\beta_2 x_{1i}+\beta_3 x_{2i})^2} + \varepsilon_{1i} \qquad (7.28)$$

The design of experiment is

$$\mathbf{x}_1 = \{1., 5., 10., 1., 5., 10., 1., 5., 10.\} \qquad (7.29)$$

$$\mathbf{x}_2 = \{1., 1., 1., 5., 5., 5., 10., 10., 10.\} \qquad (7.30)$$

$$\begin{aligned}\mathbf{y}_1 = \{&1.21 \cdot 10^{-4}, 8.01 \cdot 10^{-5}, 4.86 \cdot 10^{-5}, 5.90 \cdot 10^{-5}, 1.25 \cdot 10^{-4}, \\ &1.18 \cdot 10^{-4}, 3.14 \cdot 10^{-5}, 1.01 \cdot 10^{-4}, 1.12 \cdot 10^{-4}\}\end{aligned} \qquad (7.31)$$

It should be clear that the model is ill conditioned in the current form, especially for the product among its parameters at the numerator.

Evaluate model parameters and analyze the model. Parameters β_1, β_2, and β_3 are all surely positive for theoretical reasons.

An estimation of the experimental error variance based on 3 degrees of freedom is equal to $1.6 \cdot 10^{-11}$.

The program is

```
#include "BzzMath.hpp"
void ModelEx5(int model,int ex,BzzVector &b,
        BzzVector &x,BzzVector &y);
void main(void)
    {
    int numModels = 1;
    int numX = 2;
    int numY = 1;
    int numExperiments = 9;
    BzzMatrix X(numExperiments,numX,
         1.,1.,  5.,1.,  10.,1.,  1.,5.,  5.,5.,
         10.,5.,  1.,10.,  5.,10.,  10.,10.);
    BzzMatrix Y(numExperiments,numY,
         1.21e-04,8.01e-05,4.86e-05,5.90e-05,
          1.25e-04,1.18e-04,3.14e-05,1.01e-04,
          1.12e-04);
    BzzVector s2(1,1.6e-11);
    BzzNonLinearRegression nonLinReg(numModels,X,Y,
          ModelEx5);
    nonLinReg.SetVariance(3,s2);
    BzzVector b(3,1.,1.,1.);
    nonLinReg.InitializeModel(1,b);
    nonLinReg.LeastSquaresAnalysis();
//  nonLinReg.RobustAnalysis();
```

```
    BzzPause();
}

void ModelEx5(int model, int ex, BzzVector &b,
              BzzVector &x, BzzVector &y)
{
    y[1] = (b[1] * b[2] *b[3] * x[1] * x[2]) /
           BzzPow2(1. + b[2] * x[1] + b[3] * x[2]);
}
```

As it was foreseen, the model presents strong correlations among parameters. Actually, the condition number is

```
Condition Number 2.777116e+020 ** WARNING **
```

Even all the other indices show a strong correlation among parameters. As pointed out in the introduction of this chapter, it is essential to remove the product of parameters when possible.

Consider the following model:

$$y_{1i} = \frac{\beta_1 x_{1i} x_{2i}}{(1 + \beta_2 x_{1i} + \beta_3 x_{2i})^2} + \varepsilon_{1i} \qquad (7.32)$$

It is sufficient to modify the function

```
void ModelEx5(int model, int ex, BzzVector &b,
              BzzVector &x, BzzVector &y)
{
    y[1] = (b[1] * x[1] * x[2]) /
           BzzPow2(1. + b[2] * x[1] + b[3] * x[2]);
}
```

The resulting condition number is

```
Condition Number 7.933738e+013 ** WARNING **
```

which is only slightly better than the previous one. Even the other indices are unsatisfactory.

With the following formulation

$$y_{1i} = \frac{x_{1i} x_{2i}}{(\beta_1 + \beta_2 x_{1i} + \beta_3 x_{2i})^2} + \varepsilon_{1i} \qquad (7.33)$$

which can be implemented by means of

```
void ModelEx5(int model, int ex, BzzVector &b,
              BzzVector &x, BzzVector &y)
{
    y[1] = (x[1] * x[2]) /
           BzzPow2(b[1] + b[2] * x[1] + b[3] * x[2]);
}
```

the condition number is particularly good: `4.570677e+000`.

In addition, the other indices are satisfactory and they demonstrate that model parameters are uncorrelated. The only lack is in the *t*-test on parameters. In fact, we have

```
Par.          T-Value              P-Value
 1      -3.7527579e-001      7.2036383e-001   ** WARNING **
 2       4.1051816e+001      1.3971974e-008
 3       4.4235790e+001      8.9365662e-009
```

where the parameter β_1 seems to be insignificant.

At last, as already discussed, the model

$$y_{1i} = \frac{x_{1i}x_{2i}}{(\beta_1 + .1 \cdot \beta_2 x_{1i} + .1 \cdot \beta_3 x_{2i})^2} + \varepsilon_{1i} \qquad (7.34)$$

implemented by

```
void ModelEx5(int model,int ex,BzzVector &b,
        BzzVector &x,BzzVector &y)
    {
    y[1] = (x[1] * x[2]) / BzzPow2(b[1] +
        .1 * b[2] * x[1] + .1 * b[3] * x[2]);
    }
```

leads to no tangible improvements. Nevertheless, even the current reparameterization, the first parameter seems to be pointless. Therefore, it is possible to try to remove it. Consider that the mean square error obtained with the last two model formulations is

```
Mean Square Error = 1.7293779e-011
```

and the `F-test` results

```
F-test for the model
Fexperimental = 1.080861e+000
The probability that F with dfNum 6 dfDen 3
is greater than 1.080861e+000 is 5.162066e-001
```

Now, by removing β_1, the following model takes place:

$$y_{1i} = \frac{x_{1i}x_{2i}}{(1 + \beta_1 x_{1i} + \beta_2 x_{2i})^2} + \varepsilon_{1i} \qquad (7.35)$$

Parameter definition is to be revised:

```
BzzVector b(2,1.,1.);
```

and even the function of the model is to be changed as

```
void ModelEx5(int model,int ex,BzzVector &b,
        BzzVector &x,BzzVector &y)
    {
    y[1] = (x[1] * x[2]) /
        BzzPow2(1. + b[1] * x[1] + b[2] * x[2]);
    }
```

The condition number is even better than the previous one, $3.004466e+000$, and all other indices are satisfactory and show that model parameters are uncorrelated. The mean square error is equal to $1.6599718e$-011 and the `F-test` results

```
F-test for the model
Fexperimental = 1.037482e+000
The probability that F with dfNum 7 dfDen 3
is greater than 1.037482e+000 is 5.387844e-001
```

Therefore, this model is the best among all the alternatives proposed here.

It is also necessary to check that no outliers are present. On this subject, it is sufficient to substitute the least sum of squares method with a robust analysis, by replacing the statement

```
nonLinReg.LeastSquaresAnalysis();
```

with

```
nonLinReg.RobustAnalysis();
```

No probable outliers are identified.

Example 7.7

The model reformulation is essential even in this example, which is typical of heterogeneous kinetic problems.

The model in study is different from the previous one since kinetic constants depend on the temperature according to an Arrhenius-like form, such as

$$k \cdot \exp\left(-\frac{E}{RT}\right) \tag{7.36}$$

Often, the model presents the form

$$y_{1i} = \frac{\beta_1 \exp\left(\frac{\beta_2}{x_{3i}}\right)\beta_3 \exp\left(\frac{\beta_4}{x_{3i}}\right)\beta_5 \exp\left(\frac{\beta_6}{x_{3i}}\right)x_{1i}x_{2i}}{\left(1.+\beta_3 \exp\left(\frac{\beta_4}{x_{3i}}\right)x_{1i}+\beta_5 \exp\left(\frac{\beta_6}{x_{3i}}\right)x_{2i}\right)^2} + \varepsilon_{1i} \tag{7.37}$$

Even in this case, the single dependent variable has an experimental error with a constant variance equal to $2.2 \cdot 10^{-7}$ estimated with 6 degrees of freedom. Parameters β_1, β_3, and β_5 are surely positive for theoretical reasons.

Experimental data can be directly acquired with the following program:

```
#include "BzzMath.hpp"
void ModelEx6(int model, int ex, BzzVector &b,
        BzzVector &x, BzzVector &y);
void main(void)
```

```
{
BzzPrint("\n\nKinetic Model");
int numModels = 1;
int numX = 3;
int numY = 1;
int numExperiments = 27;
BzzMatrix X(numExperiments,numX,
      1.,1.,475.,   5.,1.,475.,  10.,1.,475.,
      1.,5.,475.,   5.,5.,475.,  10.,5.,475.,
      1.,10.,475.,  5.,10.,475., 10.,10.,475.,

      1.,1.,525.,   5.,1.,525.,  10.,1.,525.,
      1.,5.,525.,   5.,5.,525.,  10.,5.,525.,
      1.,10.,525.,  5.,10.,525., 10.,10.,525.,

      1.,1.,575.,   5.,1.,575.,  10.,1.,575.,
      1.,5.,575.,   5.,5.,575.,  10.,5.,575.,
      1.,10.,575.,  5.,10.,575., 10.,10.,575.);
BzzMatrix Y(numExperiments,numY,
    32.2826,16.9857,9.9846,22.2196,35.3511,
    29.6255,13.9274,33.9322,35.7667,.71947,
    .98679,.77448,.22245,.74184,.9792,.1182,
    .4766,.74368,.017056,.048637,.055582,
    .00463,.01721,.02962,.002451,.00943,.0178);
BzzNonLinearRegression nonLinReg(numModels,X,Y,
      ModelEx6);
BzzVector s2(1,2.2e-7);
int df = 6;
nonLinReg.SetVariance(df,s2);
BzzVector b1(6,1.,1.,1.,1.,1.,1.);
nonLinReg.InitializeModel(1,b1);
nonLinReg.LeastSquaresAnalysis();
BzzPause();
}

void ModelEx6(int model,int ex,BzzVector &b,
      BzzVector &x,BzzVector &y)
  {
  y[1] = b[1] * exp(b[2]*(1./x[3])) *
      b[3] * exp(b[4]*(1./x[3])) *
      b[5] * exp(b[6]*(1./x[3])) * x[1] * x[2] /
      BzzPow2(1. + b[3] * exp(b[4]*(1./x[3])) * x[1]
      + b[5] * exp(b[6]*(1./x[3])) * x[2]);
  }
```

The model in its original form is surely ill conditioned: the product $\beta_1 \exp(\beta_2/x_{3i})$ $\beta_3 \exp(\beta_4/x_{3i})\beta_5 \exp(\beta_6/x_{3i})$ makes parameters correlated. In fact, the analysis of the model in this form leads to the following results:

```
Condition Number 1.488210e+013 ** WARNING **
Columns correlation = Tj Tolerance
1    1.9270929e-010    ** WARNING **
2    6.0510279e-005    ** WARNING **
3    1.9275936e-010    ** WARNING **
4    1.8366614e-002
5    1.0920812e-004    ** WARNING **
6    1.1412178e-004    ** WARNING **
    ** WARNING ** Correlation between Parameters
The Tj Tolerance identifies serious multicollinearities
```

Therefore, the model must be reformulated. As already underlined in the introduction of the chapter, the product among parameters must be removed when possible. Moreover, the conventional approach to reparameterized the Arrhenius-like forms is

$$\beta_i \exp\left(\frac{\beta_j}{T_i}\right) \quad \text{into} \quad \beta_i \exp\left(\beta_j \left[\frac{1}{T_i} - \frac{1}{\bar{T}}\right]\right) \tag{7.38}$$

Therefore, a possible alternative is

$$y_{1i} = \frac{\beta_1 \exp\left(\beta_2 \left(\frac{1.}{x_{3i}} - \frac{1.}{525.}\right)\right) x_{1i} x_{2i}}{\left(1. + \beta_3 \exp\left(\beta_4 \left(\frac{1.}{x_{3i}} - \frac{1.}{525.}\right)\right) x_{1i} + \beta_5 \exp\left(\beta_6 \left(\frac{1.}{x_{3i}} - \frac{1.}{525.}\right)\right) x_{2i}\right)^2} + \varepsilon_{1i} \tag{7.39}$$

which can be easily implemented by simply modifying the function `ModelEx6`

```
void ModelEx6(int model, int ex, BzzVector &b,
        BzzVector &x, BzzVector &y)
{
static double ut = 1. / 525.;
y[1] = b[1] * exp(b[2]*(1./x[3] - ut)) * x[1] * x[2] /
    BzzPow2(1. + b[3] * exp(b[4]*(1./x[3] - ut)) *
    x[1]+ b[5] * exp(b[6]*(1./x[3] - ut)) * x[2]);
}
```

This formulation is more appealing than the previous one but still unsatisfactory. In fact, the condition number is

```
Condition Number 3.929044e+006 ** WARNING **
```

Variance inflation factors are

```
Variance inflation factor
1    4.6142809e+007    ** WARNING **
2    4.5999804e+007    ** WARNING **
3    1.3635563e+007    ** WARNING **
4    1.3487576e+007    ** WARNING **
5    1.1614805e+007    ** WARNING **
6    1.1674197e+007    ** WARNING **
```

and tolerances are

```
Columns correlation = Tj Tolerance
1    2.1671850e-008    ** WARNING **
2    2.1739224e-008    ** WARNING **
3    7.3337641e-008    ** WARNING **
4    7.4142307e-008    ** WARNING **
5    8.6097013e-008    ** WARNING **
6    8.5658998e-008    ** WARNING **

    ** WARNING ** Correlation between Parameters
    The Tj Tolerance identifies serious multicollinearities
```

It is therefore useful to try with another model formulation:

$$d = \frac{1}{x_{3i}} - \frac{1}{525.}$$
$$y_{1i} = \frac{\exp(\beta_1 + \beta_2 \cdot d) \cdot x_{1i} \cdot x_{2i}}{(1. + \exp(\beta_3 + \beta_4 \cdot d) \cdot x_{1i} + \exp(\beta_5 + \beta_6 \cdot d) \cdot x_{2i})^2} + \varepsilon_{1i} \quad (7.40)$$

which can be easily implemented by modifying the function `ModelEx6`

```
void ModelEx6(int model, int ex, BzzVector &b,
        BzzVector &x, BzzVector &y)
    {
    static double c = 1./525.;
    double d = 1./x[3] - c;
    y[1] = exp(b[1] + b[2]*d) * x[1] * x[2] /
        BzzPow2(1. + exp(b[3] + b[4]*d) * x[1]
        + exp(b[5] + b[6]*d) * x[2]);
    }
```

This formulation is slightly better than the previous one but still unsatisfactory. In fact, the condition number is still $3.929044e+006$, the maximum value of variance inflation factors is $1.2585937e+005$, and the minimum value of tolerances is $7.9453761e$-006.

At this point, it is suitable to try the formulation suggested in the introduction of the chapter:

$$c = \frac{1.}{\frac{1}{575.} - \frac{1}{475.}}$$

$$x_A = \left(\frac{1}{x_{3i}} - \frac{1}{475.}\right)$$

$$x_B = \left(\frac{1}{x_{3i}} - \frac{1}{575.}\right) \tag{7.41}$$

$$e_1 = \exp(c(\beta_1 \cdot x_A - \beta_2 \cdot x_B))$$
$$e_2 = \exp(c(\beta_3 \cdot x_A - \beta_4 \cdot x_B))$$
$$e_3 = \exp(c(\beta_5 \cdot x_A - \beta_6 \cdot x_B))$$
$$y_{1i} = \frac{x_{1i} \cdot x_{2i}}{(e_1 + e_2 \cdot x_{1i} + e_3 \cdot x_{2i})^2} + \varepsilon_{1i}$$

which can be easily implemented by modifying the function ModelEx6

```
void ModelEx6(int model, int ex, BzzVector &b,
        BzzVector &x, BzzVector &y)
    {
    static const double c = 1. / (1. / 575. - 1. / 475.);
    static double e1, e2, e3;
    static double xA;
    static double xB;
    if (ex <= 1 || ex == 10 || ex == 19)
            {
            xA = 1. / x[3] - 1. / 475.;
            xB = 1. / x[3] - 1. / 575.;
            e1 = exp(c * (b[1] * xA - b[2] * xB));
            e2 = exp(c * (b[3] * xA - b[4] * xB));
            e3 = exp(c * (b[5] * xA - b[6] * xB));
            }
    y[1] = x[1] * x[2] /
            BzzPow2(e1 + e2 * x[1] + e3 * x[2]);
    }
```

In the previous function ModelEx6, the variable ex is used to optimize the code.

In fact, the function is sequentially invoked for each experimental point from 1 to n_E. Since the variable x_{3i} is modified in correspondence with the experiments 1, 10, and 19, whereas it is kept unchanged for all other intermediate points of the index ex, the three exponentials that are the most time-consuming operations are evaluated only three times, in correspondence with these three values of ex. The case with ex equal to zero shall be considered in Chapter 8, where the model is used to predict new experimental points.

This formulation is clearly preferable than the others. In fact, the condition number is `9.388334e+003`. It is not significantly small, but the system conditioning is very good: `3.859171e+000`.

Variance inflation factors and tolerances are both satisfactory: the maximum value of inflation factors is `3.0521063` and the minimum tolerance is `.32764259`. The mean square error is

```
Mean Square Error = 2.6644668e-007
```

hence,

```
F-test for the model
Fexperimental = 1.211121e+000
The probability that F with dfNum 21 dfDen 6
is greater than 1.211121e+000 is 4.370401e-001
Mean Square Error = 2.6644668e-007
```

The model is therefore acceptable. At last, no outliers are detected by robust analysis.

Example 7.8

Even this example is typical of kinetic models. The model under study is

$$y_{1i} = k \exp\left(\frac{E}{RT}\right) p_A^\alpha p_B^\beta + \varepsilon_{1i} \tag{7.42}$$

which can be rewritten in the following form

$$y_{1i} = \beta_1 \exp\left(\frac{\beta_2}{x_{3i}}\right) x_{1i}^{\beta_3} x_{2i}^{\beta_4} + \varepsilon_{1i} \tag{7.43}$$

by adopting the notation of this book. Even in this case, the single dependent variable has an experimental error with a constant variance equal to $1.9 \cdot 10^{-2}$ estimated with 3 degrees of freedom. Parameter β_1 is surely positive for theoretical reasons. Experimental data can be directly acquired with the following program:

```
#include "BzzMath.hpp"
void ModelEx7(int model,int ex,BzzVector &b,
       BzzVector &x,BzzVector &y);
void main(void)
  {
  int numModels = 1;
  int numX = 3;
  int numY = 1;
  int numExperiments = 15;
  BzzMatrix X(numExperiments,numX,
       .01,.01,475.,   .1,.01,475.,   .01,.1,475.,
       .1,.1,475.,   .01,.01,575.,   .1,.01,575.,
```

```
            .01,.1,575.,   .1,.1,575.,    .055,.055,525.,
            .01,.055,525., .1,.055,525.,  .055,.01,525.,
            .055,.1,525.,  .055,.055,475.,.055,
            .055,575.);
        BzzMatrix Y(numExperiments,numY,
            1.967,382.55,2.885,585.71,6.67e-002,
            63.243,.385,96.954,49.553,.8803,195.74,
            36.026,55.036,132.6,22.);
        BzzNonLinearRegression nonLinReg(numModels,X,Y,
            ModelEx7);
        BzzVector s2(1,1.9e-2);
        int df = 3;
        nonLinReg.SetVariance(df,s2);
        BzzVector b1(4,1.,1.,1.,1.);
        nonLinReg.InitializeModel(1,b1);
        nonLinReg.LeastSquaresAnalysis();
    }

    void ModelEx7(int model,int ex,
            BzzVector &b,BzzVector &x,BzzVector &y)
    {
        y[1] = b[1] * exp(b[2]/x[3]) * pow(x[1],b[3]) *
            pow(x[2],b[4]);
    }
```

The condition number is significantly large

```
        Condition Number 4.555223e+004 ** WARNING **
```

and even all other indices show strong correlations among parameters. If the model is reformulated as follows:

$$y_{1i} = \exp\left(\beta_1 + \beta_2\left(\frac{1}{x_{3i}} - \frac{1}{525}\right)\right) x_{1i}^{\beta_3} x_{2i}^{\beta_4} + \varepsilon_{1i} \tag{7.44}$$

which can be implemented by means of

```
    void ModelEx7(int model,int ex,
            BzzVector &b,BzzVector &x,BzzVector &y)
    {
        y[1] = exp(b[1] + b[2]*(1./x[3] - 1./525.)) *
            pow(x[1],b[3]) * pow(x[2],b[4]);
    }
```

leads to a worst condition number

```
        Condition Number 5.177589e+004 ** WARNING **
```

and parameters are still correlated.

A novel reformulation is

$$c = \frac{1}{\frac{1}{475} - \frac{1}{575}}$$

$$e_{1i} = c\beta_1 \left(\frac{1}{x_{3i}} - \left(\frac{1}{575}\right)\right)$$

$$e_{2i} = c\beta_2 \left(\frac{1}{x_{3i}} - \left(\frac{1}{475}\right)\right) \quad (7.45)$$

$$y_{1i} = \exp(e_{1i} + e_{2i}) x_{1i}^{\beta_3} x_{2i}^{\beta_4} + \varepsilon_{1i}$$

implementable by the following code:

```
void ModelEx7(int model, int ex,
        BzzVector &b, BzzVector &x, BzzVector &y)
{
static double c = 1. / (1. / 475. - 1. / 575.);
double e1 = c * b[1] * (1. / x[3] - 1. / 575.);
double e2 = c * b[2] * (1. / x[3] - 1. / 475.);
y[1] = exp(e1 + e2) * pow(x[1], b[3]) * pow(x[2], b[3]);
}
```

The condition number is now reduced to $1.182076e+002$, whereas parameters are still correlated, as shown by tolerances

```
Columns correlation = Tj Tolerance
1    2.7569035e-003    ** WARNING **
2    4.6040677e-002
3    2.5714792e-003    ** WARNING **
4    9.9832575e-002
```

Finally, by reparameterizing it as

$$c = \frac{1}{\frac{1}{475} - \frac{1}{575}}$$

$$e_1 = c\beta_1 \left(\frac{1}{x_{3i}} - \left(\frac{1}{575}\right)\right)$$

$$e_2 = c\beta_2 \left(\frac{1}{x_{3i}} - \left(\frac{1}{475}\right)\right) \quad (7.46)$$

$$y_{1i} = \exp(e_1 + e_2)(10x_{1i})^{\beta_3}(10x_{2i})^{\beta_4} + \varepsilon_{1i}$$

and implementing it by

```
void ModelEx7(int model, int ex,
        BzzVector &b, BzzVector &x, BzzVector &y)
    {
```

```
static double c = 1. / (1. / 475. - 1. / 575.);
double e1 = c * b[1] * (1./ x[3] - 1. / 575.);
double e2 = c * b[2] * (1./ x[3] - 1. / 475.);
y[1] = exp(e1 + e2) * pow(10. * x[1],b[3]) *
    pow(10. * x[2],b[4]);
}
```

the condition number becomes $1.144072e+001$. Parameters are uncorrelated:

```
Columns correlation = Tj Tolerance
1    6.8058820e-001
2    9.5203095e-001
3    9.4583475e-001
4    6.8329632e-001
```

This formulation provides a mean square error equal to $1.5064905 \cdot 10^{-2}$ and, hence, the model is reasonably good, since it results in

```
F-test for the model
Fexperimental = 7.928897e-001
The probability that F with dfNum 11 dfDen 3
is greater than 7.928897e-001 is 6.647850e-001
```

Example 7.9

Consider the following theoretical model with one dependent variable, three independent variables, and four parameters:

$$y_{1i} = \frac{f_{1i} f_{2i}}{f_{1i} + 2.3 f_{2i}} + \varepsilon_{1i}$$

$$f_{1i} = \beta_1 x_{1i} \exp(-\beta_3/x_{3i})$$
$$f_{2i} = \beta_2 x_{2i} \exp(-\beta_4/x_{3i})$$

(7.47)

Only the dependent variable is subject to experimental error with constant variance and its estimate based on 3 degrees of freedom is equal to $5.3 \cdot 10^{-2}$. Parameters β_1 and β_2 are surely positive for theoretical reasons.

Experimental data can be directly acquired with the following program.
Evaluate the model parameters and analyze the model.

As mentioned above, there are good possibilities that this model is ill formulated both for the product of parameters $\beta_1 \beta_2$ and for the exponential form.

The program is

```
#include "BzzMath.hpp"
void ModelEx8(int model, int ex, BzzVector &b,
        BzzVector &x, BzzVector &y);
void main(void)
```

```
{
int numModels = 1;
int numX = 3;
int numY = 1;
int numExperiments = 30;
BzzMatrix X(numExperiments,numX,
        .00108,.000050,543.,   .00304,.000073,543.,
        .00612,.00012,543.,    .00923,.00035,543.,
        .01002,.00035,543.,    .00108,.000056,543.,
        .00123,.00012,543.,    .00304,.000073,543.,
        .01003,.00023,543.,    .00108,.00036,543.,
        .00108,.000050,543.,   .00304,.000073,558.,
        .00612,.00012,558.,    .00923,.00035,558.,
        .01002,.00035,558.,    .00108,.000056,558.,
        .00123,.00012,558.,    .00304,.000073,558.,
        .01003,.00023,558.,    .00108,.00036,558.,
        .00108,.000050,573.,   .00304,.000073,573.,
        .00612,.00012,573.,    .00923,.00035,573.,
        .01002,.00035,573.,    .00108,.000056,573.,
        .00123,.00012,573.,    .00304,.000073,573.,
        .01003,.00023,573.,    .00108,.00036,573.);
BzzMatrix Y(numExperiments,numY,
        99.47,148.91,245.57,702.34,703.87,110.72,
        225.62,149.11,469.31,544.19,99.67,153.54,
        253.44,725.09,727.66,113.89,233.11,
        153.24,484.46,558.68,105.84,158.75,
        261.63,747.30,750.21,117.58,239.72,
        158.35,500.07,571.98);
BzzVector s2(1,5.3e-2);
BzzNonLinearRegression
        nonLinReg(numModels,X,Y,ModelEx8);
nonLinReg.SetVariance(3,s2);
BzzVector b(4,1.,1.,1.,1.);
nonLinReg.InitializeModel(1,b);
nonLinReg.LeastSquaresAnalysis();
}
```

Even though the program finds out the function minimum

Parameters obtained by minimization	Parameters obtained with Newton method
5.19059924233773e+006	5.18826485606681e+006
7.24639722599616e+006	7.24657217426268e+006
1.18538336910187e+002	1.18288813164076e+002
6.74204697722111e+002	6.74218288282280e+002

there is a strong correlation among parameters. In fact, the condition number is $3.906911e+006$, the maximum inflation factor is $3.1890234e+003$, and the minimum tolerance is $3.1357562e\text{-}004$.

The model can be reformulated by dividing the previous function by f_{1i} and rearranging the exponential term as in the previous examples.

$$c = \frac{1}{\frac{1}{x_{3max}} - \frac{1}{x_{3min}}}$$

$$f_{1i} = \left(\frac{x_{2i}}{x_{1i}}\right) \exp\left(c\left[\beta_1\left(\frac{1}{x_{3i}} - \frac{1}{x_{3min}}\right) - \beta_3\left(\frac{1}{x_{3i}} - \frac{1}{x_{3max}}\right)\right]\right) \quad (7.48)$$

$$f_{2i} = x_{2i} \exp\left(c\left[\beta_2\left(\frac{1}{x_{3i}} - \frac{1}{x_{3min}}\right) - \beta_4\left(\frac{1}{x_{3i}} - \frac{1}{x_{3max}}\right)\right]\right)$$

$$y_{1i} = \frac{f_{2i}}{1 + 2.3 f_{1i}} + \varepsilon_{1i}$$

The program is similar to the previous one and the user must change only the function `ModelEx8`:

```
void ModelEx8(int model, int ex, BzzVector &b,
        BzzVector &x, BzzVector &y)
  {
  static double c = 1./(1./573. - 1./543.);
  double f1 = (x[2]/x[1]) * exp(c*(b[1] * (1./ x[3]
        1./573.) - b[3] *(1./ x[3] - 1./543.)));
  double f2 = x[2] * exp(c*(b[2] * (1./ x[3]
        1./573.) - b[4] *(1./ x[3] - 1./543.)));
  y[1] = f2 /(1. + .23 * f1);
  }
```

Parameters result uncorrelated and the condition number is equal to $1.265480e+001$. Inflation factors are

```
    Variance inflation factor
1   1.8588702e+000
2   1.8669735e+000
3   1.8632602e+0000
4   1.8713716e+000
```

and tolerances are

```
    Columns correlation = Tj Tolerance
1   5.3796118e-001
2   5.3562624e-001
3   5.3669370e-001
4   5.3436741e-001
```

Example 7.10

Consider the model with one dependent variable, one independent variable, and two parameters:

$$y_{1i} = \frac{\beta_1 x_{1i}}{\beta_2 + x_{1i}} + \varepsilon_{1i} \tag{7.49}$$

Only the dependent variable is subject to experimental error with constant variance.

Experimental data can be directly acquired with the following program:

```
#include "BzzMath.hpp"
void ModelEx9(int model,int ex,BzzVector &b,
        BzzVector &x,BzzVector &y);
void main(void)
    {
    BzzPrint("\n\nnumModels 1 numX 1 numY 1");
    int numModels = 1;
    int numX = 1;
    int numY = 1;
    int numExperiments = 12;
    BzzMatrix X(numExperiments,numX,
        .02,.02,.06,.06,.11,.11,.22,.22,.56,
        .56,1.1,1.1);
    BzzMatrix Y(numExperiments,numY,
        76.,47.,97.,107.,123.,139.,159.,152.,191.,
        201.,207.,200.);
    BzzNonLinearRegression nonLinReg(numModels,X,Y,
        ModelEx9);
    BzzVector b(2,1.,1.);
    nonLinReg.InitializeModel(1,b);
    nonLinReg.LeastSquaresAnalysis();
    }

void ModelEx9(int model,int ex,BzzVector &b,
        BzzVector &x,BzzVector &y)
    {
    y[1] = b[1] * x[1] / (b[2] + x[1]);
    }
```

Even though the program finds out the function minimum:

	Parameters obtained by minimization	Parameters obtained with Newton method
1	-1.99624354410029e+018	-1.99624354410029e+018
2	-8.13756961943860e+015	-8.13756961955241e+015

7.2 One Dependent Variable with Constant Variance

the values of parameters are unreasonably large and a strong correlation among parameters exists. In fact, the condition number is significantly large:

```
Condition Number 1.802830e+016 ** WARNING **
```

Even inflation factors and tolerances are unsatisfactory. Moreover, the mean square error is equal to $8.0271696 \cdot 10^3$ by indicating that either the model is inadequate or the global minimum is not yet achieved.

By reformulating the model as follow

$$y_{1i} = \frac{x_{1i}}{\beta_1 + \beta_2(x_{1i} - .5)} + \varepsilon_{1i} \tag{7.50}$$

and implementing it by replacing the function of the model

```
void ModelEx9(int model, int ex, BzzVector &b,
        BzzVector &x, BzzVector &y)
{
    y[1] = x[1] / (b[1] + b[2] * (x[1] - .5));
}
```

the condition number drops to $3.742532e+000$. In addition, all other indices for collinearity detection are satisfactory.

The mean square error is now equal to $1.1954488e+002$ and the model appears reasonably good.

It is possible to reconsider the previous formulation starting from a new initial guess, which corresponds to the values of parameters obtained by using the last formulation. On this subject, it is sufficient to introduce the following statements at the end of the program:

```
b = nonLinReg.GetParameters(1);
BzzVector c(2);
c[1] = 1./b[2];
c[2] = (b[1] - .5 * b[2]) / b[2];
c.BzzPrint("c");
```

By using the following starting point

```
1    2.12683742973300e+002
2    6.41212815804659e-002
```

inside the original model formulation, the same mean square error is obtained, but the correlation indices are even worse than the alternative formulation.

Example 7.11

Consider the model with one dependent variable, one independent variables, and two parameters:

$$y_{1i} = \frac{\beta_1 \beta_3 (x_{2i} - x_{3i}/1.632)}{1. + \beta_2 x_{1i} + \beta_3 x_{2i} + \beta_4 x_{3i}} + \varepsilon_{1i} \tag{7.51}$$

Only the dependent variable is subject to experimental error with constant variance. Experimental data can be directly acquired with the following program.

As already underlined in the introduction of this chapter, there is a high possibility to have parameter correlations due to the product among parameters at the numerator.

This formulation is therefore unsatisfactory and the product must be removed. The program is

```
#include "BzzMath.hpp"
void ModelEx10(int model,int ex,BzzVector &b,
        BzzVector &x,BzzVector &y);
void main(void)
   {
   BzzPrint("\n\nnumModels 1 numX 1 numY 1");
   int numModels = 1;
   int numX = 3;
   int numY = 1;
   int numExperiments = 24;
   BzzMatrix X(numExperiments,numX,
        205.8,90.9,37.1,  404.8,92.9,36.3,
        209.7,174.9,49.4, 401.6,187.2,44.9,
        224.9,92.7,116.3, 402.6,102.2,128.9,
        212.7,186.9,134.4, 406.2,192.6,134.9,
        133.3,140.8,87.6, 470.9,144.2,86.9,
        300.,68.3,81.7,   301.6,214.6,101.7,
        297.3,142.2,10.5, 314.0,146.7,157.1,
        305.7,142.,86.,   300.1,143.7,90.2,
        305.4,141.1,87.4, 305.2,141.5,87.,
        300.1,83.,66.4,   106.6,209.6,33.0,
        417.2,83.9,32.9,  251.,294.4,41.5,
        250.3,148.,14.7,  145.1,291.,50.2);
   BzzMatrix Y(numExperiments,numY,
        3.541,2.397,6.694,4.722,.593,.268,
        2.797,2.451,3.196,2.021,.896,5.084,
        5.686,1.193,2.648,3.303,3.054,
        3.302,1.271,11.648,2.002,9.604,
        7.754,11.59);
   BzzNonLinearRegression nonLinReg(numModels,X,Y,
        ModelEx10);
   BzzVector b(4,1.,1.,1.,1.);
// BzzVector b(3,1.,1.,1.);
   nonLinReg.InitializeModel(1,b);
   nonLinReg.LeastSquaresAnalysis();
   }
```

```
void ModelEx10(int model,int ex,BzzVector &b,
       BzzVector &x,BzzVector &y)
{
   y[1] = b[1] * b[2] * (x[2] - x[3] / 1.632) /
          (1. + b[2] * x[1] + b[3] * x[2] + b[4] * x[3]);
}
```

The condition number is

```
Condition Number 5.438352e+003
```

Correlation indices are

```
Variance inflation factor
1    2.0048796e+001
2    1.2758313e+002
3    7.9284646e+001

Columns correlation = Tj Tolerance
1    4.9878307e-002
2    7.8380267e-003   ** WARNING **
3    1.2612783e-002
```

As there are some correlations among parameters, the model is to be reformulated such as

$$y_{1i} = \frac{(x_{2i}-x_{3i}/1.632)}{\beta_1+\beta_2 x_{1i}+\beta_3 x_{2i}+\beta_4 x_{3i}} + \varepsilon_{1i} \tag{7.52}$$

It is sufficient to replace the function of the model

```
void ModelEx10(int model,int ex,BzzVector &b,
       BzzVector &x,BzzVector &y)
{
   y[1] = (x[2] - x[3] / 1.632) /
          (b[1] + b[2] * x[1] + b[3] * x[2] + b[4] * x[3]);
}
```

The condition number is equal to $1.498974e+003$. The other correlation indices are quite good and the mean square error is equal to $1.6172411 \cdot 10^{-1}$. The model seems reasonably good, except for the fact that *t*-tests point out the possibility that parameters no. 1 and 3 could be both irrelevant.

In fact, we have

```
       T-Value              P-Value
1    1.6327072e-001      8.7194382e-001   ** WARNING **
2    4.4998175e+000      2.1886427e-004
3    1.7257315e+000      9.9813962e-002   ** WARNING **
4    2.7785923e+000      1.1592520e-002
```

Reformulating the model as follows:

$$y_{1i} = \frac{(x_{2i}-x_{3i}/1.632)}{\beta_1 + \beta_2 x_{1i}/470.9 + \beta_3 x_{2i}/294.4 + \beta_4 x_{3i}/157.1} + \varepsilon_{1i} \quad (7.53)$$

where the functions at the denominator are divided by their maximum value to normalize them.

It is sufficient to replace the function of the model:

```
void ModelEx10(int model,int ex,BzzVector &b,
        BzzVector &x,BzzVector &y)
{
y[1] = (x[2] - x[3] / 1.632) /
       (b[1] + b[2] * x[1] / 470.9 +
       b[3] * x[2] / 294.4 + b[4] * x[3] / 157.1);
}
```

This formulation is better than the previous one, but it still highlights the possibility of deleting a parameter. The mean square error is equal to the previous case. If the first parameter is removed, the following form takes place:

$$y_{1i} = \frac{(x_{2i}-x_{3i}/1.632)}{\beta_1 x_{1i}/470.9 + \beta_2 x_{2i}/294.4 + \beta_3 x_{3i}/157.1} + \varepsilon_{1i} \quad (7.54)$$

It is sufficient to modify the amount of parameters involved in the program

```
BzzVector b(3,1.,1.,1.);
```

and to replace the function of the model

```
void ModelEx10(int model,int ex,BzzVector &b,
        BzzVector &x,BzzVector &y)
{
y[1] = (x[2] - x[3] / 1.632) /
       (b[1] * x[1] / 470.9 +
       b[2] * x[2] / 294.4 + b[3] * x[3] / 157.1);
}
```

The model is particularly satisfactory; the condition number is equal to 7.322354e+000; inflation factors are

```
Variance inflation factor
1    3.8507999e+000
2    5.7398475e+000
3    5.1420558e+000
```

and tolerances are

```
Columns correlation = Tj Tolerance
1    2.5968630e-001
2    1.7422066e-001
3    1.9447475e-001
```

The mean square error is $1.5532337 \cdot 10^{-1}$, which is the best one.

Example 7.12

Consider the following theoretical model (Bates and Watts, 2007) with one dependent variable, one independent variables, and four parameters:

$$y_{1i} = \frac{\beta_1}{(1.+\beta_2 \exp(-\beta_3 x_{1i}))^{\beta_4}} + \varepsilon_{1i} \qquad (7.55)$$

Only the dependent variable is subject to experimental error with constant variance. Parameter β_2 is surely positive for theoretical reasons.

Experimental data can be directly acquired with the following program:

```
#include "BzzMath.hpp"
void ModelEx11(int model,int ex,BzzVector &b,
        BzzVector &x,BzzVector &y);
void main(void)
    {
    BzzPrint("\n\nnumModels 1 numX 1 numY 1");
    int numModels = 1;
    int numX = 1;
    int numY = 1;
    int numExperiments = 15;
    BzzMatrix X(numExperiments,numX,
        .5,1.5,2.5,3.5,4.5,5.5,6.5,7.5,8.5,9.5,10.5,
        11.5,12.5,13.5,14.5);
    BzzMatrix Y(numExperiments,numY,
        1.3,1.3,1.9,3.4,5.3,7.1,10.6,16.,16.4,18.3,
        20.9,20.5,21.3,21.2,20.9);
    BzzNonLinearRegression nonLinReg(numModels,X,Y,
        ModelEx11);
    BzzVector b(4,1.,1.,1.,1.);
    BzzVector bMin(4),bMax(4);
    bMax = 100.;
    bMax[2] = 1000.;
    nonLinReg.InitializeModel(1,b,bMin,bMax);
    nonLinReg.LeastSquaresAnalysis();
    }

    void ModelEx11(int model,int ex,BzzVector &b,
            BzzVector &x,BzzVector &y)
        {
        double ax = 1. + b[2] * exp(-b[3] * x[1]);
        if(ax < 0.) BzzError();
        y[1] = b[1] /pow(ax,b[4]);
        }
```

Running the program with b = (1.,1.,1.,1.), an error message appears for the check introduced into the function ModelEx11.

It is possible to overcome this problem either by limiting parameters β during the search or by trying other initial guesses.

The former alternative requires the following statement:

```
nonLinReg.InitializeModel(1,b);
```

with the following definitions:

```
BzzVector bMin(4),bMax(4);
bMax = 100.;
bMax[2] = 1000.;
nonLinReg.InitializeModel(1,b,bMin,bMax);
```

The latter alternative requires a different initialization of the vector b:

```
BzzVector b(4,30.,.1,10.,1.);
```

In both cases, the condition number is `5.857663e+004`. The Jacobian matrix is ill conditioned.

The maximum inflation factor is `7.5557582e+002` and the minimum tolerance is `1.3234939e-003`; they both show correlations among parameters. If the model is reparameterized as

$$c = -1./14.$$
$$y_{1i} = \frac{\beta_1}{(1.+\exp(c[\beta_2(x_{1i}-.5)+\beta_3(x_{1i}-14.5)]))^{\beta_4}} + \varepsilon_{1i} \quad (7.56)$$

it is necessary to modify the function

```
void ModelEx11(int model,int ex,BzzVector &b,
       BzzVector &x,BzzVector &y)
   {
   static double c = -1./14.;
   double ax = 1. + exp(c*(b[2] * (x[1] - .5) +
       b[3] * (x[1] - 14.5)));
   if(ax < 0.) BzzError();
   y[1] = b[1]/pow(ax,b[4]);
   }
```

Adopting the following initial guess

```
BzzVector b(4,30.,5.,5.,1.);
```

the condition number is now equal to

```
Condition Number 7.989356e+001
The Jacobian matrix is well conditioned
```

and the correlation indices are

```
Variance inflation factor
1    2.8773977e+000
2    2.2605716e+001
3    1.7544708e+002
4    1.0340443e+002
```

```
Columns correlation = Tj Tolerance
1    3.4753625e-001
2    4.4236599e-002
3    5.6997245e-003      ** WARNING **
4    9.6707656e-003      ** WARNING **
   ** WARNING ** Correlation between Parameters
The Tj Tolerance identifies serious multicollinearities
```

Parameter correlations are still present, but they are weaker than the previous case. To remove completely them, it would be useful to get new experimental points; let us suppose that it is not possible to introduce new points for the time being (the problem of new additional experiments shall be discussed in detail in Chapter 8).

In any case, the analysis is showing that the model is satisfactory, as one can see looking at residuals. For confirmation, it is possible to fix the value of parameter $\beta_4 = .6178$ and to examine the model with three parameters only:

$$c = -1./14.$$
$$y_{1i} = \frac{\beta_1}{(1. + \exp(c[\beta_2(x_{1i}-.5) + \beta_3(x_{1i}-14.5)]))^{.6178}} + \varepsilon_{1i} \quad (7.57)$$

The original function must be changed:

```
void ModelEx11(int model, int ex, BzzVector &b,
       BzzVector &x, BzzVector &y)
{
  double c = -1./(14.);
  double ax = 1. + exp(c*(b[2] * (x[1] - .5) +
       b[3] * (x[1] - 14.5)));
  if(ax < 0.) BzzError();
  y[1] = b[1]/pow(ax,.6178);
}
```

and the amount of parameters must be updated:

```
BzzVector b(3,30.,5.,5.);
```

The resulting model is satisfactory and without any correlation among parameters.

Example 7.13

Consider the model (Buzzi-Ferraris and Ranzi, 1971) with one dependent variable, one independent variable, and six parameters:

$$y_{1i} = \beta_1 \exp(-\beta_2(x_{1i}-\beta_3)^2) + \beta_4 \exp(-\beta_5(x_{1i}-\beta_6)^2) + \varepsilon_{1i} \quad (7.58)$$

Only the dependent variable is subject to experimental error with constant variance. The variance estimate with 4 degrees of freedom is equal to 4.48.

Experimental data can be directly acquired with the following program:

```
#include "BzzMath.hpp"
void ModelEx12(int model,int ex,BzzVector &b,
        BzzVector &x,BzzVector &y);
void main(void)
    {
    BzzPrint("\n\nnumModels 1 numX 1 numY 1");
    int numModels = 1;
    int numX = 1;
    int numY = 1;
    int numExperiments = 33;
    BzzMatrix X(numExperiments,numX,
       0.,.2,.4,.6,.9,1.2,1.3,1.4,1.6,1.7,1.8,1.85,
       1.9,2.,2.1,2.2,2.3,2.4,2.5,2.8,2.9,3.,3.05,
       3.1,3.2,3.25,3.3,3.4,3.6,3.9,4.1,4.4,4.5);
    BzzMatrix Y(numExperiments,numY,
       8.231,16.179,25.947,41.092,73.423,111.998,
       120.489,133.816,146.209,151.585,153.411,
       155.551,151.994,148.211,139.501,144.344,
       133.32,124.068,118.724,105.406,104.309,
       106.966,106.414,102.87,109.241,114.103,
       113.973,122.406,118.859,111.482,96.311,
       65.222,53.568);
    BzzNonLinearRegression nonLinReg(numModels,X,Y,
          ModelEx12);
    BzzVector b(6,1.,1.,1.,1.,1.,1.);
    BzzVector bMin(6),bMax(6);
    bMax = 200.;
    nonLinReg.InitializeModel(1,b,bMin,bMax);
    BzzVector s2(1,4.48);
    int dof = 4;
    nonLinReg.SetVariance(dof,s2);
    nonLinReg.LeastSquaresAnalysis();
    }
```

The condition number is equal to

```
Condition Number 2.998924e+002
The Jacobian matrix is well conditioned
```

and correlation indices are

```
Variance inflation factor
1    1.6707313e+000
2    7.0996155e+000
3    5.3204706e+000
```

```
4    2.3072998e+000
5    7.8883527e+000
6    4.5085520e+000

Columns correlation = Tj Tolerance
1    5.9854030e-001
2    1.4085270e-001
3    1.8795330e-001
4    4.3340704e-001
5    1.2676918e-001
6    2.2180070e-001
```

Parameter correlations are not present. The mean square error is $5.1621685e+000$ and since the estimate of the error variance is equal to 4.48,

```
F-test for the model
Fexperimental = 1.152270e+000
The probability that F with dfNum 27 dfDen 4
is greater than 1.152270e+000 is 5.041532e-001
```

Robust analysis does not identify any outlier, thus the model is acceptable.

To plot results, the following statements must be added to the program:

```
b = nonLinReg.GetParameters(1);
BzzMatrixSparse YY(2,100);
BzzMatrixSparse XX(2,100);
double x;
int i;
for(i = 1; i <= 100; i++)
    {
    x = 4.5 * double(i - 1)/99.;
    XX(1,i) = x;
    YY(1,i) = b[1] * exp(-b[2] * BzzPow2(x - b[3]))
        + b[4] * exp(-b[5] * BzzPow2(x - b[6]));
    }
for(i = 1; i <= numExperiments; i++)
    {
    XX(2,i) = X(i,1);
    YY(2,i) = Y(i,1);
    }
BzzSave save("BFGRegression.stx");
save << XX << YY;
save.End();
system("BzzPlotSparse.exe");
```

When the `BzzPlotSparse.exe` toolkit is run, the menu item `File`, `New` must be selected and the file `BFGRegression.stx` must be indicated.

It is also possible to change the title and features of the plot.

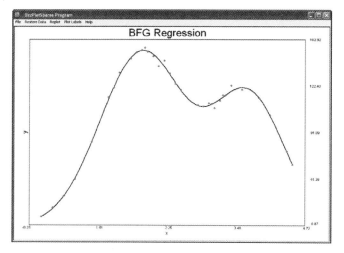

Figure 7.1 Nonlinear regression example.

Figure 7.1 shows the model obtained by the least sum of squares method (solid line) fitting experimental points (diamonds).

Example 7.14

Consider the model

$$y_{1i} = \beta_1 \exp(-\beta_2 x_{1i}) + \beta_3 + \beta_4 x + \\ -\exp(\beta_5 x_{1i} + \beta_6 (20.-x_{1i})) + \varepsilon_{1i} \tag{7.59}$$

already discussed in the stepwise analysis (see Chapter 5, Example 5.27). Evaluate parameters by using an object of the `BzzNonLinearRegression` class. Experimental data can be directly acquired with the following program:

```
#include "BzzMath.hpp"
void ModelEx13(int model,int ex,BzzVector &b,
        BzzVector &x,BzzVector &y);
void main(void)
    {
    BzzPrint("\n\nModelEx15");
    int numModels = 1;
    int numX = 1;
    int numY = 1;
    int numExperiments = 35;
    BzzVector x(numExperiments,
            0.0,.1,.2,.3,.4,.5,.6,.7,.8,.9,
            1.,2.,3.,4.,5.,6.,7.,8.,9.,10.,
```

7.2 One Dependent Variable with Constant Variance

```
            11.,12.,13.,14.,15.,16.,17.,18.,19.,20.,
            20.1,20.2,20.3,20.4,20.5);
    BzzVector y(numExperiments,
            9.750,8.75,8.12,7.881,7.657,7.466,7.425,
            7.326,7.316,7.287,7.246,7.125,7.103,
            6.941,6.818,6.716,6.634,6.531,6.409,
            6.337,6.224,6.102,6.005,5.927,5.815,
            5.711,5.567,5.379,4.517,-1.966,-3.673,
            -5.776,-8.368,-11.56,-15.50);
    BzzMatrix X(numExperiments,numX);
    X.SetColumn(1,x);
    BzzMatrix Y(numExperiments,numY);
    Y.SetColumn(1,y);
    BzzNonLinearRegression nonLinReg(numModels,X,Y,
            ModelEx13);
    BzzVector b1(6,7.,-.1,2.,-5.,1.,1.);
    nonLinReg.InitializeModel(1,b1);
    nonLinReg.LeastSquaresAnalysis();
    }

void ModelEx13(int model,int ex,BzzVector &b,
        BzzVector &x,BzzVector &y)
    {
    y[1] = b[1] + b[2] * x[1] +
    b[3] * exp(b[4] * x[1]) -
        exp(b[5] * x[1] + b[6] *(x[1] - 20.));
    }
```

The model seems to be good. Actually, it results in

```
Mean Square Error = 5.8278134e-004
F-test for the model
Fexperimental = 1.456953e+000
The probability that F with dfNum 29 dfDen 3
is greater than 1.456953e+000 is 4.323314e-001}
```

The least sum of squares drops from $1.200361e+022$ to $4.225165e+001$. The parameters that minimize the sum of squares are

```
    1   7.35686681945501e+000
    2  -1.03431429734353e-001
    3   2.37968089997977e+000
    4  -5.18540350072901e+000
    5   9.90763767950118e-002
    6   2.00177675968702e+000
```

7.3
Multicubic Piecewise Models

Sometimes, there are no models involving a single dependent variable and a single independent variable that are satisfactory; moreover, the experimental error on the dependent variable is small, rather not negligible.

In any case, when many experimental points are available, it is not reasonable to use them in an exact polynomial interpolation, through one of the methods discussed in Chapter 1, if any experimental error is present.

In such cases, the following device can be adopted: an exact interpolation is performed by using one of the possible multicubic functions passing through some support (virtual) points, rather than through the existing experiments. Values of **y** in support points must be selected in order to minimize the sum of squares between experimental points and previsions of the same multicubic function in correspondence with such points. In other words, the model is a multicubic function and model parameters are ordinates of the multicubic function in some points preventively selected.

Example 7.15

A data set containing 133 experimental points is available for this example. y are subject to a small experimental error and it is not possible to carry out an exact interpolation. Thus, 27 support abscissas x_i were chosen within the experimental domain; the corresponding ordinates must be selected to minimize the sum of squares between experimental points and estimates of the multicubic function. Among the existing multicubic functions belonging to the ***BzzMath*** library (Chapter 1), an object of the BzzCubicSmooth class is used.

The program is

```
#include "BzzMath.hpp"
void PiecewiseCubic(int model,int ex,BzzVector &b,
          BzzVector &x,BzzVector &y);
BzzCubicSmooth bc;
BzzVector xc;
void main(void)
    {
    BzzPrint("\n\nPiecewiseCubic1");
    BzzPrint("\n\nnumModels 1 numX 1 numY 1");
    int numModels = 1;
    int numX = 1;
    int numY = 1;
    int numExperiments = 131;
    BzzMatrix X(numExperiments,numX);
    int i;
    double t = 0.;
    for(i = 1;i <= 131;i++)
```

```
      {
      X(i,1) = t;
      t += .1;
      }
BzzMatrix Y(numExperiments,numY,
    5.010,5.180,5.430,5.610,5.780,6.010,6.215,6.346,
    6.588,6.771,7.010,7.286,7.535,7.891,8.128,8.310,
    8.334,8.359,8.257,8.110,8.030,7.850,7.616,7.422,
    7.212,7.010,6.782,6.543,6.403,6.272,6.310,6.492,
    6.914,7.330,7.704,8.010,8.146,8.125,8.161,8.108,
    8.080,8.117,8.138,8.074,8.091,7.990,7.879,7.678,
    7.524,7.269,7.010,6.702,6.263,5.923,5.552,5.310,
    5.124,5.090,5.034,4.992,5.010,4.973,5.016,5.044,
    5.047,5.130,5.158,5.147,5.247,5.268,5.310,5.324,
    5.256,5.286,5.234,5.210,5.132,5.130,5.042,4.916,
    4.810,4.618,4.299,4.071,3.792,3.580,3.497,3.388,
    3.294,3.271,3.210,3.152,3.078,2.988,2.982,2.910,
    2.834,2.773,2.785,2.728,2.710,2.677,2.570,2.576,
    2.517,2.510,2.461,2.496,2.472,2.451,2.510,2.534,
    2.661,2.731,2.794,2.910,2.987,2.982,3.092,3.159,
    3.280,3.500,3.747,3.949,4.264,4.490,4.738,4.932,
    5.202,5.398,5.590);
BzzNonLinearRegression nonLinReg(numModels,X,Y,
      PiecewiseCubic);
BzzVector x(27,
      0.,.5,1.,1.5,2.,2.5,3.,3.5,4.,
      4.5,5.,5.5,6.,6.5,7.,7.5,8.,8.5,
      9.,9.5,10.,10.5,11.,11.5,12.,12.5,13.);
xc = x;
BzzVector b(27,
      5.,6.,7.,8.3,8.,7.,6.3,8.,8.1,
      8.,7.,5.3,5.,5.1,5.3,5.2,4.8,3.6,
      3.2,2.9,2.7,2.5,2.5,2.9,3.3,4.5,5.6);
nonLinReg.InitializeModel(1,b);
nonLinReg.LeastSquaresAnalysis();
/////////
b = nonLinReg.GetParameters(1);
BzzMatrixSparse YY(2,200);
BzzMatrixSparse XX(2,200);
double xx;
for(i = 1; i <= 200;i++)
      {
      xx = 12.999 * double(i - 1)/199.;
      XX(1,i) = xx;
      YY(1,i) = bc(xx);
      }
```

```
    for(i = 1;i <= numExperiments;i++)
       {
       XX(2,i) = X(i,1);
       YY(2,i) = Y(i,1);
       }
    BzzSave save("CubicRegression.stx");
    save << XX << YY;
    save.End();
    system("BzzPlotSparse.exe");
    BzzPause();
    }
 void PiecewiseCubic(int model,int ex,BzzVector &b,
         BzzVector &x,BzzVector &y)
    {
    if(ex == 1)
       bc(xc,b,1.);
    y[1] = bc(x[1]);
    }
```

In the function `PiecewiseCubic`, the object `bc` is initialized in correspondence with the first experimental point only (with `ex` equal to 1):

```
    if(ex == 1)
    bc(xc,b,1.);
```

The global object `bc` preserves its data even for the successive experiments. Thus, it can be used to carry out estimations for all other experimental points:

```
    y[1] = bc(x[1]);
```

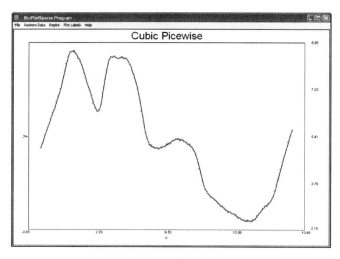

Figure 7.2 Multicubic piecewise model.

Once parameters to build the multicubic function are obtained, the same multicubic can be used to carry out estimates in other points where the model is defined. Therefore, after evaluating parameters

```
b = nonLinReg.GetParameters(1);
```

and using the object bc of the multicubic function to get model estimates, it is possible to generate the plot of Figure 7.2, which illustrates both model and experimental data.

Example 7.16

This example was proposed by Ryan (2009) as a multispline. Again, among the existing multicubic functions belonging to the *BzzMath* library (Chapter 1), an object of the BzzCubicSmooth class is adopted.
Experimental data can be directly acquired with the following program:

```
#include "BzzMath.hpp"
void PiecewiseCubic(int model,int ex,BzzVector &b,
    BzzVector &x,BzzVector &y);
BzzCubicSmooth bc;
BzzVector xc;
    {
    BzzPrint("\n\nPiecewiseCubic2");
    BzzPrint("\n\nnumModels 1 numX 1 numY 1");
    int numModels = 1;
    int numX = 1;
    int numY = 1;
    int numExperiments = 18;
    BzzMatrix X(numExperiments,numX,
        1.,2.,3.,4.,5.,5.,6.,6.,7.,8.,9.,10.,11.,
        12.,13.,14.,15.,16.);
    BzzMatrix Y(numExperiments,numY,
        10.,23.,34.,38.,44.,45.,46.,48.,47.,49.,
        50.,51.,51.,53.,54.,55.,56.,57.);
    BzzNonLinearRegression nonLinReg(numModels,X,Y,
        PiecewiseCubic);
    BzzVector x(6,
        1.,3.5,7.,10.5,13.,16.);
        xc = x;
    BzzVector b(6,10.,36.,47.,51.,54.,57.);
    nonLinReg.InitializeModel(1,b);
    nonLinReg.LeastSquaresAnalysis();
    b = nonLinReg.GetParameters(1);
    BzzMatrixSparse YY(2,200);
    BzzMatrixSparse XX(2,200);
    double xx;
```

```
        int i;
        for(i = 1; i <= 200;i++)
            {
            xx = -(double(i) - 200.)/199. +
              16. * (double(i) - 1.) / 199.;
            XX(1,i) = xx;
            YY(1,i) = bc(xx);
            }
        for(i = 1;i <= numExperiments;i++)
            {
            XX(2,i) = X(i,1);
            YY(2,i) = Y(i,1);
            }
        BzzSave save("CubicRegression2.stx");
        save << XX << YY;
        save.End();
        system("BzzPlotSparse.exe");
        BzzPause();
        }
    void PiecewiseCubic(int model,int ex,BzzVector &b,
                BzzVector &x,BzzVector &y)
        {
        if(ex == 1)
            bc(xc,b,1.);
        y[1] = bc(x[1]);
        }
```

Results are visualized in Figure 7.3.

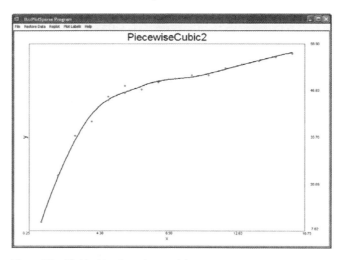

Figure 7.3   Multicubic piecewise model.

Example 7.17

Ryan (2009) also proposed an example where it is hard to find out a specific model fitting data. Again, among the existing multicubic functions belonging to the ***BzzMath*** library (Chapter 1), an object of the BzzCubicSmooth class is used. Experimental data can be directly acquired with the following program:

```
#include "BzzMath.hpp"
void PiecewiseCubic(int model,int ex,BzzVector &b,
          BzzVector &x,BzzVector &y);
BzzCubicSmooth bc;
BzzVector xc;
    {
    BzzPrint("\n\nPiecewiseCubic3");
    BzzPrint("\n\nnumModels 1 numX 1 numY 1");
    int numModels = 1;
    int numX = 1;
    int numY = 1;
    int numExperiments = 100;
    BzzMatrix X(numExperiments,numX,
         30.,40.,45.,46.,50.,53.,52.,55.,55.,57.,
         59.,60.,60.,60.,60.,62.,63.,64.,65.,66.,
         67.,68.,69.,70.,71.,73.,74.,75.,77.,79.,
         80.,82.,83.,84.,86.,88.,65.,66.,67.,69.,
         70.,74.,66.,76.,66.,67.,81.,65.,79.,80.,
         64.,64.,66.,66.,67.,67.,67.,68.,68.,69.,
         69.,70.,70.,70.,71.,71.,71.,71.,75.,77.,
         77.,77.,81.,81.,81.,70.,71.,71.,72.,89.,
         73.,73.,74.,74.,75.,75.,79.,80.,80.,82.,
         82.,83.,83.,86.,86.,89.,89.,70.,71.,72.);
    BzzMatrix Y(numExperiments,numY,
         85.,60.,90.,70.,71.,64.,91.,90.,93.,91.,
         88.,68.,74.,82.,95.,91.,91.,91.,87.,87.,
         87.,87.,87.,87.,87.,86.,86.,86.,86.,86.,
         86.,85.,85.,85.,85.,85.,82.,82.,82.,82.,
         81.,81.,81.,79.,79.,77.,77.,77.,75.,75.,
         75.,90.,90.,90.,90.,90.,90.,90.,90.,90.,
         90.,90.,90.,90.,90.,90.,90.,90.,90.,90.,
         90.,90.,90.,89.,89.,89.,94.,94.,94.,94.,
         89.,94.,94.,94.,94.,94.,94.,94.,94.,94.,
         94.,94.,94.,94.,94.,93.,93.,90.,90.,90.);
    BzzNonLinearRegression nonLinReg(numModels,X,Y,
         PiecewiseCubic);
    BzzVector x(5,
         30.,45.,60.,75.,90.);
       xc = x;
```

```
       BzzVector b(5,50.,60.,70.,80.,90.);
       nonLinReg.InitializeModel(1,b);
       BzzVector s2(1,289.);
       int df = 5;
       nonLinReg.SetVariance(df,s2);
       nonLinReg.LeastSquaresAnalysis();
       b = nonLinReg.GetParameters(1);
       BzzMatrixSparse YY(2,200);
       BzzMatrixSparse XX(2,200);
       double xx;
       int i;
       double yMin = 10000.,yMax = 0.;
       for(i = 1; i <= 200;i++)
           {
           xx = -30. * (double(i) - 200.)/199. +
               90. * (double(i) - 1.) / 199.;
           XX(1,i) = xx;
           YY(1,i) = bc(xx);
           if(YY(1,i) > yMax)
               yMax = YY(1,i);
           if(YY(1,i) < yMin)
               yMin = YY(1,i);
           }
       for(i = 1;i <= numExperiments;i++)
           {
           XX(2,i) = X(i,1);
           YY(2,i) = Y(i,1);
           }
       BzzSave save("CubicRegression3.stx");
       save << XX << YY;
       save.End();
       system("BzzPlotSparse.exe");
       double thumb = BzzPow2(.5*(yMax - yMin)) / 289.;
       if(thumb > 1.)
           ::BzzPrint("\nThumb test shows Pollice Recto %e",
               thumb);
       else
           ::BzzPrint("\nThumb test shows Pollice Verso %e",
               thumb);
       BzzPause();
       }
```

Results are visualized in Figure 7.4.

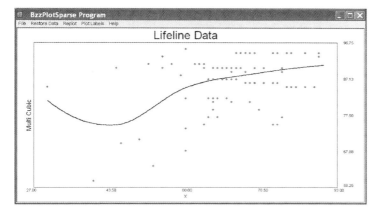

Figure 7.4 Multicubic piecewise model.

The thumb test shows that a reasonable model to fit experimental data of this problem does not exist, as it gives *pollice verso* as a result, with a value of 0.022 < 1. It is convenient to give up searching for a reasonable model with this set of data.

Example 7.18

Consider the scenario no. 1 of Section 4.3.3. By introducing new experiments, one can note that data cannot be fitted with a linear model; in addition, there is not an adequate theory that provides a reasonable nonlinear model.
An object of the `BzzCubicSmooth` class is used.
Experimental data can be directly acquired by the following program:

```
#include "BzzMath.hpp"
void PiecewiseCubic(int model,int ex,BzzVector &b,
        BzzVector &x,BzzVector &y);
BzzCubicSmooth bc;
BzzVector xc;
    {
    BzzPrint("\n\nPiecewiseCubic4");
    BzzPrint("\n\nnumModels 1 numX 1 numY 1");
    int numModels = 1;
    int numX = 1;
    int numY = 1;
```

```
       int numExperiments = 24;
       BzzMatrix X(numExperiments,numX,
    // 2.5,7.5,14.,15.,16.,22.,23.,23.,29.);
       2.5,7.5,14.,15.,16.,22.,23.,29.,
       2.7,3.8,5.4,7.02,8.4,10.,11.6,13.4,
       15.6,18.,20.,21.,23.,25.,27.,28.);
       BzzMatrix Y(numExperiments,numY,
    // 5.,2.6,2.6,3.9,5.1,13.,14.2,5.1,2.7);
       5.,2.6,2.6,3.9,5.1,13.,14.2,2.7,
       4.4,4.1,3.1,2.4,2.09,2.,2.24,2.98,
       4.3,6.27,9.3,11.8,14.2,13.8,9.5,6.69);
       BzzNonLinearRegression nonLinReg(numModels,X,Y,
          PiecewiseCubic);
       BzzVector x(5,
          2.5,10.,18.,25.,29.);
       xc = x;
       BzzVector b(5,5.5,1.,3.,15.,20.);
       nonLinReg.InitializeModel(1,b);
       nonLinReg.LeastSquaresAnalysis();
       b = nonLinReg.GetParameters(1);
       BzzMatrixSparse YY(2,200);
       BzzMatrixSparse XX(2,200);
       double xx;
       int i;
       for(i = 1; i <= 200;i++)
          {
          xx = -2.5 * (double(i) - 200.)/199. +
              29. * (double(i) - 1.) / 199.;
          XX(1,i) = xx;
          YY(1,i) = bc(xx);
          }
       for(i = 1;i <= numExperiments;i++)
          {
          XX(2,i) = X(i,1);
          YY(2,i) = Y(i,1);
          }
       BzzSave save("CubicRegression4.stx");
       save << XX << YY;
       save.End();
       system("BzzPlotSparse.exe");
       BzzPause();
       }
```

Results are visualized in Figure 7.5. The model is satisfactory.

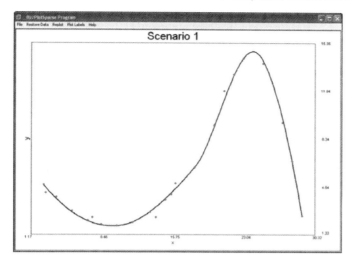

Figure 7.5 Multicubic piecewise model.

7.4
One Dependent Variable and Nonconstant Variance

Sometimes, the dependent variable is characterized by a variance that changes on the overall experimental domain. In these circumstances, it is essential to know either which variable transformation or which weights must be associated with the experimental points to make constant the variance. In this latter case, an *ad hoc* constructor is required to assign weights to experiments **y** through a matrix **W**.

Example 7.19

The experimental data analyzed here has a nonconstant, but known, variance in the experimental domain (Draper and Smith, 1998).
The model is linear (3.7). The experimental data can be directly acquired with the following program:

```
#include "BzzMath.hpp"
void ModelEx1NonConstantVariance (int model,
int ex,BzzVector &b,
BzzVector &x,BzzVector &y);
void main(void)
    {
    BzzPrint("\n\nnumModels 1 numX 1 numY 1");
```

```cpp
int numModels = 1;
int numX = 1;
int numY = 1;
int numExperiments = 35;
BzzMatrix X(numExperiments,numX,
    1.15,1.9,3.,3.,3.,3.,3.,5.34,5.38,5.4,5.4,5.45,7.7,
    7.8,7.81,7.85,7.87,7.91,7.94,9.03,9.07,9.11,9.14,
    9.16,9.37,10.17,10.18,10.22,10.22,10.22,10.18,
    10.5,10.23,10.03,10.23);
BzzMatrix Y(numExperiments,numY,
    .99,.98,2.6,2.67,2.66,2.78,2.8,5.92,5.35,4.33,
    4.89,5.21,7.68,9.81,6.52,9.71,9.82,9.81,8.5,9.47,
    11.45,12.14,11.5,10.65,10.64,9.78,12.39,11.03,8.,
    11.9,8.68,7.25,13.46,10.19,9.93);
BzzMatrix W(numExperiments,numY,
    1.24028,2.18224,7.8493,7.8493,7.8493,7.8493,
    7.8493,7.43652,6.99309,6.78574,6.78574,6.30514,
    .89204,.8442,.83963,.82171,.81296,.79588,.78342,
    .47385,.46621,.45878,.45327,.44968,.41435,.31182,
    .31079,.30672,.30672,.30672,.31079,.28033,.30571,
    .3268,.30571);
int i;
BzzNonLinearRegression nonLinReg(numModels,X,Y,W,
    ModelEx1NonConstantVariance);
BzzVector b(2,1.,1.);
nonLinReg.InitializeModel(1,b);
nonLinReg.LeastSquaresAnalysis();
b = nonLinReg.GetParameters(1);
BzzMatrixSparse YY(2,100);
BzzMatrixSparse XX(2,100);
double x;
for(i = 1; i <= 100;i++)
    {
    x = -1.10 * (double(i) - 100.)/99. +
        10.3 * (double(i) - 1.) / 99.;
    XX(1,i) = x;
    YY(1,i) = b[1] + b[2] * x;
    }
for(i = 1;i <= numExperiments;i++)
    {
    XX(2,i) = X(i,1);
    YY(2,i) = Y(i,1);
    }
BzzSave save("ModelEx1NonConstantVariance.stx");
save << XX << YY;
save.End();
```

7.4 One Dependent Variable and Nonconstant Variance | 333

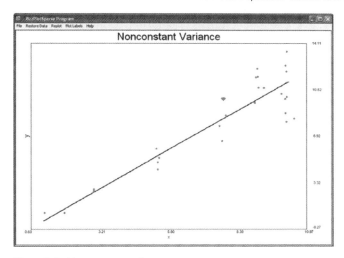

Figure 7.6 Nonconstant variance.

```
//  system("BzzPlotSparse.exe");
    }
void ModelEx1NonConstantVariance(int model, int ex,
    BzzVector &b, BzzVector &x, BzzVector &y)
    {
    y[1] = b[1] + b[2] * x[1];
    }
```

Results are visualized in Figure 7.6. The model is satisfactory.

Example 7.20

Consider the following theoretical model analyzed by Bates and Watts (2007):

$$y_{1i} = -\frac{\beta_4 + \beta_5}{\beta_1} \exp(-\beta_1 x_{1i})(1.-\exp(-\beta_1 x_{2i}))$$

$$+ \frac{\beta_4}{\beta_2} \exp(-\beta_2 x_{1i})(1.-\exp(-\beta_2 x_{2i})) \quad (7.60)$$

$$+ \frac{\beta_5}{\beta_3} \exp(-\beta_3 x_{1i})(1-\exp(-\beta_3 x_{2i}))$$

The model consists of one dependent variable and two independent variables. Only the dependent variable is subject to experimental error and the error variance is constant if the relative error is adopted. On the other hand, the variance is nonconstant by adopting the absolute error.

The experimental data can be directly acquired with the following program:

```
#include "BzzMath.hpp"
void ModelEx2NonConstantVariance (int model,
     int ex,BzzVector &b,
     BzzVector &x,BzzVector &y);
void main(void)
   {
   BzzPrint("\n\nnumModels 1 numX 1 numY 1");
   int numModels = 1;
   int numX = 2;
   int numY = 1;
   int numExperiments = 12;
   BzzMatrix X(numExperiments,numX,
       0.,.25, .25,.25, .5,.25, .75,.25, 1.,.5,
       1.5,.5,  2.,2.,  4.,2.,  6.,2.,  8.,16.,
       24.,24., 48.,24.);
   BzzMatrix Y(numExperiments,numY,
       .01563,.0419,.05328,.05226,.0885,.0634,
       .13419,.04502,.02942,.02716,.01037,.00602);
   BzzMatrix W(numExperiments,numY,
       1./.01563,1./.0419,1./.05328,1./.05226,
       1./.0885,1./.0634,1./.13419,1./.04502,
       1./.02942,1./.02716,1./.01037,1./.00602);
   BzzNonLinearRegression nonLinReg(numModels,X,Y,W,
       ModelEx1NonConstantVariance);
   BzzVector b(5,1.,1.,1.,1.,1.);
   nonLinReg.InitializeModel(1,b);
   nonLinReg.LeastSquaresAnalysis();
   }
void ModelEx2NonConstantVariance (int model,
     int ex,BzzVector &b,
     BzzVector &x,BzzVector &y)
   {
   y[1] = -(b[4] + b[5])/b[1] * exp(-b[1]*x[1]) *
       (1. -exp(-b[1]*x[2]))
   + b[4]/b[2] * exp(-b[2]*x[1]) * (1. -exp(-b[2]*x[2]))
   +b[5]/b[3] * exp(-b[3]*x[1]) * (1. -exp(-b[3]*x[2]));
   }
```

Main results are reported and discussed here.

The condition number is reasonably good if one takes into account problems caused by existing correlations among parameters that cannot be removed:

```
Condition Number 4.727130e+003
```

Contrary to what one could expect because of poor model structure, correlation indices are all good. Parameters are all well determined, but each of them is considered suspicious in the *t*-test. Unfortunately, the model does not allow any reparameterization unless its nature is changed and, in addition, it seems satisfactory by looking at residuals.

```
      Observed y       Estimated y       Residuals        rn      rw
 1  1.5630000e-002   1.8125960e-002   -2.4959597e-003   -0.27  -0.16
 2  4.1900000e-002   3.8351180e-002    3.5488202e-003    0.38   0.08
 3  5.3280000e-002   4.4618603e-002    8.6613971e-003    0.92   0.16
 4  5.2260000e-002   4.4587968e-002    7.6720323e-003    0.82   0.15
 5  8.8500000e-002   8.0110411e-002    8.3895886e-003    0.90   0.09
 6  6.3400000e-002   6.5031285e-002   -1.6312851e-003   -0.17  -0.03
 7  1.3419000e-001   1.4829365e-001   -1.4103650e-002   -1.51  -0.11
 8  4.5020000e-002   5.6431256e-002   -1.1411256e-002   -1.22  -0.25
 9  2.9420000e-002   2.2173473e-002    7.2465270e-003    0.77   0.25
10  2.7160000e-002   2.4692761e-002    2.4672391e-003    0.26   0.09
11  1.0370000e-002   1.1198570e-002   -8.2857016e-004   -0.09  -0.08
12  6.0200000e-003   5.7767225e-003    2.4327755e-004    0.03   0.04
```

Example 7.21

Consider the scenario no. 4 of Section 4.3.3. The violation of homoscedasticity condition was highlighted by introducing new experimental points.
A 2-degree polynomial is used here to fit points of the experimental data set characterized by nonconstant variance.

```
#include "BzzMath.hpp"
void ModelEx3NonConstantVariance (int model,
     int ex, BzzVector &b,
     BzzVector &x, BzzVector &y);
void main(void)
    {
    int numModels = 1;
    int numX = 1;
    int numY = 1;
    int numExperiments = 38;
    BzzMatrix X(numExperiments, numX,
        2.5,7.5,14.,15.,16.,22.,23.,23.,29.,0.,0.,0.,0.,
        2.5,4.,5.,6.,7.5,7.5,12.,12.,15.,15.,16.,16.,16.,
        19.,19.,19.,19.,22.,22.,23.,23.,23.,29.,29.,29.);
    BzzMatrix Y(numExperiments, numY,
        5.,2.6,2.6,3.9,5.1,13.,14.2,5.1,2.7,7.,7.01,7.02,
        6.98,4.95,4.,3.5,3.,2.9,2.2,2.,4.,2.5,5.,2.,3.,
        5.,2.,3.,6.,8.,3.,8.,2.,8.,12.,6.,25.,17.);
    BzzVector w(numExperiments,
        100.,50.,9.,8.,7.,4.,3.,3.,.8,160.,160.,160.,
```

```
        160.,100.,95.,90.,80.,50.,50.,11.,11.,8.,8.,7.,
        7.,7.,5.,5.,5.,4.,4.,3.,3.,3.,.8,.8,.8);
w *= .08;
BzzMatrix W(numExperiments,numY);
W.SetColumn(1,w);
BzzNonLinearRegression nonLinReg(numModels,X,Y,W,
    ModelEx3NonConstantVariance);
BzzVector b(3,1.,1.,1.);
nonLinReg.InitializeModel(1,b);
nonLinReg.LeastSquaresAnalysis();
b = nonLinReg.GetParameters(1);
BzzMatrixSparse YY(2,100);
BzzMatrixSparse XX(2,100);
double x;
int i;
for(i = 1; i <= 100;i++)
    {
    x = 30. * (double(i) - 1.) / 99.;
    XX(1,i) = x;
    YY(1,i) = b[1] + x * (b[2] + b[3] * x);
    }
for(i = 1;i <= numExperiments;i++)
    {
    XX(2,i) = X(i,1);
    YY(2,i) = Y(i,1);
    }
BzzSave save("ModelEx3NonConstantVariance.stx");
```

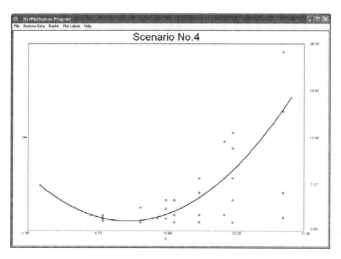

Figure 7.7 Nonconstant variance.

```
            save << XX << YY;
            save.End();
            system("BzzPlotSparse.exe");
        }
```

Results are visualized in Figure 7.7. The model is satisfactory.

7.5
More Dependent Variables and Constant Variance

Many problems involve models with many dependent variables.

Example 7.22

Consider the following theoretical model with two dependent variables, two independent variables, and four parameters:

$$y_{1i} = \frac{\beta_1 x_{1i} x_{2i}}{1 + \beta_3 x_{1i} + \beta_4 x_{2i}} + \varepsilon_{1i}$$

$$y_{2i} = \frac{\beta_2 x_{1i} x_{2i}}{1 + \beta_3 x_{1i} + \beta_4 x_{2i}} + \varepsilon_{2i}$$
(7.61)

Only dependent variables are subject to experimental error with constant variances and their estimations based on 5 degrees of freedom are equal to 0.348 and 0.0023, respectively.

Experimental data can be directly acquired from the following program:

```
#include "BzzMath.hpp"
void MultiDepenentModelEx1(int model, int ex, BzzVector &b,
        BzzVector &x, BzzVector &y);
void main(void)
    {
    BzzPrint("\n\n MultiDepenentModelEx1");
    BzzPrint("\n\nnumModels 1 numX 2 numY 2");
    int numModels = 1;
    int numX = 2;
    int numY = 2;
    int numExperiments = 13;
    BzzMatrix X(numExperiments, numX,
            20., 20.,    30., 20.,    20., 30.,
            30., 30.,    25., 25.,    25., 15.,
            25., 35.,    15., 25.,    35., 25.,
            55., 32.8,   55., 55.,    10.6, 55.,
            16., 55.);
```

```
    BzzMatrix Y(numExperiments,numY,
        3.61, 0.43,     5.42, 0.44,    5.0, 0.64,
        7.5,  0.66,     5.73, 0.55,    3.8, 0.33,
        7.3,  0.79,     4.9,  0.35,    5.9, 0.71,
        9.15, 0.926,   13.74, 1.34,    6.0, 0.70,
        8.2,  0.84);
    BzzNonLinearRegression nonLinReg(numModels,X,Y,
        ModelEx9);
    BzzVector s2(2,0.348,0.0023);
    int df = 5;
    nonLinReg.SetVariance(df,s2);
    BzzVector b(4,1.,1.,1.,1.);
    nonLinReg.InitializeModel(1,b);
    nonLinReg.LeastSquaresAnalysis();
    BzzPause();
    }
 void MultiDependentModelEx1(int model,int ex,BzzVector &b,
        BzzVector &x,BzzVector &y)
    {
    double w = x[1]*x[2]/(1. + b[3]*x[1] + b[4]*x[2]);
    y[1] = b[1] * w;
    y[2] = b[2] * w;
    }
```

Main results are reported and discussed here.

The condition number is good 5.056260e+002. The minimum condition should have been achieved:

```
         Parameters obtained       Parameters obtained
           by minimization          with Newton method
     1   4.04880050684442e-002    4.06448072930012e-002
     2   4.09115314860324e-003    4.10699739772520e-003
     3   1.16445409588136e-001    1.16937308186044e-001
     4   2.64247772668054e-002    2.66009377570498e-002
```

Correlation indices are not completely satisfactory, especially tolerances:

```
    Columns correlation = Tj Tolerance
    1  7.3576293e-003  ** WARNING **
    2  4.7750314e-003  ** WARNING **
    3  5.6361924e-003  ** WARNING **
    4  2.5016063e-002
      ** WARNING ** Correlation between Parameters
     The Tj Tolerance identifies serious multicollinearities
```

Conversely, residuals are good for both the models and the mean square errors are satisfactory too.

```
F-test for the model
Fexperimental = 9.939420e-001
The probability that F with dfNum 22 dfDen 5
is greater than 9.939420e-001 is 5.625436e-001
```

In addition, the robust analysis does not highlight any outlier and, consequently, the model is accepted even though it should be suitable to insert additional experimental points in order to reduce correlations among parameters.

Example 7.23

Consider the theoretical model:

$$y_{1i} = \frac{\beta_1 x_{1i} x_{2i}}{1. + \beta_4 x_{1i}} + \varepsilon_{1i}$$

$$y_{2i} = \frac{\beta_2 x_{1i} x_{2i}}{(1. + \beta_4 x_{1i})^2} + \varepsilon_{2i} \quad (7.62)$$

$$y_{3i} = \frac{\beta_3 x_{1i} x_{2i}}{1. + \beta_4 x_{1i} + \beta_1 x_{2i}} + \varepsilon_{3i}$$

Only dependent variables are subject to experimental errors and their variance estimate is equal to $1.68 \cdot 10^{-11}$, $1.2 \cdot 10^{-8}$, and $1.3 \cdot 10^{-4}$, respectively. Experimental data can be directly acquired with the following program:

```
#include "BzzMath.hpp"
void MultiDepenentModelEx2 (int model, int ex,
    BzzVector &b, BzzVector &x, BzzVector &y);
void main(void)
  {
  BzzPrint("\n\nMultiDependentModelEx2");
  BzzPrint("\n\nnumModels 1 numX 2 numY 3");
  int numModels = 1;
  int numX = 2;
  int numY = 3;
  int numExperiments = 17;
  BzzMatrix X(numExperiments, numX,
              .20, .20,    .50, .20,    1.0, .20,
              .20, .50,    .50, .50,    1.0, .50,
              .20, 1.0,    .50, 1.0,    1.0, 1.0,
              .25, .25,    .50, .25,    .75, .25,
              .25, .50,    .75, .50,    .25, .75,
              .50, .75,    .75, .75);
```

```
    BzzMatrix Y(numExperiments,numY,
        4.91743e-003,3.9866e-003,9.7266e-002,
        5.76934e-003,2.0880e-003,1.1538e-001,
        6.11779e-003,1.0382e-003,1.2298e-001,
        1.22943e-002,9.7065e-003,2.3446e-001,
        1.44083e-002,5.4001e-003,2.8378e-001,
        1.52995e-002,2.8755e-003,3.0495e-001,
        2.45766e-002,1.9453e-002,4.4332e-001,
        2.88377e-002,1.0480e-002,5.5177e-001,
        3.05990e-002,5.9111e-003,6.0101e-001,
        6.45962e-003,4.3567e-003,1.2763e-001,
        7.21243e-003,2.7000e-003,1.4390e-001,
        7.49460e-003,1.9980e-003,1.5035e-001,
        1.29192e-002,8.5135e-003,2.4879e-001,
        1.49937e-002,3.9560e-003,2.9772e-001,
        1.93908e-002,1.2630e-002,3.6409e-001,
        2.16193e-002,8.0201e-003,4.1971e-001,
        2.24928e-002,5.6740e-003,4.4199e-001);
    BzzNonLinearRegression nonLinReg(numModels,X,Y,
        MultiDependentModelEx2);
    BzzVector s2(3,1.68e-011,1.2e-008,1.3e-004);
    int df = 5;
    nonLinReg.SetVariance(df,s2);
    BzzVector b(4,1.,1.,1.,1.);
    nonLinReg.InitializeModel(1,b);
    nonLinReg.LeastSquaresAnalysis();
    BzzPause();
    }
  void MultiDependentModelEx2(int model,int ex,
       BzzVector &b,BzzVector &x,BzzVector &y)
    {
    double a1 = x[1] * x[2];
    double a2 = 1. + b[4] * x[1];
    y[1] = b[1] * a1 / a2;
    y[2] = b[2] * a1 / BzzPow2(a2);
    y[3] = b[3] * a1 /(a2 + b[1] * x[2]);
    }
```

The model is satisfactory even though correlations among parameters exist:

```
Variance inflation factor
1  1.7533006e+002
2  1.1760334e+000
3  1.0084795e+000
4  1.7551380e+002
```

```
   ** WARNING ** Correlation between Parameters

Columns correlation = Tj Tolerance
1  5.7035285e-003   ** WARNING **
2  8.5031597e-001
3  9.9159185e-001
4  5.6975577e-003   ** WARNING **
```

As model reparameterization are not possible, new experimental points should be added to the existing data set (see Chapter 8).

7.6
More Dependent Variables and Nonconstant Variance

Example 7.24

Let us suppose the variance of dependent variables in Example 7.22 is nonconstant and the relevance (weight) of each experimental point is known. The appropriate constructor is

```
BzzNonLinearRegression nonLinReg(numModels,X,Y,W,
        MultiDependentModelEx1);
```

where weights are collected in the `BzzMatrix W`.
The program is

```
#include "BzzMath.hpp"
void MultiDependentModelEx1(int model,int ex,
    BzzVector &b,BzzVector &x,BzzVector &y);
void main(void)
    {
    BzzPrint("\n\nMultiDependentModelEx1");
    BzzPrint("\n\nnumModels 1 numX 2 numY 2");
    int numModels = 1;
    int numX = 2;
    int numY = 2;
    int numExperiments = 13;
    BzzMatrix X(numExperiments,numX,
        20., 20.,   30., 20.,    20., 30.,
        30., 30.,   25., 25.,    25., 15.,
        25., 35.,   15., 25.,    35., 25.,
        55., 32.8,  55., 55.,    10.6, 55.,
        16., 55.);
```

```
        BzzMatrix Y(numExperiments,numY,
              3.61, 0.43,      5.42, 0.44,      5.0, 0.64,
              7.5, 0.66,       5.73, 0.55,      3.8, 0.33,
              7.3, 0.79,       4.9,  0.35,      5.9, 0.71,
              9.15, 0.926,    13.74, 1.34,      6.0, 0.70,
              8.2, 0.84);
        BzzMatrix W(numExperiments,numY,
              1.7, 21.,        1.7, 21.,        3.5, 25.,
              1.6, 21.,        1.7, 21.,        1.7, 21.,
              1.7, 21.,        1.7, 21.,        1.7, 21.,
              1.7, 21.,        1.7, 21.,        1.7, 21.,
              1.7, 21.);
        BzzNonLinearRegression nonLinReg(numModels,X,Y,W,
           MultiDependentModelEx1);
        BzzVector b(4,1.,1.,1.,1.);
        nonLinReg.InitializeModel(1,b);
        nonLinReg.LeastSquaresAnalysis();
  //    nonLinReg.RobustAnalysis();
        BzzPause();
     }
     void MultiDependentModelEx1(int model,int ex,
          BzzVector &b,BzzVector &x,BzzVector &y)
        {
        double w = x[1]*x[2]/(1. + b[3]*x[1] + b[4]*x[2]);
        y[1] = b[1] * w;
        y[2] = b[2] * w;
        }
```

This example differs from Example 7.22, as the error variance is nonconstant on the whole experimental domain; it has the task to show how to solve these problems by the `BzzNonLinearRegression` class. Note that parameters are also different with respect to the previous case, where, with constant variance, parameters were

```
1  4.04880050684442e-002
2  4.09115314860324e-003
3  1.16445409588136e-001
4  2.64247772668054e-002
```

whereas in this case parameters are

```
1  3.45231963795585e-002
2  3.57104147558715e-003
3  9.96466982573898e-002
4  2.11555260763815e-002
```

7.7
Model Consisting of Ordinary Differential Equations

When theoretical models consist of a set of differential equations, some authors call them *compartmental models*.

Example 7.25

Consider the theoretical model

$$\frac{dy_1}{dt} = -(\beta_1 + \beta_2)y_1$$

$$\frac{dy_2}{dt} = \beta_2 y_1$$

$$\frac{dy_3}{dt} = \beta_2 y_1 - \beta_3 y_3 - \beta_4 y_3 + \beta_5 y_5 \qquad (7.63)$$

$$\frac{dy_4}{dt} = \beta_4 y_3$$

$$\frac{dy_5}{dt} = \beta_4 y_3 - \beta_5 y_5$$

consisting of a system of differential equations.
Experimental data are the values of the five dependent variables at different values of t and they are reported in the following program.
As it can be seen in the program, two functions are needed. The first

```
void ModelOdeExample1(int model, int ex,
        BzzVector &b, BzzVector &x, BzzVector &y);
```

is required to evaluate the function minimum, so as to get model parameters. The second

```
void BzzOdeExample1(BzzVector &y, double t, BzzVector &f);
```

is required to integrate the ordinary differential equation system.

In the function `ModelOdeExample1`, the variable `ex` is used to optimize the code.

Since the values of **y** can be calculated with a single integration of the system, in the function `ModelOdeExample1` they are all evaluated in correspondence with the first experimental point, where `ex` is equal to 1. All the variables **y** are collected in an auxiliary `BzzMatrix Y` and they are then recovered in correspondence with the value `ex` of the experiment. Adopting this device, one has not to repeat the integration to achieve all the experimental points. The auxiliary matrix and other variables that are used at each iteration of the model are declared as `static` in order to prevent their continuous resizing.

More details on the use of the `BzzOde` class can be found in the tutorial of the ***BzzMath*** library and in Buzzi-Ferraris and Manenti (2011b).

The program is

```cpp
#include "BzzMath.hpp"
void ModelOdeExample1(int model,int ex,
        BzzVector &b,BzzVector &x,BzzVector &y);
void BzzOdeExample1(BzzVector &y,double t,BzzVector &f);
int numOdeExperiments;
BzzVector bOdeExample1,tOdeExample1;
void main(void)
    {
    BzzPrint("\n\nModelOdeExample1");
    BzzPrint("\n\nnumModels 1 numX 1 numY 5");
    int numModels = 1;
    int numX = 1;
    int numY = 5;
    int numExperiments = 18;
    BzzMatrix X(numExperiments,numX,
    1230.,1540.,2520.,3060.,3980.,4920.,6460.,7800.,
    8900.,10680.,12300.,15030.,18600.,22620.,25730.,
    29950.,32570.,36420.);
    ChangeDimensions(numExperiments,&tOdeExample1);
    for(int i = 1;i <= numExperiments;i++)
      tOdeExample1[i] = X[i][1];
    BzzMatrix Y(numExperiments,numY,
    8.701e-01,7.854e-02,3.320e-02,2.779e-03,1.562e-02,
    8.385e-01,9.668e-02,3.737e-02,4.066e-03,2.221e-02,
    7.498e-01,1.511e-01,4.531e-02,8.763e-03,4.463e-02,
    7.064e-01,1.761e-01,4.744e-02,1.176e-02,5.715e-02,
    6.354e-01,2.183e-01,4.987e-02,1.673e-02,7.735e-02,
    5.710e-01,2.592e-01,5.149e-02,2.242e-02,9.620e-02,
    4.812e-01,3.126e-01,5.255e-02,3.164e-02,1.210e-01,
    4.114e-01,3.535e-01,5.327e-02,3.960e-02,1.412e-01,
    3.650e-01,3.847e-01,5.326e-02,4.654e-02,1.515e-01,
    2.964e-01,4.249e-01,5.339e-02,5.747e-02,1.671e-01,
    2.464e-01,4.530e-01,5.283e-02,6.737e-02,1.774e-01,
    1.825e-01,4.928e-01,5.192e-02,8.363e-02,1.882e-01,
    1.220e-01,5.313e-01,4.966e-02,1.036e-01,1.953e-01,
    7.655e-02,5.580e-01,4.686e-02,1.260e-01,1.914e-01,
    5.375e-02,5.718e-01,4.473e-02,1.424e-01,1.864e-01,
    3.345e-02,5.822e-01,4.131e-02,1.652e-01,1.788e-01,
    2.467e-02,5.873e-01,3.934e-02,1.774e-01,1.720e-01,
    1.610e-02,5.946e-01,3.672e-02,1.943e-01,1.615e-01);
    BzzNonLinearRegression nonLinReg(numModels,X,Y,
            ModelOdeExample1);
    BzzVector s2(5,0.000003,0.000003,.000001,
            .000001,.000003);
```

7.7 Model Consisting of Ordinary Differential Equations

```
      int df = 5;
      nonLinReg.SetVariance(df,s2);
      BzzVector b(5);
      BzzVector bMin(5);
      BzzVector bMax(5);
      bMax = 1.e-3;
      b = 1.e-5;
      nonLinReg.InitializeModel(1,b,bMin,bMax);
      nonLinReg.LeastSquaresAnalysis();
      }
   void ModelOdeExample1(int model,int ex,BzzVector &b,
           BzzVector &x,BzzVector &y)
      {
      int i;
      static BzzOdeStiff o;
      static BzzVector y0(5,1.,0.,0.,0.,0.),yy;
      static BzzMatrix Y(18,5);
      if(ex == 1)
         {
         bOdeExample1 = b;
         o.Deinitialize();
         o.SetInitialConditions(y0,0.,BzzOdeExample1);
         for(i = 1;i <= 18;i++)
            {
            yy = o(tOdeExample1[i]);
            Y.SetRow(i,yy);
            }
         }
      Y.GetRow(ex,&y);
      }

   void BzzOdeExample1(BzzVector &y,double t,BzzVector &f)
      {
      f[1] = -(bOdeExample1[1] + bOdeExample1[2]) * y[1];
      f[2] = bOdeExample1[1] * y[1];
      f[3] = bOdeExample1[2] * y[1] - bOdeExample1[3] * y[3]
             - bOdeExample1[4] * y[3] + bOdeExample1[5] * y[5];
      f[4] = bOdeExample1[3] * y[3];
      f[5] = bOdeExample1[4] * y[3] - bOdeExample1[5] * y[5];
      }
```

The condition number is

```
   Condition Number 5.744719e+001
   The Jacobian matrix is well conditioned
```

Correlation indices are

```
Variance inflation factor
1  1.0185358e+000
2  1.0786712e+000
3  2.4463385e+000
4  3.5225331e+001
5  3.5470370e+001

Columns correlation = Tj Tolerance
1  9.8180151e-001
2  9.2706657e-001
3  4.0877417e-001
4  2.8388662e-002
5  2.8192545e-002
```

The mean square error is good and the model can be accepted.

Example 7.26

Consider the theoretical model

$$\frac{dy_1}{dt} = -(\beta_1 \exp(\beta_2/x_{1i}) + \beta_7 \exp(\beta_8/x_{1i}))y_1$$

$$\frac{dy_2}{dt} = \beta_1 \exp(\beta_2/x_{1i})y_1 - (\beta_3 \exp(\beta_4/x_{1i}) + \beta_5 \exp(\beta_6/x_{1i}))y_2 \qquad (7.64)$$

$$\frac{dy_3}{dt} = \beta_7 \exp(\beta_8/x_{1i})y_1 + \beta_3 \exp(\beta_4/x_{1i})y_2$$

consisting of a system of differential equations.

As it can be seen in the following program, two functions are needed. The first

```
void ModelOdeExample2(int model,int ex,BzzVector &b,
BzzVector &x,BzzVector &y);
```

is required to evaluate the function minimum so as to get model parameters. The second

```
void BzzOdeExample2(BzzVector &y,double t,BzzVector &f);
```

is required to integrate the ordinary differential equation system.

As in the previous Example 7.25, it is possible to optimize the code by means of the variable `ex`.

It is possible to integrate equations only when necessary, according to the value of the experimental point. Actually, in this specific problem, the variable x_{1i} changes in correspondence with experiments no. 1, 15, 27, 37, 49, and 57 only. As a result, it is possible to integrate the system in correspondence with these points only. All the variables **y** are collected in an auxiliary BzzMatrix Y and they are then recovered in correspondence with the value ex of the experiment. Two benefits come from this device.

One has not to repeat the integration to achieve all the experimental points. Exponentials, which are time-consuming operations, are evaluated in correspondence with those points only.
The auxiliary matrix and other variables that are used at each iteration of the model are declared as static in order to prevent their continuous resizing.

Experimental data adopted in the following program consists of the values of the three dependent variables at different values of x_i.

Even in this case, it is suitable to reparameterize the model through the formulation (7.5) rather than the original (7.4) or the classical one (7.7), as already seen in other examples. Parameters β_1, β_3, β_5, and β_7 are surely positive for theoretical reasons.

The program is

```
#include "BzzMath.hpp"
void ModelOdeExample2(int model, int ex,
    BzzVector &b, BzzVector &x, BzzVector &y);
void BzzOdeExample2(BzzVector &y, double t, BzzVector &f);
BzzVector kOde2(4), tOdeExample2;
void main(void)
    {
    BzzPrint("\n\nModelOdeExample2");
    BzzPrint("\n\nnumModels 1 numX 2 numY 3");
    int numModels = 1;
    int numX = 2;
    int numY = 3;
    int numExperiments = 62;
    BzzMatrix X(numExperiments, numX,
            673.,5.,        673.,7.,        673.,10.,
            673.,15.,       673.,20.,       673.,25.,
            673.,30.,       673.,40.,       673.,50.,
            673.,60.,       673.,80.,       673.,100.,
            673.,120.,      673.,150.,      698.,5.,
            698.,7.,        698.,10.,       698.,12.5,
            698.,15.,       698.,17.5,      698.,20.,
            698.,25.,       698.,30.,       698.,40.,
            698.,50.,       698.,60.,       723.,5.,
            723.,7.5,       723.,8.,        723.,9.,
            723.,10.,       723.,11.,       723.,12.5,
            723.,15.,       723.,17.5,      723.,20.,
            748.,3.,        748.,4.5,       748.,5.,
            748.,5.5,       748.,6.,        748.,6.5,
            748.,7.,        748.,8.,        748.,9.,
```

```
            748.,10.,        748.,12.5,      748.,15.,
            773.,3.,         773.,4.,        773.,4.5,
            773.,5.,         773.,5.5,       773.,6.,
            773.,6.5,        773.,10.,       798.,3.,
            798.,3.25,       798.,3.5,       798.,4.,
            798.,5.,         798.,7.);
ChangeDimensions(numExperiments,&tOdeExample2);
for(int i = 1;i <= numExperiments;i++)
        tOdeExample2[i] = X[i][2];
BzzMatrix Y(numExperiments,numY,
        83.98,1.18,14.93,       78.31,1.44,20.52,
        70.16,2.10,27.49,       59.02,2.55,38.23,
        49.61,2.92,47.34,       41.62,3.11,55.19,
        34.83,3.16,61.79,       24.41,3.08,72.01,
        17.44,2.86,79.47,       12.23,2.45,84.85,
        6.00,1.67,91.55,         2.87,1.14,95.11,
        1.42,.73,97.11,          .52,.33,98.36,
        85.23,2.05,12.68,       79.87,2.85,17.31,
        72.47,3.62,23.65,       67.19,4.54,28.47,
        61.95,4.73,33.17,       57.20,5.28,37.57,
        52.91,5.59,41.03,       45.02,6.13,48.52,
        38.18,6.25,54.82,       27.79,6.27,65.21,
        20.17,5.76,73.01,       14.63,5.28,78.99,
        85.45,3.71,10.67,       79.18,5.33,15.56,
        77.88,5.55,16.65,       75.41,6.01,18.32,
        73.02,6.52,20.12,       70.77,6.87,21.91,
        67.56,7.60,24.65,       62.45,8.62,28.76,
        57.73,9.26,32.55,       53.37,9.92,36.19,
        90.49,3.95,5.73,        85.98,5.77,8.36,
        84.55,6.24,9.18,        83.13,6.78,10.05,
        81.73,7.28,10.91,       80.15,7.74,11.76,
        79.02,8.22,12.63,       76.49,9.16,14.18,
        73.85,10.01,15.91,      71.43,10.81,17.51,
        65.63,12.66,21.32,      60.34,14.16,25.01,
        88.76,6.37,4.83,        85.33,8.19,6.45,
        83.54,9.06,7.23,        81.99,9.91,7.99,
        80.34,10.75,8.75,       78.81,11.51,9.46,
        77.27,12.38,10.21,      67.21,17.11,15.26,
        85.91,9.71,4.27,        84.86,10.49,4.61,
        83.83,11.16,4.95,       81.72,12.49,5.61,
        77.69,15.14,6.99,       70.25,19.78,9.64);
BzzNonLinearRegression nonLinReg(numModels,X,Y,
        ModelOdeExample2);
BzzVector s2(3,.6,.6,.6);
int df = 5;
nonLinReg.SetVariance(df,s2);
```

```
   BzzVector b(8,1.,1.,1.,1.,1.,1.,1.,1.);
   nonLinReg.InitializeModel(1,b);
   nonLinReg.LeastSquaresAnalysis();
   BzzPause();
   }
void ModelOdeExample2(int model,int ex,BzzVector &b,
         BzzVector &x,BzzVector &y)
   {
   int i;
   static BzzOdeStiff o;
   static BzzVector y0(3,100.,0.,0.),yy,yMin;
   static BzzMatrix Y(62,3);
   static double umin = 1. / 673.;
   static double umax = 1. / 798.;
   static double c = -1. / (umax - umin);
   int kStart,numStep;
   static BzzVector t(14);
   if(ex == 1 || ex == 15 || ex == 27 ||
         ex == 37 || ex == 49 || ex == 57)
      {
      kOde2[1] = exp(c * (b[1] * (1. / x[1] - umin)
            b[2] * (1. / x[1] - umax)));
      kOde2[2] = exp(c * (b[3] * (1. / x[1] - umin)
            b[4] * (1. / x[1] - umax)));
      kOde2[3] = exp(c * (b[5] * (1. / x[1] - umin)
            b[6] * (1. / x[1] - umax)));
      kOde2[4] = exp(c * (b[7] * (1. / x[1] - umin)
            b[8] * (1. / x[1] - umax)));
      o.Deinitialize();
      o.SetInitialConditions(y0,0.,BzzOdeExample2);
      ChangeDimensions(3,&yMin);
      o.SetMinimumConstraints(&yMin);
      }
   if(ex == 1)
      {
      kStart = 0;
      numStep = 14;
      for(i = 1;i <= numStep;i++)
         t[i] = tOdeExample2[kStart + i];
      for(i = 1;i <= numStep;i++)
         {
         yy = o(t[i]);
         Y.SetRow(kStart + i,yy);
         }
      }
   else if(ex == 15)
```

```
            {
            kStart = 14;
            numStep = 12;
            for(i = 1;i <= numStep;i++)
                t[i] = tOdeExample2[kStart + i];
            for(i = 1;i <= numStep;i++)
               {
               yy = o(t[i]);
               Y.SetRow(kStart + i,yy);
               }
            }
        else if(ex == 27)
            {
            kStart = 26;
            numStep = 10;
            for(i = 1;i <= numStep;i++)
                t[i] = tOdeExample2[kStart + i];
            for(i = 1;i <= numStep;i++)
               {
               yy = o(t[i]);
               Y.SetRow(kStart + i,yy);
               }
            }
        else if(ex == 37)
            {
            kStart = 36;
            numStep = 12;
            for(i = 1;i <= numStep;i++)
                t[i] = tOdeExample2[kStart + i];
            for(i = 1;i <= numStep;i++)
               {
               yy = o(t[i]);
               Y.SetRow(kStart + i,yy);
               }
            }
        else if(ex == 49)
            {
            kStart = 48;
            numStep = 8;
            for(i = 1;i <= numStep;i++)
                t[i] = tOdeExample2[kStart + i];
            for(i = 1;i <= numStep;i++)
               {
               yy = o(t[i]);
               Y.SetRow(kStart + i,yy);
```

7.7 Model Consisting of Ordinary Differential Equations

```
            }
        }
    else if (ex == 57)
        {
        kStart = 56;
        numStep = 6;
        for (i = 1; i <= numStep; i++)
            t[i] = tOdeExample2[kStart + i];
        for (i = 1; i <= numStep; i++)
            {
            yy = o(t[i]);
            Y.SetRow(kStart + i, yy);
            }
        }
    Y.GetRow(ex, &y);
    }
void BzzOdeExample2(BzzVector &y, double t, BzzVector &f)
    {
    f[1] = -(kOde2[1] + kOde2[4]) * y[1];
    f[2] = kOde2[1] * y[1] - (kOde2[2] + kOde2[3]) * y[2];
    f[3] = kOde2[4] * y[1] + kOde2[2] * y[2];
    }
```

Parameters obtained by the least sum of squares method are

```
    1   3.32570076289691e+000
    2   5.88407151502887e+000
    3   4.25503757947747e+000
    4   3.65241431447998e+000
    5   5.32370429545284e+000
    6   5.72194157607374e+000
    7   4.23083269579169e+000
    8   3.43104839952351e+000
```

The model does not present any correlation among parameters.

```
    Variance inflation factor
    1   2.8745046e+000
    2   4.2008193e+000
    3   6.2338244e+000
    4   2.7278662e+000
    5   2.4010523e+000
    6   1.3178591e+000
    7   5.4369891e+000
    8   2.3142644e+000
```

```
Columns correlation = Tj Tolerance
1  3.4788603e-001
2  2.3804880e-001
3  1.6041517e-001
4  3.6658689e-001
5  4.1648406e-001
6  7.5880646e-001
7  1.8392533e-001
8  4.3210274e-001

The Tj Tolerance does not identify serious
multicollinearities
```

Residuals are good and the mean square error is satisfactory.

```
Mean Square Error = 5.9438979e-003

F-test for the model
Fexperimental = 1.188783e+000
The probability that F with dfNum 178 dfDen 5
is greater than 1.188783e+000 is 4.778704e-001
```

The model is acceptable.

7.8
Model Consisting of Differential Algebraic Equations

In some circumstances, the theoretical model consists of a set of differential algebraic equations.

Example 7.27

Consider the theoretical model

$$\frac{dy_1}{dt} = -\beta_1 y_1 + \beta_2 y_2 y_3$$
$$\frac{dy_2}{dt} = \beta_1 y_1 - \beta_2 y_2 y_3 - \beta_3 y_2^2 \quad (7.65)$$
$$y_1 + y_2 + y_3 - 1 = 0$$

consisting of a system of differential algebraic equations. Experimental data consist of the values of the three dependent variables at different values of t and they are available in the following program.

7.8 Model Consisting of Differential Algebraic Equations

Theoretically, the first parameter is in the order of 1., the second is some tens larger than the first, and the third parameter is significantly larger than the others. $\beta\{1., 10., 100.\}$ is assumed as initial guess; optimal values are

1   4.13090298962625e-001
2   1.12352704754714e+003
3   1.53619407391221e+005

As it can be seen in the following program, two functions are needed. The first

```
void ModelDaeExample(int model, int ex,
        BzzVector &b, BzzVector &x, BzzVector &y);
```

is required to evaluate the function minimum for evaluating the model parameters. The second

```
void BzzDaeExample(BzzVector &y, double t, BzzVector &f);
```

is required to integrate the differential algebraic system.

As in the previous Example 7.25, it is possible to optimize the code by means of the variable `ex`.

As the values of the dependent variables can be obtained through a single integration of the system, in the function `ModelDaeExample` they are all evaluated in correspondence with the first experimental point, where `ex` is equal to 1. All dependent variables are collected in the auxiliary `BzzMatrix Y` and they are then recovered in correspondence with the value `ex` of the experimental point. Adopting this device, one has not to repeat the integration to achieve all experimental points. The auxiliary matrix and other variables that are used at each iteration of the model are declared as `static` in order to prevent their continuous resizing.

To inform the program about the nature (differential or algebraic) of the equations, the object `BzzVectorInt iDer(3,1,1,0)` is introduced in the constructor of the object `BzzDae dae`. A value equal to 1 denotes a differential equation, whereas a null value denotes an algebraic equation. More details on the use of the `BzzDae` class can be found in the tutorial of the ***BzzMath*** library and in Buzzi-Ferraris and Manenti (2011b).

The program is

```
#include "BzzMath.hpp"
void ModelDaeExample(int model, int ex,
        BzzVector &b, BzzVector &x, BzzVector &y);
void BzzDaeExample(BzzVector &y, double t, BzzVector &f);
int numDaeExperiments;
BzzVector bDaeExample, tDaeExample;
void main(void)
    {
    BzzPrint("\n\nModelDaeExample");
    BzzPrint("\n\nnumModels 1 numX 1 numY 5");
```

```
        int numModels = 1;
        int numX = 1;
        int numY = 3;
        int numExperiments = 29;
        numDaeExperiments = numExperiments;
        BzzMatrix X(numExperiments,numX,
            .1,.2,.3,.4,.5,.6,.7,.8,.9,1.,2.,3.,4.,5.,6.,7.,
            8.,9.,10.,100.,200.,300.,400.,500.,600.,700.,
            800.,900.,1000.);
        int i;
        ChangeDimensions(numExperiments,&tDaeExample);
        for(i = 1;i <= numExperiments;i++)
            tDaeExample[i] = X[i][1];
        BzzMatrix Y(numExperiments,numY,
            9.636e-001,1.488e-003,3.689e-002,
            9.338e-001,1.358e-003,6.984e-002,
            9.047e-001,1.254e-003,9.107e-002,
            8.861e-001,1.177e-003,1.148e-001,
            8.582e-001,1.109e-003,1.377e-001,
            8.464e-001,1.045e-003,1.525e-001,
            8.274e-001,1.001e-003,1.706e-001,
            8.189e-001,9.493e-004,1.832e-001,
            8.035e-001,9.122e-004,1.996e-001,
            7.872e-001,8.815e-004,2.089e-001,
            7.040e-001,6.638e-004,2.994e-001,
            6.442e-001,5.551e-004,3.563e-001,
            6.005e-001,4.802e-004,3.941e-001,
            5.735e-001,4.320e-004,4.301e-001,
            5.482e-001,3.979e-004,4.484e-001,
            5.210e-001,3.656e-004,4.766e-001,
            5.077e-001,3.437e-004,4.929e-001,
            4.838e-001,3.217e-004,5.159e-001,
            4.707e-001,3.076e-004,5.290e-001,
            1.833e-001,7.939e-005,8.166e-001,
            1.213e-001,5.093e-005,8.826e-001,
            9.502e-002,3.907e-005,9.069e-001,
            7.311e-002,2.874e-005,9.209e-001,
            6.273e-002,2.795e-005,9.372e-001,
            5.749e-002,1.654e-005,9.465e-001,
            4.821e-002,1.999e-005,9.478e-001,
            4.526e-002,1.499e-005,9.587e-001,
            3.925e-002,1.939e-005,9.557e-001,
            3.892e-002,1.607e-005,9.611e-001);
    BzzVector y0(3,1.,0.,0.),yy,yMin(3);
    BzzVectorInt iDer(3,1,1,0);
```

```
   BzzNonLinearRegression nonLinReg(numModels,X,Y,
         ModelDaeExample);
   BzzVector s2(3,5.8e-6,5.4e-12,5.6e-6);
   int df = 5;
   nonLinReg.SetVariance(df,s2);
   BzzVector b(3,1.,10.,100.);
   BzzVector bMin(3);
   BzzVector bMax(3,1.,5000.,200000.);
   nonLinReg.InitializeModel(1,b,bMin,bMax);
   nonLinReg.LeastSquaresAnalysis();
   BzzPause();
   }
void ModelDaeExample(int model,int ex,
      BzzVector &b,BzzVector &x,BzzVector &y)
   {
   int i;
   static BzzDae dae;
   static BzzVector y0(3,1.,0.,0.),yy,yMin;
   static BzzVectorInt iDer(3,1,1,0);
   static BzzMatrix Y(numDaeExperiments,3);
   if(ex == 1)
      {
      ChangeDimensions(3,&yMin);
      bDaeExample = b;
      dae.Deinitialize();
      dae.SetInitialConditions(y0,0.,iDer,
      BzzDaeExample);
      dae.SetMinimumConstraints(&yMin);
      for(i = 1;i <= numDaeExperiments;i++)
         {
         yy = dae(tDaeExample[i]);
         Y.SetRow(i,yy);
         }
      }
   Y.GetRow(ex,&y);
   }
void BzzDaeExample(BzzVector &y,double t,BzzVector &f)
   {
   double r1 = bDaeExample[1] * y[1];
   double r2 = bDaeExample[2] * y[2] * y[3];
   double r3 = bDaeExample[3] * y[2] * y[2];
   f[1] = -r1 + r2;
   f[2] = r1 - r2 - r3;
   f[3] = y[1] + y[2] + y[3] - 1.;
   }
```

Results of the model are satisfactory even though there is a clear correlation among parameters. Unfortunately, such a correlation is unavoidable because of the unbalancing of the same parameters.

7.9
Analysis of Alternative Models

The `BzzNonLinearRegression` class allows to examine even more alternative models. To do so, it is necessary to pass their amount to the object of the `BzzNonLinearRegression` class by means of the `int numModels`. Moreover, each model must be initialized through the function

```
BzzVector b1(3,1.,1.,1.);
nonLinReg.InitializeModel(1,b1);
```

The first integer in the argument of the function indicates which model is initialized, whereas the second provides the initial guess for parameters. Even in this case, it is possible to provide lower and upper bounds, which limits the values of parameters in the search for the minimum. For example,

```
BzzVector b1(3,1.,1.,1.);
BzzVector b1Min(3),b1Max(3,100.,200.,350.);
nonLinReg.InitializeModel(1,b1,b1Min,b1Max);
```

If the *j*th model is uninitialized, the successive calls of the function

```
nonLinReg.LeastSquaresAnalysis();
```

do not consider such a model in the analysis.

Conversely, all models that were properly initialized are analyzed one at a time and, besides their specific factors and indices, a comparison is provided too, in order to highlight if a model is better than the other possibilities.

Chapter 8 shall describe how it is possible to foresee which new experiments are useful both for improving the model parameter estimation and for discriminating the best model among different alternatives.

Example 7.28

Consider the following five models:

$$y_{1i} = \beta_1 + \beta_2(1.-\exp(-\beta_3 x_{1i})) + \varepsilon_{1i} \tag{7.66}$$

$$y_{1i} = \beta_1 + \beta_2 \frac{\beta_3 x_{1i}}{1. + \beta_3 x_{1i}} + \varepsilon_{1i} \tag{7.67}$$

$$y_{1i} = \beta_1 + \beta_2(\mathrm{atan}(\beta_3 x_{1i})) + \varepsilon_{1i} \tag{7.68}$$

7.9 Analysis of Alternative Models

$$y_{1i} = \beta_1 + \beta_2(\tanh(\beta_3 x_{1i})) + \varepsilon_{1i} \tag{7.69}$$

$$y_{1i} = \beta_1 + \beta_2\left(\exp\left(\frac{-\beta_3}{x_{1i}}\right)\right) + \varepsilon_{1i} \tag{7.70}$$

Only the dependent variable is subject to experimental error with constant variance and its estimate based on 5 degrees of freedom is equal to 7.5.
Experimental values can be directly acquired with the following program.
Evaluate the model parameters and analyze the model.
The program is

```
#include "BzzMath.hpp"
void MultiModelEx1(int model, int ex, BzzVector &b,
        BzzVector &x, BzzVector &y);
void main(void)
  {
  BzzPrint("\n\nMultiModelEx1");
  BzzPrint("\n\nnumModels 5 numX 1 numY 1");
  int numModels = 5;
  int numX = 1;
  int numY = 1;
  int numExperiments = 20;
  BzzMatrix X(numExperiments, numX,
        0.01,.5,1.,2.,3.,4.,6.,9.,12.,16.,18.,20.,40.,
        70.,100.,2.828355e+001,8.484864e+001,
        5.454591e+001,2.424318e+001,9.292936e+001);
  BzzMatrix Y(numExperiments, numY,
        11.115,17.588,19.863,33.547,34.178,47.872,
        57.842,78.477,86.842,92.118,100.381,98.974,
        104.995,110.968,111.999,103.133,112.994,
        105.811,101.845,111.998);
  BzzNonLinearRegression nonLinReg(numModels, X, Y,
        MultiModelEx1);
  BzzVector s2(1,7.5);
  int df = 5;
  nonLinReg.SetVariance(df,s2);
  BzzVector b1(3,1.,1.,1.);
  nonLinReg.InitializeModel(1,b1);
  BzzVector b2(3,1.,100.,1.);
  nonLinReg.InitializeModel(2,b2);
  BzzVector b3(3,1.,1.,1.);
  nonLinReg.InitializeModel(3,b3);
  BzzVector b4(3,1.,1.,1.);
  nonLinReg.InitializeModel(4,b4);
  BzzVector b5(3,1.,1.,1.);
  nonLinReg.InitializeModel(5,b5);
```

```
        nonLinReg.LeastSquaresAnalysis();
    }
    void MultiModelEx1(int model,int ex,BzzVector &b,
            BzzVector &x,BzzVector &y)
    {
        switch(model)
        {
        case 1:
            y[1] = b[1] + b[2] * (1. - exp(-b[3] * x[1]));
            break;
        case 2:
            y[1] = b[1] + b[2] * (b[3] * x[1] /
                (1. + b[3] * x[1]));
            break;
        case 3:
            y[1] = b[1] + b[2] * (atan(b[3] * x[1]));
            break;
        case 4:
            y[1] = b[1] + b[2] * (tanh(b[3] * x[1]));
            break;
        case 5:
            y[1] = b[1] + b[2] * exp(-b[3] / x[1]);
            break;
        }
    }
```

At the end of the analysis of single models, a general comparison is given.

```
==================================================
=============< Summary >==========================
==================================================
Sigma2 7.500000e+000 dof 5
    MSE    MSE/Best  Fexp      P-Value        PseudoP-Value
1   8.254  1.000000  1.100  5.016025e-001   1.000000e+000
2  20.99   2.531871  2.786  1.305477e-001   6.355786e-002
3   8.732  1.057798  1.164  4.719696e-001   9.091273e-001
4  11.10   1.345157  1.480  3.522125e-001   5.476583e-001
5  11.38   1.378995  1.517  3.407293e-001   5.147567e-001
```

The first column indicates which model is analyzed. The second reports the mean square error for each model. The third reports the ratio between the mean square error of the corresponding model and the mean square error of the best model. The fourth column reports the ratio between the mean square error and the variance of the error for each model. The fifth column reports the probability that the theoretical *F* is larger than experimental *F* just evaluated. If the probability is significantly small, it could be possible to remove the corresponding model. The last column reports the same calculation by using the value of the second column as *F* value. In addition, another table proposes the results of the fifth column by supposing the estimate of the error variance with one degree of freedom more than the real case is known. This information may be sometimes suitable as it shows if it is important to improve the error variance estimate to make reasonable the possibility to discard a model:

```
P-Values with Sigma2 7.500000e+000 d.o.f. 6
1  4.881074e-001
2  1.051872e-001
3  4.562664e-001
4  3.287071e-001
5  3.166229e-001
```

This analysis underlines that the first and third models are preferable, whereas the second model is the worst one. According to the available experimental points, one cannot clearly distinguish the best model, even though with an additional degree of freedom in the *F*-test. As a result, it is necessary to introduce new experimental points (Chapter 8).

Example 7.29

Consider the following alternative models:

$$y_{1i} = \frac{\beta_1 x_{1i} x_{2i}}{1. + \beta_3 x_{1i} + \beta_4 x_{2i}} + \varepsilon_{1i} \qquad y_{2i} = \frac{\beta_2 x_{1i} x_{2i}}{1. + \beta_3 x_{1i} + \beta_4 x_{2i}} + \varepsilon_{2i} \qquad (7.71)$$

$$y_{1i} = \frac{\beta_1 x_{1i} x_{2i}}{(1. + \beta_3 x_{1i} + \beta_4 x_{2i})^2} + \varepsilon_{1i} \qquad y_{2i} = \frac{\beta_2 x_{1i} x_{2i}}{1. + \beta_3 x_{1i}} + \varepsilon_{2i} \qquad (7.72)$$

$$y_{1i} = \frac{\beta_1 x_{1i} x_{2i}}{(1. + \beta_4 x_{2i})^2} + \varepsilon_{1i} \qquad y_{2i} = \frac{\beta_2 x_{1i} x_{2i}}{(1. + \beta_3 x_{1i})^2} + \varepsilon_{2i} \qquad (7.73)$$

$$y_{1i} = \frac{\beta_1 x_{1i} x_{2i}}{1. + \beta_3 x_{1i} + \beta_4 x_{2i}} + \varepsilon_{1i} \qquad y_{2i} = \frac{\beta_2 x_{1i} x_{2i}}{1. + \beta_3 x_{1i}} + \varepsilon_{2i} \qquad (7.74)$$

Only dependent variables are subject to experimental error with constant variance and their estimates based on 6 degrees of freedom are equal to .348 and .0023, respectively.

Experimental values can be directly acquired with the following program. Evaluate the model parameters and analyze the model.

The program is

```
#include "BzzMath.hpp"
void MultiModelEx2(int model,int ex,BzzVector &b,
        BzzVector &x,BzzVector &y);
```

```
void main(void)
   {
   BzzPrint("\n\nMultiModelex2");
   BzzPrint("\n\nnumModels 4 numX 2 numY 2");
   int numModels = 4;
   int numX = 2;
   int numY = 2;
   int numExperiments = 13;
   BzzMatrix X(numExperiments,numX,
         20.,20.,  30.,20.,  20.,30.,  30.,30.,
         25.,25.,  25.,15.,  25.,35.,  15.,25.,
         35.,25.,  55.,32.8, 55.,55.,  10.6,55.,
         16.,55.);
   BzzMatrix Y(numExperiments,numY,
         3.61,.43, 5.42,.44, 5.,.64,   7.5,.66,
         5.73,.55, 3.8,.33,  7.3,.79,  4.9,.35,
         5.9,.71,  9.15,.926, 13.74,1.34, 6.,.70,
         8.2,.84);
   BzzNonLinearRegression nonLinReg(numModels,X,Y,
         MultiModelEx2);
   BzzVector s2(2,.348,.0023);
   nonLinReg.SetVariance(6,s2);
   BzzVector b1(4,1.,1.,1.,1.);
   nonLinReg.InitializeModel(1,b1);
   BzzVector b2(4,1.,1.,1.,1.);
   nonLinReg.InitializeModel(2,b2);
   BzzVector b3(4,1.,1.,1.,1.);
   nonLinReg.InitializeModel(3,b3);
   BzzVector b4(4,1.,1.,1.,1.);
   nonLinReg.InitializeModel(4,b4);
   nonLinReg.LeastSquaresAnalysis();
   }
void MultiModelEx2(int model,int ex,BzzVector &b,
      BzzVector &x,BzzVector &y)
   {
   double a1 = x[1] * x[2];
   double a2 = b[2] * a1;
   a1 *= b[1];
   switch(model)
      {
      case 1:
         y[1] = a1 / (1. + b[3] * x[1] + b[4] * x[2]);
         y[2] = a2 / (1. + b[3] * x[1] + b[4] * x[2]);
         break;
      case 2:
         y[1] = a1 / BzzPow2(1. + b[3] * x[1] +
```

```
                b[4] * x[2]);
        y[2] = a2 / (1. + b[3] * x[1]);
        break;
    case 3:
        y[1] = a1 / BzzPow2(1. + b[4] * x[2]);
        y[2] = a2 / BzzPow2(1. + b[3] * x[1]);
        break;
    case 4:
        y[1] = a1 / (1. + b[3] * x[1] + b[4] * x[2]);
        y[2] = a2 / (1. + b[3] * x[1]);
        break;
    }
}
```

At the end of the analysis of single models, a general comparison is given.

```
==================================================
============< Summary >===========================
==================================================
d.o.f. 6

  WeightedSE  WeightedSE/Best  P-Value      PseudoP-Value
1    21.87        1.000        5.535e-001    1.00e+000
2    81.71        3.736        5.456e-002    3.10e-003
3   151.86        6.944        1.179e-002    2.61e-005 **
4    34.90        1.596        2.954e-001    2.80e-001
```

The first column indicates which model is analyzed. The second reports the weighted mean square error for each model. The third reports the ratio between the weighted mean square error of the corresponding model and the weighted mean square error of the best model. The fourth column reports the probability that the theoretical χ^2 is larger than experimental χ^2. If the probability is significantly small, it could be possible to remove the corresponding model. The last column reports the same calculation by using the value of the second column as χ^2 value. In addition, another table proposes the results of the fourth column by supposing the estimate of the error variance with one degree of freedom more than the real case is known. In this problem, one can see that, besides the model no. 3, even the model no. 2 can be reasonably discarded by improving the error variance estimation:

```
    P-Values with 7 d.o.f.
      1    5.464481e-001
      2    4.049932e-002 *** WARNING ***
      3    6.954068e-003 *** WARNING ***
      4    2.741346e-001

      *** WARNING ***
      We suggest to improve the estimation of the variance
```

This analysis underlines that first and fourth models are both preferable, whereas the second and third models are poor and, probably, they can be discarded. According to the available experimental points, one cannot clearly distinguish the best model. As a result, it is necessary to introduce new experimental points (Chapter 8).

7.10
Independent Variables Subject to Experimental Error

Even independent variables might be subject to experimental error. In this case, it is indispensable to account for it and to use the appropriate objective function (see Chapter 6).

Example 7.30

Consider the model:

$$y_{1i} = \frac{\xi_{1i}\xi_{2i}}{\sqrt{\beta_1 + \beta_2 \xi_{1i} + \beta_3 \xi_{2i} \sqrt{\xi_{1i}}}} + \varepsilon_{y_{1i}} \quad (7.75)$$

$$z_{1i} = \xi_{1i} + \varepsilon_{x_{1i}}$$

$$z_{2i} = \xi_{2i} + \varepsilon_{x_{2i}}$$

Experimental data can be directly acquired with the following program. Suppose that the dependent variable is subject to error with variance that is constant in the whole experimental domain and its estimate is equal to $2.1 \cdot 10^{-7}$. Even independent variables present an experimental error with constant variance on the whole experimental domain and their estimates are equal to $6.4 \cdot 10^{-4}$ and $7.6 \cdot 10^{-4}$.

Start examining the model by neglecting the experimental error on independent variables.

The program is

```
#include "BzzMath.hpp"
void IndependentVariablesWithErrorsEx1(int model,
    int ex,BzzVector &b,BzzVector &x,BzzVector &y);
void main(void)
    {
    int numModels = 1;
    int numX = 2;
    int numY = 1;
    int numExperiments = 25;
    BzzMatrix X(numExperiments,numX,
            8.900e-002, 8.800e-002, 2.003e+001, 8.800e-002,
            4.998e+001, 1.360e-001, 7.002e+001, 7.600e-002,
            9.996e+001, 1.120e-001, 1.330e-001, 2.002e+001,
```

```
        2.001e+001, 1.999e+001, 4.998e+001, 2.004e+001,
        7.001e+001, 1.998e+001, 1.002e+001, 2.002e+001,
        1.110e-001, 4.995e+001, 2.002e+001, 5.004e+001,
        4.999e+001, 5.001e+001, 7.003e+001, 4.998e+001,
        9.998e+001, 4.999e+001, 1.220e-001, 7.004e+001,
        1.996e+001, 6.998e+001, 5.003e+001, 7.002e+001,
        7.001e+001, 6.995e+001, 9.998e+001, 7.004e+001,
        1.330e-001, 1.000e+002, 1.998e+001, 9.998e+001,
        5.002e+001, 1.000e+002, 6.996e+001, 1.000e+002,
        1.000e+002, 1.000e+002);
    BzzMatrix Y(numExperiments,numY,
        2.316e-003,9.217e-002,2.260e-001,1.518e-001,
        2.657e-001,1.711e-001,7.105,1.372e+001,
        1.738e+001,4.298,2.391e-001,1.164e+001,
        2.282e+001,2.919e+001,3.782e+001,
        3.060e-001,1.383e+001,2.731e+001,
        3.495e+001,4.542e+001,3.901e-001,
        1.663e+001,3.289e+001,4.216e+001,
        5.489e+001);
    BzzNonLinearRegression nonLinReg(numModels,X,Y,
        IndependentVariablesWithErrorsEx1);
//  BzzVector s2(numY + numX,2.1e-7,6.4e-4,7.6e-4);
    BzzVector s2(numY,2.1e-7);
    nonLinReg.SetVariance(4,s2);
    BzzVector b(3,1.,1.,1.);
    BzzVector bMin(3),bMax(3);
    bMax = 100.;
    nonLinReg.InitializeModel(1,b,bMin,bMax);
    nonLinReg.LeastSquaresAnalysis();
    BzzPause();
    }
void IndependentVariablesWithErrorsEx1(int model,int ex,
        BzzVector &b,BzzVector &x,BzzVector &y)
    {
    y[1] = x[1] * x[2] /
      sqrt(b[1] + b[2] * x[1] + b[3] *
      sqrt(x[1]) * x[2]);
    }
```

Model parameters are

    1   6.61399525069704e+001
    2   1.54189260449999e+001
    3   3.16103582417491e+001

Condition number and correlation indices are both satisfactory.

7 Nonlinear Regression Case Studies

Conversely, the mean square error is large compared to the error variance estimate:

```
Mean Square Error = 2.7350141e-003
F-test for the model
Fexperimental = 1.302388e+004
The probability that F with dfNum 22 dfDen 4
is greater than 1.302388e+004 is 1.286132e-008
*** WARNING ***
```

Analysis of residuals is unsatisfactory too. Therefore, the model seems inadequate to represent the whole experimental data set.

To execute a model analysis that accounts for the experimental error on independent variables, the statement

```
BzzVector s2(numY,2.1e-7);
```

must be replaced with

```
BzzVector s2(numY + numX,2.1e-7,6.4e-4,7.6e-4);
```

The object `nonLinReg` realizes that the amount of variance estimates corresponds to the sum of dependent and independent variables: it accounts even for the experimental error on the independent variables and minimizes the function (6.3). As a results, model parameters are slightly different:

```
1    6.62253000366956e+001
2    1.54170877145309e+001
3    3.16105180599991e+001
```

Condition number and correlation indices are all satisfactory.

The mean square error is now significantly smaller than the previous case and the model seems adequate to fit the experimental data set.

```
Mean Square Error = 6.2189891e-008
F-test for the model
Fexperimental = 2.961423e-001
The probability that F with dfNum 22 dfDen 4
is greater than 2.961423e-001 is 9.732148e-001
```

After using the function (6.3), independent variables are modified too, besides model parameters **b**, so the model can better fit experimental data.

Example 7.31

Consider the model with one dependent variable and one independent variable:

$$y_{1i} = \beta_1 \exp\left(-\beta_2 \left(\frac{1}{\xi_{1i}} - .003\right)\right) + \varepsilon_{y_{1i}}$$

$$z_{1i} = \xi_{1i} + \varepsilon_{x_{1i}}$$

(7.76)

7.10 Independent Variables Subject to Experimental Error

Both the variables are subject to experimental error with nonconstant variance on the experimental domain. The weight associated with each experimental point is known and the function (6.2) can be adopted to estimate model parameters. Experimental data and their respective weights can be directly acquired with the following program:

```
#include "BzzMath.hpp"
void IndependentVariablesWithErrorsEx2(int model,
    int ex,BzzVector &b,BzzVector &x,BzzVector &y);
void main(void)
    {
    BzzPrint("\n\n\nWeighted variables");
    BzzPrint("\n\nnumModels 1 numX 1 numY 1");
    int numModels = 1;
    int numX = 1;
    int numY = 1;
    int numExperiments = 11;
    BzzMatrix X(numExperiments,numX,
            272.1,284.2,291.3,302.1,314.3,322.2,332.6,344.2,
            351.1,362.1,374.1);
    BzzMatrix Y(numExperiments,numY,
            1.95e+002,2.5e+002,3.6e+002,4.7e+002,
            6.0e+002,7.8e+002,9.9e+002,1.3e+003,
            1.5e+003,1.9e+003,2.1e+003);
    BzzMatrix W(numExperiments,numY + numX,
            2.58e-002,3.14e-001, 2.67e-002,3.22e-001,
            2.71e-002,3.45e-001, 2.82e-002,3.66e-001,
            2.93e-002,3.71e-001, 3.21e-002,3.84e-001,
            3.21e-002,3.95e-001, 3.34e-002,4.03e-001,
            3.41e-002,4.22e-001, 3.55e-002,4.51e-001,
            3.78e-002,4.72e-001);
    BzzNonLinearRegression nonLinReg(numModels,X,Y,W,
            IndependentVariablesWithErrorsEx2);
    BzzVector b(2,1.,1.);
    nonLinReg.InitializeModel(1,b);
    nonLinReg.LeastSquaresAnalysis();
    BzzPause();
    }

void IndependentVariablesWithErrorsEx2(int model,
    int ex,BzzVector &b,BzzVector &x,BzzVector &y)
    {
    y[1] = b[1] * exp(-b[2]* (1./x[1] - .003));
    }
```

The object `nonLinReg` receives the matrix `W` as argument. As the number of columns of this matrix is equal to the sum of the number of dependent and independent variables, the object knows that the function (6.2) is to be used to find out parameters and optimal values of **x**.

The model is satisfactory. The values of **x** were modified for minimizing the function (6.2):

```
                   Independent Variables 1
        Observed x       Estimated x         Residuals r
 1    2.7210000e+002   2.7165346e+002      4.4653547e-001
 2    2.8420000e+002   2.8224895e+002      1.9510471e+000
 3    2.9130000e+002   2.9100453e+002      2.9547071e-001
 4    3.0210000e+002   3.0130478e+002      7.9522084e-001
 5    3.1430000e+002   3.1185093e+002      2.4490677e+000
 6    3.2220000e+002   3.2152758e+002      6.7241645e-001
 7    3.3260000e+002   3.3218187e+002      4.1812564e-001
 8    3.4420000e+002   3.4512020e+002     -9.2019917e-001
 9    3.5110000e+002   3.5247503e+002     -1.3750338e+000
10    3.6210000e+002   3.6524852e+002     -3.1485163e+000
11    3.7410000e+002   3.7177276e+002      2.3272402e+000
```

Example 7.32

This example was proposed by Miller (1980), Kelly (1984), and Draper and Smith (1998). The model is

$$y_{1i} = \beta_1 + \beta_2 \xi_{1i} + \varepsilon_{y_{1i}}$$
$$z_{1i} = \xi_{1i} + \varepsilon_{x_{1i}}$$
(7.77)

with one dependent variable and one independent variable. z_{1i} are the experimental values of the independent variable.

This is a special case as the relation between variables y and x is linear and hence they can interchange their role in the model parameter evaluation. Some specific techniques that are not valid in the general case can now be adopted here (see Draper and Smith, 1998).

The general procedure of minimizing function (6.3) against parameters **b** and values of x is adopted in this example.

Therefore, both the variables are supposed to be subject to experimental error with constant variance on the experimental domain. The variance associated with each experimental point is known (equal to 8.5 for y and 3.2 for x; both the estimates were calculated with 4 degrees of freedom) and the function (6.3) can be adopted to estimate model parameters.

Experimental data can be directly acquired with the following program.

7.10 Independent Variables Subject to Experimental Error

Start examining the model by neglecting the experimental error on independent variables.

The program is

```
#include "BzzMath.hpp"
void IndependentVariablesWithErrorsEx3(int model,
    int ex,BzzVector &b,BzzVector &x,BzzVector &y);
void main(void)
    {
    BzzPrint("\n\n\nWeighted variables");
    BzzPrint("\n\nnumModels 1 numX 1 numY 1");
    int numModels = 1;
    int numX = 1;
    int numY = 1;
    int numExperiments = 20;
    BzzMatrix X(numExperiments,numX,
            23.,33.2,16.6,26.3,20.,20.,20.6,18.9,17.8,
            20.,26.4,21.8,14.9,17.4,20.,13.2,28.4,25.9,
            18.9,13.8);
    BzzMatrix Y(numExperiments,numY,
            25.2,26.,16.3,27.2,23.2,18.1,22.2,17.2,18.8,
            16.4,24.8,26.8,15.4,14.9,18.1,16.3,31.3,31.2,
            18.,15.6);
    BzzNonLinearRegression nonLinReg(numModels,X,Y,
            IndependentVariablesWithErrorsEx3);
//  BzzVector s2(numY + numX,8.5,3.2);
    BzzVector s2(numY,8.5);
    nonLinReg.SetVariance(4,s2);
    BzzVector b(2,1.,1.);
    nonLinReg.InitializeModel(1,b);
    nonLinReg.LeastSquaresAnalysis();
    nonLinReg.RobustAnalysis();
    BzzPause();
    }
void IndependentVariablesWithErrorsEx3(int model,
        int ex,BzzVector &b,BzzVector &x,BzzVector &y)
    {
    y[1] = b[1] + b[2] * x[1];
    }
```

Model parameters are

```
    1    2.78635504295908e+000
    2    8.80539198016760e-001
```

Condition number and correlation indices are both satisfactory.

The robust method does not detect any outliers.
To execute a model analysis that accounts for the experimental error on independent variables, the statement

```
BzzVector s2(numY,8.5);
```

must be replaced with

```
BzzVector s2(numY + numX,8.5,3.2);
```

The object `nonLinReg` realizes that the amount of variance estimates corresponds to the sum of dependent and independent variables: it accounts even for the experimental error on the independent variables and minimizes the function (6.3); conversely, in the former case, it minimizes the function (6.5). As a result, model parameters are different:

```
1    1.39489938404048e+000
2    9.47259680548201e-001
```

Condition number and correlation indices are all satisfactory.
The model seems adequate to fit the experimental data set.
After using the function (6.3), independent variables are modified too, besides model parameters **b**.

```
                  Independent Variables 1
         Observed x        Estimated x         Residuals r
 1  2.3000000e+001      2.3554569e+001      -5.5456911e-001
 2  3.3200000e+001      3.1655218e+001       1.5447817e+000
 3  1.6600000e+001      1.6316895e+001       2.8310513e-001
 4  2.6300000e+001      2.6622149e+001      -3.2214915e-001
 5  2.0000000e+001      2.0719206e+001      -7.1920618e-001
 6  2.0000000e+001      1.9410560e+001       5.8943982e-001
 7  2.0600000e+001      2.0927043e+001      -3.2704276e-001
 8  1.8900000e+001      1.8328161e+001       5.7183921e-001
 9  1.7800000e+001      1.7887255e+001      -8.7255380e-002
10  2.0000000e+001      1.8974345e+001       1.0256553e+000
11  2.6400000e+001      2.6083721e+001       3.1627913e-001
12  2.1800000e+001      2.3036258e+001      -1.2362576e+000
13  1.4900000e+001      1.4770062e+001       1.2993842e-001
14  1.7400000e+001      1.6576903e+001       8.2309653e-001
15  2.0000000e+001      1.9410561e+001       5.8943917e-001
16  1.3200000e+001      1.3685104e+001      -4.8510433e-001
17  2.8400000e+001      2.9299716e+001      -8.9971580e-001
18  2.5900000e+001      2.7338916e+001      -1.4389158e+000
19  1.8900000e+001      1.8533439e+001       3.6656138e-001
20  1.3800000e+001      1.3969919e+001      -1.6991936e-001
```

7.11
Variables with Missing Experiments

Sometimes, when the model is constituted by more dependent variables, usually they all cannot be measured in every experimental point. The following device to evaluate model parameters can be adopted in these cases.

Dependent variables are considered single dependent variables. Experimental data are set out so to have all the data of the first variable, then the data of the second, and so on. In the function where the model is evaluated, the appropriate variable is selected through the index `ex` of experiments.

Example 7.33

Consider the following theoretical model with two dependent variables, one independent variable, and four parameters:

$$y_{1i} = \beta_1 + \beta_2(1-\exp(-\beta_3 x_{1i})) + \varepsilon_{1i}$$
$$y_{2i} = \beta_1 + \frac{\beta_2 x_{1i}}{1+\beta_4 x_{1i}} + \varepsilon_{2i} \qquad (7.78)$$

Only dependent variables are subject to experimental error with constant variances and their estimations based on 4 degrees of freedom are equal to $7.4 \cdot 10^{-4}$ and $8.1 \cdot 10^{-4}$, respectively.

The following experimental points are related to the first variable

$$x_{1i} = \{1., 2., 3., 4., 5., 6., 7., 8., 9., 10.\}$$

$$y_{1i} = \{1.58, 1.628, 1.74, 1.81, 1.846, 1.92, 1.94, 1.99, 2.02, 2.018\}$$

whereas the following ones to the second:

$$x_{1i} = \{1., 1.5, 2., 2.5, 3., 3.5, 4., 4.5, 5., 5.5, 6., 6.5, 7., 7.5, 8., 8.5, 9., 9., 9.5, 10.\}$$

$$y_{2i} = \{1.70, 1.74, 1.718, 1.755, 1.788, 1.837, 1.735, 1.781, 1.776, 1.85, 1.833,\\ 1.786, 1.809, 1.831, 1.873, 1.875, 1.815, 1.839, 1.839, 1.814\}$$

Experiments are sorted by placing experiments of the variable y_{1i} at the first 10 values and the experiments of the variable y_{2i} at a stretch.
The program is

```
#include "BzzMath.hpp"
void MissingExperiments(int model, int ex, BzzVector &b,
     BzzVector &x, BzzVector &y);
void main(void)
   {
   BzzPrint("\n\nMissing Experiments");
```

```
      int numModels = 1;
      int numX = 1;
      int numY = 1;
      int numExperiments = 30;
      BzzMatrix X(numExperiments,1,
            1.,2.,3.,4.,5.,6.,7.,8.,9.,10.,
            1.,1.5,2.,2.5,3.,3.5,4.,4.5,5.,5.5,6.,6.5,
            7.,7.5,8.,8.5,9.,9.,9.5,10.);
      BzzMatrix Y(numExperiments,numY,
            1.58,1.628,1.74,1.81,1.846,1.92,1.94,1.99,
            2.02,2.018,1.70,1.74,1.718,1.755,1.788,1.837,
            1.735,1.781,1.776,1.85,1.833,1.786,1.809,1.831,
            1.873,1.875,1.815,1.839,1.839,1.814);
      double w1 = 1./sqrt(7.4e-4);
      double w2 = 1./sqrt(8.1e-4);
      BzzMatrix W(numExperiments,numY,
            w1,w1,w1,w1,w1,w1,w1,w1,w1,w1,
            w2,w2,w2,w2,w2,w2,w2,w2,w2,w2,
            w2,w2,w2,w2,w2,w2,w2,w2,w2,w2);
      BzzNonLinearRegression nonLinReg(numModels,X,Y,W,
            MissingExperiments);
      BzzVector b(4,1.,1.,1.,1.);
      nonLinReg.InitializeModel(1,b);
      nonLinReg.LeastSquaresAnalysis();
      }
void MissingExperiments(int model,int ex,
      BzzVector &b,BzzVector &x,BzzVector &y)
  {
  if(ex <= 10)
        y[1] = b[1] + b[2] * (1. - exp(-b[3] * x[1]));
  else
        y[1] = b[1] + b[2] * x[1] / (1. + b[4] * x[1]);
  }
```

Model analysis is satisfactory.

7.12
Outliers

Even though the outlier detection must be performed in advance, we preferred to postpone it in order to have a coherent picture of all possible situations that may occur.

Example 7.34

Consider the following theoretical model with one dependent variable, one independent variable, two parameters, and $\beta_1 > 0$:

$$y_{1i} = \beta_1 \exp(\beta_2 x_{1i}) + \varepsilon_{1i} \tag{7.79}$$

Only the dependent variable is subject to experimental error with constant variance and it estimates based on 4 degrees of freedom is equal to $9.8 \cdot 10^{-4}$.

The experimental values can be directly acquired with the following program. Evaluate the model parameters and analyze them.

```
#include "BzzMath.hpp"
void Outlier1(int model,int ex,BzzVector &b,
       BzzVector &x,BzzVector &y);
void main(void)
    {
    int numModels = 1;
    int numX = 1;
    int numY = 1;
    int numExperiments = 23;
    BzzMatrix X(numExperiments,numX,
        0.,.5,1.,1.5,2.,2.5,3.,3.5,4.,4.5,5.,5.5,
        6.,6.5,7.,7.5,8.,8.5,9.,9.5,10.,10.5,11.);
    BzzMatrix Y(numExperiments,numY,
        25.318,21.538,18.275,15.586,13.152,11.249,9.526,
        8.172,6.929,5.843,5.028,4.228,3.554,4.634,31.801,
        5.668,1.925,1.549,1.335,1.183,.997,.875,.685);
    BzzVector s2(1,9.8e-4);
    BzzNonLinearRegression nonLinReg(numModels,X,Y,
         Outlier1);
    nonLinReg.SetVariance(4,s2);
    BzzVector b(2,1.,1.);
    nonLinReg.InitializeModel(1,b);
    nonLinReg.LeastSquaresAnalysis();
    nonLinReg.RobustAnalysis();
    }
```

Results obtained with the least sum of squares method point out that the model is unable to fit experimental points and it has be removed. In fact, we have

```
Mean Square Error                   = 3.8251617e+001
Coefficient of Determination (R2)   = 7.6044155e-001
Response Variance Assigned          = 9.8000000e-004

F-test for the model
Fexperimental = 3.903226e+004
```

```
The probability that F with dfNum 21 dfDen 4
is greater than 3.903226e+004 is 1.437717e-009 *WARNING*
```

This analysis does not provide any useful information to improve the model. On the other hand, the robust analysis identifies three highly probable outliers: experiments no. 13, 14, and 15.

Parameters evaluated with the least sum of squares method are

```
1    6.50430036223173e+000
2   -2.28821103865339e-001
```

whereas the robust method leads to

```
1    4.24120762941861e+000
2   -3.24752649712914e-001
```

In other words, they are significantly far: therefore, outliers are even *influential observation* in this case (see Chapter 4). Moreover, all the residuals obtained with the robust analysis are particularly good, except for the three experiments pointed out as outliers.

After examining in depth the theoretical model, an additional term was introduced in order to get a peak in correspondence with the three outliers detected with robust analysis. The new model involves five parameters

$$y_{1i} = \beta_1 \exp(\beta_2 x_{1i}) + \beta_3 \exp(\beta_4 [x_{1i} - \beta_5]^2) + \varepsilon_{1i} \tag{7.80}$$

and it was already examined and accepted in Example 7.3.

Example 7.35

Consider the same theoretical model as Example 7.22.

$$y_{1i} = \frac{\beta_1 x_{1i} x_{2i}}{1 + \beta_3 x_{1i} + \beta_4 x_{2i}} + \varepsilon_{1i}$$

$$y_{2i} = \frac{\beta_2 x_{1i} x_{2i}}{1 + \beta_3 x_{1i} + \beta_4 x_{2i}} + \varepsilon_{2i} \tag{7.81}$$

The following gross errors are introduced into the original data set.

- In the matrix of independent variables **X**, the experiment no. 6 is modified as follows for the variable no. 2:

```
//25.,15.,
  25.,20., // Leverage
```

- In the matrix of dependent variables **Y**, the experimental point no. 1 is modified as follows for the variable no. 1:

```
        //3.61,.43,
          6.61,.43, // Outlier
```

- In the matrix of dependent variables **Y**, the experimental point no. 12 is modified as follows for the variable no. 2:

```
        //6.,.70,
          6.,1.70, // Outlier
```

The program is

```
#include "BzzMath.hpp"
void Outlier2(int model,int ex,BzzVector &b,
          BzzVector &x,BzzVector &y);
void main(void)
    {
    BzzPrint("\n\nOutlier2");
    BzzPrint("\n\nnumModels 1 numX 2 numY 2");
    int numModels = 1;
    int numX = 2;
    int numY = 2;
    int numExperiments = 13;
    BzzMatrix X(numExperiments,numX,
          20.,20., 30.,20., 20.,30., 30.,30., 25.,25.,
//        25.,15.,
          25.,20., // Leverage
          25.,35., 15.,25., 35.,25., 55.,32.8, 55.,55.,
          10.6,55., 16.,55.);
    BzzMatrix Y(numExperiments,numY,
//        3.61,.43,
          6.61,.43, // outlier
          5.42,.44, 5.,.64, 7.5,.66, 5.73,.55, 3.8,.33,
          7.3,.79, 4.9,.35, 5.9,.71, 9.15,.926, 13.74,1.34,
//        6.,.70,
          6.,1.70, // Outlier
          8.2,.84);
    BzzNonLinearRegression nonLinReg(numModels,X,Y,
          Outlier2);
    BzzVector s2(2,0.348,0.0023);
    int df = 5;
    nonLinReg.SetVariance(df,s2);
    BzzVector b(4,1.,1.,1.,1.);
    nonLinReg.InitializeModel(1,b);
    nonLinReg.RobustAnalysis();
    nonLinReg.LeastSquaresAnalysis();
    BzzPause();
    }
```

```
void Outlier2(int model,int ex,BzzVector &b,
        BzzVector &x,BzzVector &y)
{
double w = x[1]*x[2]/(1. + b[3]*x[1] + b[4]*x[2]);
y[1] = b[1]*w;
y[2] = b[2]*w;
}
```

Main results obtained by the robust analysis are reported and discussed here.

```
Outliers sorted by importance:
 12 1 6 8

These are highly probable Outliers:
Experiment 12 Variable  2

These are possible Outliers:
Experiment  1 Variable  1
Experiment  6 Variable  2
Experiment  8 Variable  2
Experiment 12 Variable  2
```

In other words, the three outliers introduced into the data set are all detected. Moreover, the parameters evaluated with the least sum of squares method are

```
         1     4.41875417805371e-002
         2     5.05787701858003e-003
         3     1.83828923672852e-001
         4    -4.64073767878442e-003
```

whereas the robust method leads to

```
         1     4.13338418954122e-002
         2     4.16277770712114e-003
         3     1.10212629717764e-001
         4     2.94838952824563e-002
```

which are significantly far from the previous ones (especially for parameters β_3 and β_4) and, therefore, outliers are even *influential observations* (see Section 4.6).

7.13
Independent Variables Subject to Experimental Error and Model with Outliers

The following example accounts for the experimental error on both the dependent and the independent variables. In addition, outliers are present in the experimental data set.

Example 7.36

Suppose that independent variables of Example 7.35 are subject to experimental error with constant variance equal to .1 and .2, respectively. It is sufficient to replace the statement

```
BzzVector s2(2,0.348,0.0023);
```

with

```
BzzVector s2(4,0.348,0.0023,.1,.2);
```

Even in this case, the robust method identifies the outliers. The parameters evaluated by the robust method and the least sum of squares method are significantly far against the previous case as independent variables **x** are also used in the minimization.

For example, the parameters evaluated by the robust method without considering any error on the independent variable were

```
1    6.03923029266595e-002
2    6.09971128074399e-003
3    1.67176217258912e-001
4    5.11907433176444e-002
```

whereas, now, they became

```
1    1.31849797362828e-001
2    1.30305779030771e-002
3    4.21896098526185e-001
4    9.97843543005157e-002
```

8
Reasonable Design of Experiments

Examples of this chapter can be found in the directory `Vol2_Chapter8` within the enclosed CD-ROM.

8.1
Introduction

This chapter deals with cases where experimental points can be selected by the experimenter.

If the experimenter cannot accordingly modify values of independent variables to get the corresponding values of dependent variables, it is not possible to appropriately select the experiments.

This problem is traditionally divided into three categories:

1) Some methods select experimental points in order to completely cover the experimental field at the best.
2) Some other methods select new experimental points in order to improve the parameter estimation of a specific model.
3) Again, other methods select new experimental points in order to discriminate among alternative models.

Methods belonging to the second category are called *Optimal Design of Experiments for Parameter Estimation* (ODE/PE).

Methods belonging to the third category are called *Optimal Design of Experiments for Model Discrimination* (ODE/MD).

This chapter is titled *Reasonable Design of Experiments* rather than the classical *Optimal Design of Experiments* for an important reason.

Usually, a design of experiments that is optimal for a specific problem might not be reasonable when considering other problems.

This aspect shall be discussed later.

Interpolation and Regression Models for the Chemical Engineer: Solving Numerical Problems
Guido Buzzi-Ferraris and Flavio Manenti
Copyright © 2010 WILEY-VCH Verlag GmbH & Co. KGaA, Weinheim
ISBN: 978-3-527-32652-5

If it is possible to plan the experiments for model analysis, the overall problem may be divided into the following steps:

1) Model collection (see Section 6.10).
2) Preliminary experiments (see Section 8.2).
3) Model analysis (see Chapters 3–7).
4) Model selection (see Sections 6.10 and 8.5).
    (a) Perform new selected experiments (see Section 8.7) and return to step no. 3.
    (b) Models' reformulation (see Chapters 3–7) and return to step no. 3.
    (c) Add new models and return to step no. 3.
    (d) Stop the search (see Section 8.7).

This chapter specifically deals with step no. 2, 4a, and 4d.

8.2
Preliminary Experiments

The problem of planning the experiments is quite old and well studied since many years (Davies, 1957).

Traditionally, who works on this problem uses a particular nomenclature; it is useful to adapt it to regression problems analyzed here.

First of all, experimental variables are called *factors*. They are generally normalized in order to get values in the range $[-1, 1]$. The effects of such factors and some of their interactions can often be manually calculated, where the effects of factors and their interactions are the parameters of linear models with intercept.

For example, consider the problem involving two factors (variables) x_1 and x_2 and the following design of experiments (two-level factorial):

```
x1 x2
+1 +1
+1 -1
-1 +1
-1 -1
```

By adopting this experimental data set, it is possible to estimate parameters of the linear model:

$$y_i = \beta_0 + \beta_1 x_{1i} + \beta_2 x_{2i} + \beta_3 x_{1i} x_{2i} \tag{8.1}$$

It appears clear that, in this case, the model would exactly interpolate experimental data. The model parameters can be manually evaluated in a simple way, as all the columns of the matrix **F** (see Chapter 3) are orthogonal to each other.

Originally, the possibility of easily evaluating the effects of factors and their interactions (in other words, the parameters of a linear model) was one of the goals of these techniques of experimental design.

Another interesting feature dealt with the possibility to know in a simple way which parameters of the linear model were independent and which were not. By doing so, multicollinearity problems were automatically taken care of.

For example, given the following set of experimental data for a problem with four factors (two-levels fractional factorial)

```
x1 x2 x3 x4
+1 +1 +1 +1
+1 +1 -1 -1
+1 -1 +1 -1
+1 -1 -1 +1
-1 +1 +1 -1
-1 +1 -1 +1
-1 -1 +1 +1
-1 -1 -1 -1
```

the effect (parameter of the linear model) for the factor x_4 is confused with the one of the x_1, x_2, x_3 interactions.

It is easy to see even which other parameters are reciprocally correlated in a linear model that involves all factors and their interactions. If two parameters are reciprocally correlated, they cannot be estimated separately.

Many features of these techniques are nowadays obsolete thanks to computer programs that avoid any manual calculation and automatically identify multicollinearity problems.

In any case, the experimental design based on these techniques is still valid in accomplishing the following essential point.

Such experimental designs allow to cover the whole experimental domain with a limited number of experiments, independent of the problem one is going to solve.

In the **BzzMath** library, the function GetGoodExperiment belonging to the BzzMatrix class, allows to find a good design of experiments, according to what is said above: experiments must uniformly cover the experimental domain. This function can be sequentially adopted by starting either from an empty matrix or from a matrix that already contains a series of experimental points. Two objects of the BzzVector class are required as argument: the first, xMin, contains the lower value of the experimental domain for each variable; the second, xMax, the upper values.

Example 8.1

Find a series of experimental points in order to cover the experimental domain $[0 \leq x_1 \leq 3; 0 \leq x_2 \leq 30]$ at the best. Consider that four experiments were already carried out in correspondence with $(0., 0.), (.1, 1.), (.5, 5.), (1., 10.)$.
The program is

```
#include "BzzMath.hpp"
void main(void)
    {
    BzzMatrix X(4,2,
            0.,0.,
            .1,1.,
```

```
                    .5.,5.,
                    1.,10.);
    BzzVector x;
    BzzVector xMin(2,0.,0.);
    BzzVector xMax(2,3.,30.);
    int i;
    for(i = 1;i <= 10;i++)
        {
        X.GetGoodExperiment(xMin,xMax,&x);
        X.AppendRow(x);
        }
    X.BzzPrint(X);
    BzzPause();
}
```

The experiments are

```
0.000 0.000
0.100 1.000
0.500 5.000
1.000 10.000
3.000 30.000
0.000 30.000
3.000 0.000
1.500 26.250
2.625 15.000
0.000 16.875
1.688 0.000
1.688 16.875
0.750 22.500
2.250 7.500
```

8.3
Using Models to Suggest New Experiments

In the literature, several strategies are proposed to improve parameter assessment and model discrimination (Box, 1949, 1971; Box and Lucas, 1959; Box and Draper, 1965; Hunter and Reiner, 1965; Draper and Hunter, 1966, 1967a, 1967b; Box and Hill, 1967; Froment and Mezaki, 1970; Fedorov, 1972; Hosten, 1974; Atkinson and Fedorov, 1975a, 1975b; Froment, 1975; Hosten and Froment, 1976; Atkinson, 1978; Hill, 1978; Buzzi-Ferraris and Forzatti, 1983; Buzzi-Ferraris *et al.*, 1984; Forzatti *et al.*, 1987; Ponce de Leon and Atkinson, 1991; Buzzi-Ferraris, 1999; Donckels, 2009).

In order to analyze some criteria adopted to propose new experimental points by exploiting features of the selected models, it is suitable to give some definitions. Some criteria require a linearization of the model in the neighborhood of the minimum point. For the sake of simplicity, it is supposed to have only one dependent variable $y = g(\mathbf{x}, \mathbf{b})$. Let $\mathbf{F}_n$ and $\mathbf{F}_{n+1}$ be matrices of the linearized model:

$$\mathbf{F}_n = \begin{bmatrix} f_1(\mathbf{x}_1) & f_2(\mathbf{x}_1) & \dots & f_p(\mathbf{x}_1) \\ f_1(\mathbf{x}_2) & f_2(\mathbf{x}_2) & \dots & f_p(\mathbf{x}_2) \\ \dots & \dots & \dots & \dots \\ f_1(\mathbf{x}_n) & f_2(\mathbf{x}_n) & \dots & f_p(\mathbf{x}_n) \end{bmatrix} \tag{8.2}$$

$$\mathbf{F}_{n+1} = \begin{bmatrix} f_1(\mathbf{x}_1) & f_2(\mathbf{x}_1) & \dots & f_p(\mathbf{x}_1) \\ f_1(\mathbf{x}_2) & f_2(\mathbf{x}_2) & \dots & f_p(\mathbf{x}_2) \\ \dots & \dots & \dots & \dots \\ f_1(\mathbf{x}_n) & f_2(\mathbf{x}_n) & \dots & f_p(\mathbf{x}_n) \\ f_1(\mathbf{x}_{n+1}) & f_2(\mathbf{x}_{n+1}) & \dots & f_p(\mathbf{x}_{n+1}) \end{bmatrix} \tag{8.3}$$

where $f_k(\mathbf{x}_i)$ coefficients are derivatives of g function with respect to parameters b_k calculated in $\mathbf{x}_i$ and for the optimal $\mathbf{b}$. If there are more then one dependent variable, for each of them there are matrices like $\mathbf{F}_n$ and $\mathbf{F}_{n+1}$.

$\mathbf{UDV}^T$ factorization (also known as singular value decomposition, SVD) returns the coefficients of $\mathbf{D}$ matrix (eigenvalues of $\mathbf{F}^T\mathbf{F}$) and $\mathbf{P}_n$ principal axes of $\mathbf{F}_n$ matrix. From the product between these two $\mathbf{F}_n\mathbf{P}_n^T$ matrices, the projection of $\mathbf{F}_n$ matrix into the space of principal axes can be obtained. The distance between one row of $\mathbf{F}_n\mathbf{P}_n^T$ matrix and $\mathbf{P}_n\mathbf{f}_{n+1}$ vector represents the distance between two points in this space.

Let $\mathbf{X}_n$ be the following:

$$\mathbf{X}_n = \begin{bmatrix} \mathbf{x}_1 \\ \mathbf{x}_2 \\ \dots \\ \mathbf{x}_n \end{bmatrix} \tag{8.4}$$

The distance between one row of this matrix and $\mathbf{x}_{n+1}$ vector is the distance between the two points estimated in the **x**-space. Also, this matrix can be factorized with *SVD* algorithm to get $\mathbf{P}_x$ principal axes.

As in the previous case, it is possible to project $\mathbf{X}_n$ matrix into the space of its principal axes by $\mathbf{X}_n\mathbf{P}_x^T$ product. By doing so, the distance between one row of this matrix and $\mathbf{P}_x\mathbf{x}_{n+1}$ vector is the distance between the two points that are estimated in this space.

8.4
New Experiments to Improve the Parameter Estimation

Based on the above definitions, it is now possible to introduce some of the most common criteria used in designing experiments with the aim of improving the model parameter estimation.

Criterion no. 1: the new point has to maximize $\prod_{i=1}^{P} d_i$ product, that is, the determinant of $\mathbf{F}_{n+1}^T\mathbf{F}_{n+1}$ matrix. It is even called *D-Optimality criterion*.

A factorization of $\mathbf{F}_{n+1}$ matrix is required for each new point $\mathbf{x}_{n+1}$. This criterion tries to minimize the confidence volume of the parameters (Box and Lucas, 1959; Box, 1971).

The volume of Ω hyper-ellipsoid is

$$\text{Vol}(\Omega) \approx \frac{1}{\sqrt{\det(\mathbf{F}_{n+1}^T \mathbf{F}_{n+1})}} \tag{8.5}$$

by neglecting a multiplicative factor.

 Criterion no. 2: the new point has to maximize the minimum d_i.

This method requires factorizing $\mathbf{F}_{n+1}$ matrix for each new point $\mathbf{x}_{n+1}$ and it tries to minimize the maximum diameter of the confidence volume of parameters (Hosten, 1974).

 Criterion no. 3: the new point has to maximize function $\phi_3 = \mathbf{f}(\mathbf{x}_{n+1})^T \times (\mathbf{F}_n^T \mathbf{F}_n)^{-1} \mathbf{f}(\mathbf{x}_{n+1})$.

This criterion adopts a simplified approach against criterion no. 4. Only one factorization of $\mathbf{F}_n$ matrix is required, but the solution of $\mathbf{F}_n^T \mathbf{w} = \mathbf{f}_{n+1}$ system is required for each new point.

 Criterion no. 4: it minimizes the maximum of function $\phi_4 = \mathbf{f}^T(\mathbf{x}_i)^T \times (\mathbf{F}_{n+1}^T \mathbf{F}_{n+1})^{-1} \mathbf{f}(\mathbf{x}_i)$ against $\mathbf{x}_i$, for each new point $\mathbf{x}_{n+1}$.

The original formulation was proposed for polynomial models with one dependent variable by Smith (1918). The method requires the factorization of $\mathbf{F}_{n+1}$ matrix, the solution of $\mathbf{F}_{n+1}^T \mathbf{w} = \mathbf{f}_i$ system, and the maximization of function $\mathbf{f}^T(\mathbf{x}_i)(\mathbf{F}_{n+1}^T \mathbf{F}_{n+1})^{-1} \mathbf{f}(\mathbf{x}_i)$ for each new point. The aim is to minimize maximum variance for the model prevision.

 Criterion no. 5: the new point has to maximize the sum $\sum_{i=1}^{P} d_i$.

Contrary to criterion 1, which tried to minimize the confidence volume of the parameters through the volume of Ω hyper-ellipsoid, this criterion operates on the perimeter of Ω.

It requires either the $\mathbf{F}_{n+1}^T \mathbf{F}_{n+1}$ product or the factorization of $\mathbf{F}_{n+1}$ matrix for each new point $\mathbf{x}_{n+1}$.

 Criterion no. 6: the new point has to maximize the inverse of condition number $\varkappa = \frac{d_{\min}}{d_{\max}}$ of the matrix $\mathbf{F}_{n+1}$.

The objective of this criterion is to minimize the condition number. For each new point $\mathbf{x}_{n+1}$, it requires the factorization of $\mathbf{F}_{n+1}$ matrix.

 Criterion no. 7: the new point has to maximize the quotient $\frac{\sum_{i=1}^{P} d_i}{\prod_{i=1}^{P} d_i}$.

The purpose of this criterion is to maximize the sphericity of the confidence volume of parameters. It factorizes the matrix $\mathbf{F}_{n+1}$ for each new point $\mathbf{x}_{n+1}$.

These methods should be used by specifically considering their objective. Actually, all the aforementioned criteria are addressed to improve the parameter estimation of a specific model and some consequences have to be accounted for.

Let us consider a trivial example: the linear model $y = a + bx$. Experiments to improve the parameter estimation all concentrate on the boundaries of the interval $x_{min} \leq x \leq x_{max}$. By introducing all experiments on the boundary of the experimental domain, it is not possible to check the validity of the model. Some experiments inside the interval range are necessary for checking its validity.

Even for single model, the selected experiments are inadequate to verify whether such a model is valid or not.

In the case of linear models, Fedorov (1972) showed that criterion 1 tend to repropose the same experiments. Really, such a behavior belongs to all criteria 1–7. Even though this cannot be demonstrated, it appears reasonable to introduce the additional experimental points on the frontier of the experimental domain to improve parameter estimation.

These criteria usually select only one or few distinct points. So, the new selected points continuously overlap the other experiments, leading to a very poor experimental design.

After executing a certain number of experiments to estimate parameters of a specific model, suppose that one wants to check whether it is preferable to use a different model.

In future, should a new model be introduced, experiments that are conceived to improve parameter estimation of a previous model may become inadequate for the new model.

When more models must be simultaneously analyzed, another problem arises.

If there is an arena of rival models, each model may require different experiments. A new criterion to select from among these different experiments has to be developed.

Criteria 1–7 may be characterized by another shortcoming occurring when the matrix **F** is significantly ill conditioned, that is, when there is a strong correlation among parameters, or, in other words, just in those cases we should use these criteria; they give a random prevision as they are strictly related to the ill-conditioning of the matrix **F**.

This is the classical vicious loop; it is not possible to use the matrix **F** to generate a new experiment if the same matrix is strongly ill conditioned.

This problem is similar to the problem of outlier detection, where some gross errors cannot be detected by using the *least sum of squares* method.

To highlight these problems, let us consider a very simple linear model, and the initial data reported in Table 8.1 and in Figure 8.1:

$$y_i = \beta_1 x_{1i} + \beta_2 x_{2i} + \varepsilon_i$$
$$0 \leq x_{1i} \leq 3 \tag{8.6}$$
$$0 \leq x_{2i} \leq 30$$

Table 8.1 Starting data.

#	x_1	x_2
1	0.	0.
2	0.1	1.
3	0.5	5.
4	1.	10.

Moreover, Figure 8.1 reports the first 15 additional experiments selected by criterion 3. Conversely, Figure 8.2 shows the first 15 points selected by the same criterion 3 and the same existing data, after a small (10^{-10}) perturbation in the initial experiments.

Experiments provided only by criterion 3 are reported here; in any case, the same problem is verified by adopting any criterion 1–7; specifically, the additional experimental points ever overlap the existing ones in every condition, and random previsions are provided when the matrix **F** is strongly ill conditioned.

Beyond previous criteria 1–7 (Buzzi-Ferraris and Manenti, 2009), four new criteria were recently implemented in the BzzNonLinearRegression class. These new criteria can be considered complementary to the previous ones, with the aim of avoiding the overlapping of experiments, by an optimal use of the experimental domain.

The BzzNonLinearRegression class was implemented to allow the user to select any of his preferred criteria 1–7 at each iteration; however, criteria 8–11 are ever taken into account.

Specifically, it is possible to overcome shortcomings of criteria 1–7 by appropriately combining criteria 10 and 11 (Section 8.7).

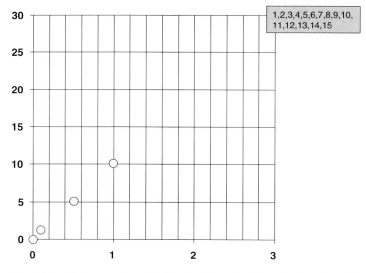

Figure 8.1 Existing experimental data (circles) and additional points selected by criterion no. 3 (squares).

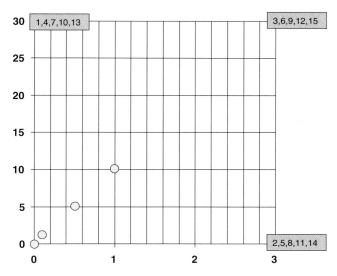

Figure 8.2 New experimental points with criterion no. 3 by perturbing (10^{-10}) the initial data.

Criterion no. 8: the new point has to maximize the minimum distance of x_{n+1} from all existing points.

This method calculates the Euclidean norm of the differences among the new point and the existing ones (Figure 8.3): although first points are badly selected, the experimental domain is appropriately filled up. One of the most important virtues of criteria 8 and 10 is that they do not depend on the specific model used, so the chosen points can be used for whatever model is proposed.

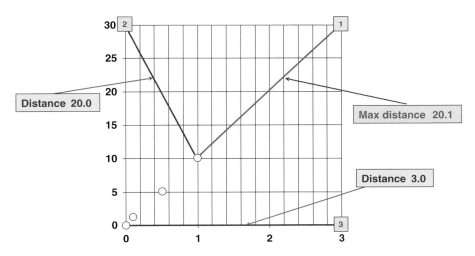

Figure 8.3 Distances of first three points in x-space.

Criterion no. 9: the new point has to maximize the minimum distance of $\mathbf{f}_{n+1}$ from the rows of the matrix $\mathbf{F}_n$.

This criterion is similar to the previous one, but it involves the matrix $\mathbf{F}_n$. Indeed, it calculates the Euclidean norm of the differences between each new vector $\mathbf{f}_{n+1}$ and each row of the matrix $\mathbf{F}_n$. Considering again the previous trivial example of Table 8.1, both the criterion 8 and the criterion 9 propose the same additional points (Figure 8.3). Both these criteria have the advantage of homogeneously filling the experimental domain. Nevertheless, they do not take into account the problem of multicollinearity: actually, looking at Figure 8.3, the first point selected is collinear with the existing data, even though it is the furthest in the experimental space, by making it useless.

Despite this disadvantage, if many experiments are selected, the experimental domain is better filled up against the aforementioned cases, but it is not at best.

 Criterion no. 10: the new point has to maximize the minimum distance of $\mathbf{P}_x\mathbf{x}_{n+1}$ from the rows of the matrix $\mathbf{X}_n\mathbf{P}_x^T$.

This is an improvement over criterion 8 (Figure 8.4): instead of calculating the distances among points in the **x**-space, it calculates the distances in the space of principal axes. In this specific space, the scale of each axis is related to the same axis importance. As a result, the distance of those points that are normal to the principal axis is greatly expanded. To get this, the program calculates Euclidean norm of the differences between each vector $\mathbf{P}_x\mathbf{x}_{n+1}$.

It requires the factorization of the matrix $\mathbf{X}_n$ in order to get $\mathbf{P}_x$.

As shown above in Figure 8.3, the distances of points $[0, 30]$, $[3, 0]$, and $[3, 30]$ in the x-space are 20.0, 3.0, and 20.1, respectively; conversely, the distances become $7.5 \cdot 10^{15}, 7.5 \cdot 10^{15}, 1.9$, respectively, in the space of the principal axes (see Figure 8.4). The points $[0, 30]$ and $[3, 0]$ are very meaningful in the space of principal axes, as they are located along a normal direction against the principal axis and allow to avoid the multicollinearity condition. The point $[3, 30]$ is the furthest one in the x-space, but it

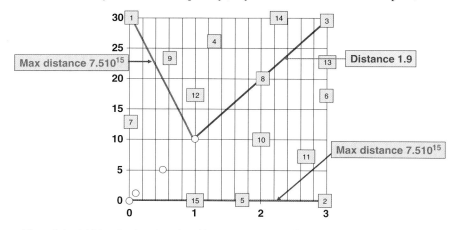

Figure 8.4 Additional points introduced by criteria no. 10 and 11.

appears very close in the principal axes space as it is located in the direction of the principal axis.

The usage of this criterion is encouraged by the fact that it covers very well the experimental domain, independent of the model selected. When a new point is proposed (even for another criterion), it is good habit to use this criterion for checking whether the new additional point is a repetition (overlapped point) or a correlated experiment.

Criterion no. 11: the new point has to maximize the minimum distance of $\mathbf{P}_n\mathbf{f}_{n+1}$ from the rows of the matrix $\mathbf{F}_n\mathbf{P}_n^T$.

The approach of criterion 10 is now applied to $\mathbf{f}_{n+1}$ instead of $\mathbf{x}_{n+1}$ (see Figure 8.4). It calculates the Euclidean norm of the differences between each new vector $\mathbf{P}_n\mathbf{f}_{n+1}$ and each row of the matrix $\mathbf{F}_n\mathbf{P}_n^T$: it requires the factorization of the matrix $\mathbf{F}_n$ in order to get $\mathbf{P}_n$. Considering the example of Table 8.1, criteria 10 and 11 are coincident (see Figure 8.4). The first point selected is set along a direction that is normal to the principal axis and it is the furthest from the principal axis, so as to avoid the problem of multicollinearity, which still affects criteria 8 and 9.

8.5
Model Selection: The Bayesian Approach

Some authors discriminate among models by calculating the probability of each model and considering as the right (or true) one the model with a probability larger than a specific threshold (Box, 1949; Box and Draper, 1965; Hunter and Reiner, 1965; Box and Hill, 1967; Draper and Hunter, 1967a, 1967b; Atkinson, 1978; Hill, 1978; Ponce de Leon and Atkinson, 1991; Schwaab *et al.*, 2006).

Section 2.10 showed how it is possible to modify the probability of an event when further information concerning such an event is known (Bayes theorem).

Section 6.10 showed that the traditional approach based on the comparison of mean square errors of various models and on considerations of the model simplicity are sometimes unable to clearly discriminate among a series of models. Bayesian approach seems to be, therefore, interesting in solving this hard problem.

The idea is particularly simple.

Once a set of models has been collected and a probability to be the right model has been assigned to each of them, such a probability is modified according to the Bayes theorem while new experimental points (or new information on the adequateness of various models) are progressively inserted.

It is necessary to answer the following three questions:

1) Is it possible to adopt such a methodology?
2) Is it correct to use it?
3) Is it a useful approach?

The first question is to be positively answered as there are many applications of such a procedure in the literature.

It is harder and philosophically controversial to answer the second question. Section 2.10 underlined the risk of improperly using the probability $P(A)$ of the event A due to a wrong selection of the population one is referring to.

In this specific case, which is the population to be inserted in the model collection and which are their initial probabilities? As highlighted by Popper (1972), the probability to be assigned to any theory, which must be deemed by a finite number of experiments, is null as there are infinite theories that can properly describe such a set of experiments. The same holds for models.

It is erroneous to consider only few models that were initially selected to evaluate their own initial probability. As there are infinite models that potentially describe well a finite number of experiments, each of them has a null probability to be the right (or true) one.

The second objection is more philosophical and it deals with the possibility to confirm a theory or, in our case, a model by means of an accumulation of confirmations.

A similar approach originates from the neopositivism of the first decades of the twentieth century. Indeed, this philosophy pointed to the induction method as a scientific way to move from experimental data to theoretical hypotheses that are true if and only if they are verified by new experimental observations. According to Carnap (1952), the induction method is to be seen as a calculus of the probability of scientific propositions.

The failure of logic positivism in developing an inductive logic led to the modern epistemology of refusing this approach: a theory is not confirmed by means of the accumulation of positive tests and it is not possible to give a theory, or a model, a probability that they are true.

About the third question, if such an approach is useful or not, it is possible to answer by tricking it: using this approach could be very dangerous. In fact, one might encounter the following possible drawbacks.

If all models proposed are poor, this approach forces the selection of the least poor model. This can deceptively lead one to think to have found a good model even though it is not.

Although only a few models can be manually formulated, it is possible to automatically generate a large number of models, which are all well supported by theory (see Section 6.10 and Buzzi-Ferraris *et al.* 1974a, 1974b).

In such a situation, it is rarely possible to discriminate among rival models that are equivalent (given a finite number of experimental points). This approach arbitrarily selects one of them, instead of proposing the whole set of equivalent (good) models.

Even for a case where the experimental data are artificially generated by using a model and this model is not included in the arena of rival models, this criterion selects one of the models by creating the illusion of having found out the true model.

To summarize: even though this approach rapidly leads to the selection of a model, this selection is arbitrary and it cannot be considered as the final selection.

8.6
New Experiments for Model Discrimination

The most modern criteria to select new experimental points in order to discriminate among rival models are based on the following properties (Buzzi-Ferraris and Manenti, 2009):

1) All selected models must be involved in the choice of new experiments.
2) New experiments have to be selected by favoring the best performing models according to the existing experiments.
3) Model predictions have to be as widely different as possible.
4) The uncertainty related to each model prediction is to be accounted for favoring those experiments where the uncertainty is smaller.
5) The criterion should return a warning when the new experiment already exists.
6) The criterion should return a warning if there are no points for an effective discrimination.

Many of these features are present in the criteria proposed by Buzzi-Ferraris and Forzatti (1983), which are based on the maximization of the following function:

$$T(\mathbf{x}) = \frac{\sum_{i=1}^{M} \sum_{j=i+1}^{M} [g_i(\mathbf{x}) - g_j(\mathbf{x})]^2}{(M-1)\left(Ms^2 + \sum_{i=1}^{M} s_i^2(\mathbf{x})\right)} \tag{8.7}$$

For the sake of simplicity, let us suppose that there are two models only with a single variable y. The original function T is

$$T_{1,2}(\mathbf{x}) = \frac{[g_1(\mathbf{x}) - g_2(\mathbf{x})]^2}{2s^2 + s_1^2(\mathbf{x}) + s_2^2(\mathbf{x})} \tag{8.8}$$

where g_1 and g_2 are the values calculated by the two models and if the estimate of the variance s^2 is known, the variance is calculated by the classical formula:

$$\begin{aligned} s_1^2 &= \left\{ \mathbf{f}_n^T (\mathbf{F}_n^T \mathbf{F}_n)^{-1} \mathbf{f}_n \right\}_1 s^2 \\ s_2^2 &= \left\{ \mathbf{f}_n^T (\mathbf{F}_n^T \mathbf{F}_n)^{-1} \mathbf{f}_n \right\}_2 s^2 \end{aligned} \tag{8.9}$$

The extension to the cases involving more than two models and/or more dependent variables is practically immediate (Buzzi-Ferraris and Forzatti, 1983; Buzzi-Ferraris et al., 1984; Forzatti et al., 1987).

8.7
Criterion Used in BzzNonLinearRegression Class to Generate New Experiments

The `LeastSquaresAnalysisAndExperimentsSearch` function of the `BzzNonLinearRegression` class evaluates the parameters of all rival models by minimizing the function that was selected by the user as per the function `LeastSquaresAnalysis`. An accurate analysis is carried out for each model. Then, new experiments are proposed in order to discriminate among rival models and, furthermore, to improve the parameter estimation of each model.

There are three versions of this function:

- The first requires as argument: two objects of the `BzzVector` class containing maximum and minimum values of the interval search for independent variables. In this case, the program automatically selects a grid to search for the most appropriate points.
- The second requires a matrix as argument. The matrix is provided by the user and contains the predetermined experimental points.
- The third is equal to the previous one, but weights to be assigned to each experimental point must be provided too. Specifically, this function must be adopted when the experimental error variance is nonconstant on the whole experimental domain and, therefore, when the function (6.4) was used to estimate model parameters.

The user has the possibility to select one of the criteria 1–7 by the function `SelectCriterion`, where the preferred selection must be inserted as int in argument. At the end of the analysis of each model, the optimal experiment shall be provided according to the selected criterion.

Independent of this choice, even optimal experiments obtained by criteria 8–11 are provided.

When there are more rival models, the function `LeastSquaresAnalysisAndExperimentsSearch` also selects the experiments to discriminate the best model among them.

Criteria are based on the Buzzi-Ferraris's method (8.7) improved by some important modifications. In the original criterion (8.7), only the models that fulfill the F-test were taken into account.

As the importance of statistical tests should be reduced, the `BzzNonLinearRegression` class searches for the best experiment among *all* couples (i,j).

Moreover, in the original criterion, variances $s_i^2(\mathbf{x})$ of the previsions y for the ith model were calculated as

$$s_i^2(\mathbf{x}) = \mathbf{f}_i^T(\mathbf{x})(\mathbf{F}_i^T\mathbf{F}_i)^{-1}\mathbf{f}_i(\mathbf{x})s^2 \tag{8.10}$$

by using an estimation of the variance s^2 of y.

In the `BzzNonLinearRegression` class, s^2 is replaced by the mean square error of the model. Poor models have large mean square errors and, consequently, their weight in the calculus of T_{ij} or T is smaller.

At the end of the analysis of each model and after printing a comparison among the models (see Section 6.9), the new experimental points that maximize the function T_{ij} for each couple of models (i,j) are proposed.

8.7 Criterion Used in BzzNonLinearRegression Class to Generate New Experiments

Beyond the evaluation of the best experimental point for each couple of models, the point that maximizes the function is also evaluated

$$T(\mathbf{x}) = \frac{2}{M(M-1)} \sum_{i=1}^{M-1} \sum_{j=1+1}^{M} T_{i,j}(\mathbf{x}) \tag{8.11}$$

where M is the number of models. The aim of the function (8.8) in the case of two models and of the function (8.11) in the case of more models is to find out new experiments where the previsions of the dependent variable g are significantly far and, at the same time, the variance of the previsions is small.

Thus, after printing out the best experimental points for each couple of models, the experiment that maximizes the mean value of T is also printed. If such a value is smaller than an assigned threshold, a warning appears to point out that, currently, no experiments for effectively discriminating among rival models exist.

At last, the experiment that maximizes the following merit function is printed out:

$$Q(\mathbf{x}) = \frac{\phi_{10}(x)}{\phi_{10,opt}} + \frac{\phi_{11}(\mathbf{x})}{\phi_{11,opt}} + \frac{T(\mathbf{x})}{T_{opt}} \tag{8.12}$$

$\phi_{10}(\mathbf{x})$ is the value of criterion no. 10; $\phi_{10,opt}$ is the best value of criterion 10; $\phi_{11}(\mathbf{x}) = \sum_{m=1}^{M} \phi_{11,m}(\mathbf{x}) \frac{MSE_{opt}}{MSE_m}$; $\phi_{11,m}(\mathbf{x})$ is the value of criterion 11 for the model m in correspondence with the point $\mathbf{x}$; $\phi_{11,opt}$ is the best value of the function $\phi_{11}(\mathbf{x})$; and T_{opt} is the best value of the function $T(\mathbf{x})$, which is defined in relation (8.11).

The function (8.12) consists of three terms:

- The first does not depend on the models and ensures that the new point is sufficiently far from the existing experiments by using criterion 10.
- The second tries to improve the parameter estimation for the best models.
- The third tries to discriminate the best models. This term is considered only when T_{opt} is greater than a threshold value (equal to 1.5).

At a certain point of the search, if the term for discriminating among rival models is neglected, it does not necessarily mean that such a term shall be ever neglected in the following.

Sometimes, new experimental points selected in an unexplored region may highlight different behaviors of the models that were never identified before.

The user has the possibility to assign a specific threshold to criterion no. 10

```
nonLinReg.SetBalance1011AndDiscrimination(.6);
```

means that $\phi_{10}/\phi_{10,opt} > 60\%$. As a result, the minimum of function (8.12) is evaluated by only using the points that fulfill such a threshold value (the default value is 0.5).

Experiments are sequentially selected and the user must decide when the selection could be stopped according to the achieved results.

The decision on the selection of the subsequent step should be based on an exhaustive analysis of all models and, if possible, on the comparison with a robust method so as to detect possible outliers.

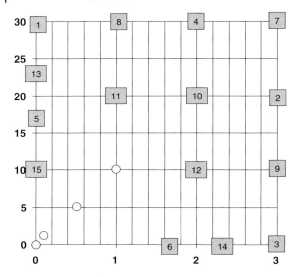

Figure 8.5 New additional points by adopting the mixed criterion (the default criterion in the **BzzMath** library).

The problem discussed in Section 8.4 can be adopted as an application of the criterion (8.12) on a single model, where the function (8.12) consists only of the first two terms.

Figure 8.5 shows new additional points proposed by the strategy employed in the `BzzNonLinearRegression` class: the experimental domain is adequately filled up. Moreover, first points are set far from the given data (additional points no. 1 and no. 3 both are far $7.5 \cdot 10^{15}$ from the existing data in the space of principal axes) and they are set along a direction normal to the principal axis, in order to avoid any collinearity.

Example 8.2

Hunter *et al.* (1968) and Himmelblau (1970) proposed the following example to test the model discrimination and, at the same time, to select new experiments for improving the parameter estimation.
Rival models are

$$y_{1i} = \exp\left(-x_{1i} \exp\left(\beta_1 - \beta_2 \left(\frac{1}{x_{2i}} - \frac{1}{525}\right)\right)\right) + \varepsilon_{1i} \tag{8.13}$$

$$y_{1i} = \frac{1}{1 + x_{1i} \exp\left(\beta_1 - \beta_2 \left(\frac{1}{x_{2i}} - \frac{1}{525}\right)\right)} + \varepsilon_{1i} \tag{8.14}$$

$$y_{1i} = \frac{1}{\left(1 + 2x_{1i} \exp\left(\beta_1 - \beta_2 \left(\frac{1}{x_{2i}} - \frac{1}{525}\right)\right)\right)^{1/2}} + \varepsilon_{1i} \tag{8.15}$$

8.7 Criterion Used in BzzNonLinearRegression Class to Generate New Experiments

$$y_{1i} = \frac{1}{\left(1+3x_{1i}\exp\left(\beta_1-\beta_2\left(\frac{1}{x_{2i}}-\frac{1}{525}\right)\right)\right)^{1/3}} + \varepsilon_{1i} \quad (8.16)$$

Note that all models (8.13)–(8.16) should be reparameterized according to the rules of Chapter 7 in order to reduce correlations among parameters at the exponent; nevertheless, their original formulation is preserved in this example.

The experimental points are artificially generated by model no. 2 (8.14) with parameters equal to -3.53235 and 5000.

If many experiments are generated without any experimental error and by appropriately covering the whole experimental domain

$$\begin{aligned} 10. &\leq x_{1i} \leq 150. \\ 450. &\leq x_{2i} \leq 600. \end{aligned} \quad (8.17)$$

the following results are obtained for the four models:

```
        MSE
1  4.512104e-003
2  1.955616e-031
3  2.088799e-003
4  5.812969e-003
```

Moreover, a robust analysis shows that no outliers are present for rival models (8.13), (8.15), and (8.16). Therefore, by adopting an experimental error variance larger than $2 \cdot 10^{-3}$ in generating the additional experiments, there is no possibility of discarding the model no. 3 (8.15) even using a large amount of experiments. An analogous reasoning may be done for the other two models. Therefore, the variance adopted in generating the new experiments is equal to $4.8 \cdot 10^{-4}$.

First four preliminary experiments are

$$\begin{aligned} x_{11} &= 25.; \ x_{12} = 575.; y_{11} = 0.3961 \\ x_{21} &= 25.; \ x_{22} = 475.; y_{21} = 0.7232 \\ x_{31} &= 125.; x_{32} = 475.; y_{31} = 0.4215 \\ x_{41} &= 125.; x_{42} = 575.; y_{41} = 0.1297 \end{aligned}$$

The program is

```
#include "BzzMath.hpp"
void ExperimentSelectionEx1 (int model, int ex,
    BzzVector &b, BzzVector &x, BzzVector &y);
BzzVector e(31,
    1.22,1.44,-1.22,1.66,-1.1,-1.22,-1.44,1.88,
    1.44,-1.24,1.66,-1.22,-1.88,1.22,1.44,-1.66,
    1.66,-1.88,-1.44,1.44,1.22,1.66,-1.44,-1.22,
    1.44,-1.22,1.22,-1.22,1.44,-1.22,-1.44);
double ExperimentalValue1 (int iex, BzzVector &x)
    {
    double x2 = 1./x[2] - 1./525.;
    return 1. / (1. + x[1] *
```

```cpp
            exp(-3.53235 - 5000.*x2)) + e[iex];
    }
 void main(void)
   {
   BzzPrint(\n\nExperimentSelectionEx1);
   BzzPrint(\n\nnumModels 4 numX 2 numY 1);
   int numModels = 4;
   int numX = 2;
   int numY = 1;
   int numExperiments = 4;
   //   int numExperiments = 5;
   //   int numExperiments = 6;
   //   int numExperiments = 7;
   BzzMatrix X(numExperiments,numX,
         25.,575.,
         25.,475.,
         125.,475.,
         125.,575.);
   e *= .015;
   BzzPrint("\nSigma %e %e",Mean(e),Variance(e));
   BzzMatrix Y(numExperiments,numY);
   Y[1][1] = 0.3961;
   Y[2][1] = 0.7232;
   Y[3][1] = 0.4215;
   Y[4][1] = 0.1297;
   BzzVector xMin(2,10.,450.);
   BzzVector xMax(2,150.,600.);
   BzzVector x(2);
   int i,j;
   for(i = 5;i <= numExperiments;i++)
         {
         x = X.GetRow(i);
         Y[i][1] = ExperimentalValue1(i - 4,x);
         BzzPrint(\n%.3e %.3e %.3e,x[1],x[2],Y[i][1]);
         }
   BzzNonLinearRegression nonLinReg(numModels,X,Y,
         ExperimentSelectionEx1);
   BzzVector s2(1,4.8e-4);
   int df = 5;
   nonLinReg.SetVariance(df,s2);
   nonLinReg.SelectCriterion(1);
   BzzVector b1(2,-5.,5000.);
   nonLinReg.InitializeModel(1,b1);
   BzzVector b2(2,1.,5000.);
   nonLinReg.InitializeModel(2,b2);
```

```
    BzzVector b3(2,1.,5000.);
    nonLinReg.InitializeModel(3,b3);
    BzzVector b4(2,1.,5000.);
    nonLinReg.InitializeModel(4,b4);
    nonLinReg.LeastSquaresAnalysisAndExperimentsSearch
         (xMin,xMax);
  }
  void ExperimentSelectionEx1(int model,int ex,
         BzzVector &b,BzzVector &x,BzzVector &y)
  {
    double x2 = 1./x[2] - 1./525.;
    double bb;
    switch(model)
      {
      case 1:
          bb = b[1] - b[2] * x2;
          y[1] = exp(-x[1] * exp(bb));
          break;
      case 2:
          bb = b[1] - b[2] * x2;
          y[1] = 1. / (1. + x[1] * exp(bb));
          break;
      case 3:
          bb = b[1] - b[2] * x2;
          y[1] = 1. / sqrt(1. + 2. * x[1] * exp(bb));
          break;
      case 4:
          bb = b[1] - b[2] * x2;
          y[1] = 1. / pow((1. + 3. * x[1] *
              exp(bb)),.333333);
          break;}
       }
```

Main results are reported in hereinafter.

At the end of the analysis of each model, the best experiments are printed out to improve parameter estimation of the specific model. As mentioned above, it is possible to select one of the first seven criteria. Criterion 1 is adopted in this example:

```
    nonLinReg.SelectCriterion(1);
```

Moreover, optimal experiments obtained by criteria 8–11 are ever provided. For example,

```
    Suggestions for model 2
    =========================
    Max determinant Criterion
    x values: 1.000000e+001 6.000000e+002
```

```
Max XDistance Criterion
x values: 7.222222e+001 5.166667e+002
Max FDistance Criterion
x values: 8.777778e+001 5.666667e+002
Max XDistance in principal axes space Criterion
x values: 7.222222e+001 5.000000e+002
Max FDistance in principal axes space Criterion
x values: 4.111111e+001 5.166667e+002
```

After analyzing all models, a comparison summarizing features of all models is printed out (see Section 6.9):

```
       MSE             MSE/Best        Fexp
1 1.301237e-002 9.887964e+000 2.710910e+001
2 1.315980e-003 1.000000e+000 2.741626e+000
3 1.382977e-003 1.050910e+000 2.881202e+000
4 4.890124e-003 3.715955e+000 1.018776e+001
```

Models no. 2 and no. 3 seem almost equivalent, whereas models no. 1 and no. 4 appear less performing.

Then, the best experimental points to discriminate between two models are printed out for each couple of selected models.

```
        Best Experiment for each Couple of Models
1 2 Tij 9.644775e-001 Experiment: 1.500000e+002 5.333333e+002
1 3 Tij 2.194696e+000 Experiment: 1.500000e+002 5.333333e+002
1 4 Tij 3.136373e+000 Experiment: 1.000000e+001 5.666667e+002
2 3 Tij 2.658859e+000 Experiment: 1.000000e+001 5.666667e+002
2 4 Tij 4.007824e+000 Experiment: 1.000000e+001 5.666667e+002
3 4 Tij 7.977618e-001 Experiment: 1.000000e+001 5.500000e+002
```

Also, the experiment that maximizes the function (8.11) is printed.

```
Suggestion:
===========
The best experiment for model discrimination is:
x values: 1.000000e+001 5.666667e+002
and it has been selected
in order to maximize Tij Mean = 2.658859e+000
```

At last, an experiment maximizing the function (8.12), which is the sum of the three contributions where the first one is independent of the selected models, is printed.

```
Suggested experiment for balanced function
(models discrimination <-> parameters estimation):
x values: 1.500000e+002, 5.000000e+002
```

8.7 Criterion Used in BzzNonLinearRegression Class to Generate New Experiments

```
Contributions
=============
Criterion 10 5.049150e+001% of its potentiality
Criterion 11 7.131010e+001% of its potentiality
Model discrimination 3.688487e+001% of its potentiality
```

In these last lines, the relevance of three contributions is explained; that is, in this specific case, the new additional point contributed for the 36% of the potentialities of the best experiment in discriminating among the rival models.

The user must face the task to select among the various experiments proposed, according to his goals and using all information coming from the model analysis.

A reasonable choice is to use the experimental points that better discriminate among models when the value of the function is sufficiently larger than 1.5; otherwise, it is preferable to choose the selected experimental point by maximizing the balanced function (8.12).

If the experimental point that optimizes the model discrimination is a duplicate of an existing experiment, it is suitable and advisable to check whether such an experiment is an outlier for some good models belonging to the arena of rival models by using a robust method. In this case, it is reasonable to repeat such an experiment.

By adopting this strategy, the following series is obtained:
New additional experiment: $1.000000e+001\ 5.666667e+002$

```
MSE MSE/Best Fexp
1 1.016548e-002 1.155068e+001 2.117809e+001 *** WARNING ***
2 8.800764e-004 1.000000e+000 1.833493e+000
3 2.272231e-003 2.581856e+000 4.733814e+000
4 7.591343e-003 8.625778e+000 1.581530e+001 *** WARNING ***
```

New additional experiment: $1.500000e+002\ 5.666667e+002$

```
1 1.110328e-002 1.585282e+001 2.313184e+001 *** WARNING ***
2 7.003980e-004 1.000000e+000 1.459162e+000
3 2.729804e-003 3.897503e+000 5.687091e+000 *** WARNING ***
4 8.918115e-003 1.273292e+001 1.857941e+001 *** WARNING ***
```

The model no. 2 is therefore the only one to be still reasonable.

Nevertheless, this means neither that the experimentation is to be stopped after six experiments only nor that the model no. 2 is the only one able to properly represent the experimental data set.

Example 8.3

Hunter and Wichern (1966) proposed even the following example to simultaneously test the model discrimination and the improvement of parameter estimation. Rival models involved are

$$y_{1i} = \frac{\beta_1\beta_3\beta_4 x_{1i}x_{2i}}{(1.+\beta_3 x_{1i}+\beta_4 x_{2i})^2} + \varepsilon_{1i} \qquad y_{2i} = \frac{\beta_2\beta_3\beta_4 x_{1i}x_{2i}}{(1.+\beta_3 x_{1i}+\beta_4 x_{2i})^2} + \varepsilon_{2i} \qquad (8.18)$$

$$y_{1i} = \frac{\beta_1\beta_3\beta_4 x_{1i}x_{2i}}{(1.+\beta_3 x_{1i}+\beta_4 x_{2i})^2} + \varepsilon_{1i} \qquad y_{2i} = \frac{\beta_2\beta_3\beta_4 x_{1i}x_{2i}}{1.+\beta_3 x_{1i}+\beta_4 x_{2i}} + \varepsilon_{2i} \qquad (8.19)$$

$$y_{1i} = \frac{\beta_1\beta_3 x_{1i}x_{2i}}{1.+\beta_3 x_{2i}} + \varepsilon_{1i} \qquad y_{2i} = \frac{\beta_2\beta_3 x_{1i}x_{2i}}{(1.+\beta_3 x_{1i})^2} + \varepsilon_{2i} \qquad (8.20)$$

$$y_{1i} = \frac{\beta_1\beta_3 x_{1i}x_{2i}}{1.+\beta_3 x_{2i}} + \varepsilon_{1i} \qquad y_{2i} = \frac{\beta_2\beta_3 x_{1i}x_{2i}}{(1.+\beta_3 x_{1i}+\beta_4 x_{1i})^2} + \varepsilon_{2i} \qquad (8.21)$$

Observe that models should be reparameterized according to the rules described in Chapter 7 in order to reduce collinearities among parameters; nevertheless, their original formulation is preserved in this example.

Experiments are artificially generated by model no. 4 (8.21) by assuming the following values of parameters: .0005, .16, 15., and 1.9. The model no. 4 was added to the models originally proposed by Hunter and Wichern as first two models (8.18) and (8.19) were too far from the model (8.20) that artificially generated the experimental data set: thus, the model discrimination was immediately accomplished as the four initial experiments were enough to discard the first two models.

The experimental domain is

$$\begin{aligned} 0.01 \leq x_{1i} \leq 2. \\ 0.01 \leq x_{2i} \leq 2. \end{aligned} \qquad (8.22)$$

The experimental error variance for the two dependent variables are $\sigma_1^2 = 8.6 \cdot 10^{-12}$ and $\sigma_2^2 = 5.4 \cdot 10^{-9}$ with four degrees of freedom.

First four preliminary experimental points are

$$\begin{aligned} x_{11} &= 0.5; x_{12} = 0.5; y_{11} = 2.230 \cdot 10^{-4}; y_{12} = 6.658 \cdot 10^{-3} \\ x_{21} &= 1.0; x_{22} = 0.5; y_{21} = 2.373 \cdot 10^{-4}; y_{22} = 3.817 \cdot 10^{-3} \\ x_{31} &= 0.5; x_{32} = 1.0; y_{31} = 4.387 \cdot 10^{-4}; y_{32} = 1.338 \cdot 10^{-2} \\ x_{41} &= 1.0; x_{42} = 1.0; y_{41} = 4.721 \cdot 10^{-4}; y_{42} = 7.551 \cdot 10^{-3} \end{aligned}$$

The program is

```
#include "BzzMath.hpp"
void ExperimentSelectionEx2 (int model, int ex,
        BzzVector &b, BzzVector &x, BzzVector &y);
```

8.7 Criterion Used in BzzNonLinearRegression Class to Generate New Experiments | 399

```
BzzVector e(31,
        1.22,1.44,-1.22,1.66,-1.1,-1.22,-1.44,1.88,
        1.44,-1.24,1.66,-1.22,-1.88,1.22,1.44,-1.66,
        1.66,-1.88,-1.44,1.44,1.22,1.66,-1.44,-1.22,
        1.44,-1.22,1.22,-1.22,1.44,-1.22,-1.44);
void main(void)
   {
   BzzPrint(\n\nExperimentSelectionEx2);
   BzzPrint(\n\nnumModels 3 numX 2 numY 2);
   int numModels = 4;
   int numX = 2;
   int numY = 2;
// int numExperiments = 4;
// int numExperiments = 5;
// int numExperiments = 6;
   int numExperiments = 7;
   BzzMatrix X(numExperiments,numX,
        .50,.50,
        1.0,.50,
        .50,1.0,
//      1.0,1.0);
        1.0,1.0,
        .01,2.,
        .01,2.,
        0.2311,2.);
BzzMatrix Y(numExperiments,numY);
BzzVector e1 = .000002* e;
BzzVector e2 = .00005 * e;
BzzPrint(\n>>>>%e %e,Variance(e1),Variance(e2));
int i,j;
double a1,a2;
BzzVector x;
for(i = 1;i <= numExperiments;i++)
     {
     x = X.GetRow(i);
     a1 = 15. * x[1] * x[2];
     a2 = 1. + 15. * x[1];
     Y[i][1] = .0005 * a1 / a2 + e1[i];
     Y[i][2] = .16 * a1 / BzzPow2(a2 + 1.9 * x[1]) + e2[31 - i];
     BzzPrint(\n%.3e %.3e %.3e %.3e,x[1],x[2],
         Y[i][1],Y[i][2]);}
BzzNonLinearRegression nonLinReg(numModels,X,Y,
     ExperimentSelectionEx2);
BzzVector s2(2,8.6e-12,5.4e-9);
int df = 4;
```

```
nonLinReg.SetVariance(df,s2);
BzzVector b1(4,0.,1.,1.,1.);
nonLinReg.InitializeModel(1,b1);
BzzVector b2(4,0.,1.,1.,1.);
nonLinReg.InitializeModel(2,b2);
BzzVector b3(3,0.0005,.16,1.);
nonLinReg.InitializeModel(3,b3);
BzzVector b4(4,0.0005,.16,1.,1.);
nonLinReg.InitializeModel(4,b4);
nonLinReg.RobustAnalysis();
BzzVector xMin(2,.01,.01);
BzzVector xMax(2,2.,2.);
nonLinReg.LeastSquaresAnalysisAndExperimentsSearch
   (xMin,xMax);
BzzPause();
}
void ExperimentSelectionEx2(int model,int ex,
          BzzVector &b,BzzVector &x,BzzVector &y)
    {
    double a1 = b[3] * x[1] * x[2];
    double a2;
    switch(model)
       {
       case 1:
           a2 = BzzPow2(1. + b[3] * x[1] + b[4] * x[2]);
           y[1] = b[1] * b[4] * a1 / a2;
           y[2] = b[2] * b[4] * a1 / a2;
           break;
       case 2:
           a2 = 1. + b[3] * x[1] + b[4] * x[2];
           y[1] = b[1] * b[4] * a1 / BzzPow2(a2);
           y[2] = b[1] * b[4] * a1 / a2;
           break;
       case 3:
           a2 = 1. + b[3] * x[1];
           y[1] = b[1] * a1 / a2;
           y[2] = b[2] * a1 / BzzPow2(a2);
           break;
       case 4:
           a2 = 1. + b[3] * x[1];
           y[1] = b[1] * a1 / a2;
           y[2] = b[2] * a1 / BzzPow2(a2 + b[4] * x[1]);
           break;
       }
    }
```

8.7 Criterion Used in BzzNonLinearRegression Class to Generate New Experiments

The following results are obtained for the analyzed models:

```
    WeightedSE    WeightedSE/              P-Value
                    Best
1  2.662613e+003 1.497936e+003 6.743521e-006 *** WARNING ***
2  9.913351e+003 5.577065e+003 4.879025e-007 *** WARNING ***
3  2.605162e+000 1.465615e+000 7.543946e-001
4  1.777521e+000 1.000000e+000 7.742769e-001
```

The experimental point to discriminate among the models coincides with the one proposed by the mixed criterion (8.12).

```
Suggestion:
============
The best experiment for model discrimination is:
x values: 1.000000e-002 2.000000e+000
and it has been selected
in order to maximize Tij Mean = 5.673662e+002
```

and it should be an important experiment in discriminating among the models by looking at the large value of the function (8.11).
Introducing such an experimental point leads to

```
    Weighted      SEWeightedSE/            P-Value
                    Best
1  3.992283e+004 7.412092e+003 6.021207e-008 *** WARNING ***
2  2.199623e+005 4.083831e+004 1.984031e-009 *** WARNING ***
3  3.431390e+001 6.370736e+000 7.176325e-002
4  5.386175e+000 1.000000e+000 5.694536e-001
```

Now, the experiments proposed by criteria (8.11) and (8.12) are different. The former one suggests to repeat the experiment:

```
The best experiment for model discrimination is:
x values: 1.000000e-002 2.000000e+000
and it has been selected
in order to maximize Tij Mean = 4.396219e+000
*** WARNING ***
The new experiment is close to an existing one
```

whereas the latter one suggests to select the following experimental point.

```
Suggested experiment for balanced function
(models discrimination <-> parameters estimation):
x values: 2.000000e+000, 2.000000e+000
Contributions
==============
Criterion 10 6.915934e+001% of its potentiality
Criterion 11 2.860608e+000% of its potentiality
Model discrimination 6.147802e+001% of its potentiality
```

By using a robust method for analyzing results, it is possible to note that the experiment no. 5, the one which criterion (8.11) suggested to repeat, is an evident outlier for the model no. 3 (8.20), which is the most competing model against model no. 4 (8.21). It can be therefore useful to duplicate such an experiment to check whether it is a real outlier for the model no. 3.

By repeating this experiment, we have

```
      WeightedSE    WeightedSE/         P-Value
                        Best
1  4.503033e+004  6.367377e+003  7.887792e-008 *** WARNING ***
2  8.235673e+004  1.164541e+004  2.358508e-008 *** WARNING ***
3  6.127272e+001  8.664084e+000  4.020041e-002 *** WARNING ***
4  7.072037e+000  1.000000e+000  5.930310e-001
```

Hence, even the model no. 3 is less performing against the model no. 4.

In a conclusive example (Buzzi-Ferraris and Manenti, 2009), let us consider the total oxidation of methane over a perovskite-type catalyst $La_{0.9}Ce_{0.1}CoO_3$. Both the experimental data and the proposed rate equations are explained elsewhere in the literature (Auer, 2001; Auer and Berger, 2002). These authors proposed the following five rival models

$$r_{CH_4,1} = \frac{k_1 k_2 P_{O_2} P_{CH_4}}{k_1 P_{O_2} + 2k_2 P_{CH_4}} \tag{8.23}$$

$$r_{CH_4,2} = \frac{k_1 k_2 P_{O_2} P_{CH_4}}{k_1 P_{O_2} + 2k_2 P_{CH_4} + \frac{2k_1 k_2}{k_3} P_{O_2} P_{CH_4}} \tag{8.24}$$

$$r_{CH_4,3} = \frac{k_1 k_2 P_{O_2} P_{CH_4}}{k_1 P_{O_2} + 2k_2 P_{CH_4}} \left(1 - \frac{k_1}{k'_1} P_{O_2}\right) \tag{8.25}$$

$$r_{CH_4,4} = \frac{k_2 P_{CH_4}}{2k_1 P_{O_2}} \left(k_1 P_{O_2} + 2k_2 P_{CH_4} - \sqrt{2k_2 P_{CH_4}(2k_2 P_{CH_4} + 4k_1 P_{O_2})}\right) \tag{8.26}$$

$$r_{CH_4,5} = \frac{1}{2} k_1 P_{O_2} \left[1 + \frac{k_1 P_{O_2}}{4k_2 P_{CH_4}} + \sqrt{\left(\frac{k_1 P_{O_2}}{4k_2 P_{CH_4}}\right)^2 + \frac{k_1 P_{O_2}}{2k_2 P_{CH_4}}}\right] \tag{8.27}$$

as tests for the simultaneous discrimination among rival kinetic models and the accurate parameter estimation; $P_{CH_4} = P_{CH_4}^{in}(1-g)$, $P_{O_2} = P_{O_2}^{in} - 2P_{CH_4}^{in} g$, and $k_j = k_{ref,j}^0 \exp\left[\frac{-Ea_j}{R}\left(\frac{1}{T} - \frac{1}{T_{ref}}\right)\right]$, with $j = 1, 1', 2, 3$.

Preliminary experimental data are reported in Table 8.2.

Parameters have to be evaluated by using relation (6.6), where

$$\frac{dg}{dt} = r, \quad 0 \leq t \leq 0.1897 \tag{8.28}$$

Table 8.2 Preliminary experimental data for the simultaneous discrimination among kinetic models and the accurate parameter estimation (for details, see Auer and Berger, 2002).

#	T	$P^{in}_{CH_4}$	$P^{in}_{O_2}$	y	Weight
1	663.1	0.01123	0.01339	0.02798	1.1550
2	663.1	0.03989	0.01335	0.04737	1.1550
3	663.1	0.04067	0.04851	0.06081	1.1550
4	693.1	0.02602	0.02230	0.09991	0.93436
5	733.1	0.01133	0.04828	0.1530	0.38619
6	733.1	0.004022	0.03075	0.2118	0.20050
7	733.1	0.02579	0.03076	0.3484	0.20050
8	733.1	0.04067	0.04851	0.3704	0.20050

The new experiments have to be selected among 43 experiments already exploited.

and

$$y = \frac{P^{in}_{CH_4} - P^{out}_{CH_4}}{P^{in}_{CH_4}} \quad (8.29)$$

Essential points are

1) Models are reparameterized as described in Chapter 7.
2) The robust search is adopted to verify if there are any outliers in the preliminary experiments. In this case, no outliers are detected.
3) The parameters are evaluated through the minimization of equation (6.6). The initial weighted mean square error, reported in the first row of Table 8.4, shows that at the beginning the best models are the model no. 3 (8.25) ($MSE^{exp_8}_{M3} = 1.249646$) and the model no. 2 (8.24) ($MSE^{exp_8}_{M2} = 6.710737$).
4) By analyzing all the indices to verify the parameter correlation (condition number, inflation factor, tolerance indices, principal diameters, and comparison between the Newton and the robust methods), no correlations are identified.
5) The experiment no. 9, which is suggested by relation (8.12), is reported in Table 8.3. The selected point discriminates among models for 66% compared to the best point. As only models 2 and 3 are reasonable for their small mean square error, only these models significantly contribute to this choice.

Table 8.3 Sequence of the new selected experiments.

#	T	$P^{in}_{CH_4}$	$P^{in}_{O_2}$	y	Weight
9	773.1	0.01859	0.01354	0.2616	0.20050
10	733.1	0.04067	0.04851	0.2314	0.38619
11	773.1	0.01133	0.04828	0.3155	0.20050
12	733.1	0.03963	0.02169	0.1863	0.38618

Table 8.4 Weighted mean square error for the five models after the *n*th experiment (first eight points are preliminary experiments).

#	1	2	3	4	5
8	38.38048	6.710737	1.249646	21.95906	335.9511
9	97.12971	6.785264	12.84385	138.6177	483.3034
10	153.3871	6.787816	20.35600	206.3668	495.3445
11	157.5478	6.923375	37.45801	210.0884	553.7219
12	168.6253	6.929506	40.88294	220.0768	668.6007

6) After the previous experiment no. 9, the model no. 2 ($MSE_{M2}^{exp_9} = 6.785264$) is better than the model no. 3 ($MSE_{M3}^{exp_9} = 12.84385$).

7) In Tables 8.3 and 8.4, both the successive experiments and the mean square error are reported, respectively. In these cases, the experiment selection suggested by relation (8.12) is mainly dictated by the accurate parameter estimation of the model no. 2 and by the best utilization of the experimental domain.

References

Arnold, S.F. (1990) *Mathematical Statistics*, Prentice-Hall, Englewood Cliffs, NJ.

Atkinson, A.C. (1978) Posterior probabilities for choosing a regression model. *Biometrika*, **65**, 39–48.

Atkinson, A.C. and Fedorov, V.V. (1975a) The design of experiments for discriminating between two rival models. *Biometrika*, **62**, 57–70.

Atkinson, A.C. and Fedorov, V.V. (1975b) Optimal design: experiments for discriminating between several models. *Biometrika*, **62**, 289–303.

Auer, R. (2001) Kinetic Study of Methane Combustion over Perovskite Catalysts, PhD Dissertation, Université Catholique de Louvain, Belgium.

Auer, R. and Berger, R. (2002) *EUROKIN – Test Case for Sequential Design of Experiments*, TU Delft, The Netherlands.

Bates, D.M. and Watts, D.G. (2007) *Nonlinear Regression Analysis and Its Applications*, John Wiley & Sons, Inc., New York.

Berenson, M.L., Levine, D.M., and Rindskopf, D. (1988) *Applied Statistics*, Prentice-Hall, Englewood Cliffs, NJ.

Box, G.E.P. (1949) A general distribution theory for a class of likelihood criteria. *Biometrika*, **36**, 317–346.

Box, M.J. (1971) An experimental design criterion for precise estimation of a subset of the parameters in a nonlinear model. *Biometrika*, **58**, 149–153.

Box, G.E.P. and Draper, N.R. (1965) The Bayesian estimation of common parameters from several responses. *Biometrika*, **52**, 355–365.

Box, G.E.P. and Hill, W.J. (1967) Discrimination among mechanistic models. *Technometrics*, **9**, 57–71.

Box, G.E.P. and Lucas, H.L. (1959) Design of experiments in nonlinear situations. *Biometrika*, **46**, 77–90.

Buzzi Ferraris, G. (1967) Ottimizzazione di funzioni a più variabili. Nota I. Variabili non vincolate. *Ingegnere Chimico Italiano*, **3**, 101.

Buzzi-Ferraris, G. (1994) *Scientific C++ - Building Numerical Libraries, The Object-Oriented Way*, 2nd edn, Addison-Wesley, Cambridge University Press.

Buzzi-Ferraris, G. (1999) Planning of experiments and kinetic analysis. *Catalysis Today*, **52**, 125–132.

Buzzi Ferraris, G. (2000) Letter to the editor. *Computers & Chemical Engineering*, **24**, 2037–2039.

Buzzi-Ferraris, G. (2009) BzzMath: numerical library in C++, Politecnico di Milano www.chem.polimi.it/homes/gbuzzi.

Buzzi-Ferraris, G. (2010) New Trends in Building Numerical Programs. *Computers & Chemical Engineering*, submitted.

Buzzi Ferraris, G., Donati, G., and Rejna, F. (1974a) European Symposium on Computer Application in Process Development, Erlangen.

Buzzi Ferraris, G., Donati, G., Rejna, F., and Carrá, S. (1974b) An investigation on kinetic models for ammonia synthesis. *Chemical Engineering Science*, **29**, 1621–1627.

Buzzi Ferraris, G. and Forzatti, P. (1983) A new sequential experimental design procedure for discriminating among rival models. *Chemical Engineering Science*, **38**, 225–232.

Interpolation and Regression Models for the Chemical Engineer: Solving Numerical Problems
Guido Buzzi-Ferraris and Flavio Manenti
Copyright © 2010 WILEY-VCH Verlag GmbH & Co. KGaA, Weinheim
ISBN: 978-3-527-32652-5

Buzzi Ferraris, G., Forzatti, P., Hemig, G., and Hofmann, H. (1984) Sequential experimental design for model discrimination in the case of multiple responses. *Chemical Engineering Science*, **39**, 81–85.

Buzzi-Ferraris, G. and Manenti, F. (2009) Kinetic models analysis. *Chemical Engineering Science*, **64** (5), 1061–1074.

Buzzi-Ferraris, G. and Manenti, F. (2010a) *Fundamentals and Linear Algebra for the Chemical Engineer. Solving Numerical Problems*, Wiley-VCH, Weinheim, Germany, ISBN: 978-3-527-32552-8.

Buzzi-Ferraris, G. and Manenti, F. (2010b) Outlier Detection. *Computers & Chemical Engineering*, submitted.

Buzzi-Ferraris, G. and Manenti, F. (2011a) Nonlinear Systems and Optimization for the Chemical Engineer. Solving Numerical Problems, in progress.

Buzzi-Ferraris, G. and Manenti, F. (2011b) Differential and Differential-Algebraic Systems for the Chemical Engineer. Solving Numerical Problems, in progress.

Buzzi-Ferraris, G. and Ranzi, E. (1971) *Programmazione della Sperimentazione Industriale*, Italcartografica, Milano.

Carnap, R. (1952) *The Continuum of Inductive Methods*, University of Chicago Press, Chicago.

Conte, S.D. and De Boor, C. (1980) *Elementary Numerical Analysis. An Algorithmic Approach*, McGraw-Hill, London.

Cook, R.D. (1977) Detection of influential observations in linear regression. *Technometrics*, **19**, 15–18.

Daniel, C., and Wood, F.S. (1980) Fitting Equations to Data, Wiley, New York.

Davies, O.L. (1957) Statistical Methods in Research and Production, Hafner Publishing Co., New York.

de Brauwere, A., De Ridder, F., Pintelon, R., Elskens, M., Schoukens, J., and Baeyens, W. (2005) Model selection through a statistical analysis of the minimum of a weighted least squares cost function. *Chemometrics and Intelligent Laboratory Systems*, **76**, 163–173.

Donckels, B. (2009) Optimal Experimental Design to Discriminate among rival dynamic mathematical models, PhD Dissertation, Gent University.

Draper, N.R. and Hunter, W.G. (1966) Design of experiments for parameter estimation in multiresponse situations. *Biometrika*, **53**, 525–533.

Draper, N.R. and Hunter, W.G. (1967a) The use of prior distributions in the design of experiments for parameters estimation in nonlinear situations. *Biometrika*, **54**, 147–153.

Draper, N.R. and Hunter, W.G. (1967b) The use of prior distributions in the design of experiments for parameters estimation in nonlinear situations: multiresponse case. *Biometrika*, **54**, 662–665.

Draper, N.R. and Smith, H. (1998) *Applied Regression Analysis*, 3rd edn, John Wiley & Sons, Inc., New York.

Fedorov, V.V. (1972) *Theory of Optimal Experiments*, Academic Press, New York.

Fisher, R. (1924) On a distribution yielding the error functions of several well known statistics. Proceedings of the International Congress of Mathematics, Toronto, vol. 2, pp. 805–813.

Fisher, R. (1925) Applications of student's distribution. *Metron*, **5**, 90–104.

Fogler, H.S. (1992) *Elements of Chemical Reaction Engineering*, Prentice-Hall, Englewood Cliffs, NJ.

Forzatti, P., Buzzi Ferraris, G., Canu, P., and Tronconi, E. (1987) Sequential design of experiments. A review of the procedures for increasing the precision of the parameter estimates. *Quaderni dell' Ingegnere Chimico Italiano*, **23**(3–4), 10–15.

Froment, G. (1975) Model discrimination and parameter estimation in heterogeneous catalysis. *AIChE Journal*, **21**, 1041–1057.

Froment, G. and Mezaki, R. (1970) Sequential discrimination and estimation procedures for rate modeling in heterogeneous catalysis. *Chemical Engineering Science*, **25**, 293–301.

Golub, G. and Van Loan, C. (1983) *Matrix Computations*, John Hopkins Press, Baltimore.

Gosset, W.S. alias Student (1908) Probable error of a correlation coefficient. *Biometrika*, **6** (2–3), 302–310.

Hamming, R.W. (1962) *Numerical Methods for Scientists and Engineers*, McGraw-Hill, New York.

Hampel, F.R., Ronchetti, E.M., Rousseeuw, P.J., and Stahel, W.A. (1986) *Robust Statistics: The Approach Based on Influence Functions*, John Wiley & Sons, Inc., New York, reprinted in 2005.

Hawkins, D.M., Bradu, D., and Kass, G.V. (1984) Location of several outliers in multiple regression using elemental sets. *Technometrics*, **26**, 197–208.

Hill, P.D.H. (1978) A review of experimental design procedures for regression model discriminating. *Technometrics*, **20**, 15–21.

Himmelblau, D.M. (1970) *Process Analysis by Statistical Methods*, John Wiley & Sons, Inc., New York.

Hines, W.W. and Montgomery, D.C. (1990) *Probability and Statistics in Engineering and Management Science*, John Wiley & Sons, Inc., New York.

Hosten, L.H. (1974) A sequential experimental design procedure for precise parameter estimation based upon the shape of the joint confidence region. *Chemical Engineering Science*, **29**, 2247–2252.

Hosten, L.H. and Froment, G.F. (1976) Non-Bayesian sequential experimental design procedure for optimal discrimination between rival models. Proceedings of Fourth International Symposium on Chemical Reaction Engineering, Heidelberg.

Huber, P.J. (1981) *Robust Statistics*, John Wiley & Sons, Inc., New York.

Hunter, W.G. and Reiner, A.M. (1965) Design for discriminating between two rival models. *Technometrics*, **7**, 307–323.

Hunter, W.G. and Wichern, D.W. (1966) Technical Report 33, Departments of Chemical. Engineering and Statistics, University of Wisconsin, Madison.

Hunter, W.G., Hill, W.J., and Wichern, D.W. (1968) A joint design criterion for the dual problem of model discrimination and parameter estimation. *Technometrics*, **10**, 152–159.

Kelly, G. (1984) The influence function in the errors in variables problem. *Annals of Statistics*, **12**, 87–100.

Kincaid, D. and Cheney, W. (1990) *Numerical Analysis*, Brooks/Cole Publishing Company, Pacific Grove, California.

Kittrell, J.R., Hunter, W.G., and Watson, C.C. (1966) Obtaining precise parameter estimates for nonlinear catalytic rate models. *AIChE Journal*, **12**, 5.

Mallows, C.L. (1973) Some comments on Cp. *Technometrics*, **15**, 661–675.

Mallows, C.L. (1995) More comments on Cp. *Technometrics*, **37**, 362–372.

Mendenhall, W., Wackerly, D.D., and Scheaffer, R.L. (1990) *Mathematical Statistics with Application*, PWS-KENT, Boston.

Miller, R.G. (1980) *Kanamycin Levels in Premature Babies, Biostatistics Casebook*, vol. **III**, 127–142, Technical Report No. 57, Division of Biostatistics, Stanford University.

Ponce de Leon, A.C. and Atkinson, A.C. (1991) Optimum experimental design for discriminating between two rival models in the presence of prior information. *Biometrika*, **78**, 601–608.

Popper, K. (1972) *Objective Knowledge: An Evolutionary Approach*, Clarendon Press, Oxford.

Press, W.H., Flannery, B.P., Teukolsky, S.A., and Vetterling, W.T. (1988) *Numerical Recipes in C*, Cambridge University Press, Cambridge.

Ralston, A. and Rabinowitz, P. (1988) *A First Course in Numerical Analysis*, 2nd edn, McGraw-Hill.

Rousseeuw, P.J. (1984a) Least median of squares regressions. *Journal of the American Statistical Association*, **79**, 871–880.

Rousseeuw, P.J. (1984b) Robust regression by means of S-estimators, in *Robust and Nonlinear Time Series Analysis* (eds J. Franke, W. Hardle, and D. Martin), Springer-Verlag, pp. New York.

Rousseeuw, P.J. (1990) Robust estimation and identifying outliers, Chapter 16, in *Handbook of Statistical Methods for Engineers and Scientists* (ed. H.M. Wadsworth), McGraw-Hill, pp. New York.

Rousseeuw, P.J. and Leroy, A.M. (1987) *Robust Regression and Outlier Detection*, John Wiley & Sons, Inc., New York.

Ryan, T.P. (2009) *Modern Regression Methods*, 2nd edn, John Wiley & Sons, Inc., NJ.

Schwaab, M., Silva, F.M., Queipo, C.A., Barreto, A.G., Jr., Nele, M., and Pinto, J.C. (2006) A new approach for sequential experimental design for model discrimination. *Chemical Engineering Science*, **61**, 5791–5806.

Schwarz, H.R. (1989) *Numerical Analysis. A Comprehensive Introduction*, John Wiley & Sons, Inc., New York.

Seber, G.A.F. (1977) *Linear Regression Analysis*, John Wiley & Sons, Inc., New York.

Seber, G.A.F., and Wild, C.J. (2003) *Nonlinear Regression*, John Wiley & Sons, Inc., New York.

Smith, K. (1918) On the standard deviations of adjusted and interpolated values of an observed polynomial function and its constants and the guidance they give towards a proper choice of the distribution of observations. *Biometrika*, **12**, 1–85.

Spriet, J. (1985) Structure characterization: an overview, in *Identification and System Parameter Estimation, Proceedings of the 7th IFAC/IFORS Symposium* (eds H.A. Baker and P.C. Young), Pergamon Press, pp. 749–756.

Stoer, J., and Bulirsch, R. (1983) *Introduction to Numerical Analysis*, Springer-Verlag, New York.

Wadsworth, H.M. (1989) *Handbook of Statistical Methods for Engineers and Scientists*, McGraw-Hill, New York.

Watts, D.G. (1981) An introduction to nonlinear least squares, in *Kinetic Data Analysis – Design and Analysis of Enzyme and Pharmacokinetic Experiments* (ed. L. Endrenyi), Plenum Press, New York, pp. 1–24.

Wilcoxson, W.L. (1965) Technical Report R419, US Naval Civil Engineering Laboratory, Port Hueneme, California.

Wilkinson, J. (1963) *Rounding Errors in Algebraic Processes*, Prentice-Hall, Englewood Cliffs, NJ.

Wonnacott, T.H. and Wonnacott, R.J. (1990) *Introductory Statistics*, John Wiley & Sons, Inc., New York.

Wood, F.S. (1973) The use of individual effects and residuals in fitting equations to data. *Technometrics*, **15**, 677–695.

Appendix A: Mixed-Language: Fortran and C++

Examples of this chapter can be found in the directory `Vol2_AppendixA` within the enclosed CD-ROM.

A.1
Mixed-Language

Up to few years ago, the language adopted in developing scientific programs and solving numerical problems was the Fortran. Especially for this reason, there is an enormous amount of programs written in this language and, consequently, many programmers do not want to switch to another language as they already have a series of code samples and programs in Fortran language.

On the other hand, the C++ gives some significant advantages even in the scientific fields as it is conceived as an object-oriented programming language, whereas the Fortran, even in its release 90/95, and the C are procedural languages.

A possible solution is to merge these languages: it is possible to implement in C++ some pieces of code already developed in Fortran and vice versa.

The mixed-language solution must be considered as a makeshift: being C++ an object-oriented language, it has potentialities that are even unthinkable in a procedural language as Fortran and for people programming in a procedural way as well (see Buzzi-Ferraris and Manenti, 2010a).

This appendix shows the mixed-language approach by means of the most typical situations:

- The program is managed by a `main` written in C++ and some classes written in this language are adopted to solve the numerical problem. The portion of code written in Fortran consists of one (or more) `SUBROUTINE` where some calculations are carried out.

- The program is managed by a PROGRAM written in Fortran. The portion where the calculations are carried out is written in Fortran too, but a C++ class is adopted to solve a specific numerical problem.

A Fortran compiler that is compatible to the C++ compiler must be adopted in compiling the portion of the Fortran program and vice versa (i.e., Visual C++ 6.0 and COMPAQ Visual Fortran 6.6 are adopted in these examples).

Example A.1: The program CppFortranRegression.exe

This example explains how to develop a program managed by a `main` written in C++, where some C++ classes and Fortran SUBROUTINES are adopted to solve a problem.

A program named `CppFortranRegression.exe` for solving the nonlinear regression problem of Example 6.1 is developed.

$$y_{1i} = \beta_1 \, e^{\beta_2/x_{1i}} + \varepsilon_{1i}$$

The program is managed by Visual C++, whereas the nonlinear regression model is developed in a Fortran SUBROUTINE.

Follow the next steps to write the mixed-language program:

- Select `New` from the menu item `File`.
- Select the screen `Projects`.
- Select `Win 32 Console Application`.
- In `Location`, select the root where the project shall be saved in.
- Write `CppFortranRegression` in the edit-box `Project name`.
- Click on the `OK` button.
- Keep the default `An Empty Project` by clicking on the `Finish` button.
- Accept the project by clicking on the `OK` button.
- Select `Win 32 Release` in the menu item: `Build, Set Active Configuration...`.
- Select `Project, Add To Project..., Files` and add the `BzzMath.lib` to the project by taking them either from the directory where it was collected or from the CD-ROM.
- Select `New` from the menu item `File`.
- Select the screen `Files`.
- Select `C++ Source File`.
- Write `CppFortranRegression.cpp` in the edit-box `File Name`.
- Keep the option of inserting the file into the project and click on the `OK` button.
- Write the following code.

```
#define BZZ_COMPILER 0
#include "BzzMath.hpp"

extern "C" {void __stdcall MODEL(int NUMMODEL,
```

```
          int EX,double *B,double *X,double *Y);}

void FirstExample(int model,int ex,BzzVector &amp;b,
      BzzVector &amp;x,BzzVector &amp;y);

void main(void)
   {
   BzzPrint("\n\nFirstExample");
   int numModels = 1;
   int numX = 1;
   int numY = 1;
   int numExperiments = 11;
   BzzMatrix X(numExperiments,numX,
      273.,283.,293.,303.,313.,323.,
      333.,343.,353.,363.,373.);
   BzzMatrix Y(numExperiments,numY,
      191.67,264.88,357.60,474.21,616.19,789.61,
      995.68,1239.71,1523.46,1850.92,2226.47);
   BzzNonLinearRegression nonLinReg(numModels,X,Y,
      FirstExample);
   BzzVector s2(1,.075);
   int df = 6;
   nonLinReg.SetVariance(df,s2);
   BzzVector b1(2,1.,1.);
   nonLinReg.InitializeModel(1,b1);
   nonLinReg.LeastSquaresAnalysis();
   }

void FirstExample(int nummodel,int ex,
      BzzVector &b,BzzVector &x,BzzVector &y)
   {
   double *vect_b = b.GetHandle();
   double *vect_x = x.GetHandle();
   double *vect_y = y.GetHandle();
   MODEL(nummodel,ex,vect_b,vect_x,vect_y);
   }
```

Note that the statement:
```
      extern "C" {void __stdcall MODEL(int NUMMODEL,
            int EX,double *B,double *X,double *Y);}
```
is adopted as it is necessary to inform the compiler that MODEL is a SUBROUTINE written in Fortran attached to the C++ program.

Moreover, note that the function GetHandle is called by an object of the BzzVector class. Such a function returns the pointer at the beginning of the vector; hence, it can be returned and used as a normal C++ pointer, with index from 0 to $n-1$ (it is worth remarking that C++ and Fortran have different indices and element accessing for vectors and matrices; see also Buzzi-Ferraris and Manenti, 2010a).

Follow the last steps to complete the merging:

- Compile the following SUBROUTINE in Fortran so to get the file FortranRegression.obj:

```
SUBROUTINE MODEL(NUMMODEL,EX,B,X,Y)
real*8 B[REFERENCE]
real*8 X[REFERENCE]
real*8 Y[REFERENCE]
dimension B(*),X(*),Y(*)
integer*4 NUMMODEL [VALUE]
integer*4 EX [VALUE]
Y(1) = B(1) * exp(B(2) / X(1))
RETURN
END
```

- Add the file FortranRegression.obj to the project by selecting the item Project, Add To Project, Files.
- Select Project, Settings and the screen Link.
- Write /force in the edit-box Project Options in order to force the linking by overcoming incompatibilities among libraries.
- Compile and run the program.

If anyone has no compatible Fortran compilers available, the file FortranRegression.obj collected in the project directory within the Appendix A folder of the enclosed CD-ROM can be used, by considering it was generated by COMPAQ Visual Fortran 6.6 (and, therefore, compatible to Visual C++ 6.0).

Example A.2: The program FortranCppRegression.exe

This situation is more complex. This example is aimed at developing a PROGRAM written in Fortran that invokes, directly or not, some C++ functions that, in turn, use one or more SUBROUTINES written in Fortran.

Follow the next steps to write the mixed-language program:

- Select New from the menu item File.
- Select the screen Projects.
- Select Win 32 Console Application.
- In Location, select the root where the project shall be saved in.
- Write FortranCppRegression in the edit-box Project name.
- Click on the OK button.
- Keep the default An Empty Project by clicking on the Finish button.

A.1 Mixed-Language

- Accept the project by clicking on the OK button.
- Select Win 32 Release in the menu item: Build, Set Active Configuration....
- Select Project, Add To Project..., Files and add the BzzMath.lib to the project by taking them either from the directory where it was collected or from the CD-ROM.
- Select New from the menu item File.
- Select the screen Files.
- Select C++ Source File.
- Write MixedRegression.cpp in the edit-box File Name.
- Keep the option of inserting the file into the project and click on the OK button.
- Write the following code.

```
// VERY IMPORTANT!
// For linking C++ with FORTRAN is necessary to
// select Project, Settings, Link
// and write /force in Project Options

#define BZZ_COMPILER 0
#include "BzzMath.hpp"

// fortran SUBROUTINE
extern "C" {void __stdcall MODEL (int model,int ex,
      double *B,double *X,double *Y);}
extern "C" {void CppFunction(int numParam,
      double *bb);}

// auxiliary function to translate data
// from C++ to FORTRAN
void RegressionFunction(int model,int ex,
      BzzVector &b,BzzVector &x,BzzVector &y);

// in argument you can transfer some information
// in this case the initial guess for parameters
void CppFunction(int numParam,double *bb)
   {
   // comment this instruction for printing
   // on file BzzFile.txt
   bzzFileOut = stdout;

   int numModels = 1;
   int numX = 1;
   int numY = 1;
   int numExperiments = 11;
   BzzMatrix X(numExperiments,numX,
```

```
            273.,283.,293.,303.,313.,323.,
            333.,343.,353.,363.,373.);
        BzzMatrix Y(numExperiments,numY,
            191.67,264.88,357.60,474.21,616.19,789.61,
            995.68,1239.71,1523.46,1850.92,2226.47);
        BzzNonLinearRegression nonLinReg(numModels,X,Y,
            RegressionFunction);
        BzzVector s2(1,.075);
        int df = 6;
        nonLinReg.SetVariance(df,s2);
        BzzVector b(numParam);
        int i;
        for(i = 1;i <= numParam;i++)
            b[i] = bb[i - 1];
        nonLinReg.InitializeModel(1,b);
        nonLinReg.LeastSquaresAnalysis();
        b = nonLinReg.GetParameters(1);
        for(i = 1;i <= numParam;i++)
            bb[i - 1] = b[i];
        }


    void RegressionFunction(int model,int ex,
            BzzVector &b,BzzVector &x,BzzVector &y)
        {
        double *vect_b = b.GetHandle();
        double *vect_x = x.GetHandle();
        double *vect_y = y.GetHandle();
        MODEL(model,ex,vect_b,vect_x,vect_y);
        }
```

Significant points to be considered are the following:

- The compiler must be informed that `CppFunction` is written in C++; this is possible by the statement: `extern "C" {void CppFunction(int numParam,double *bb);}`
- The compiler must be informed that the function `MODEL` is written in Fortran: `extern "C" {void __stdcall MODEL (int model, int ex,double *B,double *X,double *Y);}`
- It is necessary to change the vector index since they are passed as they were C/C++ vectors and used as objects of the `BzzVector` class.
- It is necessary to write the Fortran `SUBROUTINE` in capital letters as the Fortran compiler automatically makes capital all letters.

It is now necessary to write the Fortran code. Follow the next steps:

- Select New from the menu item File.
- Select the screen Files.
- Select Fortran free format Source File.
- Write FortranCppRegression.f90 in the edit-box File Name.
- Keep the option of inserting the file into the project and click on the OK button.
- Write the following code.

```fortran
PROGRAM MixedLanguage
implicit real*8(a-h,o-z)
real*8 BB(2)
common/mixed/nFunc

!this is very important
INTERFACE
 SUBROUTINE FortranFunction(numParam,pointerToBB)
  !MS$ATTRIBUTES C,ALIAS:'_CppFunction'::
FortranFunction
  !MS$ATTRIBUTES VALUE::numParam
  integer*4 numParam
  integer*4 pointerToBB
 END SUBROUTINE FortranFunction
END INTERFACE

BB(1) = 1.d0
BB(2) = 1.d0
numParam = 2
!call CPP
call FortranFunction(numParam,Loc(BB))
write(*,*)'num call model',nFunc
write(*,*)'Solution',BB(1),BB(2)
END



SUBROUTINE MODEL(NUMMODEL,EX,B,X,Y)
real*8 B [REFERENCE]
real*8 X [REFERENCE]
real*8 Y [REFERENCE]
integer*4 NUMMODEL [VALUE]
integer*4 EX [VALUE]
common/mixed/nFunc
dimension B(*),X(*),Y(*)
data nFunc/0/
nFunc = nFunc + 1
Y(1) = B(1) * exp(B(2) / X(1))
return
```

```
end
```
- Add the file `MixedLanguage.obj` to the project by selecting the item `Project, Add To Project, Files`.
- Select `Project, Settings` and the screen `Link`.
- Write/`force` in the edit-box `Project Options` in order to force the linking by overcoming incompatibilities among libraries.
- Compile and run the program.

If anyone has no compatible Fortran compilers available, the file `FortranCppRegression.obj` collected in the release folder of the project directory within the Appendix A folder of the enclosed CD-ROM can be used, by considering it was generated by COMPAQ Visual Fortran 6.6 (and, therefore, compatible to Visual C++ 6.0).

Appendix B: Basic Requirements for Using the BzzMath Library

BzzMath is available to run on

- Windows systems with Microsoft Visual C++ 6.0 or later compilers and Intel C++ 11 compiler.
- Linux systems with g++ and Intel C++ 11 compilers.

According to the compiler, some additional operations must be accomplished as described in the following.

In addition, Fortran users can either adopt all classes belonging to the *BzzMath* library through appropriate interfaces or directly use the piece of C++ codes in Fortran, by means of the so-called mixed language programming.

To use the *BzzMath* tutorial, a PC with Microsoft PowerPoint 2003 or higher is needed.

For Linux users: some graphical applications run only under Windows (.exe files).

B.1
How to Install the BzzMath Library

The following general tasks must be accomplished to use the *BzzMath* library on a computer.

- Download `BzzMath6.zip` from Buzzi-Ferraris's homepage (www.chem.polimi.it/homes/gbuzzi) or take it from the enclosed CD-ROM.
- Unzip the file `BzzMath6.zip` in a convenient directory (e.g., in `C:\NumericalLibraries\`). This directory shall be called `DIRECTORY` in the following. This unzip creates the subdirectory `BzzMath` including other five subdirectories:

  -`Lib`, `hpp`, `exe`, `Examples`, and `BzzMathTutorial` are created under the path `DIRECTORY\BzzMath`.
  -The `BzzMath` library is copied into `DIRECTORY\BzzMath\Lib` subdirectories, according to the compiler one would use (`VCPP6`, `VCPP9`, `INTEL11`, `Linuxg++`, and `LinuxIntel11`);
  -`hpp` files are copied into the directory `DIRECTORY\BzzMath\hpp`.

-exe files are copied into the directory `DIRECTORY\BzzMath\exe`.
-The overall tutorial, `.ppt` files, is copied into the directory `DIRECTORY\BzzMath\BzzMathTutorial`.
-Example files are copied into the directory `DIRECTORY\BzzMath\Examples`.

B.2
Windows Users

1. In Microsoft Developer Studio 6.0 or later, open `Options` in the `Tools` menu, then choose the `Directories` tab and add the directory specification `DIRECTORY\BzzMath\hpp` for include files.
2. Add `DIRECTORY\BzzMath\exe` and `DIRECTORY\BzzMath\BzzMathTutorial` in the operating system `PATH` option: Right click on `System Resources`. Choose the `Properties` option. Choose the `Advanced` option. Choose `Environment Variables`. Choose the `PATH` option. Add the voice

   `; DIRECTORY\BzzMath\exe; DIRECTORY\BzzMath\BzzMathTutorial;`

   Please note that when a new directory is added to the `PATH Environment Variable`, it is necessary to add a ";" character (without quotes) before specifying the new directory.

   After changing the `PATH Environment Variable`, the PC must be restarted.

B.3
Use BzzMath with Windows C++ Compilers

(A) *Visual C++ 6.0*

The proper library (`DIRECTORY\BzzMath\Lib\VCPP6\BzzMath.lib`) must be added to the project. No additional operations must be accomplished using VC++ 6.0.

The program must start with the following two statements:

```
#define BZZ_COMPILER 0 // optional (default value)
#include "BzzMath.hpp"
```

(B) *Visual C++ 7.0 (2003) and 8.0 (2005)*

Besides operations at the point A, users adopting VC++7.0 and VC++8.0 must even ignore the library `LIBC.LIB`, by selecting the menu item `Project/Properties/Linker/Input/`; there, `LIBC.LIB` must be added to the item `Ignore Specific Library`.

The program must start with the following two statements:

```
#define BZZ_COMPILER 0 // optional (default value)
#include "BzzMath.hpp"
```

(C) *Visual C++ 9.0 (2008)*

Users adopting VC++9.0 (VC++ 2008) must use the proper library (`DIRECTORY\BzzMath\Lib\VCPP9\BzzMath.lib`) and replace the default run-time library. Select

```
Project/Properties/Configuration Properties/C/C++/
Code Generation/Runtime Library
```

There, if one is working in `Release`, the `Multi-threaded (/MT)` library must be selected; if one is working in debug, the `Multi-threaded Debug (/MTd)` must be selected.

The program must start with the following two statements:

```
#define BZZ_COMPILER 1
#include "BzzMath.hpp"
```

(D) *Intel 11.0*

Users adopting this compiler must follow what described at point C and use the library (`DIRECTORY\BzzMath\Lib\INTEL11\BzzMath.lib`).

The program must start with the following two statements:

```
#define BZZ_COMPILER 11
#include "BzzMath.hpp"
```

B.4
Linux Users

Linux users have to develop their own `makefile` including the appropriate `.hpp` and `.lib PATHS` for each project. Also, the proper library has to be selected according to the compiler:

(A) *g++*

Users adopting this compiler must use the library:

```
DIRECTORY\BzzMath\Lib\Linuxg++\libBzzMath_g++.a
```

The program must start with the following two statements:

```
#define BZZ_COMPILER 101
#include "BzzMath.hpp"
```

(B) *Intel 11*

Users adopting this compiler must use the library:

```
DIRECTORY\BzzMath\Lib\LinuxIntel11
\libBzzMath_Intel.a
```

The program must start with the following two statements:

```
#define BZZ_COMPILER 111
#include "BzzMath.hpp"
```

B.5
OpenMP Windows Compatibility

(A) *Visual C++ 6, 7, and 8 users*
No parallel computing is allowed in the **BzzMath** library.

(B) *Visual C++ 9 and Intel 11 users*
People using these compilers must activate `openMP` library option for exploiting parallel computing with the **BzzMath** library.
Select in the project

```
Project/Properties/Configuration_Properties/C/C++/
Language
```

and activate `openMP Support`.

B.6
OpenMP Linux Compatibility

(A) *g++ users*
People using this compiler must enter the option `-fopenmp` in the `makefile`.

(B) *Intel 11 users*
People using this compiler must enter the option `-openmp` in the `makefile`.

B.7
Manage openMP During Computations

The **BzzMath** library uses openMP directives for parallel computing by default when the compiler supports them.

The user who wants to personally manage openMP library must deactivate the parallel computing within the **BzzMath** library to prevent any kind of parallel computing overlapping.

Inside the `main`, the first statement must be

```
bzzOpenMP = 0;
```

Appendix C: Copyrights

This software is subject to the terms of the license agreement. This software may be used or copied only in accordance with the terms of this agreement. The software is and remains the sole property of Prof. Guido Buzzi-Ferraris.

> Classes and algorithms within the *BzzMath* library are available in the enclosed CD-ROM and freely downloadable at the web site www.chem.polimi.it/homes/gbuzzi. Academies and nonprofit organizations can freely use it on the condition that whenever *BzzMath* is used to produce any piece of software (executable, library, object file, dll, and so on), a reference to the web site www.chem.polimi.it/homes/gbuzzi is reported.
> Otherwise, the author must be contacted for any other commercial and/or industrial purposes: phone + 39.02.2399.3257; fax: + 39.02.7063.8173; e-mail: guido.buzziferraris@polimi.it; address: Piazza Leonardo da Vinci, 32, 20133, Milano, Italy.

C.1
Limited Warranty

This software is provided "as is" and without warranties as to performance of merchantability or any other warranties whether expressed or implied. Because of the various hardware and software environments into which this library may be installed, no warranty of fitness for a particular purpose is offered. The user must assume the entire risk of using the library.

For any problem you may encounter using the *BzzMath* library, please contact the author at guido.buzziferraris@polimi.it.

Index

a

abscissas   1, 4, 8, 37, 38, 58
– features   4
– location   8
– values   38
Aitken method   21, 22, 27
Akaike information criterion (AIC)   273
alternative hypothesis   92, 95
alternative models   359
– analysis   356–362
– example   359–362
approximate information   263
– linearized model   263
arithmetic mean   66, 70, 93, 97
– definition   66
Arrhenius-like forms   299, 301
ASCII file   126
auxiliary BzzMatrix   347, 353–356
– program   347–351
auxiliary variable   59
auxiliary vectors   67

b

Bézier curves   2
barycentric formula   14
– Lagrange method   23
Bayesia information criterion (BIC)   274
Bayesian approach   387, 388
Bayes theorem   99, 100
best model selection   140–145
binomial distribution   80, 98
boundary conditions   11
– polynomials   52
break point   211
Bulirsch–Stoer method   39–42
– algorithm   40, 41, 42
– prevision with Bulirsch–Stoer   40
Buzzi–Ferraris's method   390

BzzCubicHermite class   46
– constructors   46
BzzCubicSmooth class   49, 329
– experimental data, program   329
BzzCubicSpline class   52
BzzFile.txt   257
BzzInterpolation class   3, 15, 22, 27, 38
– constructors   3
BzzLinearRegression   125, 126
BzzLinearRegression.exe toolkit   133, 144, 161, 218, 225, 226, 228–230, 241
– best model   230
– stepwise, analysis   229, 230
BzzLinearRegression program   124
– BzzLinearRegression class   114, 118, 119, 124, 129, 130, 132, 158, 161, 163, 190, 241
– principal components analysis   243
BzzMath library   114, 124, 127, 134, 141, 142, 145, 157, 189, 190, 247, 253, 379
– BzzCubicHermite   45
– BzzCubicSmooth   45
– BzzCubicSpline   45
– BzzOneWayFTest function   89
– BzzOneWayTest function   85
– BzzTwoWayFTest function   90
– CleverMean function   69
– CleverVariance function   72
– GetCleverMeanVarianceOutliers function   78
– mad function   71, 75
– mean function   66
– median function   67
– multicubic functions   325, 327
– remedian function   68
– robust method   157
– StandardDeviation function   74
– TrimmedMean function   68

Interpolation and Regression Models for the Chemical Engineer: Solving Numerical Problems
Guido Buzzi-Ferraris and Flavio Manenti
Copyright © 2010 WILEY-VCH Verlag GmbH & Co. KGaA, Weinheim
ISBN: 978-3-527-32652-5

– variance function   71
BzzMatrix class   188, 240
– auxiliary   347, 353
– GetGoodExperiment function   379
– principal component analysis   241
BzzMatrixSparse class   123
BzzNonLinearRegression class   247,
    251–255, 259, 261–263, 267, 384, 389,
    390, 392
– criterion   389–404
– experimental data, program   320
BzzOde class, use   343
BzzPlotSparse.exe toolkit   48, 319
BzzPlotSparse toolkit   49
– polynomials visualization   49
BzzVector class   65, 70, 238, 240, 379

c

Cartesian plane   54
Chebyshev polynomials   56, 57
– properties   57
Cholesky algorithm   107
Cholesky factorization   104
CleverLeastSquaresAnalys function   166, 167,
    170, 176, 181, 184, 206, 209, 212, 218, 224,
    233
– model selection   234
clever least squares regression analysis   203
clever mean   78
clever variance   72, 73, 75, 78
– advantage   72
– use   72
coefficient matrix   17
computational times   267
conditional probability   99, 100
– feature   99
condition number   115, 132, 139, 289,
    294, 295, 297, 299, 301, 302, 304–307, 309,
    311, 313, 314, 316, 318, 334, 338, 364,
    368
confidence region   110
continuous distribution, median   67
Cook statistics   182, 184
correlation   297, 305, 311, 312, 340
– conditioning   295
– formulation, program   312
– indices   295, 313, 318, 338, 346, 364, 368
– matrix   138, 139, 196–198, 258, 264
cubic functions   45

d

data acquisition   205
data collection   216
– exp55.lrg   228
– PiecewiseA1.lrg   220
– PiecewiseA2.lrg   221
– PiecewiseB1.lrg   222
data deletion   129, 130
data file
– building   126–128
– structure   126
data modification   128, 129
data visualization   128
2-degree interpolating polynomial   16
degree of freedom   359, 361
1-degree polynomial   10, 44
2-degree polynomial   12, 19, 335
– Lagrange form   12
3-degree polynomial   51
4-degree polynomial   11
degrees of complexity, problem solving   275
degrees of freedom   87, 88, 90, 109, 285, 288,
    369, 371
dependent variable   279, 280, 288, 291, 299,
    304, 307, 310, 312, 315, 317, 333, 341, 353,
    357, 359, 364, 369, 371, 373
– experimental data   291, 310, 315, 357, 359
– matrix   373
– parameters   279, 317
– program   292, 310, 315, 357–361, 373, 374
– variance   341
diagonal variance matrices   246
dialogue window   123, 125
– predefined regression problem.   125
differential algebraic equations   346, 353
– algebraic equations   352
discrete variable   63
– probability distribution   63
distinct point   32
D-Optimality criterion   381

e

editing program   126
– notepad   126
– wordpad   126
equivocation error   92
error variance   281, 359
Euclidean norm   103
exact interpolation method   1, 5, 8
– limitations   1
– rules   8
expected value, definition   63
experimental data   201, 219, 235, 237, 239
– CleverLeastSquaresAnalysis functions
    219
– matrix columns   219
– model comparison   239
– nonlinear dependence   219

– Principal1.lrg   241
– quadratic term   219
– RobustAnalysis functions   219
experimental domain   216
experimental error   201, 208, 239, 259, 266, 268, 271, 280, 296
– estimation   296
experimental variables   280, 296, 378
– factors   378

f
FalseLeverage2.lrg   218
F distribution,   89–91. *see also* Fisher distribution
– example   90, 91
finite elements method, feature   16
FirstExample function   257, 264, 265
– definition   264–266
F-outliers   186, 187
F-test   113, 117, 298
function approximation   2

g
Gaussian distribution   83
generic overdimensioned system   196
generic spline   50
GetGoodExperiment function   379
GetMeanSquareError function   121
GetRobustParameters function   122
GetSecludedObservations function   224
Graham–Schmidt method   145
gross error   65, 152–179

h
hat matrix   107
– calculation   107
Hermite polynomial   6, 30, 31, 32, 56
– interpolation   29–33
– Lagrange-type method   30
– Newton-type method   31–33
Hertzsprung–Russell diagram   212
heterogeneous reactions   272
heteroscedasticity condition   168, 179, 190, 191, 226, 227
– violation   335
Horner method   10, 22
– algorithm   11
– procedure   10
Hougen–Watson kinetics   272
hybrid interpolations   49
– intermediate characteristics   49
hydrodealkylation kinetic model   267
hydrogen reaction   267
hyper-ellipsoid, volume   382

i
identity matrix   16
independent variable   279, 310, 317, 371
independent variables   333, 362, 364, 367, 375
– experimental data   310
– – error   362, 365, 367
– – program   310, 362, 363, 365, 367
– parameters   279, 317
index permutations   20, 21
inflation factor   116, 196, 198, 258, 264
influential observations   182–186
– *vs.* outlier   183
InitializeModel function   270
interpolation   1, 2, 33
– features   2
– function interpolation, classes for   3
– Hermite polynomial interpolation   29–33
– introduction   1
– inverse interpolation   42–44
– Lagrange method   12–17
– Neville algorithm   26–29
– Newton method   17–26
– orthogonal polynomials   54
– polynomial   2–8
– – error in   6–8
– – Lagrange method   15
– rational functions   3, 33
– – Bulirsch–Stoer method   39–42
– – Thiele's continuous fractions   35–39
– roots-product form   8
– – form prevision   9
– standard form   9–12
– – Horner procedure, first derivative   11
– – prevision   10
– successive polynomial interpolation   44–54
– two-dimensional curves   54
inverse interpolation   42–44
– important to   43
– polynomial   43

j
Jacobian matrix   264
– conditioning   294, 295

k
k-degree polynomial   19
kinetic model   267, 295, 296, 304, 402, 403

l
Lagrange method   12–17, 197
– advantage   16
– form   266
– – coefficients   13, 14
– prevision   16

–– barycentric Lagrange formula 14
–– evaluation 15
– version 13
– weaknesses 13
Lagrange polynomial form 12, 13, 133
– barycentric form 13
Laguerre polynomials 56
least clever sum of squares 165, 166
least median of squares method 156, 168
least square analysis, functions 120
least sum of squares method 103–111, 151, 158, 204, 213, 221, 262, 263, 321, 383
– model analysis 222
– trimmed method 164
–– advantage 164
–– shortcomings 164
Legendre polynomials 55
linear model 125, 140, 162, 232, 267, 378
– data fitting 210
– parameters 378
linear problems 124
– generalized toolkit 124–128
linear regression 114, 193
– best model selection 227–241
– class 114–124
– caveat 111–114
– experimental data 208
– Ferrari F1's test 193–196
– lap time reduction 194
– model formulation 196–200
– outliers 200
–– generated by heteroscedasticity condition 226, 227
–– generated by inadequate design of experiments 224–226
–– generated by poor quality data 201–216
–– originated by inadequate models 216–223
– parameter (s) 235
– principal components 241–244
– problems solving 101, 154, 165, 196
linear system 4, 17
logic positivism 388

m

Mallow index 141
masking 155
mathematical formulation 265
mathematical model 248
matrix columns 131, 132, 196, 280, 366
matrix factorization 386
matrix range, concept 105
mean square error 108, 109, 114, 154, 199, 200, 230, 231, 234, 239, 256, 257, 262, 263, 272

M-estimators 181, 182
– problems 182
minimization program 252
– robustness of 252, 253
model analysis 119, 222, 378
– experiments, problem 377
– feature 278
– intercept 102
– techniques 119
– weighted mean square error 404
model collection, definition 272
model discrimination 389
ModelEx6 function 303
ModelEx8 function 309
model parameter estimation 224
model parsimony 273
model selection, definition 273
multicollinearity 136–140
– detection 137–140
– occurrence 137
multicubic piecewise model 322–331
multiple determination index 110, 111, 117, 138
multiple linear regression 103
multivalue methods 26
multivariate regression 103

n

n-degree polynomial 8, 9, 12, 17, 58
– Newton form 17
– standard form 9
Neville method 21, 22, 39, 40
– advantages 29
– algorithm 26–29, 39–42
– development 26
– disadvantages 28
– phases 26
– prevision with Neville method 27
– variants 28
new experiments, models 380, 381
Newton method 17–26, 250–252, 258, 263
– additional data point 23
– algorithm 24
– coefficients' evaluation 17–22
– derivatives evaluation 24
– Newton form 22
–– coefficients 20
–– previsions 22
– rules 31
nonanalytical constraints 253
nonconstant variance 333, 336
non-Gaussian distribution 94
nonlinear models 232, 247, 248, 261, 264, 272
– ad hoc constructor 247

– outlier detection   247
– problem, preventative analysis   247
– statistical analysis   94
nonlinear regressions   245, 250, 252, 257, 320
– BzzNonLinearRegression class   253–259
– introduction   275–278
– model collection   272–274
– model discrimination   267–272
– model parameters   263, 264
– model selection   272–274
– more dependent variables   337–341
– – constant variance   337–341
– multicubic piecewise models   322–331
– nonalgebraic constraints   259–261
– nonlinear models, analysis of   248–250
– one dependent variable
– – constant variance   278–321
– – nonconstant variance   331–337
– outlier detection, algorithms for   261–263
– parameter evaluation   250–253, 275–278
– preventative model analysis   264–267
– problems   245–248, 267
– rules   277, 278
– source   295
nonparametric statistics   98
nonparametric test   98
normal equations   104
normality condition   189, 190
null hypothesis   92–95
– definition   93
– error types   92
– results   92
numerical error   261
numerical rank, see pseudorank

o

object initializes parameters   257
one-way *t*-tests   95
opportune linear combinations   146
optimal design of experiments for model discrimination (ODE/MD)   377
optimal design of experiments for parameter estimation (ODE/PE)   377
OPTNOV method   157, 251
orthogonal polynomials   54, 55
– Chebyshev polynomials   56
– sets   55
outlier error, see gross error
outliers   152–179, 207, 219
– CleverLeastSquareAnalysis function   214, 215
– detection   156–168
– experimental data   208
– generation   154–156

– homoscedasticity condition   226
– mean square error   207
– model parameter estimation   224
– model variation   207
– parameter estimation   223
– real gross error   210
– robust analysis   207, 209
– – RobustAnalysis function   214
– thumb test   207
ovedimensioned system   108, 115, 131

p

parameter correlations   317, 319
parameter definition   298
parameter estimation   262, 265, 381
– improvement   381–387
parameters evaluation, value   258
parametric methods   98
piecewise models   177
plot dialogue window   134
Poisson distribution, conditions   82
pollice recto condition   113
polynomial coefficients   6, 21, 25
polynomials functions   5, 10, 24, 25, 29, 54
– approximation   5, 7, 23
– centered standard form   10
– degree   7–9, 11, 16, 24, 27
– development   29
– interpolation, error   58
– k-degree polynomial   18
– kth coefficient   18
– Newton form   24, 25
– numerical analysis   5
– properties   5
– roots   8
– successive interpolation, application   54
population   67, 91
– probability distribution   67
– variance   89
preliminary analysis   130–136
preventative model analysis   264
Principal2.lrg   243
principal component decomposition   106
probability   67, 71, 76, 80, 82, 84–86, 88, 98, 99, 361
– definition   80
– density   63
– distribution   63, 83
– function, parameters   83
problem solving   196, 232
product quality control   81
program SYSTAT   165
pseudorank   105

p-value   282
p × p linear systems   156

q
QR factorization   145
quadratic term   220

r
random variable   64, 85, 87, 89
– definition   85, 87, 89
rational functions   2, 33, 34
– asymptotical behaviors   34
– standard form   33
– techniques   34
– use, problems   34
real gross error   210
regression   151
– robust methods   151
relevant probability distributions   79–91
– binomial distribution   79–82
– – conditions   79
– F distribution   89–91
– normal Gaussian distribution   83
– Poisson distribution   82
– t-student distribution   84–87
– χ^2 distribution   87–89
rival models   280, 281, 392, 398
– kinetic models   402
– parameters   281
– square error   281
robust analysis   200, 206, 209, 212, 218, 221, 232, 262, 263, 217
– optimization algorithm   249
– outliers   209
– residuals of   202
robust estimator   65, 76, 78
robust indices   189
robust method   204, 213, 215, 263
– goal of   216
– least sum of squares method, comparison   214
– linear models, analysis   151, 152
– linear regressions   151
– outliers   211
robust minimization program   157, 252, 253
– function adoption   253
robust residuals   223
– analysis   227
– plot   227
Rousseeuw method   158

s
secluded observations   187–189
single-model analyses   267

singular value decomposition (SVD)   381
– analysis   121
– factorization   104–106, 109, 145, 188
spline functions, aim   49
spline types   53
square root argument, program   260
square system   12
standard deviation   63, 70, 74
– absolute errors sum, use   75
– estimation   74
– median, use   74
– minimum/maximum value   75
– unbiased standard deviation   74
– variance, square root   74
standardized residuals   154, 189
standardizing robust residuals   211
standard normal distribution   84
standard residual analysis   155, 217
statistical tests   61, 91–93
– alternative models analysis   356–362
– branches   61
– conditional probability   99
– confidence limits   61, 91
– correct meaning   91–98
– expected value estimation   65–70
– – arithmetic mean   66
– – clever mean   69
– – median   66
– – random selection   66
– – remedian   67
– – symmetric and nonsymmetric distributions   69
– – trimmed mean   68
– F-test   93
– fundamentals   61–65
– independent variables subject to experimental error   362–368, 374
– – example   362–366, 375
– – model with outliers   374
– model analysis   91, 116, 235
– model consisting of differential algebraic equations   352–356
– model consisting of ordinary differential equations   343–352
– more dependent variables and nonconstant variance   341
– nonparametric statistics   98
– outliers   370–374
– – detection   76–79
– – example   371–374
– relevant probability distributions   79–91
– standard deviation estimation   74
– task   61
– variables with missing experiments   369

– variance estimation 70–74
– χ^2 test 93
statistics state 62
StepwiseAnalysis function 229, 235, 236, 237
stepwise strategy 141, 166
studentized residuals analysis 179–181, 203
successive polynomial interpolation 44–54
– cubic spline 49–54
– Hermite cubic polynomials 45
swamping 155, 170

t

Taylor polynomials 6
therapeutic obstinacy 113
Thiele's series 35
– continuous fractions 35–39
– – coefficients in form 38
– – previsions 36
– rational functions 37
– – inverse rational differences, calculation 37
thumb test 113
tolerances 282, 284, 289, 291, 293, 302, 306, 311
– coefficients 138
– indices 264, 283
transcendental function 253
transcription error 201
trial-and-error method 36
tridiagonal system 50
trivial model 137
t-student distribution 84–87
– example 85–87
t-test 93, 294, 298, 335

– parameters 294
– two-way, limit condition 96
T-Value 282, 290

u

UDV^T factorization methods 381
unique n-degree polynomial 9
US Presidency election 62
– exit polls, previsions 61
– Gallup's investigation 62

v

Vandermonde matrix 4, 11
variance estimation 63, 64, 70–74, 76, 96, 286, 331, 339, 366, 368
– arithmetic mean 64, 76
– – use 70
– clever variance 72
– estimations 72
– median, use 71
variance inflation factor 138, 139, 302, 304
vector of residuals 103
vector orthogonalization 145

w

Weierstrass theorem 5

x

x-outliers 186, 187

y

y-outliers 186, 187

z

zero-degree polynomial 19